Contents

Acknowledgements		7
Preface		9
1	Generic and Specific Names	11
2	Separating the Animals into Groups	18
3	The Phyla	21
4	The Vertebrates	27
5	Birds in General—The Class Aves	30
6	Bird Orders, Families and Subfamilies	34
7	Ostriches STRUTHIONIFORMES	41
8	Rheas RHEIFORMES	43
9	Cassowaries CASUARIIFORMES	44
10	Kiwis APTERYGIFORMES	46
11	Tinamous TINAMIFORMES	48
12	Penguins SPHENISCIFORMES	50
13	Divers or Loons GAVIIFORMES	52
14	Grebes PODICIPEDIFORMES	54
15	Albatrosses, Fulmars, Shearwaters and Petrels PROCELLARIIFORMES	56
16	Tropicbirds, Pelicans, Gannets, Cormorants, Anhingas and Frigatebirds PELICANIFORMES	61
17	Herons, Storks, Flamingos and their kin CICONIIFORMES	67
18	Screamers, Geese, Swans and Ducks ANSERIFORMES	76
19	Vultures, Hawks, Eagles, Falcons and their kin FALCONIFORMES	91
20	Grouse, Pheasants, Peacocks, Guineafowls, Turkeys and their kin GALLIFORMES	105
21	Button-Quail, Cranes, Rails, Bustards and their kin GRUIFORMES	117

22	Snipe, Oystercatchers, Plovers, Curlews, Skuas, Gulls, Auks and their kin CHARADRIIFORMES	125
23	Sandgrouse, Pigeons and Doves COLUMBIFORMES	145
24	Parrots and their kin PSITTACIFORMES	150
25	Turacos, Cuckoos and their kin CUCULIFORMES	157
26	Owls STRIGIFORMES	163
27	Frogmouths, Potoos, Nightjars and their kin CAPRIMULGIFORMES	168
28	Swifts and Hummingbirds APODIFORMES	173
29	Mousebirds or Colies COLIIFORMES	180
30	Trogons TROGONIFORMES	182
31	Kingfishers, Bee-eaters, Rollers, Hornbills and their kin CORACIIFORMES	185
32	Jacamars, Honeyguides, Toucans, Woodpeckers and their kin PICIFORMES	195
33	Perching Birds PASSERIFORMES	208

Appendix   Transliteration of Greek Alphabet   324

Bibliography   325

General Index   326

Index of English Names   330

Index of Latin Names   339

To Tank

from Bill
August 1981

BIRDS—Their Latin Names Explained

BIRDS—
Their Latin Names Explained

A. F. Gotch

BLANDFORD PRESS
Poole   Dorset

First published in the U.K. 1981 by Blandford Press
Link House, West Street,
Poole, Dorset, BH15 1LL

Copyright © 1981 Blandford Books Ltd,

British Library Cataloguing in Publication Data

Gotch, Arthur Frederick
  Birds.
  1. Birds — Nomenclature
  I. Title
  598'.0142   QL677

ISBN 0 7137 1175 2

All rights reserved. No part of this book may
be reproduced or transmitted in any form or by
any means, electronic or mechanical, including
photocopying, recording or any information storage
and retrieval system, without permission in
writing from the Publisher.

Phototypeset by Oliver Burridge & Co. Ltd, Crawley, Sussex
Printed in Great Britain at The Camelot Press Ltd, Southampton

Acknowledgements

I should like to express my gratitude to the following who have given me help and advice:
L. R. Conisbee; J. Edwards Hill, British Museum (Natural History); Dr J. F. Monk; Dr J. G. Sheals; Dr Hugh Cott; Dr K. A. Joysey; Mrs Ann Datta, British Museum (Natural History); Mr R. Fish, The Zoological Society of London; Mrs Vale, Mr D. K. Read, and Mr I. C. J. Galbraith, Tring Museum; Father B. Wrighton; Lawrence Jones; Norman Kearney; Michael Gardener; Michael Tweedie; Gordon Bennett; Howard Crellin; Stuart Booth, of Blandford Press, for his help with the planning and lay-out of the book; Nicholas Burridge, of Oliver Burridge Ltd, for his advice and help with typography in the book.

Special thanks are due to my friend Ralph Conisbee without whose unfailing help, advice, and enthusiasm, the publication of this book would not have been possible.

I also wish to acknowledge the following publications which were used in research for the book:
Animal Life Encyclopaedia, Purnell & Sons Ltd., London; *Wildlife* (monthly magazine), Wildlife Publications Ltd., London; *A Source-Book of Biological Names and Terms*, E. C. Jaeger, C. C. Thomas, Springfield, Illinois; *Bibliographical Key*, Col O. E. Wynne, published by Col O. E. Wynne; *Living Invertebrates of the World*, R. Buchsbaum and L. J. Milne, Hamish Hamilton, London; *Key to the Names of British Birds*, R. D. Macleod, Pitman, London; *A Checklist of Birds of the World*, E. S. Gruson, Collins, London; *Living Birds of the World*, E. T. Gilliard, Hamish Hamilton, London; *All the Birds of the Air (British Birds)*, Francesca Greenoak, André Deutsch, London; *Birds of Britain and Europe*, Bertel Bruun, and *Birds*, John Gooder, Hamlyn Publishing Group, London; *The Dictionary of Birds*, Bruce Campbell, Michael Joseph, London; *World Atlas of Birds*, Mitchell Beazley, London; *A*

Classification of Living Animals, Lord Rothschild, Longmans, London; *Principles of Systematic Zoology*, Ernst Mayr, McGraw-Hill, New York; *Latin and Greek for Biologists*, T. H. Savory, Merrow Publishing Company, Watford; *Webster's International Dictionary*, G. & C. Merriam, U.S.A.

A.F.G.

Preface

Increasingly, books about animals make use of Latin names. This tendency must be welcomed as it enables a creature to be identified as *that particular species*, regardless of its English or vernacular name, and it is applicable throughout the world. However, many readers would have little or no idea what the names mean, or indeed why and how the names are given. Rarely is any attempt made to 'translate' the Latin names into English or to explain the reason for the names, and a great many would not be found in a Greek or Latin dictionary.

Some years ago I was studying animals which I had seen in Uganda when helping Dr Hugh Cott with some research on the Nile crocodile. Sometimes he would trot out some fascinating name like *Mabuya quinquetaeniata* when we saw a small lizard scuttling away to hide in the undergrowth. I was intrigued, but also annoyed, because not being a classical scholar these names meant little or nothing to me. After making exhaustive enquiries in bookshops and libraries, including university and zoological libraries, it became apparent that there was no book available that would solve my problem. So I decided that, as there was no such book, I had better write one.

There are about 8,600 known species of birds, and I have included 1,850 of these. Most have been selected because they are well known, and some because they are rare, or even on the point of extinction. I have tried to select birds that represent all parts of the world and even some that are known only on small remote islands. Obviously, it would be impossible to include all species of birds in a book of this scope, and an undertaking to include all known species of all animals would run to many volumes and the research would constitute a lifetime's work for a team of classicists. A Cambridge University zoologist carrying out research on beetles worked out that if he spent his entire life studying just one family, the Staphylinidae, he would only be able to devote about twenty minutes to one species!

Throughout the book, the number of species given for each Family is as given by E. S. Gruson; in many cases, they can be regarded as approximate.

The first five chapters of the book explain the system of classification started by the Swedish naturalist Carl von Linné during the eighteenth century, and which became known as the Binominal System. Chapter 6 then sets out this system with reference to the Class Aves—the birds—and each of the following chapters is devoted to one of the 27 Orders of birds. The basic principles of the system as in use today are explained, avoiding unnecessary detail as far as possible, and throughout the book running headlines at the top of each page give the classification of the birds listed on that page—the order on the left hand page and the families on the right. This makes for quick and easy reference, but the main feature is that with every bird the translation and interpretation of the Latin name is given, and when necessary an explanation of the reason for giving the species that particular name.

A. F. Gotch
Autumn 1980

1 Generic and Specific Names

The student or amateur naturalist who is interested in the study of taxonomy is faced with a formidable array of Latin and Greek words, and also with a system of grouping the animals into phyla, classes, orders and families which have little or no meaning to the layman. In this book my aim is to explain this arrangement and give a meaning to the names by translating them into English; no attempt is made to describe the animal other than the features and associations that explain the reason for the scientific name.

Carl von Linné, the Swedish botanist, born in the year 1707, was responsible for the first real attempts to classify and name living organisms—although Aristotle had done some work on a simple form of classification as long ago as 384 B.C. Linnaeus, the Latin form of the name Linné, is normally used in classification and his system of nomenclature is now in use throughout the world. The authoritative tenth edition of his *Systema Naturae* was published in 1758, and this is an all-important date, January 1st of that year being the starting point; all Latin names given before that date are considered invalid.

The Linnaean classification is known as the binominal system, i.e. 'two names'; every plant and animal must be given two names. The first is the generic name (from *genus* which is Latin for 'birth' or 'origin') and a genus comprises a group of closely related animals, or plants; the second is the specific name, the name of the actual species, which distinguishes it from any other animal in that group, and so from any other animal in the world.

The generic name should be a noun, and written with a capital letter, and the specific name should be an adjective, though sometimes it is a noun; it should be written with a small letter even though it is a proper name of a place or a person, and both names should be in *italics*. To be completely authentic, it should be followed by the name of the zoologist who first gave the animal that name, and the date of naming; for example the European Hedgehog would be:

Erinaceus europaeus Linnaeus, 1758.

The author's name and date should not be in italics; if there has been a change of the generic name, as sometimes happens, the original author's name will be given in parentheses; in written work underlining can be used to indicate *italics*. This information about the author and date is not always necessary in zoological publications and is not given in this book.

PRIORITY

The saying goes 'Priority is the basic principle of zoological nomenclature'; the first scientific name given to an animal after January 1st 1758 stands, even though eventually it turns out to be not descriptively accurate. However, by its plenary powers the International Commission on Zoological Nomenclature can moderate the application of this rule to preserve long established names, in order to avoid inconvenience and confusion. A recent ruling has discouraged zoologists from digging out and reviving forgotten names; they must not displace names that have been accepted for fifty years or more.

HOMONYMS

A new name for an animal is considered invalid if it has been used previously for some other form in the *animal* kingdom, as this would result in the same name for two different animals; it is known as a homonym. A difference of one letter is sufficient distinction, for example *Apis*, *Apos* and *Apus* are not homonyms. *Platypus* was given as the Latin name for the Duckbill in 1799, but the name had been used for a beetle some years before; it was therefore invalid and a new name had to be given; this was *Ornithorhynchus*.

SYNONYMS

In some cases alternative names are used and recognised. For example, in the primates, an author may use Prosimii and Simiae for the names of the suborders: *pro* (L) before and *simia* (L) an ape, a monkey, i.e. 'early monkeys' or 'primitive monkeys', and 'modern monkeys'; another author may use Lemuroidea and Anthropoidea: *anthrōpos*

(Gr) man and -*oides* (New L) from *eidos* (Gr) shape, resemblance, i.e. 'lemur-like' and 'man-like'. For Swainson's Francolin, a bird of the pheasant family, some authors may use *Pternistis swainsoni* and others *Francolinus swainsoni* (see p. 110). These are known as synonyms and will be shown thus: *Pternistis swainsoni* (or *Francolinus*). If a generic name has been rejected and considered invalid, but still appears in some publications, it will be shown thus: (*Calidris* formerly *Crocethia*) (see p. 133).

TAUTONYMS

It will be seen that in some cases the Latin name of an animal has the generic name repeated for the specific name, for example the Red Kite *Milvus milvus*. This is known as a tautonym, from *tauton* (Gr) the same, and *onoma* (Gr) a name; this has come about because of a change in the generic name. For example, a Linnaean specific name later used as a generic name so that the full name is a repeated word; a rule states that the specific name *may not be changed*, even though it results in a tautonym. The ruling has been modified for botanical names and tautonyms are forbidden.

I would like to quote an extract from an article by Mr Michael Tweedie which appeared in the magazine *Animals* (now *Wildlife*), and at the same time thank him for permission to do so:

'The wren was among the birds that Linnaeus himself named, and he called it *Motacilla troglodytes*. Under his genus *Motacilla* he included a number of small birds which ornithologists have now split up into several genera, reserving *Motacilla* for the wagtails. In naming the American wren-like birds in the first decade of the 19th century, the French authority Vieillot chose the Linnaean specific name *troglodytes* (troglodyte or cave-dweller, by reference to the form of the nest) as a generic name. Later it was found that the European wren was so closely allied to these that it must go in Vieillot's genus, so it became *Troglodytes troglodytes*.'

A rule states that the name of the nominate subspecies must repeat the specific name of the species (see Chapter 2, p. 19). Thus, when subspecies were named, the nominate subspecies of the wren group had to be *Troglodytes troglodytes troglodytes*. The veteran zoologists, who were classical scholars, thoroughly disliked this and there were heated interchanges of correspondence, and they refused to use these 'monstrosities'; but as they passed from the scene the modernists prevailed, the rules were accepted, and so some stability was achieved.

Some authors state that a tautonym indicates the common species in a genus, but this can be misleading; it may however, in certain cases, indicate the type species. It is true to say that quite often the common species, after a change in its generic name, does then have such a name; for example, the Common Quail *Coturnix coturnix* and the Common Snipe *Gallinago gallinago*. On the other hand the names of many common species do not have the tautonymous form; for example, the Common Kestrel *Falco tinnunculus* and the Common Curlew *Numenius arquata*.

TYPE SPECIES

The first species to be named in a particular genus is usually, though not always, the type species. Other species in that genus will resemble it more than those in a different genus and they will be distinguished by their specific names; for example *Falco dickinsoni* Dickinson's Kestrel, and *Falco peregrinus* the Peregrine Falcon.

ORIGIN OF NAMES

The Latin name of an animal might originate from the naturalist who first discovered it, but it is more likely that it would originate from a zoologist working in a laboratory, and studying the anatomy of the animal; the specific name is quite often given in honour of the person who discovered it. The kiwi has been given the generic name *Apteryx*, which is derived from the Greek *a*-, a prefix meaning 'not' or 'there is not', and *pterux* 'a wing'. The kiwi is a flightless bird, the wings being very small, hidden under the body feathers, and useless for flight; the Great Spotted Kiwi *Apteryx haasti* was named in honour of Sir Julius von Haast, the New Zealand explorer.

USE OF LATIN AND GREEK

The advantages of using languages such as Latin and Classical Greek are obvious; if Linnaeus had used the Swedish language, his system would not have been accepted internationally, and in any case other countries would not have understood it. In those days Latin was the international language of European scholars and Linnaeus wrote most of his scientific work in Latin to make it more widely read and understood. Even today there are classical scholars throughout the world who are familiar with Latin and Classical Greek and who understand the meaning of the words. It is true they would find some of the words wrongly construed and incorrectly spelt, and even hybridised, combining a mixture of Latin and Greek to form one word: anathema to the purist. Sometimes they are obscure native words which are known as 'barbarisms'. By international agreement, once these names appear in print and are accepted by the International Commission on Zoological Nomenclature, any mistakes must remain. However, the 1961-1963 revised Code permits correction of spelling; at the same time it forbids the use of hyphens, diacritic marks such as the apostrophe, the diaeresis, and the umlaut—so that *Hyperoödon* becomes simply *Hyperoodon* and *mülleri* becomes *muelleri*. The Comma Butterfly *Polygonia c-album*, meaning 'many-angled with a white 'c'', has the honour of being allowed to use the hyphen; one of the very few exceptions. The name refers to a white letter 'c' which is plainly marked on the under surface of the wing. The Thick-billed Lark *Rhamphocoris clot-bey* is another example of a hyphenated name.

The classical significance of the names is not of first importance, but some knowledge of Latin and Greek is a help in remembering the names, and will often tell you something about the animal; for instance *Aquila chrysaetos* must surely mean an eagle having some connection with gold; in fact it is the Golden Eagle of North America and Eurasia. The real importance of the names is that they are international fixed labels, identifying a particular species for zoologists throughout the world.

In many cases the names are derived from Greek words, but they are 'Latinised', that is to say they are put in a Latin form, and so are referred to as 'Latin names'; it is the popular term but rather disparaged by zoologists who prefer to call them 'scientific names'; purists even suggest that the correct term is 'Linnaean names'.

PECULIAR NAMES

Sometimes the names are just invented; the zoologist who named the Kookaburra, or Laughing Jackass as it is sometimes called, was so hard put to it in deciding on a generic name that would distinguish it from other kingfishers, that he used the word *Dacelo*; the generic name of the Common Kingfisher is *Alcedo* which is Latin for a kingfisher; *Dacelo* is simply an anagram of *Alcedo*.

There are a number of other peculiar names apart from anagrams, for instance *Ia io* for a bat, named by Oldfield Thomas; the shortest name ever given to a mammal. Ia was a young woman of classical times and Thomas says: 'Like many women of those times a bat is essentially flighty;' *io* is a Latin exclamation of joy, like hurrah! He obviously had a sense of humour, albeit a chauvinistic one. An inveterate 'coiner' of names, he also invented *Zyzomys* for an Australian mouse but never gave an explanation; perhaps he wanted to make sure that it would appear last in any index!

LOCAL AND PERSONAL NAMES

Many zoologists have used the names of little-known localities, which can make interpretation difficult, and there are references to ancient Greek mythology which may have no special significance. Very often a naturalist or collector who discovered the animal is honoured by using his or her name; the pheasant *Chrysolophos amherstiae* was named in honour of Lady Amherst. Commemorative names usually have *-i*, *-ii*, or *-iana* added to the name to form the genitive if the person is a man, and *-ae*, or *-iae* if a woman; note that in such cases the specific name is written with a small initial letter in accordance with the rules of nomenclature, although it is a personal name.

MISLEADING NAMES

Some animals have been given a name that is misleading when translated; this may have come about because they were named when knowledge of them was incomplete. Here are some examples: *sittē* (Gr) and *sittos* (Gr) have been translated by different authors as a kind of woodpecker, a kind of owl, a jay, or a hawk; and *spiza* (Gr) has been given as a small piping bird, perhaps a kind of finch, and *spizias* (Gr) a sparrowhawk. Among the mammals there are many misleading names, for instance *galē* (Gr) a weasel or marten-cat, used for a wallaby, which is a marsupial, and *kapros* (Gr) a wild boar, used for the hutiacouga, which is a rodent; *galē*, and some other names such as *kuōn* (Gr) a dog, have become conventional final elements in nomenclature for the names of small mammals quite remote from weasel, marten-cat, or dog.

The Greek word *mus*, a mouse, is used for all kinds of small mammals; consider, for instance, *Cynomys ludovicianus* the Prairie Dog; *Cynomys* means 'dog-mouse', but it is not a mouse and not even in the same family as the rats and mice, and it certainly is not a dog. It will be seen that it is spelt -*mys*, which is the Latin System of transliteration from the Greek; in the Modern System, as used in this book, it is spelt -*mus*. This is the same as the Latin word *mus* which is derived from the Greek and has the same meaning. Another example would be the generic name *Chrysococcyx*, for a cuckoo, which in the Modern System is written *khrusos* (Gr) gold, and *kokkux* (Gr) the cuckoo; the two systems of transliteration will be found in the Appendix on page 324.

2 Separating the Animals into Groups

A division or group is known as a taxon, plural taxa, from the Greek word *taxis*, an arrangement, though the term is not often used for groups higher than classes. The divisions are named as shown in the following list, the main divisions in the left-hand column:

> **KINGDOM**
>   SUBKINGDOM
> **PHYLUM**
>   SUBPHYLUM
>   SUPERCLASS
> **CLASS**
>   SUBCLASS
>   SUPERORDER
> **ORDER**
>   SUBORDER
>   SUPERFAMILY
> **FAMILY**
>   SUBFAMILY
> *Genus*
>   *Subgenus*
> *Species*
>   *Subspecies* (or *Race*)

These categories do not all have to be used in the classification of any particular group or species; each division or subdivision is given its own name as will be seen in Chapter 7 onwards. For example, the very big family Muscicapidae that includes the Thrushes, the Log-runners, the Babblers, the Flycatchers, and many others, has been divided into subfamilies, one of these being Turdinae, the Thrushes and Robins (see p. 253). A subspecies will have a subspecific name, for example the Helmeted Guinea Fowl *Numida meleagris mitrata*; this is known as trinominal, i.e. three names. It is a subspecies of the Tufted Guinea Fowl *Numida meleagris*. A rule made by the International Commission on Zoological Nomenclature states that the subspecific name of the species on which a group is founded must be the same, i.e. it must *repeat* the specific name. Thus in this case it becomes *Numida meleagris meleagris*; therefore it is easily distinguished and is known as the nominate subspecies.

A subspecies is always basically the same as the species, but there is some slight difference; it usually has a different geographical distribution and develops different characteristics. For instance the Helmeted Guinea Fowl has a bony casque on the head and the colour of the body feathers is different.

Subgenera are also sometimes recognised, and like subspecies the animal is basically the same as that in the genus; a subgenus is shown thus: *Nycticeius (Scotoecus) falabae* the Falaba House Bat. The subgeneric name is given in parentheses, and does not count as one of the words in the name—so it is not a trinominal. Some zoologists might consider this bat worthy of the status of a full genus, in which case the name would be *Scotoecus falabae*.

In deciding to which particular taxon an animal belongs, the zoologists must study its anatomy. During the early days of classification not enough attention was paid to this aspect and many animals were placed in the wrong taxon simply because of their outward appearance. These mistakes have gradually been corrected over the years, which accounts for the tautonymic names (see p. 13). However there is always likely to be a difference of opinion among the scientists concerned in this work. One of the most important parts of the anatomy of mammals which must be studied is the teeth; during a discussion on classification Baron Cuvier, the famous French zoologist, is reputed to have said:

'Show me your teeth and I will tell you what you are.'

Although birds do not have teeth, a zoologist will learn a great deal by studying the beak; Darwin's finches all appear to be much the same, small rather drab brown birds, *but their beaks are all different*. This aroused Darwin's curiosity and gave rise to his thoughts about evolution by natural selection, and it resulted in these finches being placed in various different genera with different specific names.

Apart from the anatomical structure some notice is taken of the habits of an animal: where does it live, what does it eat? As already mentioned, it is no use looking at an animal and deciding from its appearance to which group it belongs; for instance, take the lizard known in Britain as the 'slow-worm'; the uninitiated on seeing this animal would cry, 'Look, a snake'! Further, many would probably get a stick and beat the poor thing to death, though a more harmless and docile little creature it would be difficult to find; this could be one of the reasons for the decrease in numbers of the slow-worm in the British Isles!

What then makes this creature a lizard and not a snake, even though it has no legs? For one thing, it has eyelids, and snakes do not have eyelids, though lizards do; and another thing, if caught by the tail the slow-worm, like the lizard, can break it off. This is known as autotomy, from *auto-* (Gr) self, and *tomē* (Gr) a cutting off; there is a muscular mechanism in the tail which breaks it off and then actuates to prevent loss of blood; the tail then grows again. This leaves the surprised predator with only the broken-off tail, while the slow-worm makes good its escape. Indeed the Latin name *Anguis fragilis* suggests this, though it also shows that Linnaeus, who named it thought it was a snake: *anguis* (L) a snake, *fragilis* (L) brittle—the 'brittle snake'. One can imagine his surprise if he grabbed it by the tail, and was left with it wriggling in his hand; there is no doubt that the dismembered piece does wriggle, as I have seen myself, and this adds to the general surprise and confusion and gives more time for the main body to escape.

3 The Phyla

The main divisions of the Animal Kingdom are the phyla (singular, phylum) from *phulon* (Gr) a stock, race, or kind. There is not complete agreement among taxonomists as to the number of phyla, as some have separated a group and classified it as a subphylum, and it can take many years before international agreement is reached. As a result a number of different systems have become more or less established and generally recognised, and although they are basically the same there are certain differences which can be confusing; for example one well-known system is based on 22 phyla, and another on 27 phyla.

In any particular phylum there will be assembled all the animals having a common basic plan. Let us take as an example the phylum Chordata. The distinctive character of this phylum is the notochord; *nōton* (Gr) the back, and *khordē* (Gr) gut, string, giving rise to *chordata* (New L) meaning 'provided with a back-string'. This is a cord running along the back made of a special tough elastic tissue, and present in all animals in this phylum. In the humblest members of the group, such as the lancelets, small marine creatures about 5 cm (2 in) long, the notochord is retained throughout life. In the higher forms, the true vertebrates, it is present in the embryo, but is replaced more or less completely by the stronger and yet flexible spinal column of jointed vertebrae. However as all the animals in the phylum Chordata do not develop a spinal column, and there are other differences, the group is divided into four subphyla, the subphylum Vertebrata being one of these.

The system used in this book comprises 27 phyla, one of which Echinodermata, has two subphyla, and another, Chordata, four subphyla. Considering that Chordata includes such diverse animals as the acorn worms, the mice, the birds, the whales and humans, it is no wonder that subphyla are needed. Even so, the one subphylum

Vertebrata contains all the animals best known to us: birds, fishes, and reptiles; amphibians such as the frogs and newts; and mammals such as dogs, horses, antelopes, lions, whales and humans.

I do not advise anyone attempting to learn, like a parrot, the Latin and Greek names that now follow; in the course of study they will become familiar without any special effort and in any case the brain need not be packed full of words and facts; the great thing is to know how and where to look them up in appropriate books. The sequence of the animals listed is not fixed; it begins with what the compiler considers to be the most primitive forms of life and ends with the most advanced. The number of species given for each phylum is approximate; taxonomists do not always agree about the number of species in a particular group, and it can never be finally settled as new species may be discovered at any time and some species may become extinct.

The phyla are as listed below; they are known as 'invertebrates', i.e. having no backbone, with the exception of the last Subphylum, the Vertebrates:

PROTOZOA   30,000 species. Amoeba, mycetozoa, etc.
prōtos (Gr) first   *zōon* (Gr) an animal, a living thing.
amoibē (Gr) a change, an alteration. The amoeba, a tiny single-celled animal, continually changes its shape.
mukēs (Gr), genitive *mukētos*, a fungus; any knobbed body shaped like a fungus.

PORIFERA (or PARAZOA, SPONGIDA)   4,500 species. The sponges.
poros (Gr) a way through, a passage   *fero* (L) I bear, I carry.

COELENTERATA (or CNIDARIA)   9,000 species. Jellyfish, corals, etc.
koilos (Gr) hollow   *enteron* (Gr) bowel, intestine.

CTENOPHORA   80 species. Comb jellies, sea gooseberries.
kteis (Gr) genitive *ktenos*, a comb   *phora* (Gr) carrying, bearing; a reference to the rows of ciliary combs which beat and propel them through the water.

MESOZOA   7 species. Minute worms, parasites in the kidneys of squids and octopuses.
mesos (Gr) middle   *zōon* (Gr) an animal, a living thing.

PLATYHELMINTHES 9,000 species. Flatworms, liver flukes, bilharzia, etc.
platus (Gr) flat *helmins* (Gr), genitive *helminthos*, a worm.

NEMERTEA 570 species. Ribbon worms, bootlace worms.
nēma (Gr) genitive *nēmatos*, a thread.

NEMATODA (or NEMATA) 10,500 species. Roundworms, vinegar eelworms, etc.
nēma (Gr), genitive *nēmatos*, a thread *-oda* (New L) from *eidos* (Gr) form, like.

ROTIFERA (or ROTATORIA) 1,200 species. Wheel animalcules, the smallest many-celled animals about 1 mm (less than $\frac{1}{16}$ in) long, mostly living in fresh water.
rota (L) a wheel *fero* (L) I bear, I carry; they do not, of course, carry a wheel, but the first ones discovered and examined under a microscope showed tiny hairs round the mouth; these wave in a circular motion that gives the impression of a turning wheel.

GASTROTRICHA 100 species. Gastrotrichs, tiny transparent creatures less than 0·5 mm ($\frac{1}{50}$ in) long, mostly living in fresh water.
gaster (Gr) the belly, stomach *thrix* (Gr), genitive *trikhos*, hair; they have hairs on their underparts.

KINORHYNCHA (or ECHINODERA, ECHINODERIDA) 30 species. Kinorhynchs, marine animals about 1 mm (less than $\frac{1}{16}$ in) long.
kineō (Gr) I move *rhunkhos* (Gr) a snout, beak; they pull themselves along by a kind of snout.

PRIAPULIDA 6 species. Priapulids, wormlike marine animals 7·6 cm (about 3 in) long, living on muddy bottoms and sometimes at a great depth. Priapos was the god of gardens and vineyards and Priapus, in Roman mythology, meant a representation or symbol of the male generative organ, or phallus. The name priapulida probably refers to the shape of the animal, which is not unlike the human penis.
-ida (New L), from *idea* (Gr) species, sort.

NEMATOMORPHA (or GORDIACEA) 80 species. Horsehair worms, not usually marine, and very variable in length from 10 cm (4 in) upwards, and from 0·3 to 3 mm ($\frac{1}{80}-\frac{1}{8}$ in) in diameter.
nēma (Gr), genitive *nēmatos*, thread *morphē* (Gr) form, shape. Sometimes found in horse drinking troughs, hence the English name.

ACANTHOCEPHALIA 400 species. Spiny-headed worms; parasites in the intestines of vertebrates.
akantha (Gr) a thorn, prickle   *kephalē* (Gr) the head.

ENTOPROCTA (or ENDOPROCTA, CALYSSOZOA, KAMPTOZOA, POLYZOA ENDOPROCTA, POLYZOA ENTOPROCTA) 60 species. Entoprocts; a flower-like body on a stalk less than 6 mm ($\frac{1}{4}$ in) high. The anus opens within a circlet of tentacles, hence the name.
entos (Gr) within   *prōktos* (Gr) anus, hinder parts.

CHAETOGNATHA 30 species. Arrow worms; common in sea water near the shore or in the depths, from 2 to 10 cm ($\frac{3}{4}$-4 in) in length.
khaitē (Gr) hair, mane   *gnathos* (Gr) jaw; it has short bristles surrounding the mouth.

POGONOPHORA (or BRACHIATA) 22 species. Beard worms; a deep sea animal about 3 mm ($\frac{1}{10}$ in) in diameter and up to 33 cm (13 in) long. It has no digestive system and how it obtains nourishment is still a cause of further research.
pōgōn (Gr) a beard   *phora* (Gr) carrying.

PHORONIDA (or PHORONIDEA) 15 species. Phoronids; small marine animals that range from 2 to 30 cm (1-12 in) in length. They build themselves a tube in which to live, and catch their food by means of tentacles projecting from the end of the tube. The reason for their name is obscure, but is thought to originate from Phoronis, surname of Io, the daughter of Inachus; there is a strange legend which involves her wandering all over the earth.

BRYOZOA (or POLYZOA, POLYZOA ECTOPROCTA, ECTOPROCTA) 6,000 species. Moss animals; tiny animals, about 0·4 mm ($\frac{1}{64}$ in) long, which live in sea water and fresh water. You might find them attached to the bottom of your boat when you pull it ashore, and though they look rather like a mossy plant they are probably these tiny animals, the bryozoans.
bruo (Gr) I swell, sprout, giving rise to bryon, lichen or tree moss
zōon (Gr) an animal.

BRACHIOPODA 260 species. Lamp shells; the brachiopod shell is shaped somewhat like the oil lamps used by the Greeks and Romans in ancient times.

brakhus (Gr) short *pous* (Gr) genitive *podos*, a foot; they do not have feet, but this refers to a short stalk by which they attach themselves to some support.

SIPUNCULA (or SIPUNCULOIDEA) 250 species. Peanut worms; marine animals about 20 to 40 cm (8-18 in) long and 12 mm ($\frac{1}{2}$ in) in diameter. They can change their shape, and sometimes take the shape of a peanut. A peculiar feature is a pump-like action with one part of the body sliding up and down inside the posterior cylindrical part, thus collecting nourishment.
siphōn (Gr) a sucker, as of a pump   -*culus* (L) suffix meaning small; 'a little pump'.

ECHIURA (or ECHIUROIDEA, ECHIURIDA) 60 species. Curious sausage-shaped marine animals, up to about 30 cm (12 in) long, and having a proboscis which in some species may be 1 m (3 ft) long. This is used for gathering food.
ekhis (Gr) an adder, serpent   *oura* (Gr) the tail; the 'serpent' part is more a nose than a tail.

MOLLUSCA 50,000 species. Oysters, octopuses, slugs, snails, squids, etc.
mollusca (L) neuter plural of *molluscus*, soft.

ANNELIDA (or ANNULATA) 6,000 species. Leeches, earthworms, ragworms, etc.
anellus (L) a little ring; -*ida* (New L) from *idea* (Gr) species, sort; the rings that mark the body of an earthworm or a ragworm give this phylum its name.

ARTHROPODA about 815,000 species, including the insects which number about 800,000 species, possibly many more. Crustaceans, spiders, insects, etc.
arthron (Gr) a joint   *pous* (Gr) genitive *podos*, a foot; in this case it is taken to mean leg, as the arthropods have jointed legs. Some also have a hard external skeleton   *crusta* (L) a shell, crust.

ECHINODERMATA 5,500 species. Echinoderms, which are given two subphyla.

Subphylum Pelmatozoa   Sea lilies, feather stars.
pelma (Gr) genitive *pelmatos*, the sole of the foot, can mean a stalk *zōon* (Gr) an animal. The sea lily has a flower-like body supported on

a stalk, the feather star begins life on a stalk but later breaks away and is free to swim about.

Subphylum Eleutherozoa Sea urchins, sea cucumbers, starfishes, etc.

eleutheros (Gr) free, not bound as on a stalk   *zōon* (Gr) an animal   *ekhinos* (Gr) a hedgehog   *derma* (Gr) the skin; the sea urchins body is equipped with movable spikes.

CHORDATA about 44,750 species. Divided into four subphyla, each possessing the notochord.

nōtos (Gr) the back   *khordē* (Gr) gut, string   *chordata* (New L) having a notochord or backstring; the notochord, or 'back-string', is a rod-like structure made of tough elastic tissue which is present in all early embryos in the phylum Chordata.

Subphylum Hemichordata (or Stomochordata, Branchiotremata) 90 species. The acorn worms and their kin.

hēmi (Gr) prefix meaning half; suggesting halfway between primitive chordates and the next stage; the notochord is found only in the proboscis.

Subphylum Urochordata (or Tunicata) 1,600 species. Sea squirts, salps, etc.

oura (Gr) the tail   *khordē* (Gr) gut, string; the notochord extends into the tail.

Subphylum Cephalochordata (or Acrania, Leptocardii) 13 species. Lancelets, small marine animals about 5 cm (2 in) long and pointed at both ends.

lancea (L) a small spear   *kephalē* (Gr) the head   *khordē* (Gr) gut, string. The notochord extends into the head.

Subphylum Vertebrata about 43,000 species. The vertebrates: fishes, amphibians, reptiles, birds, and mammals, including humans (see below).

vertebra (L) a joint, specially a joint of the back, derived from *verto* (L) I turn. With the exception of certain fishes, such as the cartilage fishes, during development from the embryo the notochord is replaced by the bony spinal column.

4 The Vertebrates*

In the subphylum Vertebrata there is a great variety of animals, and so they are divided into groups, or taxa, called classes. There are certain recognised sequences for compiling lists of animals, but they are arbitrary, and different authors adopt different plans. It is not possible to make a linear series that is scientifically correct from the point of view of evolution, because animals have not descended one from another in a long line. The classes are as listed below.

MARSIPOBRANCHII (or AGNATHA)   Lampreys and hagfishes.

SELACHII (or CHONDROPTERYGII, CHONDRICHTHYES, ELASMOBRANCHII)   Sharks, dogfishes, rays, i.e. the cartilage fishes.

BRADYODONTI   Rabbit fishes.

PISCES (or OSTEICHTHYES)   Bony fishes.

AMPHIBIA   Frogs, toads, newts, and their kin.

REPTILIA   Tortoises, turtles, lizards, snakes, crocodiles.

AVES   Birds.

MAMMALIA   Dogs, cats, horses, whales, humans, and their kin.

The birds are divided into 27 taxa called orders, and can be distinguished by the ending -iformes. These orders are divided into a very large number of families, totalling 161, which have the ending -idae, and in some cases these are again divided into subfamilies which

---

*Including the Lampreys and Cartilage Fishes.

have the ending -inae. The complete list can be seen in Chapter 6. The names are formed by adding the suffix to the stem of the name of the type-genus. For example, the family name of the starlings is formed from the generic name *Sturnus* (L) a starling, and so becomes Sturnidae. The type-genus is that genus whose structure and characteristics are most representative of the larger group as a whole, although in some cases it may have been selected because it is the largest, best-known, or earliest-described genus.

To bring us up to date so far, let us work through an example, the owls. We will list the divisions, starting with the phylum and going through to the species.

Phylum   **CHORDATA**
Subphylum   **VERTEBRATA**
Class   **AVES**

Order   **STRIGIFORMES**

Family TYTONIDAE   Barn Owls
Genus and species   *Tyto alba*   Barn Owl
                        T. tenebricosa   Sooty Owl
                        Phodilus prigoginei   Tanzanian Bay Owl
                        (others)

Family STRIGIDAE   Typical Owls
Genus and species   *Otus albogularis*   White-throated Screech-Owl
                        Lophostrix cristata   Crested Owl
                        Uroglaux dimorpha   Papuan Hawk-Owl
                        (others)

It is considered sufficient, where the genus is the same as the one mentioned immediately before, simply to put the initial capital letter, as will be seen in the list above. The English interpretation of all the foregoing Latin names will be found in the chapter dealing with the owls.

Now let us look at another example, that of a small well-known British bird, the Chaffinch, with translations into English of each stage of its classification.

Phylum CHORDATA

khordē (Gr) gut, string; giving rise to *chordata* (New L) having a notochord or backstring *nōtos* (Gr) the back. The notochord is made of a special tough elastic tissue, and is present in the embryo of all animals in this phylum.

Subphylum VERTEBRATA

vertebra (L) a joint, specially a joint of the back, derived from *verto* (L) I turn *vertebrata* (New L) having a jointed back; in this subphylum the notochord develops into the spinal column.

Class AVES

avis (L) a bird.

Order PASSERIFORMES

passer (L) a sparrow, or other small bird *-iformes* (New L) suffix added to indicate the name of an order.

Family FRINGILLIDAE
fringilla (L) a small bird, according to some authors the chaffinch *-idae* (New L) suffix added to generic names to indicate the name of a family.

Subfamily FRINGILLINAE
-inae (New L) suffix added to generic names to indicate a subfamily.

Genus *Fringilla*
Species *coelebs* = *caelebs* (L) unmarried, single, whether a bachelor or a widower; sometimes chaffinches gather in flocks of one sex only, and at one time it was thought that the females migrated south leaving the males behind, and they became known as 'bachelor birds'. So the name of the Chaffinch is *Fringilla coelebs*—a small bird, a bachelor.

5 Birds in General—The Class Aves

This group of animals—the class Aves—have spread to almost every part of the globe; ptarmigan, with feet protected by feathers, and and ability to burrow in the snow, can live in Arctic areas; penguins in Antarctic areas live entirely on the ice and never touch land. Mountain birds have been seen at an altitude of 8,000 metres (over 26,000 feet) on Mount Everest, and some sea birds can dive to a depth of 60 metres (200 feet).

There are about 8,600 species of birds, and about 4,000 species of mammals; together they are the only warm-blooded animals. Nowadays zoologists prefer not to use the term 'cold-blooded' when referring to fish, reptiles, and their kin, because the temperature of the blood varies with the surroundings; it is known as poikilothermic, from the Greek *poikilos*, variable, and *thermē*, heat; because the temperature of the blood varies according to the surroundings. In some cases the blood can become so hot in the sun that a lizard, for instance, must seek the shade or it would perish. It is now known that the body temperature of some 'cold-blooded' animals may at times be higher than the temperature of the surroundings.

Unlike mammals, birds do not have sweat glands; the moisture produced would make the feathers useless for flight and reduce their ability to preserve warmth; they are 'warm-blooded'. This condition, in birds and mammals, is known as homeothermic (or homoiothermic) from the Greek *homoios*, like or similar; i.e. the temperature of the blood remains about the same. It is higher in birds than mammals, about 41°C (106°F), less during sleep, and higher at times of great activity. Some regulation of blood flow to the legs and feet can control temperature, being less in cold conditions and more in hot; heat loss is also helped by rapid panting, and heat preservation by 'fluffing out' the feathers.

It is generally recognised that the birds developed from the reptiles, some 200 million years ago, the feathers being a form of reptilian scales, which latter can still be seen on the legs and feet; embryonic feathers are similar to the scales of a young reptile.

The well-known fossil of a reptile-like bird, *Archaeopteryx* (from the Greek meaning 'ancient wing'), which was discovered during the year 1860 in Germany, shows characteristics of both reptiles and birds. One peculiar feature was that it had claws on the leading edge of the wings which it could use for climbing, so it was really a quadruped; a living example of this is the Hoatzin, a remarkable bird that lives in Central and northern South America. When first hatched the young hoatzin has similar claws on the fore limbs. Thus it starts life as a quadruped, using the claws for hanging on to branches and clambering about in the tree where its nest has been built.

In this respect it resembles the prehistoric semi-reptilian birds known to us only as the fossils *Archaeopteryx* (mentioned above) and *Archaeornis* ('ancient bird'). The nest is usually built over water, and when alarmed the nestling drops out of the nest into the water, swims ashore, a remarkable feat in any case, and *climbs* back to its nest. After about a week, the claws begin to disappear as the normal wing feathers develop. Thus in a matter of weeks it goes through an evolutionary change that took the 'lizards to birds' millions of years to bring about.

Chapter 6, which follows the explanatory chart overleaf, sets out the Orders, Families and Sub-families for ease of reference and in the following chapters, we look at each of the orders and the families which make up the class Aves.

32 THE ANIMAL KINGDOM

⟵ 25 other Phyla (see page 21)

Subphylum **HEMICHORDATA** *Acorn Worms*

Subphylum **UROCHORDATA** *Sea Squirts*

Class **MARSIPOBRANCHII** *Lampreys and Hagfishes*

Class **SELACHII** *Sharks, Rays and their kin*

Class **BRADYODONTI** *Rabbit fishes*

Order **STRUTHIONIFORMES** *Ostrich*

Order **RHEIFORMES** *Rheas*

Order **CASUARIIFORMES** *Cassowaries and Emu*

Order **APTERYGIFORMES** *Kiwis*

Order **TINAMIFORMES** *Tinamous*

continued from above

Order **PELECANIFORMES** *Pelicans, Boobies, Cormorants*

Order **CICONIIFORMES** *Herons, Storks and their kin*

Order **ANSERIFORMES** *Ducks, Geese, Swans*

Order **FALCONIFORMES** *Vultures, Hawks, Falcons*

Order **GALLIFORMES** *Grouse, Pheasants, Turkeys*

continued from above

Order **CUCULIFORMES** *Cuckoos, Coucals*

Order **STRIGIFORMES** *Owls*

Order **CAPRIMULGIFORMES** *Frogmouths, Nightjars and their kin*

Order **APODIFORMES** *Swifts and Hummingbirds*

COLIIFORMES *Mousebirds*

BIRD ORDERS AND FAMILIES

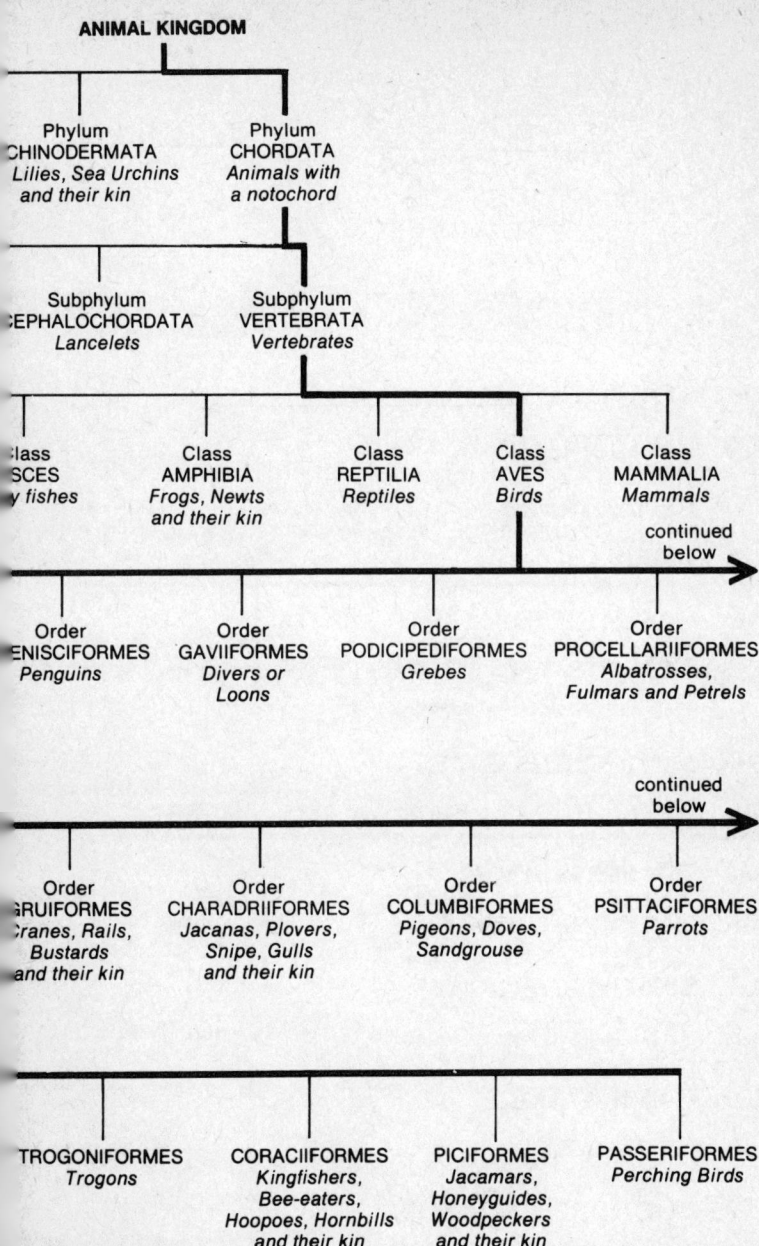

6 Bird Orders, Families and Subfamilies

Order   **STRUTHIONIFORMES**
Family   **STRUTHIONIDAE**   Ostrich

Order   **RHEIFORMES**
Family   **RHEIDAE**   Rheas

Order   **CASUARIIFORMES**
Families   **CASUARIIDAE**   Cassowaries
        DROMAIIDAE   Emu

Order   **APTERYGIFORMES**
Family   **APTERYGIDAE**   Kiwis

Order   **TINAMIFORMES**
Family   **TINAMIDAE**   Tinamous

Order   **SPHENISCIFORMES**
Family   **SPHENISCIDAE**   Penguins

Order   **GAVIIFORMES**
Family   **GAVIIDAE**   Divers, or Loons

Order   **PODICIPEDIFORMES**
Family   **PODICIPEDIDAE**   Grebes

Order PROCELLARIIFORMES

Families DIOMEDEIDAE Albatrosses
PROCELLARIIDAE Shearwaters, Fulmars, Petrels
HYDROBATIDAE Storm-Petrels
PELECANOIDIDAE Diving-Petrels

Order PELECANIFORMES

Families PHAETHONTIDAE Tropicbirds
PELECANIDAE Pelicans
SULIDAE Gannet and Boobies
PHALACROCORACIDAE Cormorants
ANHINGIDAE Darters
FREGATIDAE Frigatebirds

Order CICONIIFORMES

Families ARDEIDAE Herons, Bitterns
BALAENICIPITIDAE Whale-headed Stork
SCOPIDAE Hammerhead Stork
CICONIIDAE Storks
THRESKIORNITHIDAE Ibises, Spoonbills
PHOENICOPTERIDAE Flamingos

Order ANSERIFORMES

Families ANHIMIDAE Screamers
ANATIDAE Ducks, Geese, Swans

Order FALCONIFORMES

Families CATHARTIDAE Vultures
SAGITTARIIDAE Secretary Bird
ACCIPITRIDAE Hawks, Harriers
PANDIONIDAE Osprey
FALCONIDAE Falcons

Order GALLIFORMES

Families MEGAPODIIDAE Scrub Hens
CRACIDAE Curassows, Guans
TETRAONIDAE Grouse

PHASIANIDAE   Quails, Pheasants, Peacocks
NUMIDIDAE   Guineafowls
MELEAGRIDIDAE   Turkeys
OPISTHOCOMIDAE   Hoatzin

Order   GRUIFORMES
Families   **MESITORNITHIDAE**   Mesites
TURNICIDAE   Button-Quails
PEDIONOMIDAE   Plains Wanderer
GRUIDAE   Cranes
ARAMIDAE   Limpkin
PSOPHIIDAE   Trumpeters
RALLIDAE   Rails, Coots
HELIORNITHIDAE   Sungrebe, Finfoots
RHYNOCHETIDAE   Kagu
EURYPYGIDAE   Sunbittern
CARIAMIDAE   Seriemas
OTIDIDAE   Bustards

Order   CHARADRIIFORMES
Families   **JACANIDAE**   Jacanas
ROSTRATULIDAE   Painted Snipe
HAEMATOPODIDAE   Oystercatchers
CHARADRIIDAE   Plovers
SCOLOPACIDAE   Snipe, Woodcock
RECURVIROSTRIDAE   Avocets, Stilts
PHALAROPODIDAE   Phalaropes
DROMADIDAE   Crab Plover
BURHINIDAE   Thick-knees
GLAREOLIDAE   Pratincoles, Coursers
THINOCORIDAE   Seedsnipe
CHIONIDIDAE   Sheathbills
STERCORARIIDAE   Skuas
LARIDAE   Gulls, Terns
RYNCHOPIDAE   Skimmers
ALCIDAE   Auklets, Murres, Guillemots

Order   COLUMBIFORMES
Families   **PTEROCLIDIDAE**   Sandgrouse
COLUMBIDAE   Pigeons, Doves

Order **PSITTACIFORMES**
Family **PSITTACIDAE** Parrots

Order **CUCULIFORMES**
Families **MUSOPHAGIDAE** Touracos
CUCULIDAE Cuckoos, Coucals

Order **STRIGIFORMES**
Families **TYTONIDAE** Barn Owls
STRIGIDAE Typical Owls

Order **CAPRIMULGIFORMES**
Families **STEATORNITHIDAE** Oilbird
PODARGIDAE Frogmouths
NYCTIBIIDAE Potoos
AEGOTHELIDAE Owlet-Nightjars
CAPRIMULGIDAE Nightjars

Order **APODIFORMES**
Families **HEMIPROCNIDAE** Tree Swifts
APODIDAE Swifts
TROCHILIDAE Hummingbirds

Order **COLIIFORMES**
Family **COLIIDAE** Colies or Mousebirds

Order **TROGONIFORMES**
Family **TROGONIDAE** Trogons

Order **CORACIIFORMES**
Families **ALCEDINIDAE** Kingfishers
TODIDAE Todies
MOMOTIDAE Motmots
MEROPIDAE Bee-Eaters
LEPTOSOMATIDAE Courol
CORACIIDAE Rollers

        UPUPIDAE Hoopoe
        PHOENICULIDAE Wood-Hoopoes
        BUCEROTIDAE Hornbills

Order PICIFORMES

Families **GALBULIDAE** Jacamars
        BUCCONIDAE Puffbirds
        CAPITONIDAE Barbets
        INDICATORIDAE Honeyguides
        RAMPHASTIDAE Toucans
        PICIDAE Woodpeckers

Order PASSERIFORMES

Families **EURYLAIMIDAE** Broadbills
        DENDROCOLAPTIDAE Woodcreepers
        FURNARIIDAE Ovenbirds
        FORMICARIIDAE Antbirds
        CONOPOPHAGIDAE Gnateaters
        RHINOCRYPTIDAE Tapaculos
        PITTIDAE Pittas
        PHILEPITTIDAE Asities, False Sunbirds
        ACANTHISITTIDAE New Zealand Wrens
        TYRANNIDAE Tyrant Flycatchers
        OXYRUNCIDAE Sharpbill
        PIPRIDAE Manakins
        COTINGIDAE Contingas, Becards
        PHYTOTOMIDAE Plantcutters
        MENURIDAE Lyrebirds
        ATRICHORNITHIDAE Scrub-Birds
        ALAUDIDAE Larks
        HIRUNDINIDAE Swallows, Martins
        MOTACILLIDAE Wagtails, Pipits
        CAMPEPHAGIDAE Cuckoo-Shrikes
        PYCNONOTIDAE Bulbuls
        IRENIDAE Leafbirds
        PRIONOPIDAE Helmet Shrikes
        LANIIDAE Shrikes
        VANGIDAE Vangas or Vanga Shrikes
        PTILOGONATIDAE Waxwings

BIRD ORDERS, FAMILIES AND SUBFAMILIES

          DULIDAE Palm Chat
          CINCLIDAE Dippers
          TROGLODYTIDAE Wrens
          MIMIDAE Mockingbirds, Thrashers
          PRUNELLIDAE Accentors
          MUSCICAPIDAE 11 subfamilies
Subfamilies **TURDINAE** Thrushes, Robins
          ORTHONYCHINAE Logrunners
          TIMALIINAE Babblers, Wren-Tits
          PARADOXORNITHINAE Parrotbills
          SYLVIINAE Old World Warblers
          MALURINAE Wren-Warblers
          ACANTHIZINAE Australian Warblers
          MUSCICAPINAE Flycatchers
          RHIPIDURINAE Fantail Flycatchers
          MONARCHINAE Monarch Flycatchers
          PACHYCEPHALINAE Whistlers, Shrike-Thrushes

Families **AEGITHALIDAE** Long-tailed Tits
          REMIZIDAE Penduline Tits
          PARIDAE Tits, Titmice
          SITTIDAE Nuthatches
          CERTHIIDAE Treecreepers
          RHABDORNITHIDAE Philippine Creepers
          CLIMACTERIDAE Australian Treecreepers
          DICAEIDAE Flowerpeckers
          NECTARINIIDAE Sunbirds
          ZOSTEROPIDAE White-Eyes
          EPTHIANURIDAE Australian Chats
          MELIPHAGIDAE Honeyeaters
          EMBERIZIDAE 5 subfamilies
Subfamilies **EMBERIZINAE** Buntings, American Sparrows
          CATAMBLYRHYNCHINAE Plush-Capped Finch
          CARDINALINAE Cardinal Grosbeaks
          THRAUPINAE Tanagers, Honeycreepers
          TERSININAE Swallow-Tanager

Families **PARULIDAE** Wood Warblers

DREPANIDIDAE Hawaiian Honeycreepers
VIREONIDAE Vireos
ICTERIDAE Blackbirds, Orioles
FRINGILLIDAE 2 subfamilies
Subfamilies **FRINGILLINAE** Brambling, Chaffinch
CARDUELINAE Goldfinches and their kin

Families **ESTRILDIDAE** Waxbills
PLOCEIDAE 2 subfamilies
Subfamilies **VIDUINAE** Whydahs
PLOCEINAE Weavers, Sparrows

Families **STURNIDAE** Starlings
ORIOLIDAE Orioles
DICRURIDAE Drongos
CALLAEIDAE Wattlebirds
GRALLINIDAE Magpie Larks
ARTAMIDAE Wood-Swallows
CRACTICIDAE Butcherbirds, Currawongs
PTILONORHYNCHIDAE Bowerbirds
PARADISAEIDAE Birds of Paradise
CORVIDAE Crows, Jays, and their kin

7 Ostriches STRUTHIONIFORMES

Ostrich
Struthio camelus

This order contains only one family, and in that family only one species of ostrich is alive today. However, in the past there were quite a number ranging over Syria, Arabia, and Africa. Now, as far as we know, only the African species remains, though there are some subspecies. It is well known that they cannot fly, but with their long and powerful legs they can run very fast, and speeds of 40 mph have been recorded.

It is interesting to note that the male incubates the eggs during the night and the female during the day; the young are able to leave the nest about 24 hours after hatching. Contrary to popular belief there is no reliable evidence that ostriches hide their heads in the sand when in danger, but they might crouch down behind a tuft or hillock in which case the body could show while the head and neck could be hidden.

This group of flightless birds, including the rheas, cassowaries, emus and kiwis, are known as ratites, from the Latin *ratis*, a raft or flat-bottomed boat, a boat without a keel; the breastbone of these birds lacks the ridge or keel which serves as an attachment for the powerful flight muscles of other birds that can fly; they are known as carinates, from the Latin *carina*, a keel.

Order STRUTHIONIFORMES

struthio (L) genitive *struthionis*, an ostrich   *forma* (L) form, shape; can mean a species, a sort, a particular kind, so not necessarily referring to the actual shape.

Family STRUTHIONIDAE   1 species

Ostrich *Struthio camelus*
struthio (L) an ostrich   *camelus* (L) a camel; 'camel-like ostrich'; it seems a suitable name for this fast-running bird. Inhabiting Africa, it has been introduced to Australia where it lives wild in the south.

8 Rheas RHEIFORMES

Common Rhea
Rhea americana

Order RHEIFORMES

named after Rhea, the wife of Saturn and mother of Zeus.

Family RHEIDAE   2 species

Greater Rhea   *Rhea americana*
Sometimes known as the Common Rhea, it ranges from north-eastern Brazil to the central part of Argentina, South America.

Lesser or Darwin's Rhea   *Pterocnemia pennata*
pteron (Gr) feathers   *knēmē* (Gr) the leg between the knee and ankle; 'feather-legged'; an allusion to the feathers that cover the top part of the leg   *pennatus* (L) winged; they have wings but they are small and useless for flight; they can run very fast. Named after Charles R. Darwin (1809-1882), the English zoologist and author of the theory of organic evolution. Inhabiting South Africa.

9 Cassowaries CASUARIIFORMES

Cassowary
Casuarius casuarius

Another flightless bird order, the cassowaries are found in northern parts of Australia, in New Guinea, and adjacent islands. Like the ostrich and the rheas they have powerful legs and they are said to be able to kill a man with one blow. There are records of natives being killed by these birds, and their method is to leap into the air and strike down with their legs; the inner toe is armed with a long murderous claw, which can inflict a terrible wound. These birds are known as ratites (see notes under Ostrich on p. 42).

Order CASUARIIFORMES

from *kesuari* a Malayan word for the Cassowary.

Family CASUARIDAE 3 species

Bennett's Cassowary *Casuarius bennetti*
Dr G. Bennett (1804–1893) was an Australian surgeon, botanist, and zoologist, of New South Wales. Inhabiting New Guinea and some adjacent islands in the Pacific.

Australian Cassowary *C. casuarius*
Like all cassowaries it cannot fly, but can run very fast and is a good swimmer. Inhabiting north-eastern Queensland and New Guinea.

One-wattled Cassowary *C. unappendiculatus*
unus (L) one   *appendix* (L) genitive *appendicis*, an appendage   *-culus* (L) diminutive suffix   *-atus* (L) suffix meaning provided with. Inhabiting New Guinea.

Family   DROMAIIDAE   1 species
dromaios (Gr) running at full speed, swift.

Emu   *Dromaius novaehollandiae*
Cannot fly, but a very fast runner and a good swimmer; New Holland is an old name for part of Australia, hence the Latinised form. Unlike the cassowaries the emu is a comparatively friendly bird, and does not possess the dagger-like claw on the inner toe. This bird is known as a ratite (see notes under Ostrich on p. 42). Inhabiting dry forest and open plains in Australia.

10 Kiwis APTERYGIFORMES

Common Kiwi
Apteryx australis

The Kiwi is the national emblem of New Zealand; the name kiwi is a Maori word, and supposed to be an imitation of their cry. Unlike other birds they have a keen sense of smell; they belong to the group known as ratites (see notes under Ostrich on p. 42).

Order APTERYGIFORMES

a- (Gr) not, without   *pteron* (Gr) feathers, can mean wings   *pterugion* (Gr) a little wing; the wings of the kiwi are rudimentary and not visible on the outside of the body.

Family APTERYGIDAE   3 species

Common or Brown Kiwi   *Apteryx australis*
a- (Gr) not, without   *pterux* (Gr) a wing   *australis* does not mean Australia but derives from *auster* (L) the south wind, the south   *-alis* (L) relating to; hence *australis* (L) southern. They have a shrill cry—'kiwi' and are confined to New Zealand.

Great Spotted Kiwi *A. haasti*
Sir Julius von Haast (1824-1887) was a New Zealand explorer and geologist. He was a Director of the Canterbury Museum in 1866 and 1867.

Little Spotted Kiwi *A. oweni*
Named after Sir Richard Owen (1804-1892), an English research anatomist and explorer and author. This kiwi, and *A. haasti*, above, inhabit South Island, New Zealand.

11 Tinamous   TINAMIFORMES

Martineta Tinamou
Eudromia elegans

The Tinamous look very like guinea fowl, partridges, and other game birds, but this is only external appearance although they make good eating. The anatomy shows relationship to the rheas, and in other ways they are similar to the group known as ratites (see notes under Ostrich on p. 42). However they can fly, though only for short distances. They inhabit Central and South America.

Order   TINAMIFORMES
tinamu is a native name from the Galibi, a tribe in French Guiana.

Family   TINAMIDAE   46 species

White-throated Tinamou   *Tinamus guttatus*
gutta (L) a drop of fluid, a spot   *guttatus* (L) spotted, speckled; a reference to the inner flight feathers which are spotted pale buff; the

throat is not pure white but could be described as very pale fawn. Inhabiting southern Colombia and Venezuela, the Amazon basin, and south to northern Bolivia.

Slaty-breasted Tinamou *Crypturellus boucardi*
kruptos (Gr) covered, hidden *oura* (Gr) the tail *-ellus* (L) diminutive suffix 'a little hidden tail'; the feathers on the rump usually hide the very short tail feathers. Named after A. Boucard (1839-1904), a French ornithologist and author who was in Mexico and the Amazon area in 1877. This tinamou inhabits Mexico, Central America, and northern South America.

Kalinowski's Tinamou *Nothoprocta kalinowskii*
nothos (Gr) spurious, counterfeit *prōktos* (Gr) hindpart, tail. Sclater and Salvin, in their *Nomenclator avium neotropicalium* (London, 1873) do not explain the reason for this name, but it could refer to the small tail being covered by the body feathers, thus giving a deceptive appearance. Dr P. L. Sclater, FRS (1829-1913) was Secretary of the Zoological Society of London from 1859 to 1903; O. Salvin, FRS (1855-1898) was Curator of Ornithology at Cambridge University from 1874 to 1882. They named the bird after J. Kalinowski (1860-c. 1942), a Polish naturalist who was living in Peru from 1889 probably until his death about 1942. This tinamou inhabits the northern part of South America.

Elegant Crested Tinamou or Martineta Tinamou *Eudromia elegans*
eu- (Gr) a prefix meaning well, nicely *dromos* (Gr) a running, escape; they usually rely on running, rather than flying, as an escape from predators *elegans* (L) neat, elegant *martinete* (Sp) a night heron; this tinamou has a long slender crest similar to that of the night heron. Inhabiting the southern area of South America.

12 Penguins SPHENISCIFORMES

Rockhopper Penguin
Eudyptes crestatus

Penguins are usually associated with snow and ice, yet there are none living in the Arctic regions of the north; mostly they inhabit the Antarctic and neighbouring islands, and the southern coasts of South America, Africa, and Australia. They are not restricted to icy regions; one species, the Galapagos Penguin, lives on the shores of the Galapagos Islands, near the equator.

They are flightless, but as divers and swimmers they are probably the most accomplished of all birds; the wings are short, and useless for flight, but play the largest part in swimming.

Order SPHENISCIFORMES

sphēn (Gr) a wedge   *-iscus* (New L) a diminutive suffix, derived from the Greek *-iskos*; 'a little wedge'; a reference to the shape and shortness of the wings.

Family SPHENISCIDAE   16 species

Adélie Penguin   *Pygoscelis adeliae*
pugē (Gr) the rump, buttocks   *skelos* (Gr) the leg; a reference to the position of the legs which are set well back on the body, on the rump in fact; thus they have to adopt an upright posture: the French sector of the Antarctic where these penguins were first found was named Terre Adélie by Admiral J. S. C. Dumont d'Urville (1790-1842) after his wife Adélie.

SPHENISCIDAE 51

Emperor Penguin   *Aptenodytes forsteri*
a- (Gr) not, without   *ptēnos* (Gr) feathered, winged   *dutes* (Gr) a diver; 'a wingless diver'. Named after Johann R. Forster (1729-1798), a German traveller and ornithologist; he was on *H.M.S. Resolution* from 1772 to 1775. This is the largest penguin, more than 1 m (about four feet) tall and it lives on the coast of Antarctica.

King Penguin   *A. patagonica*
Patagonia is the region at the southern end of South America; this penguin also inhabits some islands such as South Georgia and Kerguelen, and the coasts of Tasmania and New Zealand. It is nearly as big as the Emperor Penguin.

Macaroni Penguin   *Eudyptes chrysolophus*
eu- (Gr) a prefix meaning well, nicely   *duptēs* (Gr) a diver   *khrusos* (Gr) gold   *lophos* (Gr) a crest or tuft on the head of birds; the name macaroni derives from the unusual structure of the yellow feathers that form the crest. Inhabiting the coasts of the southern parts of the Atlantic and Indian Oceans.

Rockhopper Penguin   *E. crestatus*
cristatus (L) crested; a misspelling of *crista* (L) a crest; it has an untidy crest of feathers on the forehead. Inhabiting southern islands and southern coasts of South America, South Africa, Australia, and New Zealand, in a rocky habitat.

Yellow-eyed Penguin   *Megadyptes antipodes*
megas (Gr) great   *duptēs* (Gr) a diver; it is not one of the big penguins, being about 76 cm (30 in) tall   *antipodes*, strictly speaking, means two points on opposite sides of the earth, though it is sometimes used to mean Australia or New Zealand. Inhabiting South Island, New Zealand, and Stewart, Auckland and Campbell Islands.

Jackass Penguin   *Spheniscus demersus*
Spheniscus, see notes under Order, above   *demergo* (L) I sink, I submerge   *demersus* (L) means depressed. The English name is derived from its donkey-like call. Inhabiting southern African coasts.

Galapagos Penguin   *S. mendiculus*
mendicus (L) beggerly, needy   *-culus* (L) dim. suffix; the opposite of *regillus* (L) royal, magnificent; this is taken to mean small, as it is one of the smallest penguins, only about 50 cm (20 in) tall. Inhabiting Galapagos and neighbouring islands.

13 Divers or Loons GAVIIFORMES

Red-throated Diver
Gavia stellata

Loons live almost entirely on the water, and are expert divers and swimmers like the penguins; they swim fast and deep, and it is claimed that they can go to depths of about 47 m (150 ft) when chasing fish, their main diet. They can remain submerged for long periods, some observers say as long as 15 minutes, which is remarkable if true.

The webbed feet use a sculling action something like the action of a ship's propeller, and the legs being set far back on the body the whole bird appears to be a sort of living torpedo. They inhabit northern areas and arctic seas, and are known to visit Scotland and the east coast of England.

Order GAVIIFORMES

gavia (L) a bird, perhaps the seamew.

Family GAVIIDAE 4 species

Yellow-billed Loon *Gavia adamsii*
Named after E. Adams (1824-1856), a surgeon on *H.M.S. Enterprise* from 1849 to 1855, exploring the American arctic area. Inhabiting the northern areas of Canada, Alaska and eastern Asia. The name 'loon' is of Scandinavian origin and usually used in America, meaning

an awkward person; it is an allusion to their awkward gait when on land due to the legs being set so far back on the body.

Black-throated Diver or Arctic Loon *G. arctica*
Breeding in arctic areas, it comes south in winter and may be seen on the shores of China, the Mediterranean area, and Mexico; the English name derives from a black patch on the throat.

Red-throated Diver or Loon *G. stellata*
stella (L) a star *stellatus* (L) set with stars, starry; a reference to the dark spots on the lower neck and flanks; it has a dark red throat patch. The range is similar to *G. arctica*, above.

14 Grebes PODICIPEDIFORMES

Great Crested Grebe
Podiceps cristatus

Grebes are good swimmers and divers but not so expert as the divers of the family Gaviidae, and not able to remain under water for so long; their normal time does not exceed 2 to 3 minutes. They are the only birds known to dive with their young clinging to their back, as a means of escape from danger for the whole family.

They live almost entirely on the water, sleeping, feeding, courting and mating, and are well known for their elaborate courtship display; they have a wide distribution over many parts of the world.

Order PODICIPEDIFORMES

podex (L), genitive *podicis*, the rump   *pes* (L), genitive *pedis*, the foot; 'rump-foot', an allusion to the legs being set well back on the body, on the rump in fact. In some places the local name is 'arsefoot'!

Family PODICIPEDIDAE   19 species

Horned Grebe *Podiceps auritus*
Podiceps is considered to be a contracted form of *podicipes*, which could be taken to mean 'rump-foot' (see above), but *-ceps* (L) as a suffix means 'headed', so this would translate as 'rump-headed', so the contraction is unfortunate   *auris* (L) the ear   *auritus* (L) having ears; a

PODICIPEDIDAE 55

reference to the conspicuous ear tufts, and these give rise to the English name 'horned'. Inhabiting temperate and subarctic regions of North America and Eurasia and migrating south in winter to subtropical areas.

Great Crested Grebe *P. cristatus*
cristatus (L) crested; it has a prominent crest, in fact most grebes have a crest: the English name 'great' has been given because it is the largest grebe, being about 48 cm (19 in) long. It inhabits most of Europe including the British Isles, but not northern Scandinavia; it is found in many parts of Asia, Africa, Australia, and New Zealand.

Madagascar Little Grebe *P. pelzelnii*
Named after A. von Pelzeln (1825-1891), a German zoologist and author who was Custodian of the Royal Museum in Vienna from 1859 to 1883. This grebe is confined to Madagascar.

Little Grebe or Red-throated Dabchick *P. ruficollis*
rufus (L) red   *collum* (L) the neck; a reference to the chestnut-coloured throat patch; it is the smallest grebe, about 25 cm (10 in) long. Inhabiting Europe, including the British Isles, and southern Sweden, most of Africa, and ranging across Asia as far as the East Indies and Japan.

Western Grebe *Aechmophorus occidentalis*
aikhmē (Gr) the point of a spear, a spear   *phora* (Gr) a carrying, bearing; a reference to the tarsal bones of the foot which are narrow and shaped like a blade   *occidentalis* (L) western. Inhabiting western North America and ranging south to southern Mexico.

Flightless or Short-winged Grebe *Centropelma micropterum*
kentron (Gr) a spur, spike   *pelma* (Gr) the sole of the foot, a reference to the bones of the foot (see above)   *mikros* (Gr) small   *pteron* (Gr) wings; the wings are very small and useless for flight. It is found only in South America on Lake Titicaca in the Andes.

Atitlán Grebe *Podilymbus gigas*
Podilymbus is a combination of *Podiceps* (see under Order and Horned Grebe, above) and *kolumbis* (Gr) a diving bird; another coined word and a mixture of Latin and Greek which really has no meaning   *gigas* (Gr) a giant; it is one of the biggest grebes, about 46 cm (18 in) long. This is a very rare grebe, probably almost flightless, and confined to Lake Atitlán in Guatemala.

15 Albatrosses, Fulmars, Shearwaters and Petrels PROCELLARIIFORMES

Black-footed Albatross
Diomedea nigripes

The Order Procellariiformes includes the albatrosses, fulmars, shearwaters, and petrels; they are sea birds and masters of flight 'par excellence', ranging over vast areas of the oceans. The albatross spends its life at sea, sleeping on the surface, feeding at sea, and only returning to land to breed.

Taken as a whole birds of this order, particularly the albatrosses, like stormy weather, as the gusts and upcurrents caused by the wind and waves enable them to stay airborne and glide for long distances; they do this apparently without effort, and with hardly a movement of their wings. Our most experienced glider pilots, their cockpits packed with modern instruments, have yet to achieve the mastery of flight and navigation demonstrated by these birds.

Order PROCELLARIIFORMES

procella (L) a violent wind, a storm; they like stormy weather at sea (see above).

Family DIOMEDEIDAE 13 species

Diomedes, according to the Greek legend, was driven by a storm on to the coast of southern Italy, where he remained and died an old man; his companions were turned into birds.

Grey-headed Albatross   *Diomedia chrysostoma*
khrusos (Gr) gold   *stoma* (Gr) the mouth; the upper surface of the beak is golden yellow and the head is grey merging into white at the neck. Inhabiting subantarctic islands and ranging north into temperate regions.

Wandering Albatross   *D. exulans*
exul = *exsul* (L) an exile, a wanderer; it inhabits southern oceans and is given to widespread wandering, travelling great distances; the enormous wingspan may be more than 3 m (11 ft) which enables it to remain airborne for long periods in almost effortless gliding flight (see introductory notes, above).

Sooty Albatross   *D. fusca*
fuscus (L) dark-coloured; the plumage has a grey-brown tinge which distinguishes it from the usual white albatross. Inhabiting southern oceans and ranging north as far as the southern parts of South America, South Africa, and Australia and New Zealand.

Black-browed Albatross   *D. melanophrus*
melas (Gr), genitive *melanos*, black   *ophrus* (Gr) the eyebrow; an allusion to the dark plumage round the eye. Inhabiting southern oceans but sometimes seen north of the equator.

Black-footed Albatross   *D. nigripes*
niger (L) black   *pes* (L) the foot. Inhabiting the Pacific Ocean from the southern part of the Bering Sea to the coasts of Asia and North America, the Hawaiian Islands, and ranging south to the equator.

Family PROCELLARIIDAE   53 species
procella (L) a storm, a violent wind; they like stormy weather and are 'at home' at sea like the albatrosses.

Giant Petrel or Giant Fulmar   *Macronectes giganteus*
makros (Gr) long; in general can mean large   *nēktēs* (Gr) a swimmer   *giganteus* (L) gigantic; the largest fulmar, and may be up to nearly 1 m (38 in) long. The name petrel is said to come from St Peter, and the gospel story of his walking on the water; fulmar is from Old Norse *full*, meaning foul, and *mar*, a gull; it derives from the bird's ability to spit

a foul-smelling oily liquid at intruders. Inhabiting the southern oceans and coasts of South America, South Africa, Australia and New Zealand.

Northern Fulmar *Fulmarus glacialis*
Fulmarus, see above   *glacialis* (L) glacial, icy; it is widespread in the northern hemisphere inhabiting small arctic islands and ranging south to temperate regions including the coasts of the British Isles.

Dove or Antarctic Prion *Pachyptila desolata*
pakhus (Gr) thick, stout   *ptilon* (Gr) a feather; a reference to the soft dense feathers, a characteristic of the dove prion   *desolatus* (L) forsaken, desolate; a reference to the habitat, the lonely uninhabited antarctic region: the name dove refers to its appearance, about the size of a dove at 28 cm (11 in) and having blue-grey upperparts and pale grey underparts. Prion is from the Greek *priōn*, a saw, and refers to the bill which has serrated saw-like edges. Inhabiting the antarctic sea and islands.

Parkinson's Petrel *Procellaria parkinsoni*
procella (L) a storm   *-arius* (L) suffix meaning pertaining to; they are associated with stormy weather (see introductory notes about albatrosses. Named after S. Parkinson (c. 1745-1771); a draughtsman to Sir J. Banks FRS who was with Capt Cook on *H.M.S. Endeavour* in 1770. Inhabiting antarctic regions and the southern coasts of South America and Australia.

Greater Shearwater *Puffinus gravis*
Puffinus, a Latinized form of the vernacular name puffin (see p. 144), originally *pophyn* (Middle English)   *gravis* (L) heavy, ponderous; a large bird, measuring about 46 cm (18 in). The English name derives from their manner of flight, very near the surface of the water and tilting the body from side to side, 'shearing' the water with their wings. Inhabiting the Tristan da Cunha group of islands in the South Atlantic, and the Falkland Islands off the southern coast of South America, they have a wide range wandering north possibly as far as the arctic circle.

Wedge-tailed Shearwater *P. pacificus*
pacificus (L) of the Pacific; it inhabits small islands in the southern Pacific and Indian Oceans: the English name refers to the long wedge-shaped tail.

Short-tailed or Tasmanian Shearwater   *P. tenuirostris*
tenuis (L) thin, slender   *rostrum* (L) the beak; it has a more slender beak than other shearwaters and a shorter tail. It breeds in Tasmania but has a wide migratory range circumnavigating almost the whole of the Pacific Ocean.

Bermuda Petrel or Cahow   *Pterodroma cahow*
dromos (Gr) a course, a race, usually of horses; can mean any quick movement, e.g. flight   *pteron* (Gr) feathers, wings; 'fast on the wing'; the name cahow is an imitation of the peculiar mating cry. It is confined to Bermuda, in the North Atlantic, and the surrounding sea and small islands.

Dark-rumped Petrel   *P. phaeopygia*
phaios (Gr) dusky, brown   *pugē* (Gr) the rump, buttocks. This petrel is widespread in the southern Pacific, ranging to the west coasts of Central and South America and across to the small islands off the west coasts of New Guinea and Australia.

Solander's Petrel   *P. solandri*
Named after Dr D. C. Solander FRS (1733-1782), a Swedish botanist on *H.M.S. Endeavour* from 1768 to 1771 and for a number of years he was working for the British Museum (Natural History). This petrel inhabits the southern coast of Australia and the Indian Antarctic Sea.

Snow Petrel   *Pagodroma nivea*
pagos (Gr) ice   *dromos* (Gr) a running course   *nix* (L) genitive *nivis*, snow   *niveus* (L) snowy; the name is not only suitable for its habitat but the plumage which is almost entirely white. Widespread in the oceans of the Antarctic and ranging north to about the southern tip of New Zealand and South America, and further north after breeding.

Family   HYDROBATIDAE   20 species
hudor (Gr) water   *batēr* (Gr) the threshold on which one treads.

Wilson's Storm Petrel   *Oceanites oceanicus*
oceanus (L) the ocean, derived from Ōkeanos, in Greek mythology the god of the river which was believed to encircle the earth   *-ites* (L) suffix meaning having to do with, belonging to   *-icus* (L) suffix meaning belonging to; the Storm Petrel is the smallest of the ocean birds and spends most of its life at sea; sailors associate its appearance at sea with stormy weather (see introductory notes to the Albatrosses).

Named after Alexander Wilson (1766-1813), the Scottish-American ornithologist; he wrote the nine volume *American Ornithology* published in 1805. This petrel is widespread in the Antarctic, breeding on the many islands and migrating north into the Indian Ocean, the Pacific, and the Atlantic.

White-faced Storm-Petrel   *Pelagodroma marina*
pelagos (Gr) the sea, especially the open sea, the high sea   *dromos* (Gr) a running course   *marinus* (L) of the sea. Breeding on islands in the southern oceans and migrating northwards.

Storm-Petrel   *Hydrobates pelagicus*
hudor (Gr) water   *batēs* (Gr) one that treads or covers; a reference to the petrel's habit of apparently treading on the water with a 'pattering' of feet when hunting for food   *pelagos*, see above   *-icus* (L) suffix meaning belonging to. Inhabiting the North Atlantic, including the sea around the British Isles, and the Mediterranean.

Markham's Storm-Petrel   *Oceanodroma markhami*
oceanus (L) the ocean, derived from Ōkeanos, in Greek mythology the god of the river which was believed to encircle the earth   *dromos* (Gr) a running course. Named after Sir C. R. Markham FRS (1830-1916), a naturalist and explorer and author of the book *Travels in Peru and India*. This petrel inhabits the seas around the coasts of North America, Central, and South America.

Family PELECANOIDIDAE   4 species
pelekan (Gr) a water-bird of the pelican kind   *-oides* (New L) from *eidos* (Gr) apparent shape, resemblance; it does not actually resemble the pelican in appearance, but like the pelican it has an extensible throat pouch used for holding food while hunting.

Peruvian Diving-Petrel   *Pelecanoides garnotii*
Named after Dr P. Garnot (1794-1838), a French author and ornithologist. It ranges along the western coast of South America as far north as northern Peru.

Subantarctic Diving-Petrel   *P. urinatrix*
urinator (L) a diver   *-atrix* (L) suffix denoting feminine; probably suggested by the smallness of the bird, only about 18 cm (7 in). Breeding on remote islands in the Subantarctic and migrating north to the open sea.

16 Tropicbirds, Pelicans, Gannets, Cormorants, Anhingas and Frigatebirds PELECANIFORMES

European White Pelican
Pelecanus onocrotalus

The pelicans, in spite of their rather ungainly appearance, are graceful fliers and good swimmers and divers; their enormous pouch, attached to the lower bill and throat, is too well known to need description. They hunt for fish in fresh water and sea water. Although all the birds in this group inhabit the sea or inland waters, the frigatebird cannot swim; it feeds mostly by frightening other birds into dropping their prey which it then catches in mid-air, hence 'frigatebird' because the pirates used frigates. It also picks up small marine creatures from the surface of the sea, and it is said that if it accidentally comes down on the water it cannot rise again, and may perish.

The anhingas, sometimes known as snakebirds because of their long neck, frequent inland waters. They catch fish by spearing them with their beak; the pronounced 's-bend' in the snake-like neck can be straightened, like a spring suddenly released, and thus they impale a fish.

The gannets, and also the brown pelican, have an unusual way of catching their prey: they dive from a height and strike the water with such force that it can stun a fish just below the surface.

Tropicbirds also dive from a height, but instead of hitting the water they dive cleanly, and plunge some distance below the surface. Cormorants, on the other hand, swim on the surface before diving, and then under water using both the wings and the webbed feet. In China, Japan, and India they are trained to catch fish for their owners, in some cases swimming quite a distance under water on a long leash.

Order PELECANIFORMES

pelecanus (L) a pelican   *forma* (L) form, shape; can mean sort, kind.

Family PHAETHONTIDAE   3 species
phaethōn (Gr) shining, radiant; Phaethōn was the Greek sun god
phaethontis (Gr) a poetical form with a similar meaning; an allusion to the pure white plumage which reflects the fluorescent greens and blues of the water when the birds are hovering near the surface.

White-tailed Tropicbird   *Phaethon lepturus*
leptos (Gr) slender   *oura* (Gr) the tail; a reference to the tail which consists of two long white and slender tail feathers, which stream out behind to a length greater than that of the body. Worldwide distribution in tropical waters and breeding on islands in the Caribbean, Bermuda, and far and wide in the Atlantic and Pacific Oceans.

Red-tailed Tropicbird   *P. rubricauda*
ruber (L) red   *cauda* (L) the tail of an animal. Ranging over great distances and breeding on islands in the warm areas of the Pacific and Indian Oceans.

Family PELECANIDAE   7 species
pelecanus (L) a pelican.

American White Pelican   *Pelecanus erythrorhynchos*
eruthros (Gr) red   *rhunkhos* (Gr) the beak; the large beak with its enormous pouch is red; this is one of the big pelicans with a wingspan of about 3 m (10 ft). Inhabiting inland waters and lakes in North and Central America.

Brown Pelican   *P. occidentalis*
occidentalis (L) western; inhabiting the south Atlantic coast of North America, the Gulf coast, the West Indies, the Pacific coast from Cali-

fornia south to Chile, and the Galapagos Islands. It is a sea bird but never ventures far from land and breeds on small off-shore islands.

European White Pelican   *P. onocrotalus onocrotalus* (L) the pelican. An almost pure white pelican inhabiting rivers, lakes, and some coasts in south-east Eurasia, Africa, and to some extent India and Malaysia. The name European is too restrictive; it is sometimes known as the Old World White Pelican.

Family   SULIDAE   7 species
sula is an Icelandic name for the gannet or booby and means a foolish person, probably because of their stupid-looking and ungainly gait on land, but also because they are so indifferent to the approach of people that it is possible to walk up to one and seize it in the hand. Some authors give the genus as *Morus*, for instance the Common Gannet as *Morus bassanus*, and the Cape Gannet as *M. capensis*; this is incorrect; at one time the scientific name for the genus was *Morus*, until it was discovered that an earlier name *Sula* had been given. According to the international rules the first name given as the genus is the correct one, so the name is *Sula   Mōros* (Gr) means foolish, stupid, so that name seems to agree with the general idea that the birds looked foolish or behaved in a foolish manner.

Common Gannet   *Sula bassana*
-anus (L) suffix meaning belonging to   *bassana* is a coined name meaning belonging to the Bass Rock, in the Firth of Forth, Scotland. Inhabiting the northern Atlantic ranging from Newfoundland across to the British Isles and the Channel Isles; some authorities now consider *S. capensis* of South Africa and *S. serrator* of southern Australia, Tasmania, and New Zealand, to be conspecific; they breed on rocky islands and coastal cliffs. *Sula bassana* is sometimes known as the Solan Goose; gannets are about the size of a goose.

Brown Booby   *S. leucogaster*
leukos (Gr) white   *gastēr* (Gr) the belly; the plumage is dark brown above with a white breast and belly. Worldwide distribution breeding on tropical islands right round the globe; when not breeding gannets spend their life at sea covering vast distances.

Red-footed Booby   *S. sula*
It has red feet and the bare skin on the face is sometimes red; the only booby that perches and builds its nest in trees. Inhabiting southern

regions of the Atlantic, Pacific, and Indian Oceans, and breeding on islands where there are trees.

Family PHALACROCORACIDAE   30 species
phalakros (Gr) bald-headed   *korax* (Gr), genitive *korakos*, a raven, a crow; anything hooked like a raven's beak; cormorants have a sharply hooked bill and usually part of the face is naked. The name cormorant is derived from a combination of the two Latin words corvus marinus, a 'sea-crow'.

Galapagos Flightless Cormorant   *Nannopterum harrisi*
nannos = *nanos* (Gr) a dwarf; strictly speaking it means one whose limbs are too small for his body   *pteron* (Gr) wings; the small rounded wings are useless for flight: named after Charles M. Harris (fl 1890–1899), Chief Naturalist in the Galapagos Islands in 1897 and 1898; he collected for the Tring Museum, Hertfordshire, England. Confined to Galapagos and neighbouring small islands.

Long-tailed Cormorant   *Phalacrocorax africanus*
Phalacrocorax, see under Family, above   *africanus* (L) of Africa; it has a longer tail than other cormorants. Living on lakes and rivers in Egypt and south of the Sahara ranging west across Africa to Gambia; also Madagascar.

Blue-eyed Shag   *P. atriceps*
ater (L) black   *ceps* (New L) from *caput* (L) the head; the head, and the upperparts, are black, but the eyes are not blue, they are brown; the name is an allusion to the eyelids which are blue and the bare patch on the face is quite a bright blue. There is no basic difference between a shag and a cormorant, but the shag is slightly smaller, however in some countries the name of a particular bird may be a shag and in others a cormorant. Inhabiting southern oceans and inland waters in Chile, Argentina, and Uruguay.

Peruvian Cormorant   *P. bougainvillii*
Named after Adm H. Y. P. Baron de Bougainville (c. 1781–1846), the French naturalist and author. This cormorant is found only on the coasts of Peru and Chile and sometimes Colombia.

Great Cormorant   *P. carbo*
carbo (L) coal, charcoal; i.e. black, a reference to the glossy blue-black plumage. The biggest cormorant, about 1 m (38 in), with a very wide

distribution from Atlantic coasts in northern North America, Greenland, Iceland, Scandinavia, the British Isles, and east through Africa and India on coasts and some inland waters as far as Japan, Australia, and New Zealand.

Auckland Island Shag   *P. colensoi*
Named after the Rev. W. Colenso FRS (1811-1899), a naturalist and missionary in New Zealand, it inhabits Auckland Island which lies to the south of South Island, New Zealand.

Little Pied Cormorant   *P. melanoleucos*
melas (Gr), genitive *melanos* black   *leukos* (Gr) white. Inhabiting Indonesia, Papua New Guinea, some of the Pacific Islands, and Australia.

Spotted Shag   *P. punctatus*
punctum (L) a hole, a prick   *punctillum* (L) a dot, a spot   *punctatus* spotted; the upper parts and wings are marked with little dark spots. Inhabiting the coasts of New Zealand.

Family ANHINGIDAE   4 species
Anhinga is a Tupi-Guarani word of the tribes living in the Amazon regions of South America, meaning 'water-turkey', and this English name is sometimes used in America; it has been suggested that the word is derived from *anguinus* (L) snaky, on account of the long snake-like neck.

Anhinga   *Anhinga anhinga*
Inhabiting the southern part of the USA, the Galapagos Islands, Central and South America ranging south to Argentina.

Asian Darter   *A. melanogaster*
melas (Gr), genitive *melanos* black   *gastēr* (Gr) the belly. Inhabiting India, the Burma-Vietnam area, and Malaysia and Indonesia.

Australian Darter   *A. novaehollandiae*
New Holland was at one time a name for part of Australia (see p. 231). This anhinga inhabits Australia and Papua New Guinea. Darter is probably the name usually used in several countries but in the USA it is called the Anhinga.

African Darter   *A. rufa*
rufus (L) red, ruddy; a reference to the chestnut-coloured neck. Inhabiting parts of the Middle East, Africa south of the Sahara, and Madagascar.

Family FREGATIDAE 5 species
fregata (New L) from *fregata* (It) a frigate; they often feed by frightening other birds into dropping their prey which they then catch in mid-air, hence 'frigatebirds' because of their piratical behaviour and the pirates used frigates.

Christmas Island Frigatebird *Fregata andrewsi*
Named after Dr C. W. Andrews FRS (1866-1924), a zoologist who was working at the British Museum (Natural History) in 1892 and visited Christmas Island in 1892 and 1897; it is in the Indian Ocean about 200 miles south of Java. This frigatebird breeds only on this island and some neighbouring small islands.

Ascension Island Frigatebird *F. aquila*
aquila (L) an eagle; an allusion to the hooked beak and its generally ferocious attack to obtain food. It breeds on Ascension Island far out in the South Atlantic, mid-way between Africa and South America.

Magnificent Frigatebird *F. magnificens*
magnificus (L) eminent, magnificent; an allusion to its great size, the largest frigatebird, it can measure over 1 m (45 in). Inhabiting the tropical part of the Atlantic on the coasts of North, Central, and South America and some small islands, and the same in the eastern Pacific Ocean.

Greater Frigatebird *F. minor*
minor (L) lesser, smaller; it is smaller than *magnificens*, at about 1 m (40 in); the English name 'greater' means it is not 'the greatest'. Inhabiting the tropical parts of the coasts and islands of the Atlantic, Indian, and Pacific Oceans.

17 Herons, Storks, Flamingos and their kin CICONIIFORMES

White Spoonbill
Platalea leucorodia

There are six families of birds in the order Ciconiiformes, and they are all associated with inland waters. They have long legs for wading, and some have partially webbed feet, and they frequent rivers, lakes, and marshy areas in most countries throughout the world.

Herons, egrets and bitterns eat mainly fish, and other aquatic animals; they have powder downs and a special serrated claw which are connected with preening. The powder down is an area of small feathers that easily crumble into a powder, and the feathers are continuously replaced by new growth. The beak is used to crumble the feathers, and the powder is then spread on those feathers that have been soiled by the slime and oil of fish. The powder soaks up the oil and the feathers are then 'combed out' with the special claw. The whale-headed stork also has powder downs, but other storks and the remainder of the birds in this group do not possess this specialised equipment. It is quite rare among birds but there are others that have it, for example the toucans and parrots.

Order CICONIIFORMES

ciconia (L) a stork   *forma* (L) form, shape; can mean a sort, kind, so not necessarily referring to the actual shape.

Family ARDEIDAE   62 species
ardea (L) a heron.

Grey Heron *Ardea cinerea*
cinereus (L) ash-coloured. Inhabiting the British Isles, part of Iceland, Scandinavia, and northern Africa, and ranging across Eurasia to Japan, India, and south-east Asia.

Goliath Heron *A. goliath*
In the Old Testament, Goliath was the Philistine giant who was killed by the boy David with a stone from his sling. This is a big heron which may be as much as 1·5 m (5 ft) in height. Inhabiting Senegal, Egypt, Madagascar, South Africa and parts of the Red Sea region.

Great Blue Heron *A. herodias*
erōdios (Gr) a heron; a big heron with pale blue wings and upperparts inhabiting the southern part of North America, and Central America.

Little Green Heron *Butorides virescens*
butio (L) a bittern *-ides* (L) suffix denoting a relationship; a reference to the herons being related to the bitterns *viridis* (L) green *-escens* (L) suffix meaning beginning to, somewhat; 'greenish'. Inhabiting the southern part of North America and ranging south through Central America to the northern part of South America.

Madagascar Squacco Heron *Ardeola idae*
ardea (L) a heron *-olus* (L) diminutive suffix; a small heron: named after Frau Ida R. Pfeiffer (1797-1858), a German traveller and authoress who was in Madagascar from 1856 to 1858. The name squacco is from Italian dialect *sguacco*.

Squacco Heron *A. ralloides*
rale (Fr) a rail, a water rail *Rallus aquaticus* *-oides* (New L) from *eidos* (Gr) likeness of form, can mean a type of; an allusion to this heron being similar to the water rail. Inhabiting southern Europe, Turkey, parts of East Africa, and Madagascar.

Cattle Egret *Bubulcus ibis*
bubulcus (L) a ploughman that ploughs with oxen; in a general sense a herdsman. It is an allusion to the habit of this egret of following buffalo or herds of domestic cattle searching for the insects that are disturbed by their hooves, or perching on their backs to find the insects that plague the cattle; a mutual benefit *ibis* (Gr) an Egyptian bird that feeds on aquatic animals and to which divine honours were paid; this is not an ibis but an egret that feeds on insects. Originally inhabiting only Africa and southern Asia, it has spread to parts of North,

Central, and South America, Indonesia and Australia; in Africa it is found to the north and south of the Sahara, ranging south to Madagascar and South Africa.

Great White Heron or Great Egret   *Egretta alba*
aigrette (Fr) a tuft of feathers or plume, an egret; derived from the plume of feathers worn by the male bird during the breeding season   *albus* (L) white; a large white heron measuring up to 89 cm (35 in) of which the body is probably less than 46 cm (18 in). Inhabiting North, Central, and South America, Africa south of the Sahara and Madagascar, large areas of central Asia, India, southern Asia, Malaysia, Indonesia, Papua New Guinea, and Australia.

Little Blue Heron   *E. caerulea*
caeruleus (L) dark blue. Inhabiting the southern part of North America, Central America, and the northern part of South America.

Chinese Egret   *E. eulophotes*
eu (Gr) prefix meaning nicely, well, often used to mean typical   *lophos* (Gr) a crest   *-otēs* (Gr) suffix meaning possession of; many thousands of egrets of all species have been slaughtered in the past to obtain the crests for decoration, mostly for women's hats. Inhabiting China, south-eastern Asia, and ranging to Australia.

Little Egret   *E. garzetta*
garza (It) derived from *garza* (Sp) an egret   *-etto* (It) diminutive suffix; 'little egret'. An almost world-wide distribution but not known in Central and South America; it ranges across southern Europe and Asia, Africa, south-east Asia to Papua New Guinea and Australia.

Boat-billed Heron   *Cochlearius cochlearius*
coclearum (L) a spoon; the bill is more like an upturned boat than a spoon; this heron must not be confused with the spoonbills in the family Threskiornithidae. Inhabiting the mangrove swamps of central Mexico and ranging south through Central America and Brazil to northern Argentina.

White-backed Night Heron   *Nycticorax leuconotus*
nux (Gr), genitive *nuktos*, night   *korax* (Gr) a raven, a crow; usually only seen during the hours of twilight, it has a harsh crow-like call   *leukos* (Gr) white   *notos* (Gr) the back. Inhabiting Africa.

Black-crowned Night Heron   *N. nycticorax*
It has a glossy black head and neck. Inhabiting the temperate regions

of North America and ranging south to Argentina, the southern part of Eurasia and part of northern Africa, India, the Burma-Vietnam area, Japan, Hawaii, Malaysia and the Philippines.

Banded Tiger Heron *Tigrisoma lineatum*
tigris (L) a tiger   also *tigris* (Gr) a tiger   *soma* (Gr) the body   *linea* (L) a string, a line   *-atus* (L) suffix meaning provided with; the body has dark bands or stripes on a brownish background giving very good protective colouring among the reeds. Inhabiting Central America and the northern part of South America.

Least Bittern *Ixobrychus exilis*
ixos (Gr) mistletoe   *brukhō* (Gr) I roar, I howl; *ixos* probably means a reed, so the name would mean a 'reed-howler', and is a reference to the booming call for which bitterns are famous. The name *Ixobrychus* was given by G. J. Billberg in 1828, but he never gave a proper explanation. It used to be thought that the booming sound was made by the bittern blowing into the hollow stem of a reed, as with a reed instrument like the bassoon; several different explanations have been suggested but the most likely one is that the male's throat is specially modified to produce this sound; it is quite remarkable and has been compared to a distant foghorn, and in fact can be heard over a distance of nearly 5 km (3 miles)   *exilis* (L) thin, slender; it is one of the small bitterns at about 31 cm (12 in), even smaller than *minutus*, below. Inhabiting the tropical parts of America and ranging south to Brazil.

Little Bittern *I. minutus*
minutus (L) small, minute; it is about 35 cm (14 in) long, very small compared to the Eurasian Bittern at 76 cm (30 in). It is occasionally seen in south-east England, and ranges across Eurasia, Africa, India, the Burma-Vietnam area, and Australia.

American Bittern *Botaurus lentiginosus*
boo (L) I cry aloud, I roar   *taurus* (L) a bull; a reference to the booming call for which bitterns are famous; it is the large bitterns like this one, measuring about 66 cm (26 in), that are the real exponents of booming; the small bitterns really only make a deep croak   *lentigo* (L) genitive *lentiginis*, a lentil-shaped spot, a freckle   *-osus* (L) suffix meaning full of, very spotted; a reference to the spotted brown plumage. Inhabiting the southern part of North America and ranging south through Central America to the northern part of South America.

Eurasian Bittern *B. stellaris*
stella (L) a star *stellaris* (L) starry; the plumage is more streaked than starred though it does have brown spots. Inhabiting the south-eastern part of England, the temperate and tropical areas of Eurasia, Africa, India, the Burma-Vietnam area, Malaysia, and Indonesia.

Family BALAENICIPITIDAE 1 species
balaena (L) a whale *caput* (L), genitive *capitis*, the head; the head and huge beak are said to resemble the head of a whale.

Whale-headed Stork or Shoebill *Balaeniceps rex*
ceps (New L) from *caput* (L) the head *rex* (L) a king; the bill is rather like a shoe but is not much like that of a whale except that it is unusually large. For anatomical reasons it has been difficult to place this bird except in a family on its own. Inhabiting Sudan, Uganda, and Zaire, and probably other parts of Africa where it has not yet been recorded.

Family SCOPIDAE 1 species
scopae (L) a besom, a broom made of twigs; the tufts of feathers which project from the back of the head together with the large beak in front give the appearance of a hammer.

Hammerhead Stork or Anvilhead *Scopus umbretta*
umbra (L) a shade *-etta* (New L) from *-etto* (It) diminutive suffix; a small shade; a reference to the crest and beak together giving the appearance of a sunshade or umbrella. Anatomically it is neither a stork nor a heron though it bears a close resemblance to both, so it is placed in a family on its own. Widespread in Africa from southern Sudan to South Africa, Madagascar, and also parts of Arabia.

Family CICONIIDAE 17 species
ciconia (L) a stork.

Yellow-billed Stork *Mycteria ibis*
ibis (Gr) an Egyptian bird that feeds on worms and aquatic animals, to which divine honours were paid; it has also been translated as a stork; this is a misleading name as it is not an ibis, of the family Threskiornithidae. A white bird with a red face and a yellow bill, it lives in Africa and Madagascar.

Painted Stork *M. leucocephala*
leukos (Gr) white *kephalē* (Gr) the head; mainly a white bird display-

ing various colours such as red legs, an orange bill, and yellow and red skin on the bare face. Inhabiting India and ranging through the Burma-Vietnam area and south-western China.

Asian Open-billed Stork   *Anastomus oscitans*
anastomōsis (Gr) an opening   *oscitans* (L) listless, sluggish, from *oscito* (L) I gape, I yawn; these names refer to the peculiar bill which never closes except at the tip, and it has been suggested that this assists the stork when picking up snails and mussels, which form part of its diet. Inhabiting the Indian subcontinent, Sri Lanka, the Burma-Vietnam area, and south-east China.

Abdim's Stork   *Ciconia abdimii*   (formerly *Sphenorhynchus*)
ciconia (L) a stork; named after Bey Al-Arnaut Abdim (1780-1827), at one time Governor of the Wadi Halfa area in northern Sudan. Inhabiting Sudan and other parts of tropical Africa.

White Stork   *C. ciconia*
This is the well-known stork that sometimes builds its nest on the roofs of houses, is supposed to bring good luck, and is strictly protected throughout Europe and Africa. Widespread in Eurasia from Denmark and Holland south to southern Iberia, north-western Africa, east through Asia Minor, central Asia, India and Japan.

Saddle-bill Stork   *Ephippiorhynchus senegalensis*
ephippios (Gr) for putting on a horse, a saddle   *rhunkhos* (Gr) the beak; a reference to the black band round the middle of the large orange-red bill   *-ensis* (L) suffix meaning belonging to; named from Senegal in West Africa, it is widespread in Africa except the extreme south.

Marabou   *Leptoptilos crumeniferus*
leptos (Gr) slender   *ptilon* (Gr) a wing   *crumena* (L) a small money purse or bag, usually hanging from the neck   *fero* (L) I bear; an allusion to the naked pink throat-pouch hanging from the neck about 46 cm (18 in) long; a rather ugly appendage which has some connection with the breathing: *marabout* (Fr) a priest; can mean an ugly and mis-shapen man; this stork is ugly and grotesque when seen on the ground but is graceful in the air. The range is similar to the saddle-bill stork, above.

Family THRESKIORNITHIDAE   31 species
thrēskos (Gr) religious   *ornis* (Gr), genitive *ornithos*, a bird. The most famous species of ibis, the Sacred Ibis *Threskiornis aethiopica*, was

formerly worshipped by the Egyptians and was supposed to preserve the country from plagues and serpents. It was zealously preserved in temples, and numerous mummified remains of ibises wrapped in linen in the ordinary way have been found at Memphis near Cairo, and Thebes in Upper Egypt.

Sacred Ibis *Threskiornis aethiopica*
See above *-icus* (L) suffix meaning belonging to; of Ethiopia. Although once common in Egypt this ibis is no longer found there; it inhabits Ethiopia, from where it takes its name, and is widespread in the wetter regions of Africa including Madagascar; it also inhabits parts of south-east Asia, Malaysia, Indonesia, and some Pacific islands.

Indian White Ibis *T. melanocephalus*
melas (Gr), genitive *melanos*, black, dusky *kephalē* (Gr) the head; the body feathers are white but the naked areas of the head are bluish black. In addition to India it inhabits parts of Malaysia and Indonesia.

Australian White Ibis *T. molucca*
The Moluccas are a group of islands in the Banda Sea, about 960 km (600 miles) to the north of Australia; it also inhabits Papua New Guinea and parts of Australia, and occasionally Tasmania.

Bald Ibis *Geronticus calvus*
gerōn (Gr) genitive *gerontos*, an old man *-icus* (L) suffix meaning belonging to or pertaining to *calvus* (L) bald. Inhabiting South Africa.

Hermit Ibis *G. eremita*
erēmitēs (Gr) a hermit. Sometimes known as the Waldrapp, it inhabits Africa and parts of southern Asia; known to have bred in central and southern Europe until about 1800.

Japanese Ibis *Nipponia nippon*
Nippon is the Japanese name for Japan. This ibis is now very rare.

White Ibis *Eudocimus albus*
eudokimos (Gr) to be of good repute, famous *albus* (L) white. Inhabiting southern parts of North America and the north of South America, and Central America.

Scarlet Ibis *E. ruber*
ruber (L) red; the bright red plumage of this ibis is quite remarkable. Inhabiting the northern part of South America.

74 CICONIIFORMES

Glossy Ibis *Plegadis falcinellus*
plēgas (Gr), genitive *plēgados*, a sickle   *falx* (L), genitive *falcis*, a sickle, shaped like a sickle; a reference to the curved beak   *-ellus* (L) diminutive suffix, 'a little sickle'. It has a wide range including southern Europe, Africa, Asia, the East Indies and Australia; an occasional visitor to the south of England in the autumn.

Roseate Spoonbill *Platalea ajaja*   (formerly *Ajaia*)
platalea (L) a water bird, the spoonbill   *ajaja* is a South American native name for the spoonbill. Unlike the other spoonbills, which are almost pure white, this bird is tinged with pink and darkening to red in some parts. Inhabiting the southern part of North America, Central America, and the northern half of South America.

African Spoonbill *P. alba*
albus (L) white. Inhabiting Africa and Madagascar.

Yellow-billed Spoonbill *P. flavipes*
flavus (L) yellow   *pes* (L) the foot; it has yellow legs and feet as well as the yellow bill. Inhabiting Australia.

White Spoonbill *P. leucorodia*
leukos (Gr) white   *rodeos* (Gr) of roses; *leucorodia* could mean rose-pink but the name is misleading as the plumage is white, however an orange patch can be seen on the throat during summer. Inhabiting southern Europe, Asia, north-eastern Africa, and may visit south-eastern England in the winter.

Lesser Spoonbill *P. minor*
minor (L) smaller. Inhabiting eastern China and Japan.

Royal Spoonbill *P. regia*
regius (L) royal. Inhabiting New Guinea and Australia.

Family PHOENICOPTERIDAE   4 species
phoinix (Gr), genitive *phoinikos*, deep purple or crimson; the word derives from the fact that the discovery of this colour was ascribed to the Phoenicians   *pteron* (Gr) feathers, can mean a wing; 'red-feathered': hence *phoinikopteros* (Gr) the flamingo.

Flamingos, in spite of their long legs and neck which give them a heron-like appearance, are related to the geese, ducks and swans, of the order Anseriformes. The evidence is not only anatomical, but in their habits, and the behaviour of the newly hatched chicks. Sometimes they have been placed in a separate order, the Phoenicopteriformes, but now they are usually placed in the order Ciconiiformes, with the herons and storks.

They are gregarious birds, flying in large formations and feeding and breeding together in their thousands. They like shallow water, scooping and dredging the mud with their specially shaped beaks they sieve out the small invertebrates and vegetable matter on which they feed. Their red plumage gives a wonderful colour to huge areas of the lakesides where they congregate.

Lesser Flamingo *Phoeniconaias minor*
phoinix (Gr), genitive *phoinikos*, deep purple or crimson   *naias* (L) a water nymph   *minor* (L) smaller. Inhabiting the southern part of Africa and some parts of India.

Greater Flamingo *Phoenicopterus ruber*
ruber (L) red, ruddy. This bird is an example of the confusion that can occur when using the English names of animals. In books on ornithology it is variously referred to as the Greater, the Common, the American, and the European Flamingo; the only way to establish for certain the species referred to is to use the Latin name. It has been said that the name 'flamingo' is derived from *flamenco* (Sp) an Andalusian folk-song, and another possible source is *flamma* (L) a flame, a fire. This flamingo is widespread and inhabits the Bahama Islands, parts of Mexico, the Galapagos Islands, the southern part of South America, southern Europe, Africa, India, and the Burma-Vietnam area.

Andean Flamingo *Phoenicoparrus andinus*
parra (L) a bird of ill omen, and variously translated as 'perhaps the owl', and 'perhaps the wheatear'; any connection is obscure. Inhabiting the Andes in southern Peru, western Bolivian plateaus, and the Andes in northern Chile and north-western Argentina. It is the largest species.

James's Flamingo *P. jamesi*
Named after H. B. James (1846-1892), a naturalist and a business man living in Chile. Inhabiting high Andean lakes, possibly up to about 11,000 feet (3,500 m), and now a very rare species.

18 Screamers, Geese, Swans and Ducks
ANSERIFORMES

Black Swan
Cygnus atratus

The three species of screamers have been allotted a family on their own as there seems no obvious position for them with the other birds in the order Anseriformes. They are a peculiar mixture of game birds, soaring birds of prey, and waterfowl, the latter being the reason why they are placed in this order; they possess various peculiar anatomical features including a pair of sharp spurs on the shoulder of each wing.

The English name 'screamer' arises from their harsh screaming calls which carry a great distance, probably up to 3 km (2 miles); when many of them assemble in groups they all take up the cries and the resulting noise is almost unbearable.

The geese, swans, and ducks is a large group of waterfowl with an almost world-wide distribution, though mainly in the Northern Hemisphere. Ancient literature tells us that as long ago as the year 500 B.C. these birds were known about and recorded—no doubt because, as we know today, they make good eating.

Geese and swans have a close relationship among individuals, sometimes the 'pair bond' lasting for life, which in the case of swans could be 40 to 50 years or more. They communicate by a posture and voice language, for instance when the gander has driven off an intruder he utters a special cry, and the female repeats the cry as if to show her approval, and stretches out her neck parallel to the ground; even the baby goslings copy their parents by making this gesture. There are birds other than geese and swans that show a similar behaviour.

Many species, notably the Greylag Goose *Anser anser*, fly in 'V' and other special formations now adopted by man in aeroplanes; it is tiring for the leaders and sometimes they are changed during flight.

Order   ANSERIFORMES

anser (L) a goose.

Family   ANHIMIDAE   3 species
anhima (New L) derived from a Portuguese word, derived from *anhuma*, a Tupi native name for the bird.

Horned Screamer   *Anhima cornuta*
cornutus (L) horned; a reference to the remarkable horn about 10 cm (4 in) long curving forward from the top of the head. Inhabiting Venezuela, Bolivia, and the southern part of Brazil.

Northern Screamer   *Chauna chavaria*
khaunos (Gr) gaping; metaphorically can mean foolish, silly   *chavaria* is a coined name probably from *charivari* (Fr) rough music, cacophonous noise, a reference to their harsh cries. Inhabiting Colombia and Venezuela.

Southern Screamer   *C. torquata*
torquatus (L) wearing a collar; a reference to the band of dark feathers round the neck. Inhabiting Bolivia, Brazil, and Argentina.

Family   ANATIDAE   146 species
anas (L), genitive *anatis*, a duck.

Magpie Goose   *Anseranas semipalmata*
Anseranas, see above   *semi-* (L) prefix meaning half   *palma* (L) the palm of the hand; this is a reference to the feet, which are only partly webbed. Any ornithologist could be forgiven for not knowing where to place this bird in the scheme of classification; it has certain characteristics typical of swans, geese, and ducks, and it has been suggested that it should be placed in an order on its own; among other peculiarities it perches in trees, like the Tree Ducks (below). The name

Magpie derives from the colour of the plumage; it has a black head and neck, a white body, and a black rump and tail; it inhabits southern Papua New Guinea and the northern part of Australia.

Black-billed Tree Duck *Dendrocygna arborea*
dendron (Gr) a tree *kuknos* (Gr) a swan *cycnus* = *cygnus* (L) a swan; the tree ducks and the swans are alike in some of their habits *arbor* (L) a tree; some species of tree ducks may be seen perching in trees. Inhabiting North and Central America.

Black-bellied Tree Duck *D. autumnalis*
autumnalis (L) relating to autumn; probably a reference to the brownish colour of the back and breast. They have a distinctive whistling call and are sometimes known as Whistling Ducks. Inhabiting North, Central, and South America.

Fulvous Tree Duck *D. bicolor*
bicolor (L) of two colours; it is light brown with a dark brown back and pale stripes on the flanks *fulvous* means dull yellow, tawny, from *fulvus* (L) yellowish brown, tawny. Ranging from California in North America to Argentina in South America, and also inhabiting Africa and India.

Eyton's Tree Duck *D. eytoni*
Named after T. C. Eyton (1809-1880), a naturalist and author; he founded the Eyton Hall Museum. Inhabiting Australia and New Guinea.

Spotted Tree Duck *D. guttata*
gutta (L) a drop of fluid, a spot *guttatus* (L) spotted, speckled. Inhabiting islands in the south-west Pacific.

Indian Tree Duck *D. javanica*
Sometimes known as the Lesser Whistling Duck, it is not restricted to Java and inhabits India, southern China, and other areas of south-east Asia.

Coscoroba Swan *Coscoroba coscoroba*
coscoroba (Sp) probably derived from *cosaroba*, a Tupi native name for 'a swan-like diving bird'. This swan has a shorter neck than other swans, and really looks more like a duck; for several reasons it is considered to be intermediate between the ducks and the swans. Inhabiting southern South America, ranging from southern Brazil to Tierra del Fuego and including the Falkland Islands.

Black Swan *Cygnus atratus*
cygnus (L) a swan   *ater* (L) black   *atratus*, clothed in black as for mourning. Inhabiting Australia.

Whooper Swan   *C. cygnus*
It has a 'whooping' type of call and is sometimes known as the Whistling Swan. Inhabiting Scandinavia and Iceland and may visit the British Isles in winter.

Black-necked Swan   *C. melanocoryphus*
melas (Gr), genitive *melanos*, black   *koruphē* (Gr) the head, the top part. Inhabiting South America, the range is similar to the Coscoroba Swan (above).

Mute Swan   *C. olor*
olor (L) a swan. This is the common swan that originally bred in Europe and Asia and has now been introduced to many parts of the world by man; it is the one usually seen on lakes and rivers in the British Isles. It is not entirely mute as it can make grunting and hissing noises.

White-fronted Goose   *Anser albifrons*
anser (L) a goose   *albus* (L) white   *frons* (L) forehead, brow. Inhabiting western North America, Central America, Africa, parts of Eurasia including the British Isles, India, and the Burma-Vietnam area.

Greylag Goose   *A. anser*
The plumage is predominantly grey to greyish-brown, and it is suggested that 'lag' came about because it lags behind when other kinds of geese have departed for their breeding grounds. It breeds in northern parts such as Iceland and Scandinavia, also northern Scotland and ranging east to the Balkans and the Black Sea area; it winters in southern Europe, northern Africa, and an eastern race ranges across southern Asia to China. It can sometimes be seen migrating across England in huge formation flights; I have seen over 100 flying south in three large 'V' formations of more than 30 birds each.

Pink-footed Goose   *A. brachyrhynchus*
brakhus (Gr) short   *rhunkhos* (Gr) the beak; this is a close relative of the Bean and Greylag but with a shorter beak, and is sometimes considered to be a subspecies of the Bean Goose *A. fabalis* (below). Breeding in Greenland, Iceland, and the Norwegian archipelago of Spitzbergen, and migrating south to Scotland, England, Wales, and coastal areas in northern France.

Snow Goose   *A. caerulescens*
caeruleus (L) dark blue   *-escens* (L) suffix meaning beginning to, somewhat; the plumage is almost white, hence the English name, but there is a grey variety usually known as the Blue Goose in which the main body colour is blue-grey. Inhabiting North America and an occasional visitor to western Europe, and also known in southern parts of Asia.

Lesser White-fronted Goose   *A. erythropus*
eruthros (Gr) red   *pous* (Gr) the foot; it is similar to the White-fronted Goose (above) only smaller, and there is a larger patch of white on the forehead extending onto the crown. Breeding in northern Scandinavia and Eurasia and migrating south to Romania, Bulgaria, Asia Minor, and other areas of southern Asia including India and the Burma-Vietnam area.

Bean Goose   *A. fabalis*
faba (L) the broad bean   *-alis* (L) suffix meaning pertaining to; the name was given by Dr Thomas Pennant FRS (1726-1798) and refers to its habit of feeding on the beans and other crops left in the fields after the harvest. Breeding in northern areas from Greenland to eastern Siberia and migrating to southern Europe (and occasionally Britain), to North America and to parts of southern Asia.

Brent (or Brant) Goose   *Branta bernicla*
Branta is a name coined from the Anglo Saxon *brennan*, to burn, and refers to the reddish-brown colour   *bernicla* (New L) from *bernicle* (Fr) a barnacle (see Barnacle Goose, below). Inhabiting North and Central America, northern Europe including the British Isles and Scandinavia, and ranging south-east to the Burma-Vietnam area.

Canada Goose   *B. canadensis*
-ensis (L) suffix meaning belonging to; inhabiting Canada and northern areas of North America and migrating south to the Gulf of Mexico and other southern areas. It is now a familiar sight in Britain with its graceful black neck and white chin; it was introduced to Europe in the seventeenth century.

Barnacle Goose   *B. leucopsis*
leukos (Gr) white   *opsis* (Gr) aspect, appearance; 'white-faced'; it has a white forehead and face. The name arises from an ancient belief that this goose was an offspring of the barnacle, and even more bizarre the belief that these barnacles grew on trees. In fact, when the shell of a

barnacle is broken open the body shows a distinct resemblance to a goose. It is a mutual exchange of names, as there is the Goose Barnacle *Lepas anatifera lepas* (Gr) a limpet *anas* (L), genitive *anatis*, a duck *fero* (L) I bear, I bring forth. The Barnacle Goose inhabits Greenland, Iceland, Spitzbergen, and Norway and migrates south in winter to Ireland and parts of northern France.

Red-breasted Goose *B. ruficollis*
rufus (L) red *collus* = *collum* (L) the neck of man and animals; not only the neck but also the breast is quite a striking red in marked contrast to the brown and white body. Inhabiting northern areas of western Asia and migrating south to Asia Minor, India, and other parts of southern Eurasia.

Ne-ne or Hawaiian Goose *B. sandvicensis*
-ensis (L) suffix meaning belonging to. The Hawaiian Islands were formerly known as the Sandwich Islands, a territory of the USA; they were named by Capt James Cook (1728-1779) the explorer and navigator, after John Montagu Sandwich, the 4th Earl of Sandwich (1718-1792). Ne-ne is the Hawaiian name for this goose; it is found only in Hawaii except that some pairs were brought to the Wildfowl Trust in England for breeding, to rescue them from extinction; still very rare.

Andean Goose *Chloephaga melanoptera*
khloē (Gr) the tender shoot of plants *phagein* (Gr) to eat; in addition to various grasses they are fond of seaweed *melas* (Gr), genitive *melanos*, black *pteron* (Gr) feathers, or can mean wings. Inhabiting rocky shores along the west coast of South America.

Upland Goose *C. picta*
pictus (L) painted; a reference to the colour pattern of the plumage which is white above with narrow black lines across and a yellow to buff-coloured breast. Named Upland Goose because it usually lives on higher ground and not near the sea; it inhabits Chile and southern Argentina and ranges south to Tierra del Fuego.

Ruddy-headed Goose *C. rubidiceps*
rubidus (L) red, reddish *ceps* (New L) from *caput* (L) the head. Inhabiting South America.

Blue-winged Goose *Cyanochen cyanoptera*
kyaneos (Gr) dark blue, glossy blue *khēn* (Gr) a goose *pteron* (Gr)

feathers, can mean wings. Inhabiting Africa; really a sheldrake but superficially rather like a goose.

Ruddy Shelduck   *Tadorna ferruginea*
tadorna (New L) derived from *tadorne* (Fr) a sheldrake   *ferrugineus* (L) rusty, 'rust-coloured'   *sheld* (Old E) variegated, particoloured (see below). Inhabiting southern parts of Eurasia, northern Africa, and ranging east to China.

Shelduck   *T. tadorna*
Sometimes known as the Sheld Duck which is probably a better name, from *sheld* (Old E) variegated, particoloured; the plumage includes the colours black, white, chestnut, and dark green, and is more colourful than *ferruginea* (above). Widespread in Eurasia including the British Isles and Scandinavia, breeding coastal areas; also Mediterranean, northern Africa, and ranging east to Arabia, India, China, and Japan.

Paradise Duck   *T. variegata*
varius (L) variegated   *varie* (L) with diverse colours   *variegatus* (L) provided with diverse colours. The name Paradise Duck arises from the colourful plumage, like the Bird of Paradise. Inhabiting Australia.

Patagonian Crested Duck   *Lophonetta specularioides*
lophos (Gr) the crest of birds, and other crests   *nētta* (Attic Gr) a duck, derived from *neō* (Gr) I swim   *speculum* (L) a mirror; the English word speculum can mean the bright patch on a bird's wing, specially a duck's wing   *-oides* (New L) derived from *eidos* (Gr) apparent shape, resemblance; on a mostly brown and dark brown plumage a pink patch, or speculum, shows up on the wings. Inhabiting western Argentina, southern Chile, Patagonia, and ranging south to Tierra del Fuego and the Falkland Islands.

Falkland Island Flightless Steamer Duck   *Tachyeres brachypterus*
takhus (Gr) swiftness, speed   *eressō* (Gr) I row   *takhuērēs* (Gr) fast-rowing   *brakhus* (Gr) short   *pteron* (Gr) feathers, can mean wings. This flightless duck with only small wings can achieve quite a speed on the surface of the water by beating the water with its wings as though rowing, and this causes much flying spray and general commotion which has given rise to the name 'steamer duck'; an allusion to the paddle steamers in general use when the name was given. It is confined to the Falkland Islands.

ANATIDAE 83

Flying Steamer Duck   *T. patachonicus*
-icus (L) suffix meaning belonging to   *patachonicus*, of Patagonia (the southern part of Argentina). Only this one of the three Steamer Ducks is able to fly, having larger wings, but even so often prefers to escape from intruders by 'steaming' along the surface of the water. Inhabiting southern Chile and Argentina and ranging south to Tierra del Fuego, and the Falkland Islands.

Magellan Flightless Steamer Duck   *T. pteneres*
ptēna (Gr) fowls, birds   *pteneres* is a coined word intended to mean 'rowing birds' (see *T. brachypterus* above). Inhabiting coastal areas along the Magellan Straits and ranging north to some extent, and the islands around Tierra del Fuego.

Pintail   *Anas acuta*
anas (L) a duck   *acutus* (L) sharp, pointed; the central tail feathers are elongated and sharply pointed, forming the 'pintail'. It has a widespread distribution in the Northern Hemisphere.

American Wigeon   *A. americana*
-anus (L) suffix meaning belonging to; inhabiting North, Central, and South America.

Bahama Pintail   *A. bahamensis*
-ensis (L) suffix meaning belonging to, usually referring to a place. Not entirely confined to the Bahamas, and known in North and South America.

Madagascan Teal   *A. bernieri*
Named after Dr J. A. Bernier, a French naval surgeon and botanist; he spent three years in Madagascar from 1831 to 1834.

Chestnut Teal   *A. castanea*
kastana (Gr) the chestnut tree; an allusion to the chestnut-coloured plumage. Inhabiting Australia.

Northern Shoveler   *A. clypeata*
clypeus = *clipeus* (L) a shield   *-atus* (L) suffix meaning provided with; probably a reference to the white breast which stands out in contrast to the darker plumage of the body; it has a shovel-like broad-fronted bill. Widespread throughout the northern part of the world including North, Central and South America, Europe, including south-east England, parts of Scandinavia, Africa, Asia, including India and the Burma-Vietnam area.

South American or Speckled Teal *A. flavirostris*
flavus (L) yellow   *rostrum* (L) the beak. Inhabiting South America.

Baikal Teal   *A. formosa*
formosus (L) finely formed, beautiful; the English name is from Lake Baikal, a very large fresh-water lake in southern Siberia. It also lives in parts of North America, south-east Asia, and is a very rare visitor to Europe.

South Georgia Pintail   *A. georgica*
South Georgia is a British island about 1,287 km (800 miles) to the east of the Falkland Islands in the South Atlantic; it is a very remote place, but although named from this island other subspecies of this pintail duck inhabit parts of South America and Africa.

Meller's Duck   *A. melleri*
Named after Dr C. J. Meller (c. 1836–1869), who was Superintendent of the Botanical Gardens in Mauritius in 1865; Mauritius is one of the Mascarene Islands in the Indian Ocean about 1,126 km (700 miles) to the east of Madagascar. This duck inhabits Africa.

Eurasian Wigeon   *A. penelope*
penelops (Gr) a kind of duck; Penelope was the wife of Odysseus, and there is a Greek legend about her being thrown into the sea as a baby and rescued by sea-birds, but whether the bird was named after her or she was named after the bird is not known. This duck is widespread in areas of North and Central America, Europe, Asia, Africa, India, the Burma-Vietnam area, Malaysia, Indonesia, and New Guinea.

Mallard   *A. platyrhynchus*
platus (Gr) wide or flat   *rhunkhos* (Gr) the beak; a reference to the heavy and rather flat beak. Widespread distribution similar to *A. penelope*, above, and including Australia.

Garganey   *A. querquedula*
querquedula (L) a kind of duck: garganey is the Italian name used in the area of the lakes of northern Italy. Inhabiting Europe but only the south-eastern part of England; Africa, Asia, India, the Burma-Vietnam area, Malaysia, Indonesia, New Guinea and Australia.

Gadwall   *A. strepera*
strepo (L) I make a noise, I rattle; a reference to the call which has also been described as reedy. Inhabiting North and Central America, Europe including the British Isles but little known in Scandinavia;

Africa, Asia, India, and the Burma-Vietnam area. The origin of the name Gadwall is obscure, but was first used in the seventeenth century.

Torrent Duck   *Merganetta armata*
mergus (L) a diver, a water fowl   *nētta* (Attic Gr) = *nēssa* (Gr) a duck, from *nēo* (Gr) I swim   *armatus* (L) armed; a reference to the sharp spurs on its wings. The name Torrent Duck has been given because it frequents rapid mountain streams and likes the rough tempestuous water because it finds the essential small invertebrate food there; these streams are in the Andes Mountains and the birds range along the whole of the western part of South America.

Freckled Duck   *Stictonetta naevosa*
stiktos (Gr) dotted, dappled   *nētta* (Gr) see above   *naevus* (L) a mole or wart on the body; can mean a spot, a blemish   *-osus* (L) suffix meaning full of; 'very spotted'. Inhabiting Australia.

Steller's Eider   *Polysticta stelleri*
polus (Gr) many, much   *stiktos* (Gr) dotted, dappled; not a very apt name as the drake does not appear to be spotted though the duck has a mottled brown plumage, however the drake takes on the brown colour in winter. George W. Steller (1709-1769) was a German zoologist and traveller; several other animals have been named after him. This eider inhabits arctic Canada and Siberia, and ranges south as far as the northern coasts of the Atlantic and Pacific Oceans.

Common Eider   *Somateria mollissima*
sōma (Gr), genitive *sōmatos*, the body   *erion* (Gr) wool   *mollis* (L) soft, *mollissima*, very soft; 'very soft body-wool'. Noted for the very soft down, hence the name eiderdown, or quilt. Inhabiting the colder parts of the Northern Hemisphere including the British Isles.

Redhead   *Aythya americana*
aythya (New L) from *aithuia* (Gr) a sea-gull or diving bird; an important American game bird akin to the Canvasback and European Pochard but with a brighter rufous head. Inhabiting North and Central America.

Australian Pochard   *A. australis*
auster (L), genitive *austri*, the south   *-alis* (L) suffix meaning relating to   *australis* (L) southern; it does not necessarily mean Australia. This pochard inhabits Indonesia, New Guinea, some of the small Pacific islands, and Australia.

Baer's Pochard   *A. baeri*
Named after Prof K. E. V. Baer (1792-1876), a German Professor of Zoology, of Königsberg. This pochard inhabits North America, Eurasia, India, and the Burma-Vietnam area.

Common Pochard   *A. ferina*
ferina (L) the flesh of wild animals, game. Widespread distribution including North America, Eurasia, Africa, India, the Burma-Vietnam area, Malaysia, and Indonesia. It is considered an important game bird and makes good eating.

Tufted Duck   *A. fuligula*
fuligo (L) soot   *-ulus* (L) dim. suffix; can also mean somewhat, a tendency; 'somewhat sooty'; it is mostly black except for the white flanks, and has a trailing crest at the back of the head, hence the English name. The distribution is similar to *A. ferina* (see above), ranging from North America, and including Iceland, across Eurasia to Kamchatka, the peninsula at the eastern end of the USSR.

New Zealand Scaup   *A. novaeseelandiae*
Scaup is a Scottish word for scalp, the mussel-scalp or mussel-scaup; this pochard has been given the name because it feeds on mussel-scaups.

Canvasback   *A. valisineria*
Indirectly named after Prof Antonio Vallisnieri (1661-1730), an Italian naturalist who was a Professor of Medicine in Padua; its favourite food is the waterweed *Vallisnera spiralis*, named after him. The name canvasback derives from the colour and the marking of grey and white on the back. Inhabiting North and Central America, it is an important game bird, and considered one of the best ducks for the table.

African or Red-eyed Pochard   *Netta erythrophthalma*
nētta (Attic Gr) = *nēssa* (Gr) a duck, from *nĕo*, I swim   *eruthros* (Gr) red   *ophthalmos* (Gr) the eye; the eye is quite a bright red in the drake, but brown in the duck. Inhabiting Africa and South America.

Red-crested Pochard   *N. rufina*
rufus (L) red   *-inus* (L) suffic meaning like, pertaining to; a reference to the crest. It is known in East Anglia, and found in various regions of Eurasia, but local.

ANATIDAE

Maned Goose *Chenonetta jubata*
khēn (Gr), genitive *khēnos*, a goose *nētta* (Attic Gr) see under African Pochard, above *juba* = *iuba* (L) the mane of an animal *iubatus* (L) maned; a reference to the crest. Inhabiting Australia.

Brazilian Teal *Amazonetta brasiliensis*
nētta (Attic Gr) see above; 'Amazon duck' *-ensis* (L) suffix meaning belonging to; it is not confined to Brazil and ranges from the northern part of South America south to Buenos Aires.

Mandarin Duck *Aix galericulata*
aix (Gr) a water bird of the goose kind; the appearance is more that of a typical duck rather than a goose *galerum* (L) a skull cap *galericulum* (L) a small cap for the head *galericulata*, provided with a small cap; an allusion to the colouring of the head and a crest which give the impression of a cap. The name Mandarin has been given because of the brilliant and decorative plumage, and for this reason it has been introduced to many countries and domesticated and can often be seen on ponds in parks and gardens. Originally inhabiting China and other far-eastern countries.

Wood Duck *A. sponsa*
sponsa (L) a betrothed woman, a bride; the name is taken from the Mandarin Duck, above; in the old days in China a pair was given as a traditional wedding present to symbolise marital fidelity. Although living in quite different parts of the world these two ducks are very closely related and the females appear to be almost identical. Inhabiting the temperate regions of North America.

Knob-billed Goose *Sarkidiornis melanotos*
sarx (Gr), genitive *sarkos*, flesh *idios* (Gr) separate, distinct; hence strange *ornis* (Gr) a bird; a reference to the peculiar knob on the bill of the male *melas* (Gr), genitive *melanos*, black *nōton* (Gr) the back; it has a black back in contrast to the white breast and grey flanks.

Muscovy Duck *Cairina moschata*
-inus (L) suffix meaning belonging to; it is unlikely that this duck is named from Cairo, Egypt, as it inhabits Central and South America; it could be from Cairu, Brazil *moschatus* (New L) musky; originally known as the 'musk-duck', it has a strong musky smell; 'Muscovy' does not suggest any connection with Moscow.

Spur-winged Goose *Plectropterus gambensis*
plēktron (Gr) a cock's spur *pteron* (Gr) feathers, can mean wings; a reference to the spur on the wing shoulder *-ensis* (L) suffix meaning belonging to; it is not confined to Gambia although named from there; it ranges across Africa from Sudan and Ethiopia south to the Zambesi.

Barrow's Goldeneye *Bucephala islandica*
bu = bous (Gr), genitive *boos*, a bull *kephalē* (Gr) the head; 'bull-headed' is a reference to the large head on a rather short neck *-icus* (L) suffix meaning belonging to; named from Iceland it is not confined to that island; it breeds there and also in Greenland and other parts of northern North America but in winter it ranges further south. It is named in honour of Sir John Barrow (1764-1848), an English explorer and Admiralty official; the small town of Barrow in northern Alaska, and Barrow Point, are named after him.

Smew *Mergus albellus*
mergus (L) a sea bird, a diver, from *mergo* (L) I dip, I plunge in *albus* (L) white *-ellus* (L) diminutive suffix, used here to suggest 'whitish'; the male is mostly white with grey flanks and black marking. The name smew derives from the Old German word *smiehe*. Breeding in northern Scandinavia and northern Asia and ranging south in winter to southern Europe, northern India, China, and Japan; an occasional visitor to southern England.

Auckland Island Merganser *M. australis*
auster (L), genitive *austri*, the south *australis*, southern; it does not necessarily mean Australia; Auckland Island is about 483 km (300 miles) south of New Zealand. The name merganser is derived from *mergus* and *anser* (L) a goose; this merganser is very rare and may even now be extinct.

Hooded Merganser *M. cucullatus*
cucullus (L) a hood *-atus* (L) suffix meaning provided with; a reference to the fan-shaped crest which is white with a black border and has the appearance of a hood. Inhabiting North America from the southern part of Canada ranging south to Central America.

Goosander or Common Merganser *M. merganser*
merganser, see *M. australis*, above. The name goosander is probably from goose combined with *and* (Old Norse), plural *ander*, a duck; 'goose-duck' would suggest a large duck and this is the largest of all

the ducks. Inhabiting North America, Europe including Iceland, Scandinavia, and the British Isles, though not Ireland, and ranging east across Asia to Kamchatka, China, and Japan.

Red-breasted Merganser *M. serrator*
serratus (L) toothed like a saw; a reference to the bill which has backward-pointing serrations which enable it to hold the slippery fish on which it feeds; all the mergansers have the serrated bill. *M. serrator* breeds in the northern parts of North America and Eurasia including Iceland, Scandinavia, and the northern parts of the British Isles, and ranges south throughout the whole of this area in the winter.

Blue-billed Duck *Oxyura australis*
oxus (Gr) sharp, pointed *oura* (Gr) the tail; a reference to the tail consisting of stiff feathers and this group of ducks are sometimes known as 'stifftails' *auster* (L), genitive *austri*, the south -*alis* (L) suffix meaning relating to; southern; it does not necessarily mean Australia although in fact this duck does live in the southern part of Australia. The male has a pale blue bill.

Ruddy Duck *O. jamaicensis*
-*ensis* (L) suffix meaning belonging to; named from Jamaica it also inhabits Canada, the USA, Central America, and parts of South America.

White-headed Duck *O. leucocephala*
leukos (Gr) white *kephalē* (Gr) the head. Inhabiting certain isolated areas in southern Europe, most of the northern part of North Africa, and some areas in Asia including India.

Lake Duck *O. vittata*
vitta (L) a chaplet, a ribbon *vittatus*, bound with a ribbon, can mean striped. Inhabiting South America.

White-backed Duck *Thalassornis leuconotus*
thalassa (Gr) the sea *ornis* (Gr) a bird; it seems a strange name for a bird that usually frequents inland waters rather than the sea *leukos* (Gr) white *nōton* (Gr) the back. Inhabiting Africa.

Musk Duck *Biziura lobata*
Bizi, obscure *oura* (Gr) the tail; the origin of 'bizi' has not been traced but is probably an obscure coinage by Shaw; the stiff tail has an unusual shape and is normally held upright *lobatus* (New L) lobed, from *lobos* (Gr) a lobe; a reference to the strange lobe under the

bill. In the Official Checklist of the Birds of Australia, H. Wolstenholme, BA, of Wahroonga, Sydney, referred to the MS of Dr Herbert Langton (deceased), an expert on the derivation of bird names; he says: 'Like myself he could not find the origin of certain obscure names, such as *Biziura, Epthianura,* and *Aplonis*.' Dr G. Shaw, FRS (1751–1813) was a professor at the British Museum (Natural History) from 1807 until his death in 1813. This duck has a musk gland which produces an unpleasant odour; it inhabits southern Australia and Tasmania.

Black-headed Duck   *Heteronetta atricapilla*
heteros (Gr) other, different   *nētta* (Attic Gr) = *nēssa* (Gr) a duck, from *nēo*, I swim   *ater* (L) fem. *atra*, black   *capillus* (L) the hair of the head, usually of men, can mean the hair of animals: 'a different duck'; it is not closely related to other stifftails and is unique in being the only truly parasitic member of the duck family, laying its eggs in other birds' nests. Inhabiting the southern part of the Andes, South America.

19 Vultures, Hawks, Eagles, Falcons and their kin FALCONIFORMES

Goshawk
Accipiter gentilis

This group consists of the big vultures, the scavengers, and the diurnal birds of prey. The word diurnal comes from the Latin *diurnus*, meaning belonging to a day, as these birds hunt in the daytime, unlike the owls for instance, who hunt at night. It includes the Osprey and the Secretary Bird.

They range in size from the Falconets, about 80 cm (7 in) long, to the huge Andean Condor, *Vultur gryphus*, with a wingspan of about 3·5 m (12 ft); it is the largest flying bird in the world still alive today. There is no doubt that the vultures, although they look rather repulsive, do a good job; I know of someone who says they clean up his ranch, and when they visit his ranch-house to see what there is to scavenge, he refers to them as 'my refuse disposal unit'. They rank among the finest soaring birds in the world as demonstrated by their effortless circling in thermals.

Order FALCONIFORMES

phalkōn (Gr) = *falco* (L), genitive *falconis*, a falcon, derived from *falx* (L), genitive *falcis*, a sickle; said to be on account of the curved talons.

Family CATHARTIDAE   7 species
kathartēs (Gr) a cleanser, a purifier; being scavengers they clear up rotting carcases and other refuse.

Lesser Yellow-headed Vulture   *Cathartes burrovianus*
-anus (L) suffix meaning belonging to; a curious alteration of the spelling, it is named after a Dr Burrough but further details about him are not known; the name was given in 1845. This vulture inhabits South America.

Black Vulture   *Coragyps atratus*
korax (Gr) a raven, a crow   *gups* (Gr) a vulture; 'a raven-vulture'; the black plumage and general appearance is that of a raven   *ater* (L) black   *atratus* (L) clothed in black as for mourning. Inhabiting the middle areas of North America and ranging south through Central America to Patagonia.

California Condor   *Vultur californianus*
vultur (L) a vulture   *-anus* (L) suffix meaning belonging to. Inhabiting the western part of North America and ranging south to Central America, but now almost extinct.

Andean Condor   *V. gryphus*
grupos (Gr) hook-nosed, with an aquiline nose. The largest flying bird in the world with a wing-span of about 3·5 m (12 ft), it ranges along the entire length of the Andes from sea level up to about 3,047 m (10,000 ft).

Family SAGITTARIIDAE   1 species
sagitta (L) an arrow   *sagittarius* (L) an archer, a bowman; '... from the way their upright carriage and dignified stride reminded people of an archer about to loose an arrow' (Purnell's *Encyclopedia of Animal Life*). In appearance and anatomy it does not have any obvious affinities that would place it in any particular group so it has been given a family on its own; its proper place in classification remains in doubt.

Secretary Bird   *Sagittarius serpentarius*
-arius (L) suffix meaning pertaining to; it is associated with snakes because it is adept at killing them and they form part of its diet: the name 'secretary' is an allusion to the spray of quills projecting from the back of the head, reminiscent of the old-fashioned quill pens that were tucked behind the ears of secretaries. Widespread throughout most of Africa.

Family ACCIPITRIDAE 211 species
accipiter (L), genitive *accipitris*, a hawk.

Honey Buzzard *Pernis apivorus*
pernis (New L), said to be a corruption of *pternis* (Gr) a bird of prey *apis* (L) a bee *voro* (L) I devour; it eats bees and wasps, nipping off the tail before eating, and the honey, and also eats frogs and lizards and small mammals. Inhabiting most of Europe and occasionally breeding in southern England, ranging east across Russia to the eastern side of the Ural Mountains.

Barred Honey Buzzard *P. celebensis*
-ensis (L) suffix meaning belonging to; inhabiting Celebes, now known as Sulawesi, one of the islands of Indonesia; it also inhabits the Philippines. The name 'barred' is a reference to the dark brown markings in the plumage.

Swainson's Kite *Gampsonyx swainsonii*
gampsos (Gr) bowed, curved *onux* (Gr) a claw; a reference to the strongly hooked talons: named after W. Swainson, FRS (1789-1855), a zoologist, artist, and taxidermist; he spent a number of years in Brazil, Sicily, Africa, and New Zealand. This kite inhabits Central and South America.

Swallow-tailed Kite *Elanoides forficatus*
elanus (New L) derived from *elanos* (Late Gr) a kite *-oides* (New L) from *eidos* (Gr) apparent shape, resemblance *forficatus* (New L) forked, derived from *forfex* (L), genitive *forficis*, scissors; a very beautiful bird with a deeply forked tail; the whole appearance in silhouette is that of a large swallow. Inhabiting the southern part of the USA and ranging south to southern South America.

White-tailed Kite *Elanus leucurus*
Elanus, see above *leukos* (Gr) white *oura* (Gr) the tail. Inhabiting the southern borders of the USA and ranging south through Central and much of South America.

Snail Kite *Rostrhamus sociabilis*
rostrum (L) the beak *hamus* (L) a hook; the upper mandible is slender and strongly hooked, a real 'winkle-picker', which enables it to extract the snails on which it feeds, and this is its only food *sociabilis* (L) easily united, compatible; a reference to its habit of nesting in colonies up to 100 strong, the nests being in close proximity; an unusual breeding behaviour for kites. Ranging from Mexico to Argentina; an

isolated group, sometimes known as Everglade Kites, live in the Everglades of Florida, but these are now very rare.

Mississippi Kite   *Ictinia mississippiensis*
iktinos (Gr) a kite or hen-harrier   *-ensis* (L) suffix meaning belonging to; named from the River Mississippi, it is found in North, Central, and South America.

Square-tailed Kite   *Lophoictinia isura*
lophos (Gr) the crest of birds   *iktinos* (Gr) a kite or hen-harrier; 'a crested kite'   *isos* (Gr) equal   *oura* (Gr) the tail; a reference to the tail feathers being of equal length, thus forming the square tail. Inhabiting Australia.

Black-breasted Buzzard   *Hamirostra melanosternon*
hamus (L) a fish-hook; can mean anything hooked   *rostrum* (L) the beak   *melas* (Gr), genitive *melanos*, black   *sternon* (Gr) the chest or breast. Inhabiting the Australian region.

Black Kite   *Milvus migrans*
milvus (L) a bird of prey, a kite   *migro* (L) I move from place to place; migrans, wandering; '. . . encountered almost everywhere throughout the warmer parts of the Old World' (*Living Birds of the World*, Gilliard); northern populations migrate south in winter. The plumage is very dark brown above and rufous brown below, rather than black.

Red Kite   *M. milvus*
It is not red but the plumage is more rufous than the Black Kite (above); common, and the range is similar.

Brahminy Kite   *Haliastur indus*
hals (Gr) the sea   *astur* (L) a species of hawk: named from the River Indus, it has a wide distribution from India to the Solomon islands and the Philippines. Sometimes known as a Sea Eagle, it often frequents rivers and sea coasts. Brahman or Brahmin means having to do with prayer; this kite is held sacred by the Hindus.

White-tailed Eagle   *Haliaeetus albicilla*
hals (Gr), genitive *halos*, the sea   *aietos* = *aetos* (Gr) an eagle; the birds in this genus are sometimes known as sea-eagles as they usually inhabit sea coasts, rivers, and lakes, to obtain the fish which they snatch from the water with their claws; mammals and birds also form part of their diet   *albus* (L) white   *-illus* (L) diminutive suffix; this is supposed to mean 'white-tailed' but it does not; the mistake may

originate from the name of the wagtail, *Motacilla* (for explanation see Motacillidae p. 236). Ranging from Greenland, Iceland, and Norway through Eurasia to Japan and usually migrating south in winter to the Oriental region.

Bald Eagle   *H. leucocephalus*
leukos (Gr) white   *kephalē* (Gr) the head; it is not bald, but the white head and neck give it the appearance of being bald. It is the national emblem of the USA and appears on the dollar bill; at one time it was widespread in North America but owing to shooting and destruction of habitat it is now very rare, and only seen in any quantity in Alaska and Florida.

White-bellied Sea Eagle   *H. leucogaster*
leukos (Gr) white   *gastēr* (Gr) the belly. Ranging from India to southern China, Papua New Guinea and nearby islands, Australia and Tasmania.

Steller's Sea Eagle   *H. pelagicus*
pelagos (Gr) the sea   *-icus* (L) suffix meaning belonging to: named after George W. Steller (1709-1769), a well-known German zoologist and traveller; a number of other animals have been named in his honour. Inhabiting the Pacific coast of Asia.

African Fish Eagle   *H. vocifer*
vociferor (L) to cry aloud, shout; a very noisy bird calling with a clear, yelping voice. Inhabiting rivers, lakes, and swamps as high as 1,219 m (4,000 ft), in Africa.

Grey-headed Fishing Eagle   *Ichthyophaga ichthyaetus*
ikhthus (Gr) a fish   *phagein* (Gr) to eat   *aetos* (Gr) an eagle; 'a fish-eating fish eagle'. Inhabiting India and ranging south-east to Indonesia.

Palm-nut Vulture   *Gypohierax angolensis*
gups (Gr) a vulture   *hierax* (Gr) a hawk or falcon   *-ensis* (L) suffix meaning belonging to; named from Angola it is found in other parts of Africa where there are oil palms; although the husks of oil palm nuts appear to be its favourite food it also eats other food such as fruit, molluscs, and locusts.

Bearded Vulture or Lammergeier   *Gypaetus barbatus*
gups (Gr), genitive *gupos*, a vulture   *aetos* (Gr) an eagle   *barbatus* (L) bearded; a reference to the black feathers under the beak that form

the beard. The name lammergeier comes from the German *lammer*, lambs, and *geier*, a vulture; they are reputed to carry off live lambs for food but this has never been recorded by reliable observers. Inhabiting southern parts of Eurasia and northern Africa ranging from the Pyrenees to China in mountainous areas.

Indian White-backed Vulture *Gyps bengalensis*
gups (Gr) a vulture *-ensis* (L) suffix meaning belonging to; it ranges from the Indian sub-continent to Burma, Laos, Cambodia, and Vietnam. The plumage is almost black with a conspicuous white patch on the lower back.

Cape Vulture *G. coprotheres*
kopros (Gr) dung; can mean dirt in general   *thēreuō* (Gr) I hunt; a reference to its habit of feeding on decaying carcases. Inhabiting Africa.

Indian Black Vulture *Sarcogyps calvus*
sarx (Gr), genitive *sarkos*, flesh   *gups* (Gr) a vulture   *calvus* (L) bald; it has a bare head and neck of a reddish orange colour and the body is black with some white markings. Inhabiting India and the Burma-Vietnam area.

White-headed Vulture *Trigonoceps occipitalis*
trigōnos (Gr) three-cornered, triangular   *ceps* (New L) from *caput* (L) the head; a reference to the white down on the head which gives it a triangular outline   *occiput* (L), genitive *occipitis*, the back part of the head, can mean the head as a whole   *-alis* (L) suffix meaning relating to. Ranging from Eritrea in East Africa to the Orange River in South West Africa.

Snake Eagle *Circaetus cinereus*
kirkos (Gr) a kind of hawk or falcon that flies in circles   *aetos* (Gr) an eagle   *cinereus* (L) ash-coloured; the plumage is a dark slaty-brown: a fearless hunter of snakes, it has been seen to kill and eat a large poisonous snake about 1 m (3 ft) in length. Inhabiting Africa.

Philippine Serpent Eagle *Spilornis holospilus*
spilos (Gr) a blemish, a spot   *ornis* (Gr) a bird   *holos* (Gr) whole, entire; a brown plumage almost entirely spotted with white: it eats small mammals, lizards, and other reptiles, chiefly snakes. Inhabiting the Philippines.

Marsh Harrier *Circus aeruginosus*
kirkos (Gr) a kind of hawk or falcon that flies in circles; in fact this harrier is seldom seen soaring and flying in circles; it usually flies low over marshy ground searching for frogs, small mammals, small waterfowl, and fish   *aerugo* (L) rust of copper   *aeruginosus* (L) full of copper-rust, rusty; can mean the red rust of iron, being a reference to the upper plumage which is a reddish brown. It has a wide distribution in Europe and Asia, including the south of England, Africa including Madagascar, India, ranging south-east through Burma, Malaysia, the Philippines, New Guinea, and Australia.

Pallid Harrier *C. macrourus*
makros (Gr) long   *oura* (Gr) the tail; actually the tail is not much longer than other closely related harriers: the plumage is distinctly pale with grey above and a white breast. It has a wide distribution rather similar to the Marsh Harrier (above), but not extending so far west in Europe and not to the south-east in Australasia.

Montagu's Harrier *C. pygargus*
pugē (Gr) the rump   *argos* (Gr) shining, bright   *pugargos* (Gr) has been used to mean a type of eagle, one with a white rump, probably the White-tailed Eagle *Haliaeetus albicilla*; this harrier, *C. pygargus*, has a well-defined white rump. Inhabiting Eurasia including the southern part of England, Africa, India, and the Burma-Vietnam area. Named after Col George Montagu (1751-1815), a writer on natural history and an early member of the Linnaean Society; he had a fine collection of animals including birds which was eventually purchased by the British Museum (Natural History).

Pale Chanting Goshawk *Melierax canorus*
melos (Gr) a song   *ierax* (Gr) a hawk or vulture   *cano* (L) I sing   *canorus* (L) melodious; it does not sing like an ordinary song-bird but has a melodious whistle and calls from a tree-top; the plumage above is pale grey. Inhabiting the eastern and southern part of Africa.

Cooper's Hawk *Accipiter cooperii*
accipiter (L) the common hawk: named after W. Cooper (1798-1864), an American zoologist; he founded the New York Lyceum of Natural History. In most species the female is larger than the male and in this hawk the female is about one-third larger than the male; it inhabits North and Central America.

Red-thighed Sparrowhawk *A. erythropus*
eruthros (Gr) red   *pous* (Gr) the foot; in this case taken to mean the leg. Inhabiting Africa.

Goshawk   *A. gentilis*
gentilis (New L) noble; it has been given this name due to its prowess at hunting in the days of falconry; it has been described as 'the most noble of all falcons' (R. D. Macleod). Inhabiting North and Central America, Europe including occasionally the British Isles, Asia to India and the Burma-Vietnam area.

Black-mantled Goshawk   *A. melanochlamys*
melas (Gr), genitive *melanos*, black   *khlamus* (Gr) a short cloak or mantle; a reference to the black plumage that forms a short 'cape' round the head and neck. Inhabiting New Guinea.

Sparrowhawk   *A. nisus*
According to the Greek legend Nisus, king of the Megara, was changed into a sparrowhawk. Widespread and common in Europe including the British Isles, Africa, ranging east to Japan, including India, the Burma-Vietnam area, and Indonesia.

African Long-tailed Hawk   *Urotriorchis macrourus*
oura (Gr) the tail   *triorkhos* (Gr) a kind of falcon or kite   *makros* (Gr) long   *oura* (Gr) the tail. Inhabiting Africa.

Rufous-winged Buzzard-Eagle   *Butastur liventer*
buteo (L) a kind of falcon or hawk   *astur* (L) a kind of hawk   *livens* (L), genitive *liventis*, bluish, the colour of lead. Inhabiting Indonesia.

White Hawk   *Leucopternis albicollis*
leukos (Gr) white   *pternis* (Gr) a bird of prey   *albus* (L) white   *collum* (L) the neck. Inhabiting Central and South America.

Slate-coloured Hawk   *L. schistacea*
skhistos (Gr) divided, cleft   *schist* (New L) slate   *-aceus* (L) suffix meaning made of, like; slate-coloured. Inhabiting South America.

Black Hawk   *Buteogallus anthracinus*
buteo (L) a kind of falcon or hawk   *gallus* (L) a cock   *anthrax* (Gr), genitive *anthrakos*, coal or charcoal   *-inus* (L) suffix meaning like; coal-coloured. Inhabiting North, Central, and South America.

Solitary Eagle   *Harpyhaliaetus solitarius*
harpē (Gr) a bird of prey   *haliaetos* (Gr) a sea-eagle   *solitarius* (L)

solitary. Inhabiting Central and South America.

White-tailed Hawk *Buteo albicaudatus*
buteo (L) a kind of falcon or hawk *albus* (L) white *cauda* (L) the tail of an animal *-atus* (L) suffix meaning provided with; the underparts, rump, and tail are white. Ranging from Texas, through Central America to South America.

Common Buzzard *B. buteo*
Although most of the birds in this genus are known as hawks, those that live in Europe or Africa are often known as buzzards; this one is common and widespread in Africa and Europe including the British Isles though not Ireland; it ranges through southern Asia to India, the Burma-Vietnam area, Malaysia, and Indonesia.

Galapagos Hawk *B. galapagoensis*
-ensis (L) suffix meaning belonging to, usually referring to a place; it is confined to Galapagos and the surrounding small islands.

Red-tailed Hawk *B. jamaicensis*
-ensis (L) see above; it has a rather short reddish-brown tail. It ranges from Alaska south to Panama and the West Indies.

Rough-legged Hawk *B. lagopus*
lagōs (Gr) a hare *pous* (Gr) the foot; 'hare-footed'; a reference to the legs being feathered more extensively than others in the genus. Inhabiting Europe including the eastern part of the British Isles but not Spain, and ranging east to the Burma-Vietnam area.

African Mountain Buzzard *B. oreophilus*
oros (Gr), genitive *oreos*, a mountain *philos* (Gr) loved, pleasing; a 'mountain-lover'. Inhabiting Africa.

Harpy Eagle *Harpia harpyia*
Arpuiai (Gr) the Snatchers, derived from *arpazō* (Gr) I snatch away, carry off; there are various interpretations but in late mythology they appear as hideous winged monsters; a very large eagle and able to carry off various mammals such as monkeys, opossums, and agoutis. It ranges from southern Mexico to southern Brazil and northern Argentina.

Monkey-eating Eagle *Pithecophaga jefferyi*
pithekos (Gr) an ape *phagein* (Gr) to eat: named after Jeffrey Whitehead (fl 1840-1909), an English naturalist. A very large eagle feeding

on various mammals in addition to monkeys and also birds. Very rare and probably now found only on Mindanao in the Philippines.

Wedge-tailed Eagle *Aquila audax*
aquila (L) an eagle   *audax* (L) bold, audacious. Inhabiting New Guinea, Australia, and Tasmania.

Golden Eagle *A. chrysaetos*
khrusos (Gr) gold   *aetos* (Gr) an eagle; the colour is mostly dark tawny to brown with a golden crown and nape. A widespread species but becoming rare in places; inhabiting North America and ranging south to Mexico, Eurasia including Scandinavia and Scotland and ranging south to northern Africa, and east to Arabia, India, and the Burma-Vietnam area.

Gurney's Eagle *A. gurneyi*
Named in honour of J. H. Gurney Jnr (1848-1922), an ornithologist and author, it lives in New Guinea.

Tawny Eagle *A. rapax*
rapax (L), genitive *rapacis*, rapacious, grasping: the plumage is rufous brown, or tawny. Inhabiting most of Africa and ranging east to Arabia, the southern part of India, and the Burma-Vietnam area.

Bonelli's Eagle *Hieraaetus fasciatus*
hierax (Gr) a hawk or falcon   *aetos* (Gr) an eagle   *fascia* (L) a band or girdle; *fasciatus*, banded; it has bars across the long tail terminating with a wide black band. Named after Prof F. A. Bonelli (1784-1830), an Italian Professor of Natural History. It inhabits southern parts of Europe and northern Africa and ranges east to southern India and the Burma-Vietnam area.

Long-crested Eagle *Lophaetus occipitalis*
lophos (Gr) the crest of birds, and other crests   *aetos* (Gr) an eagle   *occiput* (L), genitive *occipitis*, the back part of the head   *-alis* (L) suffix meaning relating to; the plumage is very dark brown or black with a prominent crest on the head. Widespread in Africa south of the Sahara.

Hodgson's Hawk-Eagle *Spizaetus nipalensis*
spizias (Gr) the sparrow-hawk   *aetos* (Gr) an eagle   *-ensis* (L) suffix meaning belonging to; named from Nepal it inhabits southern Asia, India, and the Burma-Vietnam area: the English name is in honour

of B. H. Hodgson, FRS (1800-1894) who was Resident in Nepal from 1833 to 1843.

Ornate Hawk-Eagle *S. ornatus*
ornatus (L) dress, ornament; a reference to the very colourful plumage and striking crest. Not a well-known hawk-eagle although fairly widespread from Mexico to Argentina.

Crowned Eagle *Stephanoaetus coronatus*
stephanos (Gr) a crown, garland *aetos* (Gr) an eagle *corona* (L) a crown *-atus* (L) suffix meaning provided with; it has a prominent black and white double crest. Inhabiting Africa.

Family PANDIONIDAE 1 species
Named after Pandion, a legendary king of Athens.

Osprey *Pandion haliaetus*
haliaeetos (L) the osprey or sea-eagle. Widespread in almost the whole of the northern hemisphere and migrating south in winter; it breeds in America, south to Brazil, Africa and Australasia.

Family FALCONIDAE 61 species
falx (L), genitive *falcis*, a sickle, a reference to the bird's curved talons.

Red-throated Caracara *Daptrius americanus*
daptēs (Gr) fem *daptria*, an eater, bloodsucker *-anus* (L) suffix meaning belonging to; it inhabits Central and South America from southern Mexico to Peru and southern Brazil. It has a naked red area on the face and throat *caracara* is an Argentinian word for this bird of prey and said to be an imitation of its call.

White-throated Caracara *Phalcoboenus albogularis*
phalkōn (Gr) a falcon (= *falco* (L), genitive *falconis*, a falcon) *boenus*, derived from *bainō* (Gr) I walk, step; 'a walking falcon'; with their long legs they are quite at home on the ground and frequently search for their prey on foot; 'characteristic head-bobbing walk' (*World Atlas of Birds*, Mitchell Beazley); 'caracaras run rapidly on the ground' (*Living Birds of the World*, Gilliard) *albus* (L) white *gula* (L) throat *-aris* (L) suffix meaning pertaining to. Ranging from Florida and southern Texas through South America to Tierra del Fuego.

Common Caracara *Polyborus plancus*
poluborus (Gr) much-devouring; *plancus* (L) flat-footed. Ranging from

the southern part of North America, through Central America including Cuba, south to Tierra del Fuego including the Falkland Islands.

Chimango Caracara *Milvago chimango*
milvus (L) a bird of prey, a kite   -*ago* (New L) suffix meaning resemblance   *chimango* (Argentine/Spanish) a beetle-eater. Inhabiting South America.

Laughing Falcon *Herpetotheres cachinnans*
herpeton (Gr) a creeping thing, a reptile   *thēraō* (Gr) I hunt, chase, wild beasts; can mean I catch, take, wild beasts; an allusion to its main prey which is snakes and lizards   *cachinno* (L) one who laughs violently, a laugher; a reference to the two-note call which is usually repeated many times. Inhabiting Mexico and ranging south to Bolivia, Paraguay, Brazil, and northern Argentina.

Barred Forest-Falcon *Micrastur ruficollis*
mikros (Gr) small   *astur* (L) a species of hawk; at about 36 cm (14 in) it is one of the smaller falcons   *rufus* (L) red   *collum* (L) the neck; the upperparts, throat, and breast are a rufous brown; the underparts have black and white bands and there are white bands across the black tail. Inhabiting the southern part of Mexico and ranging south through Panama to Brazil and northern Argentina.

African Pygmy Falcon *Polihierax semitorquatus*
polios (Gr) hoary, grey, usually referring to the hair   *hierax* (Gr) a hawk or falcon; a reference to the blue-grey upperparts   *semi-* (L) prefix meaning half   *torquatus* (L) wearing a collar; a reference to the white collar. A very small falcon measuring about 20 cm (8 in); it inhabits Somalia and Sudan ranging south to southern Africa but not the extreme south.

Pied Falconet *Microhierax melanoleucos*
mikros (Gr) small   *hierax* (Gr) a hawk or falcon   *melas* (Gr), genitive *melanos*, black   *leukos* (Gr) white; a reference to the black and white plumage. The falcons in this genus, known as falconets, are quite small being only about 18 to 23 cm (7 to 9 in) long; they range through southern Asia and the oriental region from India to the Philippines, Malaysia, and Indonesia.

Fox Kestrel *Falco alopex*
falx (L), genitive *falcis*, a sickle; a reference to the birds curved talons

alōpēx (Gr) a fox; a reference to the plumage which is 'fox-red'. Inhabiting western and northern Central Africa.

Merlin   *F. columbarius*
columba (L) a pigeon, a dove   *-arius* (L) suffix meaning pertaining to; referring to its occasional capture of a pigeon: Merlin is from Old French *esmerillon*. Widespread in the Northern Hemisphere including the British Isles, and moving south in winter.

African Hobby   *F. cuvieri*
Named after the French zoologist and author M. F. Cuvier (1775–1838), brother of the more well-known Baron Georges Cuvier. The name hobby, through various changes, is said to come from Old French *hober*, to move. Inhabiting Africa.

Dickinson's Kestrel   *F. dickinsoni*
Named after Dr J. Dickinson (1832–1863), at one time a missionary and doctor in Nyasaland, now known as Malawi. Inhabiting Africa.

Grey Falcon   *F. hypoleucus*
hupo (Gr) under, less than usual   *leukos* (Gr) white; i.e. less than white, 'off-white'. Inhabiting Australia.

Prairie Falcon   *F. mexicanus*
This falcon usually favours bare and arid regions; it inhabits Mexico and parts of Central America.

Peregrine Falcon   *F. peregrinus*
peregrinus (L) that comes from foreign parts, strange, foreign; here taken to mean a wanderer; it is known throughout the world except in the polar regions.

Gyrfalcon   *F. rusticolus*
rusticola (L) an inhabitant of the country. The derivation of gyrfalcon is obscure but could be from the German *gier*, greedy; the German name for the bird is *gierfalke*. Inhabiting the Arctic round the world and sometimes migrating south in winter.

American Kestrel or American Sparrowhawk   *F. sparverius*
sparver (Middle E) from *esprevier* (Middle F) the sparrowhawk   *sparverius* (New L) pertaining to sparrows; the sparrow is one of the birds that form its prey. Inhabiting North, Central, and South America, ranging from Alaska to Tierra del Fuego.

Common Kestrel *F. tinnunculus*
tinnio (L) I ring, tinkle   *tinnulus* (L) ringing, tinkling   *tinnunculus* (L) a kind of hawk, the kestrel; the name means 'little bell-ringer' and refers to the birds repeated high-pitched call. Inhabiting North America, Eurasia including the British Isles, Africa, and ranging east to India, the Burma-Vietnam area, Malaysia, and Indonesia.

20 Grouse, Pheasants, Peacocks, Guineafowls, Turkeys and their kin
GALLIFORMES

Bobwhite
Colinus virginianus

The order Galliformes includes the well-known game birds and also the domestic hen. Then there are the curassows which also make good table birds, but living in forests in uninhabited territory, perhaps 2,400 m (8,000 ft) above sea level, they are not a popular source of food. In addition there are the little-known megapodes (from the Greek 'big-feet'), a strange assortment consisting of the brush turkeys, mallee fowls, incubator birds and others that incubate their eggs by heat, but not heat from their own bodies. In some cases it is the heat generated by a mound of rotting vegetation, which they build for the purpose; or it can be the heat of the sun on sand, or, most surprising of all, the heat from underground volcanic action.

Finally there is the hoatzin, a most remarkable bird, in some respects resembling the others in this order, but with certain marked differences. For example when first hatched the young hoatzin is practically naked, but has claws on the fore limb. Thus it starts life as a quadruped, using the claws for hanging on to branches or clambering about in the trees where its nest has been built. In this respect it resembles certain prehistoric semi-reptilian birds, known to us only as fossils; equally remarkable the young bird can swim. After about a week the claws begin to disappear as the normal wing feathers develop, thus in a few days it goes through an evolutionary change that took the lizard-like birds millions of years to bring about.

Order GALLIFORMES

gallus (L) a cock (pertaining to poultry)   *forma* (L) form, shape; can mean sort, kind, so not necessarily referring to the actual shape.

Family MEGAPODIIDAE   12 species
megas (Gr) large   *pous* (Gr), genitive *podos*, a foot; an allusion to their unusually large and strong legs and feet.

Marianas Scrub Hen   *Megapodius laperouse*
Capt J. F. Comte de la Pérouse (1741-1788) was a French naturalist: Marianas is the name of the group of islands in the Pacific Ocean to the north of New Guinea where these birds live.

Mallee Fowl   *Leipoa ocellata*
leipō (Gr) I leave, I abandon   *ōon* (Gr) an egg, plural *ōa*; 'a deserter of eggs'; a reference to their habit of leaving the eggs to be hatched by the heat of the sun or of rotting vegetation   *ocellatus* (L) spotted with eyes; a reference to the spotted plumage   *mallee* is a native Australian name for scrubby kinds of eucalyptus, and probably refers to their habitat. They live in Australia.

Brush Turkey   *Alectura lathami*
alektōr (Gr) a cock   *oura* (Gr) the tail: named after Dr John Latham, FRS (1740-1837) an English zoologist. Inhabiting Australia.

Red-billed Brush Turkey   *Talegalla cuvieri*
tale, a New Guinea native name for a water-hen   *gallus* (L) a cock: named after Baron Georges Cuvier (1769-1832) the famous French anatomist and zoologist; he was at one time Professor of Natural History in the Collège de France. Inhabiting New Guinea.

Bruijn's Brush Turkey   *Aepypodius bruijnii*
aipus (Gr) high   *pous* (Gr), genitive *podos*, a foot; another way of saying 'big feet': named after Dr J. Bruijn (1811-1895) a Dutch zoologist and botanist. Inhabiting New Guinea.

Family CRACIDAE   44 species
krazō (Gr) I croak, scream   *crax* (New L), genitive *cracis*, a screamer;

a reference to their noisy call which is magnified by a special formation of the unusually long trachea.

Plain Chachalaca   *Ortalis vetula*
ortalis (Gr) a young bird   *vetula* (L) a little old woman. It inhabits North America, Central America, and other lands bordering the Caribbean Sea   *Chachalaca* is Spanish from Nahuatl, meaning the twittering of a bird.

Crested Guan   *Penelope purpurascens*
Pēnelopē (Gr) a feminine name, actually a weaver   *purpurascens* (L) purplish; this bird has a variety of colours, with a dark greenish olive back with bronze reflections, and the naked part of the face a slaty blue. It is wide-ranging from Mexico to Argentina.   *Guan* is an American-Spanish name for the bird.

Horned Guan   *Oreophasis derbianus*
oros (Gr), genitive *oreos*, a mountain   *phasianos* (Gr) the Phasian bird or pheasant; the name comes from the River Phasis, in Colchis (see *Phasianus colchicus* p. 114). Named after the 13th Earl of Derby, formerly the Hon. E. S. Stanley (1775-1851). He was President of the Zoological Society of London from 1831 until his death in 1851. This guan inhabits the mountain forests from southern Mexico to Guatemala.

Crested or Black Curassow   *Crax alector*
crax (New L) see above, under Family   *alektōr* (Gr) a cock. Inhabiting South America and particularly widespread in Amazonia. The name *curassow* is said to derive from the island of Curacao, in the West Indies, but it is not known that any of the curassows ever lived there.

Red-wattled Curassow   *C. globulosa*
globus (L) a ball, globe   *-osus* (L) suffix meaning full of, prone to; the wattle takes the form of red globules round the base of the beak. Inhabiting South America.

Helmeted Curassow   *C. pauxi*
Paoxi is a native bird name in the northern part of Venezuela. This curassow lives in Venezuela and a large area in Bolivia, South America.

Family   TETRAONIDAE   16 species
tetraōn (Gr) a bird of the grouse kind.

Siberian or Black-billed Capercaillie *Tetrao parvirostris*
parvus (L) small   *rostrum* (L) the beak. Inhabiting eastern Siberia.

Black Grouse *Lyrurus tetrix*
lura (Gr) a lyre   *oura* (Gr) a tail; it has lyre-shaped tail feathers: *tetrix* = *tetrax* (Gr) a kind of grouse. Inhabiting Europe and parts of Asia.

Willow Ptarmigan *Lagopus lagopus*
lagōpous (Gr) the ptarmigan; literally 'hare-foot', from *lagōs* (Gr) a hare, and *pous* (Gr) a foot; this is a reference to the lower leg and foot, which in winter is covered with feathers, like a gaiter. Inhabiting Arctic areas in both the New and Old World.

White Tailed Ptarmigan *L. leucurus*
leukos (Gr) white   *oura* (Gr) the tail. Inhabiting Alaska, Canada, and ranging south to the Rockies. The name ptarmigan is derived from the Gaelic *tarmachan*.

Rock Ptarmigan *L. mutus*
mutus (L) dumb, silent; it is not dumb but the call is rough and unmusical. Widespread in the far north around the world and the mountains of Eurasia.

Spruce Grouse *Dendragapus canadensis*
dendron (Gr) a tree   *agapaō* (Gr) I love, I welcome   *-ensis* (L) suffix meaning belonging to; 'of Canada'. It is widespread in North America.

Blue Grouse *D. obscurus*
obscurus (L) obscure, secret, reserved; it lives high in the Rocky Mountains of North America, and is seldom seen, unlike the Spruce Grouse (above) which is often seen in bush camps and is comparatively tame.

Ruffed Grouse *Bonasa umbellus*   (replaces *Tetrastes*)
bonasus (L) a species of bison; probably a reference to the low hooting noises and drumming sounds made by the male   *umbella* (L) a parasol or umbrella; during courtship display the male raises the tail feathers to make a fan-like shape. Inhabiting the northern part of North America.

Prairie Chicken *Tympanuchus cupido*   (includes *T. pallidicinctus*)
tumpanon (Gr) a drum + *-ochos* (New L) from *ekhō* (Gr) I hold = drum-

holding; a reference to the drumming sounds made by the male during courtship display *cupido* (L) physical desire, love. Inhabiting the central part of the USA.

Sharp-tailed Grouse *T. phasianellus* (replaces *Pediocetes*) *phasianus* (L) the pheasant (see p. 114) *-ellus* (L) dim. suffix, 'a small pheasant'; grouse are among the smallest in the family Tetraonidae. Inhabiting North America.

Sage Grouse *Centrocercus urophasianus* *kentron* (Gr) a spike, a spur *kerkos* (Gr) the tail *oura* (Gr) the tail *phasianos* (Gr) the pheasant (see p. 114). Inhabiting North America.

Family PHASIANIDAE 183 species *phasianus* (L) a pheasant *phasianos* (Gr) the Phasian bird or pheasant (see p. 114 under *Phasianus colchicus*).

Bearded Wood Partridge *Dendrortyx barbatus* *dendron* (Gr) a tree *ortux* (Gr) the quail *barbatus* (L) bearded. Inhabiting Mexico, Central America, and parts of the Greater and Lesser Antilles.

Mountain Quail *Oreortyx pictus* *oros* (Gr), genitive *oreos*, a mountain *ortux* (Gr) the quail *pictus* (L) painted; a reference to its bright colours. Inhabiting the mountains of California and Nevada.

California Quail *Lophortyx californica* *lophos* (Gr) a crest *ortux* (Gr) the quail *-icus* (L) suffix meaning belonging to; 'of California'. From the south-western part of the USA it ranges south to Mexico.

Bobwhite *Colinus virginianus* *colín* (Sp) derived from the Nahuatl zolin, a partridge; in Mexico colín means a quail *-anus* (L) suffix meaning belonging to; 'of Virginia'. The male has black and white stripes on the head and a white throat patch; inhabiting the eastern part of the USA.

Marbled Wood Quail *Odontophorus gujanensis* *odous* (Gr), genitive *odontos*, a tooth *phora* (Gr) carrying, bearing; it has tooth-like markings on the plumage *-ensis* (L) suffix meaning belonging to, usually referring to a place; 'of Guiana'. Inhabiting Central and South America.

Stripe-faced Wood Quail *O. balliviani*
Named in honour of Gen. J. Ballivian (1804-1852), President of the Bolivian Republic from 1842 to 1847. Range as above.

Ocellated Quail *Cyrtonyx ocellatus*
kurtos (Gr) curved *onux* (Gr) talon, claw *oculus* (L) the eye; dim. *ocellus*, a little eye *-atus* (L) suffix meaning provided with; a reference to the 'eye-like' markings. Inhabiting south-western USA and ranging south to Mexico.

Himalayan Snowcock *Tetraogallus himalayensis*
tetraōn (Gr) a bird of the grouse kind; also *tetrao* (L) a heath-cock *gallus* (L) a cock *-ensis* (L) suffix meaning belonging to, usually referring to a place. Inhabiting the Himalayan area and Tibet.

Szecheny's Pheasant Grouse *Tetraophasis szechenyii*
tetraōn (Gr) a bird of the grouse kind *phasianos* (Gr) the Phasian bird, or pheasant: named after Count Bela Szecheny (1837-1918), a naturalist and author who was in Central Asia from 1877 to 1880. Ranging through the Himalayan area from eastern Afghanistan to Bhutan.

Red-legged Partridge *Alectoris rufa*
alektōr (Gr) a cock *rufus* (L) red. Inhabiting western Europe, Corsica, and the Canary Islands.

Black Francolin *Francolinus francolinus*
francolin (Fr) from *francolino* (Old It) a partridge. Ranging from Cyprus through western Asia to Assam.

Hartlaub's Francolin *F. hartlaubii*
Named after Dr K. J. G. Hartlaub (1814-1900), at one time Prof. of Zoology at Bremen. This francolin inhabits South Africa.

Somali Greywing Francolin *F. lorti* (or *africanus*)
Named after E. E. Lort Phillips (1857-1944), a big game hunter and collector in East Africa; he spent many years attempting to establish the identity of this bird and finally succeeded during a special expedition to Somaliland about the year 1895. Inhabiting East Africa.

Swainson's Francolin *Pternistis swainsoni* (or *Francolinus*)
pterna (Gr) the heel *pternistēs* (Gr) one who strikes with the heel; the legs have sharp spurs on them used in fighting. Named after W. Swain-

son, FRS (1789-1855) a much travelled English zoologist and artist. This francolin inhabits South Africa and is particularly common in the Kruger National Park.

Common or Grey Partridge   *Perdix perdix*
perdix (L) a partridge. Inhabiting Europe including the British Isles, southern Scandinavia, northern Spain, and ranging across Europe to Asia Minor and Central Asia.

Mrs Hodgson's Partridge   *P. hodgsoniae*
Named in honour of Mrs Hodgson in 1857, the wife of B. H. Hodgson, FRS (1800-1894), Resident in Nepal from 1833 to 1843. This partridge lives in Tibet.

Madagascar Partridge   *Margaroperdix madagascarensis*
margarōdēs (Gr) pearl-like   *perdix* (L) = *perdix* (Gr) a partridge; a reference to the grey plumage   *-ensis* (L) suffix meaning belonging to, usually referring to a place. Inhabiting Madagascar.

Common Quail   *Coturnix coturnix*
coturnix (L) a quail. Inhabiting Europe including the British Isles, Asia, and Africa.

Swamp Quail   *C. ypsilophorus*
Upsilon (Gr) the letter u   *phoreō* I bear; a reference to the markings on the back which resemble the Greek capital letter U; it is rather like our capital letter Y. Inhabiting Australia and Papua New Guinea.

Stubble Quail   *C. novaezealandiae*
Although originally inhabiting New Zealand and Australia it has not been seen in New Zealand for the past 100 years.

Manipur Bush Quail   *Perdicula manipurensis*
perdix (L) a partridge   *-culus* (L) diminutive suffix; 'a little partridge' *-ensis* (L) suffix meaning belonging to, usually referring to a place; named after Manipur in southern Assam, this quail inhabits southern Assam and northern Burma.

Tree Partridge   *Arborophila torqueola*
arbor (L), genitive *arboris*, a tree   *philos* (Gr) dear, pleasing   *torques* (L) a twisted necklace or collar   *-olus* (L) diminutive suffix, 'a little collar'; a reference to the dark ring round the neck. Tree partridges live in the forests of eastern India ranging to southern China and Malaya.

Bamboo Partridge *Bambusicola fytchii*
bambu (Malayan) probably from Tulu; the generic name of the plant is *Bambusa colo* (L) I inhabit: named after Maj Gen A. Fytche (1820-1892), Commander in Chief of the British Army in Burma from 1867 to 1871. This partridge inhabits Assam and possibly northern Burma.

Ceylon Spur-fowl *Galloperdix bicalcarata*
gallus (L) a cock   *perdix* (L) a partridge   *bi-* (L) prefix meaning two   *calcar* (L) a spur   *-atus* (L) suffix meaning provided with; it has two spurs on the legs. Inhabiting Ceylon, now known as Sri Lanka.

Western Tragopan *Tragopan melanocephalus*
tragos (Gr) a he-goat: Pan is a Greek god of pastures and woods, and is usually represented with horns and goats legs; the name tragopan is a reference to the two fleshy erectile horns on the head of the male bird   *melas* (Gr), genitive *melanos*, black   *kephalē* (Gr) the head; the head is not entirely black but has black markings. At one time tragopans were widespread from western Pakistan to Burma and China, but many are now rare and only found in certain areas; the Western Tragopan probably still inhabits parts of Pakistan and Kashmir.

Satyr Tragopan   *T. satyra*
The Satyr is a mythical Greek god, half man and half beast, with a goat's horns, ears and tail; the name is a reference to the two fleshy erectile horns on the head of the male, but in fact all male tragopans have the two horns. Inhabiting Nepal and Bhutan.

Temminck's Tragopan   *T. temminckii*
Named after Prof C. J. Temminck (1778-1858), a Dutch zoologist at one time Director at the Natural History Museum, Leyden. Inhabiting eastern India and Burma and ranging to central China.

Cabot's Tragopan   *T. caboti*
Named after Dr S. Cabot (1815-1885) an American zoologist and Curator of the Boston Natural History Society in 1845. Inhabiting eastern China.

Himalayan Monal or Impeyan Pheasant   *Lophophorus impejanus*
lophos (Gr) the crest of birds   *phoros* (Gr) a bearing, carrying: named in honour of Sir Elijah Impey (1732-1809) and Lady Impey who introduced the bird into England; Sir Elijah was Chief Justice in

Bengal from 1774 to 1789   *Monāl* is a Nepalese name for the bird. Ranging from Afghanistan to Assam.

Chinese Monal   *L. lhuysii*
Named after E. Drouyn de L'Huys (1805-1881) a French zoologist *Monāl* is a Nepalese name for this pheasant; it inhabits China.

Brown Eared Pheasant   *Crossoptilon mantchuricum*
krossoi (Gr) a fringe, tassels   *ptilon* (Gr) feathers, a wing; a reference to the two brown 'earlike' tufts of feathers on the head   *-icus* (L) suffix meaning belonging to; 'of Manchuria'. Inhabiting the mountains of north-eastern China and Manchuria.

Kalij Pheasant   *Lophura leucomelana*
lophos (Gr) the crest of birds   *oura* (Gr) the tail; 'tail-crest'   *leukos* (Gr) white   *melas* (Gr), genitive *melanos*, black; the males are white above and black underneath   *Kalij* or *Kaleege* (Nepali and Pahari) is the native name for this pheasant inhabiting India.

Crested Fireback   *L. ignita*
ignitus (L) fiery, glowing; the male has a glowing crimson back and rump. Inhabiting Borneo and Sumatra.

Red Jungle Fowl   *Gallus gallus*
gallus (L) a cock; this is the ancestor of domestic poultry; a very colourful bird with bright red plumage and iridescent green. It is widespread in northern India ranging to southern China and Malaysia but not Borneo.

Domestic Hen   *G. domesticus*
Most zoologists give it the name *G. domesticus*. Widespread throughout the world, it is descended from *G. gallus*, above.

Ceylon Jungle Fowl   *G. lafayetii*
Named in honour of M. J. P. La Fayette, Marquis (1757-1834) the French politician. It is found only in Ceylon, now Sri Lanka.

Grey Jungle Fowl   *G. sonneratii*
Named after P. Sonnerat (1745-1814), French Navy and naturalist; he was in the Philippines in 1771 and India in 1775. Inhabiting Afghanistan, West Pakistan, and India.

Koklass Pheasant   *Pucrasia macrolopha*
Pucrasia is derived from *pukras* (Nepalese) a pheasant   *makros* (Gr) long   *lophos* (Gr) a crest   *koklass* is a native name in Nepal for this

pheasant, inhabiting northern India and the Himalayas.

Common or Ring-neck Pheasant *Phasianus colchicus*
phasianos (Gr) the Phasian bird or pheasant; the name comes from the River Phasis in Colchis, which flows into the Black Sea; also *phasianus* (L) the pheasant: Colchis is an ancient territory in Asia situated between the Black Sea and the Caspian Sea; it does not appear on modern maps and only exists as a Greek legend, and once famous as a home of sorcery -*icus* (L) suffix meaning belonging to. Known as 'ring-necks' because there is usually a prominent white collar, these game birds are now widespread in Eurasia and America but originally came from Asia.

Reeves's Long-tailed Pheasant *Syrmaticus reevesii*
surma (Gr), genitive *surmatos*, a robe that trails -*icus* (New L) a suffix sometimes used to emphasize a certain characteristic; 'a long robe that trails': named after J. Reeves (1774-1856), an English naturalist who was in China from 1812 to 1831. This pheasant inhabits the mountainous regions of eastern Asia.

Mrs Hume's Long-tailed Pheasant *S. humiae*
Named in honour of Mrs Mary Hume (1880-1890), the wife of A. O. Hume (1829-1912) naturalist and author; they lived in India. This pheasant inhabits eastern India and Burma and Thailand.

Elliot's Long-tailed Pheasant *S. ellioti*
Named after Dr D. G. Elliot (1835-1915), an American zoologist, who was Curator of the Chicago Field Museum from 1894 to 1908. A rare pheasant inhabiting a small area in south-western China.

Golden Pheasant *Chrysolophys pictus*
khrusos (Gr) gold *lophos* (Gr) a crest *pictus* (L) painted; a reference to the bright colours of this bird with its fine golden crest. Inhabiting the mountainous regions of eastern Asia.

Lady Amherst's Pheasant *C. amherstiae*
Named in honour of Lady Sarah Amherst, Countess (1762-1838) the wife of William Pitt Amherst, 1st Earl (1773-1857) British diplomat. He was in China in 1816 and later became Governor-General of India from 1823 to 1828. The range is similar to *C. pictus*, above.

Bronze-tailed Peacock Pheasant *Polyplectron chalcurus*
polus (Gr) many *plēktron* (Gr) anything to strike with, a cock's spur; the male has two and often three spurs on each leg *khalkos* (Gr)

copper   *oura* (Gr) the tail. Inhabiting Malaysia, probably mainly the mountains of Sumatra.

Crested Argus Pheasant   *Rheinardia ocellata*
Capt Rheinard, a French Army officer, was in Annam from 1880 to 1883; it is now usually known as Vietnam   *ocellata* (L) provided with little eyes; a reference to the 'eyelike' markings. Ranging from Vietnam to the Malay Peninsula.

Argus Pheasant   *Argusianus argus*
Named after Argus, the mythical son of Arestor, who had 100 eyes, and Hera transplanted his eyes to the tail of the peacock. The inner wing feathers of the Argus Pheasant show rows of colourful 'eyelike' markings   *-anus* (L) suffix meaning belonging to. Inhabiting Malaya and Borneo.

Common or Blue Peafowl   *Pavo cristatus*
pavo (L) a peacock   *cristatus* (L) crested. Usually known as the Peacock, and Peahen; inhabiting India and Ceylon, now known as Sri Lanka.

Congo Peafowl   *Afropavo congensis*
pavo (L) a peacock; 'African peacock'   *-ensis* (L) belonging to; it inhabits the forests of Congo, now known as Zaire.

Family   NUMIDIDAE   8 species
Numidea is an old Roman name for a district in north-west Africa, now the Morocco area; a flock of *Numida meleagris* still live there.

Black Guineafowl   *Agelastes niger*
agelastikos (Gr) disposed to herd together; flocks of these birds can number several hundred   *niger* (L) black. Inhabiting Africa south of the Sahara.

Tufted Guineafowl   *Numida meleagris meleagris*
The nominate subspecies. *Numida*, see above under Family. Meleagros was the son of Oeneus, king in Calydon; according to the legend his sisters were changed to guineafowls on his death. It has a tuft on the head. Inhabiting Africa south of the Sahara and an isolated flock in the Morocco area; the English name derives from Guinea in West Africa.

Helmeted Guineafowl   *N. m. mitrata*
mitratus (L) wearing a turban or high head-dress; a reference to the

bony casque on the head; this is a subspecies that some authors classify as a separate species. Inhabiting Africa south of the Sahara.

Kenya Crested Guineafowl   *Guttera pucherani*
gutta (L) a drop of fluid   *guttatus* (L) spotted, speckled; a reference to the speckled plumage; Dr J. Pucheran (1817-1894) was a French zoologist who was working at the Natural History Museum in Paris in 1843. This guineafowl inhabits East Africa.

Vulturine Guineafowl   *Acryllium vulturinus*
akron (Gr) highest, topmost; can mean a point, a peak   *-illion* (Gr) diminutive suffix, 'a small point'; a reference to the pointed tail *vulturinum* (L) vulture-like; a reference to its appearance, having the head and upper part of the neck nearly naked. Inhabiting Africa.

Family   MELEAGRIDIDAE   2 species
meleagris (Gr), genitive *meleagridos*, a sort of guineafowl; Meleagros was the son of Oeneus, king in Calydon; according to the legend his sisters were changed into guineafowls on his death.

Turkey   *Meleagris gallopavo*
meleagris (Gr) a sort of guineafowl   *gallus* (L) a cock (of poultry)   *pavo* (L) a peacock; a misleading mixture of names; the turkey, although related, is not any of these birds. Inhabiting North America and Mexico and parts of Central America.

Ocellated Turkey   *Agriocharis ocellata*
agrios (Gr) wild, living in the fields   *kharis* (Gr) grace, beauty   *ocellus* (L) dim. of *oculus*, a little eye   *-atus* (L) provided with; it has eye-like markings on the tail feathers. Inhabiting the Yucatan Peninsula, Guatemala, and Honduras, Central America.

Family   OPISTHOCOMIDAE   only 1 species
opisthokomos (Gr) wearing the hair long at the back; this strange bird, the Hoatzin, has a long straggly crest of feathers on the top and at the back of the head.

Hoatzin   *Opisthocomus hoatzin*
opisthokomos (Gr) see above   *uatzin* (Nahuatl) a pheasant; the Nahuatl are a people of southern Mexico and Central America. The hoatzin inhabits the northern part of South America. For more information about this unusual and interesting bird see page 105.

21 Button-Quail, Cranes, Rails, Bustards and their kin GRUIFORMES

Spotted Crake
Porzana porzana

Order GRUIFORMES
grus (L) a crane.

Family MESITORNITHIDAE (or MESOENATIDAE)
3 species
Dr A. L. Rand says that 'mesite' is a 'classical word of irrelevant meaning'. *ornis* (Gr), genitive *ornithos*, a bird. Dr Rand is a U.S. ornithologist and author of *The New Dictionary of Birds*.

Brown Mesite   *Mesitornis unicolor*
unicolor (L) of one colour. Inhabiting eastern Madagascar.

White-breasted Mesite   *M. variegata*
vario (L) I variegate; it is reddish brown above, a grey collar, white on the chest spotted with black. Inhabiting Madagascar.

Bensch's Monias   *Monias benschi*
monias (Gr) solitary; although they sometimes gather in flocks of 30 or more, the male works alone to construct the nest; J. H. E. Bensch

(born 1868) was a Colonial Administrator in Madagascar in 1903. The three mesites are found only in Madagascar.

Family TURNICIDAE 15 species
from *coturnix* (L), genitive *coturnicis*, a quail *turnix* (New L) a shortened form, said to indicate that they lack the hind toe; the hind toe is missing.

Black-breasted Bustard-Quail *Turnix melanogaster*
turnix (New L) see above *melas* (Gr) black *gaster* (Gr) the belly. Inhabiting Australia.

Bustard-Quail *T. suscitator*
suscito (L) I arouse *suscitator* (L) an awakener; the female makes a booming call at dawn. Inhabiting the Philippines, also India, Malaysia, China and Japan.

Little Button-Quail *T. sylvatica*
silva (L) a wood *-icus* (L) suffix meaning belonging to. Inhabiting southern Spain, Africa, and ranging across Asia to the Philippines.

Quail Plover or Lark Quail *Ortyxelos meiffrenii*
ortux (Gr) the quail *elos* (Gr) low ground by rivers, marsh-meadows; it is sometimes known as the Marsh Quail. Baron Meiffren-Laugier de Chartreuse (fl. 1829) was a French zoologist and author of several books on ornithology. This lark-like quail inhabits Senegal to Uganda.

Family PEDIONOMIDAE 1 species
pedion (Gr) a plain *nomos* (Gr) an abode, a feeding place.

Plains Wanderer *Pedionomus torquatus*
torquatus (L) having a necklace; it has a white collar spotted with black. Inhabiting the south-eastern part of Australia.

Family GRUIDAE 14 species
grus (L) a crane.

Whooping Crane *Grus americana*
This crane, inhabiting North America and parts of Central America, is now very rare, and possibly only about 50 are still in existence. It is named for its loud call; the trachea, or windpipe, is about 1·5 m (5 ft) long and partly coiled within the breast bone, which helps to produce

the loud 'trombone-like' noise. All cranes have an unusually long trachea.

Common Crane *G. grus*
grus (L) a crane. Widespread in Eurasia and ranging south as far as South Africa in winter.

Japanese Crane *G. japonensis*
Inhabiting eastern Asia and Japan, it is becoming rare.

Brolga *G. rubicunda*
rubicundus (L) red, ruddy *brolga* is a native Australian name. Inhabiting New Guinea and Australia.

Crowned Crane *Balearica pavonina*
The generic name is based on hearsay, and is a mistake; Howard Saunders writes: 'I am not aware of the existence of a single authentic specimen of *Balearica pavonina* either on the mainland of Southern Spain or in the Balearic Islands.' *pavoninus* (L) of a peacock; can mean coloured like a peacock's tail; a reference to the colourful plumage and crown, or crest. It ranges all across Africa north of the equator from Senegal on the west coast to Ethiopia and Somalia in the east.

Family ARAMIDAE 1 species
aramus a bird name of unknown origin.

Limpkin *Aramus guarauna*
The specific name probably refers to *Guarauno*, American Spanish for the Warrau, a people of Venezuela and Guyana; the English name *limpkin* is said to refer to the peculiar gait which gives the impression of limping. Inhabiting the northern part of South America, the Caribbean Islands, Central America, and the southern part of North America.

Family PSOPHIIDAE 3 species
psophos (Gr) a noise; they make loud trumpeting noises.

Common Trumpeter *Psophia crepitans*
crepito (L) I rattle, I clatter *crepitans*, clattering; the call is more a deep booming sound rather than a rattle. Inhabiting the northern part of South America.

White-winged Trumpeter *P. leucoptera*
leukos (Gr) white   *pteron* (Gr) feathers; can mean wings. Inhabiting South America, particularly the Amazon region.

Green-winged Trumpeter *P. viridis*
viridis (L) green. Inhabiting Brazil.

Family RALLIDAE 124 species
rallus (New L) from *rallus* (Medieval L) a rail, for example the Water Rail or the Clapper Rail.

Water Rail *Rallus aquaticus*
aquaticus (L) living in water, belonging to water; usually seen among reeds in swampy areas or ponds. Inhabiting Europe, including Great Britain, and ranging across Asia to Japan.

Cape Rail *R. caerulescens*
caeruleus (L) blue   *-escens* (L) suffix meaning beginning to, slightly; 'bluish'. Found in the southern part of Africa.

Virginia Rail *R. limicola*
limus (L) mud   *colo* (L) I dwell in, I inhabit. Found in the southern part of Canada and ranging south to South America.

Clapper Rail *R. longirostris*
longus (L) long   *rostrum* (L) the beak. The English name is a reference to its rattling call; it inhabits both the east and west coasts of North America, ranging south through Central and South America.

Slate-breasted Rail *R. pectoralis*
pectus (L) the breast   *pectoralis*, relating to the breast. Inhabiting New Guinea and Australia.

White-striped Rail *Rallicula leucospila*
rallus, see above   *-culus* (L) dim. suffix; 'a small rail'   *leukos* (Gr) white   *spilos* (Gr) a mark, a blemish. Inhabiting New Guinea.

Brown Wood-Rail *Aramides wolfi*
aramus is a bird name of unknown origin: Dr T. Wolf (born 1841) a geologist in Ecuador in 1883, named this bird in 1884. It inhabits South America.

Mountain-Rail *Edithornis sylvestris*
Edith, a female name + *ornis* (Gr) a bird; named in honour of Mrs

Edith Baker in 1937, the wife of G. F. Baker (1878-1937) a New York banker and Trustee of the American Museum of Natural History *silvestris* (L) belonging to woods. This mountain-rail inhabits Malaysia.

Weka   *Gallirallus australis*
gallus (L) a cock (of poultry)   *rallus*, see above   *australis* does not necessarily mean Australia   *auster* (L) the south   *-alis* (L) suffix meaning relating to; hence southern *Weka* is the Maori name for the flightless rail; although the wings seem well developed it does not fly. Inhabiting New Zealand.

Corncrake   *Crex crex*
crex (Gr) a bird with a sharp knotched bill and long legs; Liddell & Scott's Greek Lexicon says—'This description does not suit the *crex rallus* Linn., our rail, though its cry is well expressed by the name (which is onomatopoeic)'. The main food is insects and other invertebrates though it does eat corn and other seeds when available. Inhabiting northern parts of Europe including the British Isles and ranging south in winter to Africa, Madagascar, and parts of Arabia.

African Black Crake   *Limnocorax flavirostra*
limnē (Gr) a marsh, a pond   *korax* (Gr) a raven or crow   *flavus* (L) yellow   *rostrum* (L) the beak; it is a black moorhen-like bird that lives in swamps and on lakesides; the beak is greenish-yellow. Common in Africa south of the Sahara, specially in the area of the lakes of Central Africa.

Carolina Crake   *Porzana carolina*
porzana (New L) from Italian, a crake; not confined to Carolina, it inhabits northern parts of North America and ranges south to northern South America.

Spotted Crake   *P. porzana*
Inhabiting North America, Europe, Africa, western Asia, India, and the Burma-Vietnam area. It has brown upper parts and a grey white-speckled breast.

Baillon's Crake   *P. pusilla*
pusillus (L) very small; a small crake, about the size of a starling; named after L. A. F. Baillon (1778-1851), a French zoologist from Abbeville. Inhabiting Eurasia, Africa, the Oriental Region, New Guinea, and Australia.

Galápagos Rail *Laterallus spilonotus*
latus (L) side, flank   *rallus* (New L) from *rallus* (Medieval L) a rail; a reference to the white bars on the back and sides   *spilos* (Gr) a mark, blemish   *nōtos* (Gr) the back. Inhabiting South America.

Moorhen *Gallinula chloropus*
gallina (L) a hen (of poultry)   *-ulus* (L) diminutive suffix   *khlōros* (Gr) greenish-yellow   *pous* (Gr) the foot; it has greenish-yellow legs and feet. The distribution is almost world-wide but not the Australian region.

Purple Gallinule *Porphyrula martinica*
porphurula, dim. of *porphuriōn* (Gr) a red-coloured water bird   *porphureōs* (Gr) purple; the plumage is dark purple rather than red: named from the island Martinique, in the West Indies, it is also found in North America, Central, and South America.

Purple Gallinule or Swamp Hen *Porphyrio porphyrio*
Porphyrio, see above. Distribution is widespread, ranging through southern Europe, Asia, India and Malaysia, Australia and New Zealand.

Takahe *Notornis mantelli*   (or *Porphyrio*)
notos (Gr) the south   *ornis* (Gr) a bird: named after W. D. B. Mantell (1820-1895) a New Zealand naturalist   *takahe* is a Maori name for this flightless bird, now almost extinct. Inhabiting New Zealand.

Coot *Fulica atra*
fulica (L) a coot   *atra* (L) black. Distribution is widespread in Europe and Asia, parts of Africa north of the Sahara, and ranging east to Japan.

Horned Coot *F. cornuta*
cornutus (L) horned. Inhabiting the Andes area in Bolivia, Chile and northern Argentina.

Crested or Knob-billed Coot *F. cristata*
cristatus (L) having a crest. Inhabiting the northern part of Africa, and Spain.

Giant Coot *F. gigantea*
gigas (L) a giant   *gigantea* (L) belonging to the giants. Inhabiting the Andes area of South America, mainly in Peru.

Family HELIORNITHIDAE 3 species
hēlios (Gr) the sun   *ornis* (Gr), genitive *ornithos*, a bird; from the original vernacular name 'sunbird', but records do not explain the name; it is now called 'finfoot', or 'sungrebe'.

African Finfoot   *Podica senegalensis*
pous (Gr), genitive *podos*, a foot; hence *podicus* (New L) belonging to the foot; a reference to the long lobed toes, the lobes acting as paddles instead of webbed feet which gives it greater agility when running on land; this also gives it the name 'finfoot'   *-ensis* (L) suffix meaning belonging to; it is not confined to Senegal and is widespread in Africa south of the Sahara.

Asian or Masked Finfoot   *Heliopais personata*
hēlios (Gr) the sun   *pais* (Gr) a child; 'child of the sun'   *personatus* (L) wearing a mask; it has a black front to the face. Inhabiting Bengal and Malaya.

Sungrebe   *Heliornis fulica*
Heliornis, see above under Family   *fulica* (L) a coot. Inhabiting Mexico, Central America, and ranging south through South America.

Family RHYNOCHETIDAE 1 species
rhis (Gr), genitive *rhinos*, the nose   *khaitē* (Gr) flowing hair or mane; it has a long shaggy crest, on the head rather than on the nose, which is raised when the bird is excited.

Kagu   *Rhynochetos jubatus*
jubatus = *iubatus* (L) having a mane, crested. Found only on the island New Caledonia, off the east coast of Australia, it is very rare. Kagu is a local native name.

Family EURYPYGIDAE 1 species
eurus (Gr) wide   *pugē* (Gr) the rump; 'wide-rumped'.

Sunbittern   *Eurypyga helias*
hēlios (Gr) the sun   *hēlias*, daughter of the sun. Inhabiting Central America and the Amazon area; it is very rare.

Family CARIAMIDAE 2 species
cariama and *seriema* are Portuguese forms of a native word (prob. *Tupi*) for this bird.

Crested Seriema *Cariama cristata*
cristata (L) having a crest. Inhabiting the southern half of South America including part of Brazil.

Burmeister's Seriema *Chunga burmeisteri*
Chunga is a native name in Argentina for a crane-like bird: Dr K. H. K. Burmeister (1807-1892) was Director of the Zoological Museum at Halle University from 1842 to 1848. This seriema inhabits the southern half of South America.

Family OTIDIDAE 21 species
ōtis (Gr), genitive *ōtidos*, a bustard with long ear feathers.

Little Bustard *Otis tetrax*
tetrax (Gr) name of two kinds of birds, one probably of the grouse kind (*tetrao* L). Inhabiting Europe, northern Africa, and ranging to the south-west of Asia.

Denham's Bustard *Neotis denhami*
neos (Gr) new, recent *ōtis* (Gr) a bustard: Lt Col D. Denham (1786-1826) explored north-west Africa from 1822 to 1825; he named this bustard in 1826. Inhabiting Africa.

Australian Bustard *Ardeotis australis* (formerly *Choriotis*)
ardea (L) a heron *auster* (L) the south *-alis* (L) suffix meaning belonging to; 'southern'. Found only in Australia.

Crested Bustard *Eupodotis ruficrista* (formerly *Lophotis*)
eu- (Gr) prefix meaning well, nicely; often used to indicate typical *pous* (Gr), genitive *podos*, the foot, claws, + *ōtis*; 'a bustard having strong or typical claws'; they are fast runners: *ruficrista* (coined from L) red-crested. Inhabiting Africa.

22 Snipe, Oystercatchers, Plovers, Curlews, Skuas, Gulls, Auks and their kin CHARADRIIFORMES

Avocet
Recurvirostra avosetta

The order Charadriiformes includes many familiar birds, and they are mostly to be found by the sea or near fresh-water lakes, rivers, and marshes. Almost without exception they eat various crustaceans, and the diet includes worms and insects; in some cases, for example the plovers and lapwings, they also eat seeds.

The Jacana, or Lily-trotter, is interesting for its enormously long toes and nails, which enable it to walk about on floating vegetation, hence the name 'lily-trotter'. Some species in this order change the usual role of male and female, for instance in the case of the American Painted Snipe *Nycticryphes semicollaris* the male incubates the eggs and feeds and cares for the young. This is also the case with the Dotterel *Eudromias morinellus*, and even more surprising the female Phalarope *Phalaropus lobatus* also initiates the courtship display. She is larger and more colourful than her different mate, who might almost be called 'hen-pecked'.

Order CHARADRIIFORMES

kharadra (Gr) a mountain stream, a ravine   *kharadrios* (Gr) a bird dwelling in clefts, perhaps the lapwing or the curlew; a misleading name as they do not live in clefts or frequent mountain streams, and usually the nest is a ground-scrape or an open cup.

Family JACANIDAE   7 species
jaçanã (Port) a name used for these birds, probably by the South-American Indians; in English the soft 'c' is usually replaced by a hard 'k' sound.

African Jacana   *Actophilornis africanus*
aktē (Gr) a headland on the coast; can mean the rugged banks of rivers   *philos* (Gr) loved, pleasing   *ornis* (Gr) a bird; although sometimes seen on mossy rocks and river banks, the jacana is usually found walking about on floating vegetation, made possible by its enormously long toes and nails. Inhabiting Africa south of the Sahara.

Australian Jacana   *Irediparra gallinacea*
Named after Tom Iredale in 1911, an English naturalist from Cumberland   *parra* (L) a bird of ill omen; can mean the lapwing   *gallus* (L) a cock   *gallinaceus* (L) of poultry. Inhabiting Indonesia, New Guinea, and Australia.

Pheasant-tailed Jacana   *Hydrophasianus chirurgus*
hudor (Gr) water   *phasianos* (Gr) from the River Phasis, the Phasian bird (see p. 114) 'a water-pheasant'; jacanas always live on or near water   *kheirourgos* (Gr) working or doing by hand, a surgeon; the reason for the specific name is obscure. From the Indo-Malayan region eastwards to Taiwan and southwards to the Philippines.

Bronze-winged Jacana   *Metopidius indicus*
metopidios (Gr) on the forehead; the jacana has a frontal shield on the forehead   *indicus* (L) of India. Inhabiting India, the Thailand and Vietnam area and Malaysia.

American Jacana   *Jacana spinosa*
jacana (see above, under Family)   *spinosus* (L) thorny, prickly; jacanas have a spike on the front edge of the wing, said to be used in fighting. Ranging from southern Texas to Argentina.

Family ROSTRATULIDAE   2 species
rostrum (L) the beak   *-atus* (L) suffix meaning provided with   *-ulus*

(L) dim. suffix; 'provided with a small beak'; the beak could not be described as small, but it is shorter than that of the true snipe (Family Scolopacidae).

Painted Snipe *Rostratula benghalensis*
-ensis (L) suffix meaning belonging to; in addition to the Bengal area of India it is found in the southern part of Asia ranging from Asia Minor and Africa, including Madagascar, to Japan, Malaysia, the Philippines, Indonesia, and Australia, but rarely in Sarawak and Borneo.

South American Painted Snipe *Nycticryphes semicollaris*
nux (Gr), genitive *nuktos*, night *kruphios* (Gr) hidden, secret; active only at dawn and dusk, they are secretive and solitary *semi-* (L) half *collare* (L) a chain for the neck *collaris*, pertaining to the neck; it has a white collar which does not completely encircle the neck. Inhabiting southern South America.

Family   HAEMATOPODIDAE   6 species
haima (Gr), genitive *haimatos*, blood *pous* (Gr), genitive *podos*, the foot; 'blood-coloured feet'; oystercatchers have pink legs and feet.

Black Oystercatcher *Haematopus ater*
ater (L) black. Inhabiting southern South America.

European Oystercatcher *H. ostralegus*
ostreon (Gr) oyster *legō* (Gr) I gather, I pick up; oystercatcher is a misnomer as they do not eat oysters, but they do open and eat various shell-fish, probably mostly mussels and cockles. This oystercatcher has a wide range apart from Europe, including the Canaries, North and South America, South Africa, Asia, Australia, and New Zealand.

American Oystercatcher *H. palliatus*
palliatus (L) clad in a Greek mantle. Inhabiting New Jersey and California ranging to northern South America.

Family   CHARADRIIDAE   62 species
(see notes under Order, opposite).

Southern Lapwing *Vanellus chilensis*
vanellus (New L) from *vanneau* (Fr) the lapwing, from *van* (Fr) a winnowing fan, a reference to the slow flapping of the wings in flight

-ensis (L) suffix meaning belonging to; named from Chile as it inhabits South America.

Spur-winged Lapwing   *V. spinosus*
spinosus (L) thorny, prickly; there is a spur on the front edge of the wing. Inhabiting southern Europe, the Middle East, and northern and central Africa.

Common Lapwing   *V. vanellus*
Wide distribution including Europe, Africa, southern Asia including the Thailand and Vietnam area.

Golden Plover   *Pluvialis apricaria*
pluvialis (L) relating to rain, bringing rain; several explanations of this name have been given by various authors, all having some connection with rain. The Oxford English Dictionary suggests that it is because the birds foretell rain by their restlessness; the German name for the plover means 'rain-piper' because they are known to sing in the rain   *apricus* (L) places open to the sun; can mean loving the sun *-arius* (L) suffix meaning belonging to; probably a reference to the bird's golden colour. Inhabiting Eurasia and India.

American Golden Plover   *P. dominica*
-icus (L) suffix meaning belonging to; a reference to the Dominican Republic, where the typical specimen was found probably during migration as they do not live there. The Golden Plovers are widespread, breeding in the Arctic around the world and migrating south in winter to tropical countries including South America, Africa, and Australia.

Grey or Black-bellied Plover   *P. squatarola*
squatarola (New L) from Italian dialect, the black-bellied plover. Inhabiting northern coastal areas of Siberia, Alaska, Canada and some islands, migrating south and wintering all round the world from South America to Australia.

Little Ringed Plover   *Charadrius dubius*
kharadrios (Gr) a bird living in clefts (see under Order p. 126)   *dubius* (L) uncertain, doubtful; J. A. Scopoli (1723-1788) a professor of botany in Padua, who named the typical form, was doubtful whether it was a distinct species. Widespread in Europe including the southeastern part of England, northern Africa, Asia and ranging to Malaysia and New Guinea. Given its English name because of the

white and black bands round the neck.

Ringed Plover   *C. hiaticula*
hiatus (L) a cleft, an opening (cf. *karadrios*, under Order p. 126) *cula*, probably a misspelling of *colo* (L) I inhabit, I dwell (see p. 126). Widespread, breeding in the north around the world and migrating south in winter to South America, Africa, and southern Asia.

Mountain Plover   *C. montana*
montanus (L) of a mountain. Inhabiting North and Central America.

Killdeer   *C. vociferus*
vociferor (L) I cry aloud, I shout; they are noisy birds, the call sounding like 'kill-dee', hence the vernacular name Killdeer. Ranging from Canada to Mexico and the West Indies, and coasts of Peru and Chile.

Dotterel   *Eudromias morinellus*
eu- (Gr) prefix meaning well, nicely   *dromeus* (Gr) a runner; when hunting they run in short bursts, halt and freeze, pick up an insect, then dash off in a new direction   *morinellus* (New L) according to Dr Gesner (1516-1565), and Webster's International Dictionary, it is a coined word, a diminutive of *mōros* (Gr) stupid, foolish, and in part refers to the Morini, an ancient name for the people of Flanders where the bird used to be very common; it has a reputation for stupidity (see Australian Dotterel, p. 137). Inhabiting scattered areas of North America, northern Europe especially Scandinavia, Scotland, the Netherlands, and migrating south in winter to southern Italy, Greece, North Africa, and ranging south-east to Thailand and Vietnam.

Wrybill   *Anarhynchus frontalis*
ana- (Gr) prefix meaning up, upon, back   *rhunkhos* (Gr) snout, beak; there is a most peculiar shape to the beak, the outer or distal part being bent to the right; it is thought that in some way this helps the bird to obtain insects that hide under stones   *frons* (L), genitive *frontis*, the forehead   *-alis* (L) suffix meaning relating to; it has a white forehead. Inhabiting New Zealand.

Family SCOLOPACIDAE   81 species
skolopax (Gr), genitive *skolopakos*, a bird of the snipe kind, perhaps a woodcock.

Upland Sandpiper   *Bartramia longicauda*
Named after W. Bartram (1739-1823) in 1851, an American natu-

ralist *longus* (L) long *cauda* (L) the tail of an animal. Inhabiting North, Central, and South America.

Common Curlew *Numenius arquata*
noumĕnius (Gr) derived from *neo-mĕnios*, meaning used at the new moon; can also mean the curlew on account of the bird's crescent-shaped bill *arcus* (L) a bow *-atus* (L) provided with, hence *arquata* (New L) provided with a bow, another reference to the bird's crescent-shaped bill. Inhabiting the northern parts of Eurasia including the British Isles and ranging south in winter to Africa and southern Asia as far as Malaysia and Borneo.

Long-billed Curlew *N. americanus*
-anus (L) suffix meaning belonging to. Breeding in the western part of North America and migrating south in winter to southern Mexico.

Eskimo Curlew *N. borealis*
boreus (L) pertaining to the north wind *borealis* (L) northern. This curlew is very rare; it breeds in Alaska and northern North America and migrates south in winter to southern South America.

Far Eastern Curlew *N. madagascariensis*
-ensis (L) suffix meaning belonging to; the name is a mistake, it does not belong to Madagascar and has never lived there; it breeds in eastern Siberia and ranges south in winter to Malaysia, New Guinea and many islands in that part of the Pacific Ocean, and Australia.

Whimbrel *N. phaeopus*
phaios (Gr) dusky, grey *pous* (Gr) the foot; the legs are greenish grey. Breeds in parts of Alaska, Greenland, Iceland, Scandinavia, and northern USSR and migrates south in winter to South America, Africa and Australia.

Bristle-thighed Curlew *N. tahitiensis*
-ensis (L) suffix meaning belonging to. Breeding in the mountains of Alaska it migrates across the Pacific Ocean to winter in Tahiti and other islands of the Polynesian group as far south as New Caledonia.

Bar-tailed Godwit *Limosa lapponica*
limus (L) mud *-osus* (L) suffix meaning full of, prone to; they often inhabit mud flats and marshy places *-icus* (L) suffix meaning belonging to; 'of Lapland'. Breeding in northern areas of Europe, and occasionally Britain, it migrates south in winter sometimes as far as South Africa, Australia and New Zealand. The tail is white with black

bars. The name godwit is obscure, but is said to come from Old English meaning 'good creature', a reference to it being good to eat.

Black-tailed Godwit *L. limosa*
Breeds in northern Eurasia and migrates south in winter to south-eastern Asia, Africa and Australia.

Wood Sandpiper *Tringa glareola*
trungas (Gr) a white-rumped water bird, the sandpiper *glarea* (L) gravel *-olus* (L) dim. suffix, 'little gravel', to indicate sand, though they tend to inhabit marshy places rather than sandy places. Breeding in the northern part of Eurasia and migrating south in winter to south-east Asia, Africa, and Australia.

Yellowshank *T. melanoleuca*
melas (Gr) black *leukos* (Gr) white; it has a white upper rump and black tips to the wings. Inhabiting North America and migrating south in winter to Central and South America.

Greenshank *T. nebularia*
nebula (L) mist *-arius* (L) suffix meaning belonging to; a reference to the bird's habitat on marshy ground where it is often misty. Inhabiting Europe including the British Isles and northern Asia, and migrating south in winter to southern Europe, Africa, south-east Asia, Malaysia, New Guinea, and Australia.

Green Sandpiper *T. ochropus*
ōkhros (Gr) pale, yellow *pous* (Gr) foot, talons or claws; actually the feet and legs are a greenish colour. Wide distribution in the northern part of Eurasia and migrating south in winter to Africa, south-east Asia and Malaysia.

Solitary Sandpiper *T. solitaria*
Inhabiting North America and migrating in winter to Central and South America. Usually seen singly or at the most in pairs.

Common Snipe *Gallinago gallinago*
gallinago, a coined word derived from *gallina* (L) a hen (poultry). Almost world-wide distribution migrating south in winter.

Japanese Snipe *G. hardwickii*
Named after Maj. Gen. T. Hardwick, FRS (1756-1835) a naturalist in India. This snipe inhabits Japan, Vietnam, Thailand, New Guinea and Australia.

Swinhoe's Snipe   *G. megala*
megalē (Gr) great: R. Swinhoe, FRS (1836-1877) was in the Consular Service in China. Inhabiting eastern Siberia and migrating south to India, the Vietnam-Thailand area, Malaysia, New Guinea and neighbouring small islands, and Australia.

Pintail Snipe   *G. stenura*
stenos (Gr) narrow   *oura* (Gr) the tail. Breeds in Siberia and migrates to India and south-east Asia.

Ruddy Turnstone   *Arenaria interpres*
arena (L) sand   *arenarius* (L) relating to sand, sandy; it is found on rocky and pebbly shores and also on sandy flats   *interpres* (L) a negotiator, a messenger; an allusion to the alarm call which warns other birds of the approach of danger. Breeds on the coasts of Alaska, northern Canada, Greenland, Scandinavia and Siberia, and migrates south to an almost world-wide distribution including South America, South Africa, Australia and New Zealand.

Black Turnstone   *A. melanocephala*
melas (Gr), genitive *melanos*, black   *kephalē* (Gr) the head; the head and breast are mainly black. Breeds in Alaska and migrates south in winter to southern California and Central America.

Short-billed Dowitcher   *Limnodromus griseus*
limnē (Gr) a marsh, a pond   *dromeus* (Gr) a runner; 'marsh-runner'   *griseus* (New L) grey. The name *dowitcher* is of Iroquoian origin; the Iroquois are an American-Indian people. This snipe breeds in North America and winters in Central and South America.

American Woodcock   *Scolopax minor*   (formerly *Philohela*)
skolopax (Gr) a woodcock   *minor* (L) lesser. Inhabiting the south-eastern part of North America.

Eurasian Woodcock   *S. rusticola*
rusticola (L) an inhabitant of the country; a reference to the bird's habitat, woodland rather than marshes. Breeds in Europe though not in the far north or south, and ranging across Asia to Japan, also some islands such as the Canaries, Maderia, and Azores and parts of Asia Minor and the Himalayas; it does not migrate far.

Jack Snipe   *Lymnocryptes minimus*
limnē (Gr) a marsh, a pond   *kruptos* (Gr) secret, hidden; an allusion

to the bird's habit of hiding among reeds *minimus* (L) smallest; it is the smallest snipe. Breeds in north-east Europe and northern Asia migrating south in winter to Africa, India, Vietnam and Thailand, and Malaysia.

Surfbird *Aphriza virgata*
aphros (Gr) froth, sea foam *zaō* (Gr) I live; they hunt for prey very close to the surf as they seem to prefer rocks and pebbles that have just had a wave break over them *virga* (L) a twig; *virgatus*, made of twigs, can mean striped; the bird is usually mottled black and white rather than striped. Breeds in Alaska and migrates south in winter to Central and South America as far as Chile.

Sanderling *Calidris alba* (formerly *Crocethia*)
Calidris is a coined word derived from *skalidris* (Gr) a spotted bird *albus* (L) white; a reference to the birds plumage in winter. Sanderling is derived from an Icelandic name for the sandpiper. Almost world-wide distribution, breeding in the Northern Hemisphere and migrating south in winter to all southern countries.

Baird's Sandpiper *C. bairdii*
Named after Spencer Fullerton Baird (1823-1887) the American ornithologist. Breeds in the far north of North America and migrates south to South America.

Purple Sandpiper *C. maritima*
maritimus (L) of the sea; apart from the breeding season it is always found along the shore or nearby, and prefers rocky coasts. Breeds in Arctic areas on coasts and islands of the Arctic Sea and migrates south in winter.

Temminck's Stint *C. temminckii*
Named after Prof C. J. Temminck (1778-1858) the Dutch zoologist at one time Director of the Natural History Museum, Leyden. The origin of the name stint is obscure. Breeds subarctic and arctic areas from Scandinavia to the Bering Straits, and occasionally in Britain and migrates south in winter mainly to Africa and south-east Asia as far as Malaysia.

Spoonbilled Sandpiper *Eurynorhynchus pygmeus*
eurunō (Gr) I make wide or broad *rhunkhos* (Gr) the beak *pugmaios* (Gr) a foot tall, dwarfish. Breeding in northern North America and

Eurasia and migrating south in winter, the Siberian species to India, and the Thailand-Vietnam area.

Ruff *Philomachus pugnax*
philos (Gr) loving   *makhē* (Gr) battle, combat   *pugnax* (L) fond of fighting, quarrelsome; there is ritual fighting among the males as part of the courtship ceremony but it is really only pretence and bravado. Breeding in the far north of Eurasia and migrating south in winter to South Africa and the Oriental region.

Family   RECURVIROSTRIDAE   7 species
recurvo (L) I curve backwards   *rostrum* (L) a beak; only the avocets have the upward-curved bill from which the name is derived.

Ibisbill   *Ibidorhyncha struthersii*
ibis (L), genitive *ibidis*, a sacred Egyptian bird that lived on water animals, the ibis   *rhunkhos* (Gr) a beak, bill; the beak is curved downward like that of the ibis, quite different from the avocet's beak which is curved upward: named after Dr John Struthers (fl 1855), a Scottish zoologist who was at Glasgow University in 1831. Inhabiting the mountains of central Asia, and ranging to Kashmir and Burma.

Black-winged Stilt   *Himantopus himantopus*
himas (Gr), genitive *himantos*, a leather thong   *pous* (Gr) the foot; 'strap-leg'; a reference to the slender lower leg. Almost world-wide distribution with slight variations in different countries which would be classified as sub-species or races. The name 'stilt' is a reference to the long thin legs.

Banded Stilt   *Cladorhynchus leucocephalus*
klados (Gr) a shoot, a twig   *rhunkhos* (Gr) the beak; a reference to the long slender beak which resembles a long thin shoot or twig   *leukos* (Gr) white, pale   *kephalē* (Gr) the head. Inhabiting Australia. It has a chestnut-brown band across the breast.

American Avocet   *Recurvirostra americana*   (includes *H. mexicanus*) *Recurvirostra*, see notes under Family, above. Inhabiting North and Central America. Avocet is from the Italian *avosetta*.

Avocet   *R. avosetta*
Inhabiting Eurasia, Africa, India, and the Vietnam-Thailand area.

Family   PHALAROPODIDAE   3 species
phalaris (Gr) a coot, so called from its bald white head (*phalakros* (Gr)

bald)   *pous* (Gr), genitive *podos*, the foot, 'coot-footed'; an allusion to the lateral lobes on the feet which resemble those of coots and form paddles that assist when swimming.

Red or Grey Phalarope   *Phalaropus fulicarius*
fulica (L) a coot   *-arius* (L) suffix meaning belonging to (see above). The plumage is red in summer and grey in winter. Breeds in arctic areas almost throughout the northern hemisphere, and migrates south in winter ranging to South America, Africa, the oriental region, and Australia.

Northern Phalarope   *P. lobatus*   (formerly *Lobipes*)
lobatus (New L) lobed (see above). The range is similar to the Red Phalarope, above.

Wilson's Phalarope   *P. tricolor*   (formerly *Steganopus*)
In summer the female has a white rump, dark grey wings, and reddish-brown patterns on the side of the neck and wing coverts. Named after Alexander Wilson (1766-1813) an American ornithologist. Breeds inland in central Canada and USA and migrates to South America. All three phalaropes are occasionally seen in Britain.

Family   DROMADIDAE   1 species
dromas (Gr), genitive *dromados*, running; spends a lot of time walking and running looking for crabs, its favourite food. Can fly and also swims well.

Crab Plover   *Dromas ardeola*
ardeola (L) a little heron; it is rather like a small heron. Inhabiting Africa, parts of southern Asia including India.

Family   BURHINIDAE   9 species
bous (Gr) an ox   *rhis* (Gr), genitive *rhinos*, the nose; 'bull-nosed'; the head is relatively large and the bill short and thick.

Double-striped Thick-knee   *Burhinus bistriatus*
stria (L) a furrow, a channel   *striatus* (New L) striped; *bi-striatus*, having two stripes; there are two stripes on the head. Thick-knee is a misleading name; it refers to the bulging joint between the tibia and tarsus which is in fact the ankle. Inhabiting Mexico and Central America and the northern part of South America.

Southern Stone-Curlew   *B. magnirostris*
magnus (L) great   *rostrum* (L) the beak; the beak is short and thick.

The name 'stone-curlew' refers to their liking for stony and pebbly ground. Inhabiting Australia.

Stone-Curlew   *B. oedicnemus*
oidos (Gr) a swelling   *knēmē* (Gr) the knee, lower part of the leg; 'a thick knee'. Ranging from south-east England southern Eurasia and India to Africa.

Peruvian Thick-knee   *B. superciliaris*
supercilium (L) the eyebrow   *-arius* (or *aris*) (L) suffix meaning belonging to; there is a white streak above the eye. Ranging from Ecuador to Peru.

Beach Stone-Curlew   *Esacus magnirostris*   (or *Orthorhamphus*)
Esacus, obscure; evidently a coined name and not explained in the ornithological records in the British Museum (Natural History) *magnus* (L) great   *rostrum* (L) the beak; the beak is short and thick; note that the Southern Stone-Curlew has the same specific name. Inhabiting the Indo-Australasian region.

Family   GLAREOLIDAE   17 species
glarea (L) gravel   *-olus* (L) diminutive suffix   *glareola* (New L) a coined word to indicate dry sandy places; 'small gravel'; the family frequent dry stony places, deserts, ploughed land, etc.

Egyptian Plover   *Pluvianus aegyptius*
pluvius (L) rainy, bringing rain   *-anus* (L) suffix meaning belonging to; a coined word, 'associated with rain' (see Golden Plover p. 128) *Aegyptus* (L) Egypt   *-ius* (L) suffix meaning belonging to. Inhabiting Egypt and ranging south across Africa from Senegal to Ethiopia, and south to Uganda.

Indian Courser   *Cursorius coromandelicus*
cursor (L) a runner   *-ius* (L) suffix meaning belonging to; they are good runners, usually running rather than flying when escaping from danger; most coursers can run faster than a man: the Coromandel Coast is the east coast of India, forming part of the Bay of Bengal *-icus* (L) suffix meaning belonging to. Inhabiting India.

Cream Coloured Courser   *C. cursor*
cursor (L) a runner (see above). Mainly found in Africa, but sometimes ranging to southern Europe and south-west Asia.

Temminck's Courser *C. temminckii*
Named after Prof C. J. Temminck (1778-1858) a Dutch zoologist. The distribution is widespread in Africa except the Congo forests, the north-east area, and the south-west.

Australian Dotterel *Peltohyas australis*
peltē (Gr) a small shield; Sharpe gives no explanation of *Peltohyas* but it may refer to a shield-shaped mark at the base of the beak *auster* (L) the south *-alis* (L) suffix meaning relating to. Inhabiting Australia. Dotterel is derived from *dote*, and the diminutive suffix *-rel*; 'a little fool'; they have a reputation for stupidity, being so tame and easily caught. Here the name is incorrect, as it is not in the same family as the lapwings, plovers, and dotterels, the Charadriidae. Dr R. B. Sharpe (1847-1909) was an ornithologist in the British Museum (Natural History) from 1872 to 1909.

Black-winged Pratincole *Glareola nordmanni*
Glareola, see under Family (p. 136): named after Alexander v. Nordmann (1803-1866), a Russian zoologist who travelled in southern Russia and Crimea in 1842. Inhabiting southern Eurasia and Africa. Pratincole is a name derived from Latin *pratum*, a meadow, and *incola* (L) a dweller, alluding to a common habitat.

White-collared Pratincole *G. nuchalis*
nuchalis (New L) of the neck; a reference to the white line round the neck. Inhabiting Africa.

Pratincole *G. pratincola*
pratincola, see above under Black-winged Pratincole. Inhabiting southern Eurasia, Africa and India.

Family THINOCORIDAE 4 species
this (Gr), genitive *thinos*, the beach, shore   *korax* (Gr) a raven; they inhabit rocky shores but can also be found high in the mountains.

Gay's Seedsnipe *Attagis gayi*
attagas (Gr) a long-billed bird fond of the water, perhaps the godwit: named after Dr Claude Gay (1800-1873), a French botanist who lived in Chile from 1824 to 1841. Inhabiting western South America along the Andes, ranging south from Ecuador. The English name seedsnipe is a reference to its diet which is mainly seeds and occasionally some vegetable matter and insects.

D'Orbigny's Seedsnipe *Thinocorus orbignyianus*
Thinocorus, see above under Family: named after Prof A. D. d'Orbigny (1803-1857), a French zoologist who was in South America from 1826 to 1833 and was Professor at the Museum of Natural History, Paris, in 1854. Inhabiting Peru and ranging south to Tierra del Fuego.

Pygmy or Patagonian Seedsnipe *T. rumicivorus*
rumex (L), genitive *rumicis*, sorrel   *voro* (L) I devour; a reference to their liking for the sorrel plant. Breeding in the southern part of South America it migrates north to Argentina and some valleys in the high Andes. The smallest seedsnipe, about 18 cm (7 in) long; Patagonia is the southern part of Argentina.

Family   CHIONIDIDAE   2 species
khiōn (Gr) snow; a reference to the completely white plumage and to their habitat in lands of snow, ice and rock.

Snowy Sheathbill *Chionis alba*
albus (L) white. Inhabiting sub-antarctic islands such as South Georgia, South Orkneys, and other small islands off the tip of southern South America, it migrates north as far as Uruguay. The name sheathbill derives from a horny casing that covers the base of the bill.

Lesser Sheathbill *C. minor*
minor (L) smaller, less; actually very little smaller than *C. alba*. Inhabiting sub-antarctic islands such as Prince Edward, Crozet, Kerguelen and Heard; these lie between the southern part of the Indian Ocean and the Antarctic.

Family   STERCORARIIDAE   5 species
stercus (L), genitive *stercoris*, dung   *stercorarius* (L) having to do with dung; with reference to their fondness of offal and carrion.

Long-tailed Jaeger *Stercorarius longicaudus*
longus (L) long   *cauda* (L) the tail; the central tail feathers are much lengthened. Breeds in northern arctic areas of North America and Eurasia and migrates to tropical areas in the southern Hemisphere where it spends a lot of its time at sea. The name jaeger is from *jäger* (G) a hunter, and derives from the fierce attacks it makes on other sea birds, causing them to drop or even disgorge their prey; however apparently *S. longicaudus* is less ferocious than its relatives.

Pomarine Jaeger *S. pomarinus*
pōma (Gr) a cover, a lid   *rhis* (Gr), genitive *rhinos*, the nose; an allusion to the rim over the base of the bill which appears in summer. The range is similar to *S. longicaudus*, above.

MacCormick's Skua *S. maccormicki*
Dr R. MacCormick (1800-1890) was surgeon with the British Antarctic Expedition in 1839-1843. This skua breeds in the Antarctic and migrates to Australia, New Zealand and surrounding islands, but like other skuas spends much of its time at sea. The name skua is derived from *skufr*, the Icelandic name for the bird.

Great Skua *S. skua*   (or *Catharacta*)
skugvur (Old Norse) = *skufr*, a predatory gull. The range differs from other skuas in that it breeds in both the Arctic and Antarctic; in the north, Iceland, the Faeroes and Scotland, and in the south Antarctic and Sub-antarctic islands, the southern tip of South America and the Falkland Islands and the extreme south of New Zealand; both kinds migrate to warmer areas in winter and spend much of their time at sea.

Family   LARIDAE   86 species
laros (Gr) a sea bird, probably the gull or cormorant.

Herring Gull   *Larus argentatus*
argentatus (L) ornamented with silver; a reference to the silvery-grey plumage. Widespread on the sea coasts of the Northern Hemisphere.

Red-legged Kittiwake   *L. brevirostris*
brevis (L) short   *rostrum* (L) the beak. Breeds in the Bering Straits area and North Pacific and migrates south in winter. The name kittiwake is imitative of the bird's call.

Common Gull   *L. canus*
canus (L) hoary, grey; a reference to the predominant colour; like several other gulls that have grey wings with black wing-tips, these gulls are difficult to distinguish one from another. The range is similar to *L. argentatus*, above, and often seen inland on lakes and rivers and scavenging on rubbish dumps.

Lesser Black-backed Gull   *L. fuscus*
fuscus (L) dark-coloured. Inhabiting mainly the eastern Atlantic shores from Scandinavia ranging south to Africa.

Ross's Gull   *L. rosea*   (or *Rhodostethia*)
roseus (L) red; a white gull strongly tinged with pink. Discovered by and named after Rear Admiral Sir James C. Ross (1800-1862), the Arctic and Antarctic explorer. This gull is rarely seen south of the Arctic area; it breeds in the Kolyma River area in north-eastern Siberia and migrations in winter do not reach very far south.

Black-headed Gull   *L. ridibundus*
rideo (L) I laugh   *ridibundus* (L) laughing; an allusion to its supposedly laughing call. Breeds in Britain, Ireland and western Europe ranging to eastern Asia, migrating in winter to northern Africa, and ranging to Asia, Persian Gulf, India, Philippines, China and Japan.

Black-legged Kittiwake   *L. tridactylus*
tria (Gr) three   *daktulos* (Gr) a finger, a toe; the three front toes are of normal size but the hind toe is small and almost rudimentary. Breeding on North Atlantic coasts and migrating south in winter. The name kittiwake is an imitation of their call.

White-winged Black Tern   *Chlidonias leucoptera*
Chlidonias is actually a misspelling; it should be *khelidonios* (Gr) of the swallow, like the swallow, a reference to the tern's swallow-like wings and forked tail; there is a rare Greek word *khelidonias*, meaning the spring wind because the swallows come with it   *leukos* (Gr) white *pteron* (Gr) feathers, can mean wings. Widespread distribution including sea coasts of Eurasia, Africa, the Oriental Region, New Guinea and Australia. The name tern is of Scandinavian origin, akin to Old Norse *therna*, a tern.

Black Tern   *C. nigra*
niger (L) black. Breeds in south-western Europe ranging to western Asia, and winters on coasts and inland waters of Africa ranging south to Angola and Tanzania.

Bridled Tern   *Sterna anaethetus*
sterna (New L) a tern, of Scandinavian origin, cf. *therna* (Old Norse) a tern; *anaethetus* is a misspelling of *anaisthētos* (Gr) without feeling, without sense of a thing; can mean without common sense, stupid; an allusion to its stupidity in allowing people to approach so near; English sailors called it a 'noddy', Linneus named a related bird *Sterna solida*, 'the dense tern'. Very widespread distribution and known in almost every country in the world though rare in some parts. The

name bridled refers to a bridle-like black line from the base of the bill past the eyes.

Greater Crested Tern   *S. bergii*
Named after Dr F. G. Berg (1843-1902), a zoologist and Director of the Buenos Aires Museum from 1892 to 1901. Range is similar to *S. anaethetus*, above, but not recorded in the Americas.

Caspian Tern   *S. caspia*
Named from the Caspian Sea, the distribution is widespread, similar to above and including the Americas.

Roseate Tern   *S. dougallii*
Named after Dr Patrick Macdougall (c. 1770-c. 1817) a Scottish zoologist; Glasgow University in 1808   *roseus* (L) rose-coloured. Worldwide distribution, like *S. anaethetus*, above.

Forster's Tern   *S. forsteri*
Thomas Nuttall (1786-1859), the English ornithologist and botanist, described this tern and it was named after Dr Johann Reinhold Forster (1729-1798), the German naturalist who accompanied Capt Cook on his voyage to the Pacific on *HMS Resolution* in 1772. Inhabiting North America and South America.

Sooty Tern   *S. fuscata*
fuscus (L) dark, dusky; it has very dark wings and back. Inhabiting southern seas around the world.

Common Tern   *S. hirundo*
hirundo (L) a swallow; a reference to the swallow-like wings and the deeply-forked tail. It has a world-wide distribution.

Gull-billed Tern   *S. nilotica*
niloticus (L) of the Nile; the bird takes the name from the River Nile but it is known in most parts of the world, although rare in the New Guinea-Australia-Pacific Islands area. The bill is noticeably heavier than in other terns.

Trudeau's Tern   *S. trudeaui*
Named after Dr J. de B. Trudeau (1817-1887) a New York doctor, naturalist, and author of books on zoology. Inhabiting South America.

Inca Tern   *Larosterna inca*
'A gull-tern': the Incas were an American-Indian tribe of Peru. This

interesting tern, with its red beak and feet and long white trailing moustache, inhabits the coasts of Ecuador, Peru and Chile.

Brown Noddy *Anous stolidus*
anous (Gr) without understanding, silly   *stolidus* (L) dull, slow of mind; authors of Latin names seem determined to condemn some birds as stupid just because they are not afraid of man! (cf *S. anaethetus*, p. 140). Inhabiting the Southern Hemisphere around the world.

Black or Lesser Noddy   *A. tenuirostris*
tenuis (L) thin, slender   *rostrum* (L) the beak; noddies have a slender pointed beak. The Black Noddy, although smaller than the Brown Noddy, is not one of the smallest. Found in most tropical and sub-tropical areas.

White Tern *Gygis alba*
gugēs (Gr) a water-bird   *albus* (L) white. Found in most tropical and sub-tropical seas.

Family   RYNCHOPIDAE   3 species
rhunkhos (Gr) snout, beak   *ops* (Gr) eye, face, appearance; 'snout-like'; they have a compressed and blade-like bill, the lower mandible being longer than the upper to assist in skimming their prey from the surface of the water.

Indian Skimmer *Rynchops albicollis*
albus (L) white   *collum* (L) the neck; it has a white neck and breast and upper parts dark to black. Inhabiting the coasts and inland waters of India, Burma, Vietnam, Thailand and Cambodia.

African Skimmer   *R. flavirostris*
flavus (L) yellow   *rostrum* (L) snout, beak; the beak is yellow and red. Inhabiting coasts and inland waters of Africa south of the Sahara.

Black Skimmer   *R. nigra*
niger (L) black; it is not entirely black, having a white breast and neck. It is found only in the New World, ranging from New Jersey in North America to the Amazon Basin and Argentina.

Family   ALCIDAE   21 species
alka (Icelandic) the auk.

Dovekie *Alle alle*
allex (L) the great toe; probably a reference to the lack of the hind toe,

the 'x' being deleted to show that the toe is missing. Sometimes known as the Little Auk, dovekie is the diminutive of dove; the Great Auk is now extinct. Breeds in the Arctic on coasts of Greenland and groups of islands such as Spitzbergen and Franz Joseph Land, migrating south in winter to coasts of the British Isles and France, and from Greenland to the northern parts of the east coast of North America.

Razorbill *Alca torda*
alka (Icelandic) the auk *torda* is a local name for this auk, the general Swedish name being *tordmule*. Breeds on coasts of the northern Atlantic such as New England, western Greenland, Iceland, Scandinavia and the British Isles, migrating south in winter when much of the time is spent far out to sea. The name razorbill is a reference to the compressed unusually sharp bill.

Common Murre or Guillemot *Uria aalge*
ouria (Gr) a water bird *aalge* (Dan) the murre, a type of guillemot; the origin of the word murre is obscure. Inhabiting northern seas and ranging south to North Korea and San Francisco in the Pacific, and Portugal in the Atlantic; it is known on the coasts of Scandinavia, Iceland, the British Isles, northern France, and Newfoundland.

Brünnich's Guillemot *U. lomvia*
lomvia (D dialect) a bird. Named after M. T. Brünnich (1737-1827), a Danish zoologist and Director of the Natural History Museum, Copenhagen, in 1772. Sometimes known as the Thick-billed Murre, it breeds in islands in the Arctic seas such as Baffin Island, Spitzbergen and Franz Joseph Land, migrating south in winter.

Black Guillemot *Cepphus grylle*
kepphos (Gr) a sea-bird of the petrel kind *gryllus* (L) a cricket, a grasshopper; can mean a kind of comic figure; on land, standing upright like a small penguin and its long webbed feet sticking out in front, it is a comical sight; it sits down on the tarso-metatarsus bone giving it a flat-footed appearance. The range is similar to *U. aalge* and *U. lomvia*, above.

Kittlitz's Murrelet *Brachyramphus brevirostris*
brakhus (Gr) short *rhamphos* (Gr) beak, bill *brevis* (L) short *rostrum* (L) beak, snout; the name in Greek and repeated in Latin for the species, 'short-billed'. Named after F. H. Kittlitz (1779-1874) the Russian zoologist on the expedition to Kamchatka from 1826 to 1829. From arctic eastern Sibera ranging to Alaska and wintering in Kam-

chatka, the Aleutian Islands, and ranging as far south as Japan. Murrelet, dim. of murre; see *Uria aalge*, above.

Cassin's Auklet *Ptychoramphus aleuticus*
ptux (Gr), genitive *ptukhos*, the folds of a garment, anything that appears to be in folds   *rhamphos* (Gr) the crooked beak of birds; generally a beak, bill; a reference to the compressed beak which appears to be in folds   *-icus* (L) suffix meaning belonging to; it ranges from the Aleutian Islands along the Alaska Peninsula and the Pacific shores of British Columbia and migrating south in winter to Central America. It is named after John Cassin (1813-1869), Curator of Birds, Philadelphia Academy of Sciences, who described many species of birds.

Crested Auklet *Aethia cristatella*
aithuia (Gr) a seagull or diver   *crista* (L) the crest of an animal   *-ellus* (L) diminutive suffix, 'little crest'; it has a small crest just above the base of the beak. Inhabiting the Bering Straits area, the Aleutian Islands, the Kamchatka Peninsula, and the Kuril Islands, and migrating south in winter.

Puffin *Fratercula arctica*
fraterculus (New L) a friar; considered to be an allusion to the birds habit of clasping its feet together as though in prayer when rising from the sea   *-icus* (L) suffix meaning belonging to; 'of the Arctic'. Range similar to *Alca torda* (p. 143) but extending to Spitzbergen. The origin of the name puffin is obscure, but Francesca Greenoak in her book, *All the Birds of the Air*, says that she has read about a puffin, kept for a time in captivity, that would cry—'pupin, pupin'!

Horned Puffin *F. corniculata*
cornu (L) the horn of an animal   *-culus* (L) diminutive suffix   *-atus* (L) suffix meaning provided with; 'having a little horn'; it has small fleshy horns above the eyes. Inhabiting coasts of the northern Pacific in the area of the Bering Straits and the Bering Sea and moving south in winter although some puffins remain in the breeding areas all the year round.

23 Sandgrouse, Pigeons and Doves
COLUMBIFORMES

Pallas's Sandgrouse
Syrrhaptes paradoxus

Pigeons and doves, in the order Columbiformes, are all basically the same, and all have similar characteristics; but the sandgrouse are a problem for taxonomists; they are not grouse. Although they resemble them in general shape and colour, and they live in sandy places which gives them their English name, they are related to the pigeons and doves. Some authors place them in an order on their own, the Pteroclidiformes. They frequent mostly desert and grassy areas whereas the pigeons and doves are to be found in almost all land habitats and have an almost world-wide distribution; the diet is mostly seeds and berries, though insects are also taken by sandgrouse, and insects and worms by the doves and pigeons.

The various kinds of domestic pigeons kept by pigeon fanciers and those seen in European city streets are descended from the rock-pigeon, or rock-dove, *Columba livia*; this process of selective breeding has probably been going on for some 5,000 years.

Order COLUMBIFORMES
columba (L) a pigeon or dove.

Family PTEROCLIDIDAE 16 species
pteron (Gr) feathers, can mean wings; Temminck says 'The generic name *Pterocles* that I propose for this genus indicates that there is something special about the wings; that is the unusual length of the feathers, the primary being the longest'. He gives no explanation for the second element, *cles*.

Pallas's Sandgrouse *Syrrhaptes paradoxus*
syr- = *syn-* (Gr) prefix meaning together *rhapto* (Gr) I sew; a reference to the vestigial web joining the toes *paradoxos* (Gr) contrary to opinion, strange; a reference to the web and other unusual abnormal anatomical features. Named after Prof P. S. Pallas (1741-1811), a German zoologist and explorer and a professor at St Petersburg University; he made contributions to most of the natural sciences. This sandgrouse inhabits a large area in Asia to the east of the Caspian Sea and migrates south in winter as far as northern India and China.

Tibetan Sandgrouse *S. tibetanus*
-anus (L) suffix meaning belonging to. It breeds high in the mountains of Central Asia and migrates south in winter to India, Burma, and the Thailand-Vietnam area.

Variegated Sandgrouse *Pterocles burchelli*
Pterocles, see under Family, above: named after Dr W. J. Burchell (1782-1863), an English zoologist who made an expedition to Africa in 1811. Inhabiting Africa including parts of the Sahara and the Kalahari Desert.

Namaqua Sandgrouse *P. namaqua*
Namaqualand is on the western side of South Africa and is partly a desert area. Towards the end of the nineteenth century the naturalist E. G. B. Meade-Waldo asserted that desert-living sandgrouse deliberately soak their breast feathers in water and in this manner carry it many miles to water their young, though other naturalists at the time considered this to be nonsense. The idea ceased to be seriously considered until quite recently ornithologists observing the Namaqua and other desert-living sandgrouse have actually seen this water-carrying system being used by the bird, including the deliberate soak-

ing of the feathers at the water hole and the chicks taking the water from the feathers at the nest.

Madagascar or Masked Sandgrouse *P. personatus*
persona (L) a mask *personatus* (L) masked; it has a black border round the beak. Inhabiting Madagascar.

Family COLUMBIDAE 280 species
columba (L) a pigeon or dove.

Nilgiri Wood Pigeon *Columba elphinstonii*
Named after the Hon M. Elphinstone (1779-1859), in Afganistan in 1808 and Governor of Bombay from 1819 to 1827, and author of books on natural history. This pigeon inhabits India and is named from the Nilgiri District in the south-west.

Rock Dove *C. livia*
Livius is a Roman name; in this case it is coined from *lividus* (L) bluish-grey. Originally from Eurasia, and the ancestor of the domestic pigeon, the distribution is now almost world-wide.

Wood Pigeon *C. palumbus*
palumbes (L) a wood pigeon, a ring dove. Inhabiting Europe including the British Isles but not northern Scandinavia; the Mediterranean islands and ranging east into Russia and part of Asia and south to India and Cambodia.

Collared Turtle Dove *Streptopelia decaocto*
streptos (Gr) a necklace *peleia* (Gr) a dove or wood-pigeon *dekaoktō* (Gr) 18; a Greek legend says that a servant girl was once employed for a miserable 18 pieces a year, and she prayed to the gods to let the world know of this meanness; they took pity on her and created a dove that calls 'dekaokto, dekaokto'; it is not much like the dove's call which is more like 'coo-COO-cook', but the Latin name is derived from the legend. Originally inhabiting Asia it is now fairly widespread in Europe.

Laughing Dove *S. senegalensis*
-ensis (L) suffix meaning belonging to, usually in relation to a place, 'of Senegal'. Though named from Senegal it inhabits much of Africa except desert areas and is not known in Madagascar; found in Turkey and Arabia and ranging to eastern India, it has been introduced to

western Australia. The call usually consists of five 'coos' which sounds as though the bird is laughing.

Turtle Dove *S. turtur*
turtur (L) a turtle dove. Inhabiting Europe including the British Isles and ranging east into Asia beyond the Caspian Sea, south to northern Africa, the Middle East, India and the Burma area.

Barred or Zebra Ground-Dove *Geopelia striata*
gē (Gr) the earth, ground   *peleia* (Gr) a dove or wood-pigeon   *stria* (L) a furrow, a groove   *striatus* (New L) striped. An eastern bird, inhabiting the Burma area, Indonesia, Malaysia, the Philippines, Australia, New Guinea, and the Pacific islands. Known as a ground-dove because it spends a lot of its time on the ground, but it is capable of flight.

Namaqua Dove *Oena capensis*
oinas (Gr) the vine; can mean a kind of wild pigeon the colour of ripening grapes   *-ensis* (L) suffix meaning belonging to, usually in relation to a place, 'of The Cape'. Though named from South Africa it inhabits a large part of Africa including the Red Sea coast and south-western Arabia; Namaqualand is a little-known coastal region in south-west Africa.

Brush Bronzewing *Phaps elegans*
phaps (Gr) a kind of wild dove or pigeon   *elegans* (L) neat, elegant. Inhabiting the southern part of Australia.

Crested Pigeon *Ocyphaps lophotes*
ōkus (Gr) swift, fast   *phaps* (Gr) a kind of wild dove or pigeon; it is reputed to be able to outpace the Little Falcon *Falco longipennis* *lophos* (Gr) a crest   *lophōtos* (Gr) crested. Inhabiting Australia, mostly western area.

Blue or Common Crowned Pigeon *Goura cristata*
Goura is a native name in New Guinea for the crowned pigeons *cristata* (L) crested. Inhabiting New Guinea.

African Green Pigeon *Treron australis*
trērōn (Gr) timid, shy   *australis* (L) southern; this Latin word does not indicate Australia; it is derived from *auster* (L) the south wind. Inhabiting Africa.

Golden Dove *Ptilinopus luteovirens*
ptilon (Gr) feathers   *pous* (Gr) the foot; 'feather-footed'; a reference to the upper half of the leg (tarsus) being covered with feathers   *luteus* (L) golden-yellow, saffron-yellow   *virens* (L) becoming green. It is found only on Viti Levu, one of the Fiji Islands.

Comoro Blue Pigeon *Alectroenas sganzini*
alektoris (Gr) a hen (poultry), there is a rare form *alektruonis*; or the final element could be from *oinas* (Gr) a kind of wild pigeon: named after Capt Victor Sganzin (fl 1830 died 1841), a German zoologist who was in Madagascar in 1831-1832. The Comoro Islands lie between the northern tip of Madagascar and the mainland of Africa.

Baker's Imperial Pigeon *Ducula bakeri*
dux (L), genitive *ducis*, a leader, cf English duke (imperial)   *ducula* (New L) a little duke: named after Dr J. R. Baker, FRS (born 1900) an Oxford zoologist and at one time President of the Microscopic Society. This pigeon inhabits the New Hebrides.

Topknot Pigeon *Lopholaimus antarcticus*
lophos (Gr) the crest or tuft on the head of birds   *laimos* (Gr) the throat, can also mean the neck; there is a crest on the head and on the back of the neck   *-icus* (L) suffix meaning belonging to, 'of the Antarctic'. Inhabiting the east coast of Australia from Cape York to Victoria.

24 Parrots and their kin PSITTACIFORMES

Masked Lovebird
Agapornis personata

In the order Psittaciformes and the family Psittacidae are all the parrot-like birds, including the well known budgerigar; they live in tropical and sub-tropical forests so are not known in the wild in Europe. Almost without exception they are brightly coloured and the sexes are usually alike, and they range in size from the little pygmy parrots of New Guinea to the huge macaws of South America.

Distinctive features are the feet with two toes turned forward and two backward, the powerful hooked beak which is also used for climbing, and the habit of holding up food in one foot to eat it. They are mostly vegetarian, and the diet consists of fruit, berries, seeds, nuts, etc., though some eat insects and occasionally carrion.

Some have become well known as mimics, the two best 'talkers' being the African Grey and the Budgerigar; one parrot kept as a pet earned a reputation by giving a good imitation of the flushing of a lavatory!

Order PSITTACIFORMES

psittacus (L) a parrot.

Family PSITTACIDAE 328 species

Black Lory *Chalcopsitta atra*
khalkos (Gr) copper, can mean bronze coloured *psitta*, abbreviated form of *psittacus* (L) a parrot *ater* (L) black. Inhabiting New Guinea.

Duivenbode's or Brown Lory *C. duivenbodei*
Named after C. W. R. v. Duivenbode, a well-known merchant of Ternate; sometimes known as 'King of Ternate', the dates of his birth and death are obscure, but his son L. D. H. A. v. Duivenbode was born in 1831 which gives some idea of his age. Ternate is an island in the Moluccas, Indonesia. Inhabiting New Guinea, where most lories are found.

Scaly-breasted Lorikeet *Trichoglossus chlorolepidotus*
thrix (Gr), genitive *trikhos*, hair *glossa* (Gr) the tongue; this lorikeet likes nectar and it forms a large part of its diet; it has a 'brush-tipped' tongue for seeking and lapping up the nectar *khlōros* (Gr) pale green, can mean yellow *lepidōtos* (Gr) scaly, covered with scales; a reference to the breast feathers, which have the appearance of overlapping scales. Inhabiting Australia.

Yellow and Green Lory *T. flavoviridis*
flavus (L) yellow *viridis* (L) green. Inhabiting the Indonesian area.

Stresemann's Lory *Lorius amabilis*
luri = *lori* (Malay) a lory or parrot *amabilis* (L) worthy of love, lovely: named after Prof Dr Erwin Stresemann (born 1889), a German zoologist, Director of the Ornithological Dept Zoological Museum Berlin in 1921. This lory inhabits New Britain.

Purple-crowned Lorikeet *Glossopsitta porphyrocephala*
glossa (Gr) the tongue *psitta*, abbreviated form of *psittacus* (L) a parrot; like the Scaly-breasted Lorikeet, above, it has a brush-tipped tongue for collecting nectar *porphureos* (Gr) purple *cephalē* (Gr) the head. Ranging across southern Australia.

Little Lorikeet *G. pusilla*
pusillus (L) small. Inhabiting the Malay Archipelago, Polynesia, and Australia.

Black or Great Palm Cockatoo *Probosciger aterrimus*
pro- (Gr) a prefix with many meanings, e.g. forward, for *boskō* (Gr) I feed *gero* (L) I bear, carry; hence *proboscis* + *ger*, 'carried for feed-

ing'; a reference to the thick prehensile tongue   *ater* (L) black
aterrimus (L) very black; the name 'cockatoo' is probably derived
from the call. Inhabiting Australia and New Guinea.

Galah   *Eolophus rosiecapillus*
ēōs (Gr) dawn, the red colour at dawn   *lophos* (Gr) the crest of birds
roseus (L) red   *capillus* (L) hair; in this case taken to mean feathers;
it has pink breast feathers and a white crest with a pink tinge; the
crest is erectile. This cockatoo lives in Australia and Galah is the native
name.

Sulphur-crested Cockatoo   *Cacatua galerita*   (formerly *Kakatoe*)
Cacatua is from a Malayan name kakatoe or kokatua, derived from the
birds call, hence the English cockatoo   *galeritus* (L) wearing a skull-
cap or hood; it has a bright yellow crest. Inhabiting Australia, New
Guinea, and nearby islands.

Little Corella   *C. sanguinea*
sanguis (L) blood   *sanguinea* (L) blood red; sometimes known as the
Blood-stained Cockatoo on account of the red plumage; Corella is a
native name in Australia. Inhabiting Australia and New Guinea.

Kaka   *Nestor meridionalis*
Nestor was a legendary Greek hero known for long life and wisdom,
and the name is often used to mean a wise counsellor, a leader; there
is probably no special reason for the name. In 1758 Linnaeus used
several names from classical mythology for the generic or specific
names of animals and other authors have done the same; it is probable
that they were given without thought of any special significance
meridies (L) mid-day, noon   *-alis* (L) suffix meaning relating to;
meridionalis (L) southern; it is found only in New Zealand, South
Island, and lives in the southern part, and the Stewart Islands. Kaka
is the Maori name.

Geelvink Pygmy Parrot   *Micropsitta geelvinkiana*
mikros (Gr) little, small   *psitta*, abbreviated form of *psittacus* (L) a
parrot; these are the smallest birds in the parrot family, only about
9 cm (3½ in) long: the Geelvink Channel separates the Houtman
Abrolhos group of islands from the west coast of Australia, where these
miniature parrots live.

Meek's Pygmy Parrot   *M. meeki*
Named after Albert G. Meek (1871–1943), a London-born Australian

naturalist and author; he lived in the New Guinea area from 1894 to 1913 and collected for Lord Rothschild. This Pygmy Parrot lives in New Guinea and there are other species living in the Pacific islands.

Crimson Rosella *Platycercus elegans*
platus (Gr) flat, can mean broad   *kerkos* (Gr) the tail; it has a broad tail   *elegans* (L) neat, elegant: the name rosella may be an allusion to the bright red plumage, but it is also suggested that it derives from Rosehill, a district near Sydney in south-east Australia; certainly the Crimson Rosella is known in that area, and it ranges from the northeast part of Queensland to near Adelaide.

Bourke's Parrot *Neophema bourkii*
neos (Gr) new, recent   *phēmē* (Gr) a voice, a word; indicating a newly discovered parrot and named after Maj Gen Sir R. Bourke (1777-1855), Governor of New South Wales, Australia, 1831 to 1837. This parrot inhabits a large area in the southern part of Australia including part of New South Wales.

Turquoise Parrot *N. pulchella*
pulcher (L) beautiful, handsome   *-ellus* (L) diminutive suffix, hence small and beautiful, 'a little beauty'; certainly an apt name for this small colourful parrot. Inhabiting a large area in the west of Australia from the North West Cape south to Perth, and ranging east to the Mount Heuglin area.

Budgerigar *Melopsittacus undulatus*
melos (L) a tune, a song   *psittacus* (L) a parrot   *undulatus* (L) waved, undulated; a reference to the dark wavy lines on the back of the head and neck and the adjacent part of the wings. Fairly widespread in Australia but only coastal in the south.

Night Parakeet *Geopsittacus occidentalis*
ge (Gr) earth, ground   *psittakos* (Gr) a parrot; sometimes known as the ground parakeet because it is an almost flightless bird, and spends much of its time on the ground   *occidentalis* (L) western. The name Night Parakeet refers to its nocturnal habits as it usually hunts at night; it is very rare and possibly extinct. Inhabiting Australia.

Kakapo *Strigops habroptilus*
strix (Gr), genitive *strigos*, a night bird, the owl   *ops* (Gr) the eye, face, 'owl-faced'; the head and face have the appearance of an owl   *habros* (Gr) soft, delicate   *ptilon* (Gr) feathers; the feathers are unusually

soft, like those of an owl which enable it to fly almost silently and so useful when catching prey; however the kakapo is now a flightless bird and eats fruit, leaves and roots of grasses. It is rare and found only in one small area in the south-west of South Island, New Zealand; *kakapo* is a Maori name for this bird.

African Grey Parrot *Psittacus erithacus*
psittacus (L) a parrot   *erithakos* (Gr) a solitary bird that could be taught to speak; sometimes it is taken to mean the robin-redbreast. Very well known as a domestic pet, in the wild it lives in West and Central Africa.

Madagascar or Grey-headed Lovebird *Agapornis cana*
agapē (Gr) love   *ornis* (Gr) a bird   *canus* (L) hoary, grey-haired. Known as lovebirds because of their sociable habits; pairs will spend hours sitting together preening each other or just sitting bill-to-bill. Inhabiting Madagascar.

Fischer's Lovebird *A. fischeri*
Named after Dr Gustav A. Fischer (1848-1886), a German zoologist who explored East Africa during the years 1876 to 1886. Inhabiting Africa south of the Sahara.

Masked Lovebird *A. personata*
personatus (L) masked; it has a black face, the remainder of the plumage being bright yellow and green. Inhabiting Africa, mainly in the Tanzania area.

Philippine Hanging Parrot *Loriculus philippensis*
lori (Malay) a lory or parrot   -*culus* (L) diminutive suffix, 'a little parrot'; the parrots in the genus *Loriculus* are very small, some being no bigger than a sparrow, and some have developed a habit of hanging upside down like bats and even sleeping in this position   -*ensis* (L) suffix meaning belonging to. It inhabits islands in the Philippine group.

Blossom-headed Parakeet *Psittacula cyanocephala*
psittacus (L) a parrot   -*culus* (L) diminutive suffix   *kuaneos* (Gr) blue   *kephalē* (Gr) the head. Inhabiting India and Sri Lanka.

Ring-necked Parakeet *P. krameri*
Named after W. H. Kramer (fl. 1740-died 1765), an Austrian zoologist and author. This parakeet has a rosy half-collar; it inhabits Africa, India, and the Burma to Vietnam area.

Hyacinthine Macaw   *Anodorhynchus hyacinthinus*
anodous (Gr) without teeth   *rhunkhos* (Gr) the beak; the original description is in Latin: '. . . *rostrum totum nigrum, quam maxime crassum, compressum, altum, superius apice uncinatum, edentatum* . . .' which briefly translated means 'beak black, thick, compressed, upper hooked, toothless'. When Spix gave this name in 1824 it was probably not generally recognised that recent birds do not have teeth, although ancient birds such as *Archaeornis* did   *hyacinthinus* (L) belonging to the hyacinth, can mean blue; the entire plumage is bright blue, a very beautiful macaw, inhabiting the tropical forests of eastern Brazil. Dr J. B. v. Spix (1781-1826) was a German zoologist and Professor of Zoology at the Munich Museum; he was in Brazil from 1817 to 1820.

Red-and-Green Macaw   *Ara chloroptera*
ara (New L) probably an abbreviation of *arara* (Tupi) a macaw   *khlōros* (Gr) green   *pteron* (Gr) wings; the plumage is red with green wings. Inhabiting South America ranging from Panama to Brazil.

Coulon's or Blue-headed Macaw   *A. couloni*
Named after Dr L. Coulon (1804-1894), a French zoologist who was for many years President of the Society for Natural Sciences in Neuchatel. The Blue-headed Macaw inhabits South America.

Red-masked Parakeet   *Aratinga erythrogenys*
ara (New L) probably an abbreviation of *arara* (Tupi) a macaw   *tinga* (Tupi) bright, ornamented   *eruthros* (Gr) red   *genus* (Gr) cheek, jaw. A macaw-like parrot inhabiting South America.

Thick-billed Parrot   *Rhynchopsitta pachyrhyncha*
rhunkhos (Gr) the beak   *psittakos* (Gr) a parrot   *pakhus* (Gr) thick. Inhabiting Central America, Mexico, and ranging north to Arizona.

Hoffmann's or Sulphur-winged Parakeet   *Pyrrhura hoffmanni*
purros = *purrhos* (Gr) red, flame-coloured   *oura* (Gr) the tail; named after Dr Carl Hoffmann (1823-1859), a German zoologist who was in Costa Rica with Dr A. von Frantzius from 1854 to 1859. This parakeet is found in Central America.

Slender-billed Parakeet   *Enicognathus leptorhynchus*
henikos (Gr) single   *gnathos* (Gr) jaw; Gray does not explain the peculiar name 'single jaw'   *leptos* (Gr) small, slender   *rhunkhos* (Gr) the snout, beak. Inhabiting Chile. G. M. Gray, FRS (1808-1872) was an ornithologist at the British Museum (Natural History) from

1831 until his death in 1872; he published *The Genera of Birds* in 1840.

Monk or Grey-breasted Parakeet   *Myiopsitta monachus*
muia (Gr) a fly   *psitta* is an abbreviated form of *psittakos* (Gr) a parrot; 'a fly-parrot'; it is not established that this parakeet eats flies though many parrots eat insects of various kinds   *monakhos* (Gr) a monk, solitary; the name seems inappropriate as these parakeets are known to breed and move about in large flocks and are considered to be gregarious. Inhabiting Bolivia, Paraguay, Uruguay, and Argentina.

Golden-winged Parakeet   *Brotogeris chrysopterus*
brotogērus (Gr) with human voice; a word probably only used in connection with parrots   *khrusos* (Gr) gold   *pteron* (Gr) wings. Inhabiting the northern part of South America.

White-fronted Parrot or Amazon   *Amazona albifrons*
albus (L) white   *frons* (L) forehead, brow. Inhabiting southern Mexico and Central America.

St Vincent Parrot   *A. guildingii*
Named after The Rev L. Guilding (1798-1831), a naturalist and chaplain on St Vincent Island in the West Indies group; this parrot inhabits this island.

Yellow-headed Parrot   *A. ochrocephala*
ōkhros (Gr) pale, pale yellow   *kephalē* (Gr) the head; one of the largest Amazons, about 38 cm (15 in) long, a green bird with a pale yellow head. Inhabiting Mexico and ranging south to Brazil.

25 Turacos, Cuckoos and their kin
CUCULIFORMES

Common Cuckoo
Cuculus canorus

The turacos are cuckoo-like birds, and although usually placed in the order Cuculiformes there is some question as to whether this is correct, and at least one zoologist who has studied their anatomy gives them a separate order, Musophagiformes. Included in this could be the Hoatzin *Opisthocomus hoazin*, of the order Galliformes; the young of both these birds have an unusual claw on the wing which assists them to scramble about in the trees before they can fly.

Turacos are specially noted for their bright red and green plumage; the red pigment turacin gets its name from these birds, and the green pigment is called turacoverdin. It is the only true green pigment found in birds, as other birds with green colouring get it from the actual structure of the feathers, or from a mixture of other pigments.

Cuckoos are familiar to us through their unusual song, which gives them their common name in many countries, being an imitation of this song. The parasitic habit of using another bird's nest is well known, but by no means all the birds in the family Cuculidae use this rather unpleasant anti-social method of rearing their young. When a cuckoo lays its egg in another birds nest it means certain death to the host bird's own chicks, as they are thrown out by the fledgling cuckoo, possibly in the egg before it has time to hatch.

Some cuckoos exhibit most remarkable forms of migration, for example the Bronzed Cuckoo *Chrysococcyx lucidus*, from the islands off the coast of New Zealand. The parent birds, having laid their eggs in the host-bird's nest, depart to the Solomon Islands some 3,220 km (2,000 miles) away. Then, by some quite incredible instinct of navigation, the young birds follow them soon after they have learnt to fly, accomplishing this dog-leg journey via Australia without parental guidance.

The anis are unlike the true cuckoos, in that they build their nests, sometimes many birds sharing one large nest and all taking turns with the incubation. The coucals and couas also build their own nests; the couas live only on the island of Madagascar, while the coucals have a wide range, including Africa, Asia and Australia.

Order CUCULIFORMES
cuculus (L) the cuckoo *forma* (L) form, shape; can mean sort, kind, so not necessarily referring to the actual shape.

Family MUSOPHAGIDAE 22 species
musa (New L) derived from the Arabic *môza*, a banana, a plantain *phagēma* (Gr) food; turacos are fruit-eating birds but they do not confine their diet entirely to bananas or plantains; some will eat small animals such as insects, snails, and other invertebrates.

Knysna Turaco *Tauraco corythaix*
touraco (Fr) an imitation of the bird's cry *koruthaix* (Gr) helmet-shaking, i.e. with waving plume; the prominent crest on these birds gives the head the appearance of wearing a military-type helmet. Knysna is a small town on the south coast of South Africa famous for its forests of hardwood trees, used for making furniture; the turacos live in these forests.

Hartlaub's Turaco *T. hartlaubi*
Named after Dr K. J. G. Hartlaub (1814-1900) a German zoologist of Bremen who explored and collected in Africa in 1857. Inhabiting the mountain forests of Kenya and northern Tanzania.

White-cheeked Turaco *T. leucotis*
leukos (Gr) white *ous* (Gr), genitive *ōtos*, the ear; it has white patches on the sides of the head. Inhabiting north-east Africa.

Livingstone's Turaco *T. livingstonii*
Named after the famous missionary and explorer Dr David Livingstone (1813-1873), he travelled extensively in Central Africa during the years 1840 to 1873. It inhabits the forests of Tanzania, Mozambique and Zimbabwe.

Prince Ruspoli's Turaco *T. ruspolii*
Named after Prince E. Ruspoli (1866-1893), an Italian zoologist who was in north-eastern Africa from 1891 to 1893. This turaco is confined to a small area of Ethiopia (formerly Abyssinia).

Black-billed Turaco *T. schuettii*
Named after O. Schutt (1843-c.1888), a railway engineer who worked in various parts of the world, and in Angola from 1877 to 1879. Inhabiting Zaire and southern Uganda.

Lady Ross's Turaco *Musophaga rossae*
Musophaga, see notes under Family, above. Named after Lady J. C. Anne Ross (c. 1810-1857), wife of Rear Admiral Sir James C. Ross (1800-1862) the Arctic and Antarctic explorer and navigator. Inhabiting high mountain forests in Zaire, Africa.

Great Blue Turaco *Corythaeola cristata*
korus (Gr) a helmet *koruthaiolos* (Gr) moving the helmet quickly, waving *cristata* (L) crested; a reference to the large black crest; the plumage is mostly blue. Inhabiting equatorial Africa from the west coast to western Kenya.

Eastern Grey Plantain-eater *Crinifer zonurus*
crinis (L) hair *fero* (L) I bear *zonē* (Gr) a girdle, a band *oura* (Gr) the tail; references to the prominent crest and a white band on the tail. Inhabiting East Africa particularly Uganda and surrounding areas.

White-bellied Go-away Bird *Corythaixoides leucogaster*
koruthaix (Gr) helmet shaking *-oides* (New L) from *eidos* (Gr) shape, form; can mean resemblance; a reference to the crest being like the top of a military-type helmet *leukos* (Gr) white *gastēr* (Gr) the belly; with a pale grey back, head, and chest, it has a pure white belly. It has earned the name Go-away Bird because of its loud nasal cry 'g'way gwaay'; inhabiting Ethiopia and southern Sudan and ranging south to northern Tanzania.

Family CUCULIDAE 127 species
cuculus (L) the cuckoo.

Red-winged Indian Cuckoo *Clamator coromandus*
clamator (L) a shouter, a noisy speaker: *coromandus* refers to the Coromandel Coast of south-eastern India. Inhabiting India and ranging east through Burma, and south to the Thailand-Vietnam area and Malaysia.

Common Cuckoo *Cuculus canorus*
canorus (L) melodius, sweet-sounding. Ranging from western Europe to Asia and migrating south in winter.

Pallid Cuckoo *C. pallidus*
pallidus (L) pale; it is a light brownish-grey with pale underparts. It inhabits New Guinea, Australia and Tasmania.

Long-tailed Cuckoo *Cercococcyx mechowi*
kerkos (Gr) the tail *kokkux* (Gr) the cuckoo: a reference to the long tail: named after Maj A. von Mechow (born c. 1840), an Austrian zoologist who was in Angola from 1878 to 1881. Inhabiting Africa south of the Sahara.

Emerald Cuckoo *Chrysococcyx cupreus*
khrusos (Gr) gold *kokkux* (Gr) the cuckoo *cuprum* (L) copper *cupreus* (L) coppery. Inhabiting Africa south of the Sahara.

Golden Bronze Cuckoo *C. lucidus* (formerly *Chalcites*)
lucidus (L) shining. Inhabiting New Guinea, some small Pacific islands, Australia, Tasmania and New Zealand.

Black-billed Cuckoo *Coccyzus erythropthalmus*
kokkux (Gr) the cuckoo *kokkuzō* (Gr) I cry cuckoo *eruthros* (Gr) red *ophthalmos* (Gr) the eye; it has a black beak and a red ring round the eye; it breeds in North America and migrates to South America in winter.

Pearly-breasted Cuckoo *C. euleri*
Named after Carlos Euler (1834-1901), a Swiss naturalist; he was in Brazil in 1853 and later became Vice Consul in Rio de Janeiro from 1867 to 1901. Inhabiting South America.

Koel *Eudynamis scolopacea*
eudunamos (Gr) powerful *skolopax* (Gr) the woodcock *-aceus* (L) suffix forming an adjective from a noun, 'woodcock-like'. Inhabiting

India, Burma and the Thailand-Vietnam area, Malaysia, New Guinea, and some Pacific islands. *Koel* is a Hindustani name for the cuckoo.

Great Lizard Cuckoo   *Saurothera merlini*
sauros (Gr) a lizard   *thērao* (Gr) I hunt; lizards form part of the diet: named after Comtesse M. de la Mercedes de Jaruco Merlin (1788–1852), a Cuban naturalist who married General Count Merlin in 1811. Inhabiting Central America, and the Greater Antilles.

Leschenault's Cuckoo   *Phaenicophaeus leschenaultii*
phaeinos (Gr) shining, especially of burnished metal   *phaios* (Gr) dusky, brown; a reference to the shining bronze effect of the bird's plumage: named after J. B. Leschenault de la Tour (1773–1826), a French naturalist who was in India from 1816 to 1822. Inhabiting India.

Smooth-billed Ani   *Crotophaga ani*
krotōn (Gr) a louse, a tick   *phagein* (Gr) to eat   *-phagos* as a suffix means '-eating'; tick-eating: *ani* is a Spanish-American name for this cuckoo in Mexico and Brazil; insects of various kinds form the main diet. Known as smooth-billed as opposed to the groove-billed (below) this ani inhabits the southern part of North America, Mexico, Central America, Cuba and the West Indies, ranging south to Argentina.

Groove-billed Ani   *C. sulcirostris*
sulcus (L) a furrow   *rostrum* (L) the beak. Inhabiting the southern part of North America and ranging south through Central America to Argentina.

Greater Roadrunner   *Geococcyx californianus*
gē (Gr) the earth   *kokkux* (Gr) the cuckoo   *-anus* (L) suffix meaning belonging to, 'of California': not confined to California it inhabits the southern part of North America and ranges south to Central America. Can run, assisted by the wings, at speeds up to about 20 mph, and is reluctant to fly.

Lesser Roadrunner   *G. velox*
velox (L) rapid, swift; see notes above re *G. californianus*. Inhabiting Mexico and Central America.

Crested Coua   *Coua cristata*
Coua is a native Malagasy name and is probably an imitation of the call   *crista* (L) the crest of an animal   *-atus* (L) suffix to form an

adjective from a noun *cristatus* (L) crested. Found only on the island of Madagascar.

Red-capped Coua *C. ruficeps*
rufus (L) red *ceps* (New L) derived from *caput* (L) the head. All couas, ten species, are confined to the island of Madagascar.

Pheasant Coucal *Centropus phasianinus*
kentron (Gr) a spur *pous* (Gr) the foot or claw; a reference to the murderous-looking long hind claw *phasianos* (Gr) the Phasian bird or pheasant (see p. 114 under *Phasianus colchicus*) *phasianus* (L) a pheasant *-inus* (L) suffix forming an adjective from a noun; 'pheasant-like'; a reference to the long tail, unusually long even for a cuckoo. Inhabiting New Guinea and Australia.

Common Coucal *C. sinensis*
Sinai (Gr) the Chinese *-ensis* (L) suffix meaning belonging to; 'of the Chinese'. Inhabiting south-east Asia, including part of China and ranging south to India, the Burma-Thailand-Vietnam area, and Malaysia.

Steere's Coucal *C. steerei*
Named after Prof J. B. Steere (1842–1940), an American naturalist and author who was in the Philippines area from 1874 to 1875, and 1887 and 1888. Inhabiting the Philippine Islands, Malaysia and Indonesia.

White-browed Coucal *C. superciliosus*
supercilium (L) the eyebrows *-osus* (L) suffix meaning prone to, full of; it has distinct white eyebrows. Inhabiting the southern part of Arabia and most of Africa. The name coucal is French and is thought to derive from *coucou*, the French for a cuckoo, with the addition of the 'al' from *alouette*, a lark.

26 Owls STRIGIFORMES

Little Owl
Athene noctua

In the order Strigiformes there are two families, but only small differences separate the 10 Barn Owls in the family Tytonidae from the 123 species in the main family Strigidae. Nearly all have the typical flat round face, but in Tytonidae the face is more heart-shaped; one exception is the Hawk Owl *Surnia ulula* in which the face is more hawk-like. Some zoologists think that the flat round face has a part to play in the acute sound reception.

They are all carnivorous, with a varied diet including mammals, fish, crustaceans, lizards, insects, and birds and their eggs. In most species the plumage is unusually soft, resulting in almost noiseless flight, and this combined with an acute sense of hearing and keen eyesight makes them very efficient predators; they are mostly nocturnal.

Order STRIGIFORMES

strix (L), genitive *strigis*, a screech owl.

Family TYTONIDAE   10 species
tutō (Gr) a night-owl   *tuton* (New L), genitive *tutonis*.

Barn Owl   *Tyto alba*
albus (L) white; it is not entirely white, the upper parts are an orange

to buff colour; the face, front and belly are white. It has an almost world-wide distribution including Australia and Tasmania but not New Zealand or the Antarctic; it is not found in northern parts such as Alaska, northern Canada, northern Scandinavia, and northern Asia.

Sooty Owl *T. tenebricosa*
tenebrae (L) darkness, especially of night *tenebricosus* (L) full of darkness, shrouded in darkness; a reference to its nocturnal habits. Inhabiting New Guinea and Australia.

Tanzanian Bay Owl *Phodilus prigoginei*
phaos = *phōs* (Gr) light, especially daylight *deilos* (Gr) cowardly, craven, 'afraid of light'; a reference to its nocturnal habits. Named after Dr A. Prigogine (born 1913), a Belgian Doctor of Science and author. The name 'bay' refers to the chestnut colour of this owl which inhabits eastern Zaire.

Family STRIGIDAE   123 species
strix (L), genitive *strigis*, a screech owl.

White-throated Screech-Owl *Otus albogularis*
otus (L) a horned owl, an owl with ear-tufts *albus* (L) white *gula* (L) the throat *-aris* (L) a suffix meaning pertaining to: owls are well known for their fearful screeching and hooting noises. Inhabiting South America.

Flores Scops-Owl *O. alfredi*
Named after Alfred H. Everett (1848-1898), a zoologist who was in Sarawak from 1869 to 1890; the owl takes its name from the island of Flores, Indonesia, and the name 'scops-owl' from *skōps* (Gr) a kind of owl, probably the little horned owl; the owls in the genus *Otus*, of which there are about 36, have ear-tufts of feathers that look like horns. Inhabiting parts of Indonesia.

Crested Owl *Lophostrix cristata*
lophos (Gr) the crest of an animal *strix* (Gr) an owl *cristata* (L) crested. Inhabiting Central and South America.

Great Eagle-Owl *Bubo bubo*
bubo (L) a horned owl; a rare Latin word probably incorrectly used; it really means to cry like a bittern; this owl has a deep hooting cry.

One of the largest owls, and known to take a roe deer fawn, it inhabits Eurasia, from Scandinavia and Spain in the west to the Pacific in the east, northern Africa, and India.

Great Horned Owl *B. virginianus*
Although named from Virginia it ranges from Alaska and northern Canada south to Tierra del Fuego in South America.

Pel's Fishing Owl *Scotopelia peli*
skotos (Gr) darkness *peleia* (Gr) a wood-pigeon: named after H. S. Pel (fl 1854) a Dutch naturalist; he was Governor of the Dutch Gold Coast from 1840 to 1850. This rare owl hunts for fish at night, catching them with its claws; it inhabits the rivers and lakes of western Africa.

Rufous Fishing Owl *S. ussheri*
Named after H. T. Ussher (1836-1880), an English naturalist who was in the Gold Coast from 1866 and Governor from 1879 to 1880. Inhabiting the forested waterways of western Africa.

Snowy Owl *Nyctea scandiaca*
Nyctea (New L) from *nukteros* (Gr) by night; a misleading name as this owl is known to be a daytime hunter of lemmings and other small mammals: named from northern Scandinavia but not confined to that area, it also inhabits northern Siberia, Spitzbergen, Iceland, northern Greenland, and the Hudson Bay area. It is almost pure white or creamy, sometimes with brown spots.

Hawk Owl *Surnia ulula*
Surnia is a coined name for this owl given in 1806 by Prof A. M. C. Duméril (1774-1860), the French zoologist *ulula* (L) a screech owl whose cry was an ill omen; it lacks the flat round face of the typical owls and resembles a hawk more than an owl. Inhabiting the forests of northern North America and Eurasia and not usually migrating south in winter.

Collared Pygmy-Owl *Glaucidium brodiei*
glaukos (Gr) glancing, gleaming, originally without notion of colour, later pale blue, grey *glaux* (Gr) an owl, so called from its glaring eyes; *glaukidion*, dim., suggesting a small owl: named after Sir B. C. Brodie, Bart. FRS (1783-1862), President of the Royal College of Surgeons in 1844. Inhabiting central parts of Eurasia, ranging south to India, the Burma-Vietnam-Thailand area, and Malaysia.

Papuan Hawk-Owl *Uroglaux dimorpha*
oura (Gr) the tail   *glaukos* (Gr) pale blue, grey; it has a silvery-grey tail   *dis-* or *di-* (Gr) two   *morphē* (Gr) form, shape; can mean sort, kind; a reference to the two kinds of marking, horizontal bars on the back and vertical streaks on the front. A rare nocturnal hunter inhabiting the forests of New Guinea, and having the appearance of a hawk rather than an owl.

Solomon Islands Hawk-Owl *Ninox jacquinoti*
Ninox (New L) a coined name for this genus of 16 hawk-like owls: named after Vice-Admiral C. H. Jacquinot (1796-1879). Inhabiting the Solomon Islands in the Pacific; they lie to the east of New Guinea.

Little Owl *Athene noctua*
The name refers to Pallas Athene, the Goddess of Wisdom; 'As wise as an owl'; *nox* (L), genitive *noctis*, night   *noctua* (L) a night-owl; in spite of this name it is less nocturnal than many of the owls and may often be seen perched on posts or telegraph poles, and hunting in daylight. Inhabiting Europe including Denmark and the southern part of England where it was introduced about 1880; it ranges east to central Russia and Arabia and south to Italy, Spain, and northern Africa.

African Wood Owl *Ciccaba woodfordii*
kikkabau (Gr) a cry in imitation of the screech-owl, hence *kikkabē* (Gr) the screech-owl: named in honour of Col E. J. A. Woodford (c. 1761-c. 1825) Adj 5th Foot Guards, 1888.

Tawny Owl *Strix aluco*
strix (L) a screech-owl   *alucus* = *ulucus* (L) a screech-owl; a very rare word and probably only used once by Vergil. Widespread in Europe including the British Isles, but not Ireland; parts of Asia as far as the eastern Himalayas and the northern part of Africa.

African Marsh Owl *Asio capensis*
asio (L) a horned owl; it has small rather inconspicuous ear-tufts that resemble horns   *-ensis* (L) suffix meaning belonging to; 'of The Cape'; it is not confined to South Africa and has even been seen on rare occasions in southern Spain, it is fairly widespread in Africa but not in the east. Marsh Owl refers to the habitat, which is marshy grassland and waterways.

Long-eared Owl   *A. otus*
ous (Gr), genitive *ōtus*, the ear; it has bigger ear-tufts than *A. capensis* (above). A wide distribution, including North and Central America, Eurasia from Ireland to Japan, part of China, and the northern part of Africa.

Fearful Owl   *Nesasio solomonensis*
nēsos (Gr) an island   *asio* (L) a horned owl   *-ensis* (L) suffix meaning belonging to; 'of the Solomon Islands'. The name fearful is probably taken from its screeching cry in the night; owls have long been known as birds of ill omen.

Buff-fronted Owl   *Aegolius harrisi*
aegolius = *aigōlios* (Gr) a night-bird of prey: named after Edward Harris (1799-1863); he was with Audubon on his Missouri River trip in 1843. A number of birds named by Audobon bear Harris's name, which he gave to commemorate their friendship. This buff-coloured owl lives in South America.

27 Frogmouths, Potoos, Nightjars and their kin CAPRIMULGIFORMES

Tawny Frogmouth
Podargus strigoides

The order Caprimulgiformes contains some unusual and rare birds such as the Oilbird, the Potoos, and the Owlet Nightjars. The place in classification of the unique Oilbird, with affinities to the owls, is still under discussion among ornithologists and is given a family on its own; the fat of the young birds can be made into a fine oil suitable for cooking and lighting, and which keeps well without turning rancid.

As suggested by the name nightjar all the birds in this order are nocturnal, though some in the family Caprimulgidae are also crepuscular (appearing at twilight). With the exception of the Oilbird, which eats fruit, they are all insect eaters, although the Frogmouth's diet is more varied and may include fruit, small mammals, and even reptiles.

Order CAPRIMULGIFORMES

caprimulgus (L) a milker of goats; can be used to mean a countryman. There was an ancient idea that the nightjars could suck milk from domestic goats, hence an alternative name for the birds is goatsucker; it has never been authenticated and today the idea is discounted, though it would be almost impossible to prove that it never happens

forma (L) form, shape; can mean sort, kind, so not necessarily referring to the actual shape.

Family STEATORNITHIDAE 1 species
stear (Gr) genitive *steatos*, fat, tallow   *ornis* (Gr) genitive *ornithos*, a bird.

Oilbird *Steatornis caripensis*
In ancient times the natives penetrated the caves where the oilbirds live and slaughtered the chicks by the thousand to obtain the oil (see introductory notes, above)   -*ensis* (L) belonging to; the name refers to the Caripe Caves; Caripe is a small town in the hills of northeastern Venezuela, and thousands of the birds live in these caves. Oilbirds also inhabit Trinidad, Colombia, Ecuador and Peru. Also known by the Spanish native name *Guacharo*.

Family PODARGIDAE 12 species
podargos (Gr) swift-footed; however *argos* (Gr) can mean lazy, slow, so *podargos* could mean slow-footed; except when flying they are sluggish birds and seldom move in daylight.

Papuan Frogmouth *Podargus papuensis*
-*ensis* (L) suffix meaning belonging to; 'of Papua', New Guinea; it is also found in Australia.

Tawny Frogmouth *P. strigoides*
strix (Gr), genitive *strigos*, an owl   -*oides* (New L) derived from *eidos* (Gr) form, shape, resemblance; they are like owls in size, plumage, and colouring. In habiting Australia and Tasmania.

Hodgson's Frogmouth *Batrachostomus hodgsoni*
batrakhos (Gr) a frog   *stoma* (Gr) the mouth: named after B. H. Hodgson, FRS (1800-1894), a naturalist who was in Nepal from 1833 to 1843. This frogmouth inhabits India and the Burma to Vietnam area.

Javan Frogmouth *B. javensis*
-*ensis* (L) suffix meaning belonging to; in addition to Java it is found in the Burma to Thailand area and other parts of Malaysia.

Family NYCTIBIIDAE 5 species
nux (Gr), genitive *nuktos*, night   *bios* (Gr) living, a means of living *nuktibios* = *nuktobios* (Gr) living at night, seeking one's food by night.

Great Potoo *Nyctibius grandis*
grandis (L) large, great. Ranging from Panama to Peru and Brazil.

Common Potoo *N. griseus*
griseus (New L) grey. The name potoo is derived from an imitation of the birds call. Ranging from Mexico to Argentina, and Trinidad and some islands in the West Indies.

Family AEGOTHELIDAE 7 species
aegos (Gr) a goat *thēlē* (Gr) a nipple; apparently a Greek form of Caprimulgidae, suggesting that the birds use a goat's nipple to obtain milk (see p. 168).

Mountain Owlet-Nightjar *Aegotheles albertisi*
Named after C. Luigi M. d'Albertis (1841-1901), a zoologist and botanist who was in New Guinea from 1871 to 1877. Anatomically these birds seem to be a mixture between the owls, the frogmouths, and the nightjars, hence the name 'owlet nightjar', and sometimes the name 'owlet frogmouth'; this one inhabits New Guinea.

Owlet Frogmouth *A. cristatus*
cristatus (L) crested; the crest consists of small plumes on the head, and hardly noticeable. Inhabiting Papua New Guinea, Australia and Tasmania. Frogmouth is a reference to the very wide gape.

New Caledonian Owlet-Nightjar *A. savesi*
Named after Théo Savés (1855-1918), a French zoologist; he was in New Caledonia from 1873 to 1885. Inhabiting New Caledonia and other islands in the Pacific.

Family CAPRIMULGIDAE 72 species
capra (L) a she-goat *mulgeo* (L) I milk *caprimulgus* (L) a milker of goats; can be used to mean a countryman (see notes under Order Caprimulgiformes, p. 168).

Archbold's Nightjar *Eurostopodus archboldi*
eurōstos (Gr) stout, strong *pous* (Gr), genitive *podos*, the foot: a reference to the feet which are bigger than usual for this family, which have rather small feet. Named after R. Archbold (born 1907), an American zoologist who was in the Mammals Dept of the American Museum of Natural History in 1928, and in New Guinea in 1933 and 1934. Inhabiting New Guinea.

Spotted Nightjar *E. guttatus*
gutta (L) a drop, a spot *-atus* (L) suffix meaning provided with, i.e. spotted. Inhabiting Australia, and Aru Island and New Ireland.

White-throated Nightjar *E. mystacalis*
mustax (Gr), genitive *mustakos*, the upper lip, moustache *-alis* (L) suffix meaning pertaining to; it has bristles surrounding the mouth, considered to be an aid to catching insects. Inhabiting Australia and some of the Pacific islands.

Poor-will *Phalaenoptilus nuttallii*
phallaina or *phalaina* (Gr) a sea monster, a whale; strangely, can mean a butterfly or a moth, and used in this sense by Aristotle *ptilon* (Gr) feathers, or a wing; the flight of the poor-will is moth-like and wavering as it chases flying insects: Thomas Nuttall (1786-1859) was an English ornithologist, botanist and author who lived in the USA from 1808 until his death in 1859; several other birds were named after him. The poor-will ranges from south-west Canada through North Dakota and central parts of the USA, west to the Pacific and south to Mexico. The English name is an imitation of its cry.

Egyptian Nightjar *Caprimulgus aegyptius*
caprimulgus (L) a milker of goats, can be used to mean a countryman (see notes under Order Caprimulgiformes, p. 168). It is a rare visitor to Egypt and the Mediterranean area in summer, from Africa, and southern Asia as far east as the Burma area.

Common Nightjar *C. europaeus*
It is widespread in Europe including the British Isles and southern Scandinavia, and ranging east to Eurasia as far as India and the Burma area, and south to Africa; it migrates in winter to the southern areas, flying at night.

Long-tailed Nightjar *C. macrurus*
makros (Gr) large, long *oura* (Gr) the tail. Inhabiting India, the Burma-Thailand-Vietnam area, Malaysia, New Guinea and Australia.

Rufous Nightjar *C. rufus*
rufus (L) red, ruddy. Inhabiting Central and South America.

Whip-poor-will *C. vociferus*
vocifero (L) I cry aloud, I vociferate; the whip-poor-will is well-known

for its continuous calling during the night, and the English name is an imitation of this call. It inhabits southern Canada and the USA and migrates south in winter to Mexico and parts of Central America.

Standard-winged Nightjar   *Macrodipteryx longipennis*
makros (Gr) large, long   *dis = di-* (Gr) two   *pterux* (Gr) a wing   *longus* (L) long   *penna* (L) a feather, a wing; these two names do not refer to the main wings but to the two much lengthened primaries of the male. During courtship flight these are trailed behind the main wing like two streamers, pennants or flags; i.e. the 'standard' in the English name; in order better to display these spectacular pennants the birds often fly in daylight which is most unusual for nightjars; after the mating period they are moulted and disappear. Inhabiting the southern part of Africa and migrating north in winter to the north of the equator.

Pennant-winged Nightjar   *M. vexillarius*
vexillum (L) a standard, a flag   *vexillarius* (L) a standard-bearer; see notes above with reference to the remarkable lengthened primary feathers. Inhabiting Africa, similar to *M. longipennis*.

Ladder-tailed Nightjar   *Hydropsalis climacocerca*
hudōr (Gr) water   *psalis* (Gr) a pair of shears or a single-bladed shearer like a razor; it opens and shuts the long rectrices when over water; these are the 'rudder' feathers of the tail   *klimax* (Gr), genitive *klimakos*, a ladder   *kerkos* (Gr) a tail; 'ladder-tailed'; the bars on the tail resemble the rungs of a ladder. Inhabiting South America.

28 Swifts and Hummingbirds
APODIFORMES

Long-tailed Sylph
Aglaiocercus kingi

The order Apodiformes is divided into three families, though there are only three recorded species of crested swifts, 71 species of swifts, and over 300 species of hummingbirds, their nearest relatives. They seem a strange assortment to be grouped together, but they are all related for various anatomical reasons; superficially the swifts are like the swallows but they are not closely related.

It has long been a popular belief that once a swift is on the ground it cannot take off again, on account of its very small and weak legs, but this is not true, although they rarely land on the ground and then probably by accident. The very small and inconspicuous legs have given rise to the scientific name *Apus*, meaning 'without feet'; when resting it would normally cling to the side of a tree, a cliff, or possibly a wall; it cannot perch in the normal way. They spend most of their life in the air, in which element they are completely at home and highly efficient, their manoeuvrability only exceeded by the humming birds which can fly forwards or backwards or remain completely stationary, like a helicopter. This is necessary for birds that obtain all their nourishment from the nectar in flowers or the insects they find there; to assist in the process the end of the tongue has developed many different shapes, including in one case a tubular tip.

Order   APODIFORMES

a- (Gr) prefix meaning not, without   *pous* (Gr), genitive *podos*, a foot; 'without feet' (see notes above)   *forma* (L) form, shape; can mean sort, kind.

Family   HEMIPROCNIDAE   3 species
hemi- (Gr) prefix meaning half; according to the Greek legend Proknē was transformed by the gods into a swallow and her sister Philomela into a nightingale, though some writers have Proknē the nightingale and Philomela the swallow. The prefix *hemi-* would not mean 'half a swallow' but 'like a swallow'; in any case this is misleading, as mentioned above, because although the swifts resemble swallows superficially, they are not swallows and are not even closely related.

Crested Tree Swift   *Hemiprocne longipennis*
longus (L) long   *penna* (L) a feather, a wing; it has long pointed wings and a long tail. The crest, a tuft of feathers on the head at the base of the beak, is erectile. Widespread in the oriental region from India to Malaysia where there are trees; unlike the swiftlets and swifts with their small weak legs it can perch in the trees, its favourite position.

Whiskered Tree Swift   *H. mystacia*
mustax (Gr), genitive *mustakos*, the upper lip, a moustache; it has long white whiskers at the side of the head. Inhabiting the Papua New Guinea area.

Family   APODIDAE   71 species
a- (Gr) prefix meaning not, without   *pous* (Gr), genitive *podus*, a foot; 'without feet'; the legs are small, weak and inconspicuous, and cannot be used for perching in the normal way.

White-bellied Swiftlet   *Collocalia esculenta*
kolla (Gr) glue   *kalia* (Gr) a dwelling, a bird's nest   *esculentus* (L)

good to eat; the nest is made entirely of saliva, which solidifies and hardens, and is used to make the well-known bird's nest soup. Widespread in the oriental region from India to Papua New Guinea, the Pacific Islands, and Australia.

Giant Swiftlet   *C. gigas*
gigas (Gr) a giant; swiftlets, as the name suggests, are small birds with an average length of about 10 cm (4 in); this one may measure 15 cm (6 in) or more. Inhabiting Malaysia.

Spot-fronted Swift   *Cypseloides cherriei*
kupselos (Gr) the sand-martin   *-oides* (New L) from *eidos* (Gr) apparent shape, form; can mean resemblance; the sand-martin, the swallows, and the swifts all look much alike with their forked tails and long pointed wings: named after G. K. Cherrie (1865-1948), an American ornithologist and author; he was Curator of the Costa Rica Nature Museum from 1894 to 1897. It inhabits Central and South America.

Black Swift   *C. niger*
niger (L) black. Inhabiting North, Central, and South America.

André's Spine-tailed Swift   *Chaetura andrei*
chaeta (New L) a bristle from *khaitē* (Gr) flowing hair, a mane   *oura* (Gr) the tail; a reference to the stiff spine-like projecting shafts of the tail feathers: named after Eugene André (1861-1922), a French naturalist who was in Venezuela from 1897 to 1900. Inhabiting Central and South America.

Vaux's Spine-tailed Swift   *C. vauxi*
William S. Vaux (1811-1882), was an American zoologist and a member of the Philadelphia Academy of Natural Sciences; this swift was named in his honour in 1839 by his friend J. K. Townsend, an American ornithologist and author. It lives in south-west Canada and north-west USA and migrates south in winter, probably as far as Central America and northern South America. The swifts in the genus *Chaetura*, of which there are about 19, are often known as Spinetails without adding the name 'swift'.

Dark-backed Swift   *Apus acuticaudus*
a- (Gr) prefix meaning not, without   *pous* (Gr) a foot (see introductory notes on page 173)   *acutus* (L) sharp, pointed   *cauda* (L) the tail; a reference to the pointed tail feathers. Inhabiting India.

House Swift   *A. affinis*
affinis (L) adjacent, a neighbour. Inhabiting Eurasia, Africa, the Oriental Region from India to Malaysia.

Common Swift   *A. apus*
Widespread and common in Europe including the British Isles, ranging east as far as China and migrating south in winter to Africa including Madagascar.

Pallid Swift   *A. pallidus*
pallidus (L) pale; nearly all swifts have a dark or even black plumage; this species is pale brown with white on the throat. Inhabiting Mediterranean coasts, North Africa, and Asia Minor.

White-throated Swift   *Aeronautes saxatilis*
aēr (Gr), genitive *aeros*, the air   *nautēs* (Gr) a sailor; swifts spend a great deal of their lives in the air, and are famous for their skill and speed; this one is considered to be the fastest North American swift *saxatilis* (L) dwelling among rocks; a reference to its habitat, rocky places and cliffs, where it builds a nest composed of saliva, plant debris, and feathers, in a crevice on a rock face or in a cave. Inhabiting North and Central America.

Pygmy Swift   *Tachornis furcata*
takhus (Gr) fast, swift   *ornis* (Gr) a bird   *furca* (L) a fork   *-atus* (L) suffix meaning provided with; a reference to the forked tail. One of the smallest swifts, about 9 cm ($3\frac{1}{2}$ in) in length. Inhabiting northwestern South America.

Palm Swift   *Cypsiurus parvus*
kupselos (Gr) a bird, the sand-martin   *oura* (Gr) the tail; 'sand-martin-like tail'; the sand-martins, swallows and swifts all have rather similar forked tails, but the swift, in the family Apodidae, is not closely related to them; they belong to the family Hirundinidae   *parvus* (L) small. Inhabiting Africa, and the Oriental Region from India to Malaysia.

Family   TROCHILIDAE   315 species
trokhilos (Gr) a small bird of the wagtail or sandpiper kind; has also been used to mean the wren; this can be misleading as the hummingbird is not closely related to any of these birds.

Pale-bellied Hermit   *Phaethornis anthophilus*
phaethōn (Gr) beaming, radiant   *ornis* (Gr) a bird; an allusion to the

brilliant plumage   *anthos* (Gr) a flower   *philos* (Gr) dear, pleasing; hummingbirds spend much of their time hovering close to flowers to obtain the nectar with their specially adapted beaks. The name hermit is used for the hummingbirds in the genus *Phaethornis* on account of their habit of frequenting dark forest recesses. Inhabiting northern South America.

Broad-tipped Hermit   *P. gounellei*
Named after E. Gounelle (1850-1914) a French zoologist from Paris who visited Brazil in 1887. Inhabiting South America.

Long-tailed Hermit   *P. superciliosus*
supercilium (L) the eye-brow   *-osus* (L) suffix meaning full of; it has very noticeable white stripes above the eye. The proper meaning of the Latin word *superciliosus* is haughty, disdainful. Inhabiting southern Mexico, Central America, the north-west part of South America including the Amazon Basin in Brazil.

White-tipped Sicklebill   *Eutoxeres aquila*
eu- (Gr) prefix meaning well, nicely   *toxērēs* (Gr) furnished with the bow (the bow as in archery); a reference to the remarkable sharply curved sickle-like bill   *aquila* (L) an eagle; an allusion to the eagle's curved bill: white-tipped refers to the tips of the tail feathers. From Costa Rica in Central America south to Colombia, Ecuador, and north-eastern Peru in South America.

Lazuline Sabrewing   *Campylopterus falcatus*
kampulos (Gr) bent, curved   *pteron* (Gr) feathers or wings; a reference to the thickened bent shafts of the primary feathers which resemble sabres   *falx* (L), genitive *falcis*, a sickle   *falcatus* (L) sickle-shaped. Inhabiting northern Venezuela, Colombia, and eastern Ecuador. Lazulite is a blue mineral; the name refers to the iridescent dark violet blue of the throat and breast plumage.

Glittering-bellied Emerald   *Chlorostilbon aureoventris*
khloros (Gr) green   *stilbōn* (Gr) the planet Mercury; in this case taken to mean the shining or glittering one   *aurum* (L) gold   *aureus* (L) golden   *venter* (L), genitive *ventris*, the belly. Inhabiting South America.

Fork-tailed Emerald   *C. canivetii*
Named after E. Canivet De Carentan (fl 1876) a French amateur collector. Inhabiting Mexico to Trinidad.

White-bellied Hummingbird *Amazilia chionogaster*
amazilia (New L) probably derived from a Spanish-American word and has some connection with the River Amazon; the name was given to this genus of 30 hummingbirds by Lesson, the French zoologist. *khiōn* (Gr) snow   *gastēr* (Gr) the belly. Inhabiting South America.

Honduras Emerald   *A. luciae*
Named in honour of Lucy Brewer, the daughter of Dr T. M. Brewer (1814-1880) an American ornithologist and author. Inhabiting the Honduras area in Central America.

Amethyst-throated Hummingbird   *Lampornis amethystinus*
lampē (Gr) a torch   *ornis* (Gr) a bird: amethyst, a bluish-violet quartz *-inus* (L) suffix meaning like; 'amethyst-coloured'. Inhabiting Central America.

Sword-billed Hummingbird   *Ensifera ensifera*
ensifera (L) sword-bearing; an allusion to the remarkably long bill, longer than the head and body together, for obtaining nectar from flowers with a long tube. Inhabiting Venezuela, Colombia, Ecuador and Peru.

Chestnut-breasted Coronet   *Boissonneaua matthewsii*
Named after A. Boissonneau (fl 1839) a French ornithologist and author, and Andrew Mathews (fl 1825-1841) a botanist and gardener at Chiswick in 1825; he was in Peru and Chile from 1830 to 1841 where he died. This chestnut-breasted hummingbird inhabits Ecuador and Peru.

Black-tailed Trainbearer   *Lesbia victoriae*
lesbias (L) a precious brilliant coloured stone found on the island of Lesbos: named after Mde Victoire Mulsant, dates not recorded but the name was given in 1846. The name 'trainbearer' refers to the trailing central pair of tail feathers, about 15 cm (6 in) long. Inhabiting the Ecuador area in South America.

Long-tailed Sylph   *Aglaiocercus kingi*
aglaia (Gr) beauty, adornment   *kerkos* (Gr) the tail; a reference to the long tail, about 13 cm (5 in), the upper parts being an iridescent purple: named after Rear Admiral P. P. King, FRS (1791-1856), on a government survey in command of HMS *Adventure* in South America in 1825 to 1830. Inhabiting Venezuela, Colombia, Ecuador, eastern Peru and Bolivia.

Racket-tailed Hummingbird *Loddigesia mirabilis*
Named after G. Loddiges (1784-1846), a taxidermist who collected about 1,000 hummingbirds in the Americas   *mirabilis* (L) wonderful; the tail has only four feathers as against the usual ten in hummingbirds, the outer feathers being elongated; they take the shape of sickles furnished with a purple flag at the tip and inverted so that the flags are carried out to the sides. A rare species and only known from a small valley 2,133 m (7,000 ft) up in the Andes in a wild part of Peru.

Amethyst Woodstar *Calliphlox amethystina*
kallos (Gr) a beauty   *phlox* (Gr) a flame, reddish: amethyst, a bluish-violet quartz   *-inus* (L) suffix meaning like; 'amethyst-coloured'. Inhabiting South America.

Bee Hummingbird *Mellisuga helenae*
mel (L) honey   *sugo* (L) I suck: named after Princess Hélène d'Orleans (1814-1858) of Mecklenburg, East Germany; she married the Duke of Orleans in 1837. This tiny bird is reputed to be the smallest bird in the world, the male being only about 5 cm (2 in) long including the bill and tail; the female is slightly larger. It is confined to Cuba and the Isle of Pines, in the Greater Antilles.

Broad-tailed Hummingbird *Selasphorus platycercus*
selas (Gr) light, brightness   *phoreō* (Gr) I bear, I carry; 'light-bearing'; a reference to the bright iridescent plumage   *platus* (Gr) broad, flat   *kerkos* (Gr) the tail. Inhabiting western North America and ranging from Alaska south to Mexico.

Rufous Hummingbird *S. rufus*
rufus (L) red, ruddy. Inhabiting western North America and Mexico.

29 Mousebirds or Colies COLIIFORMES

Red-faced Mousebird
Colius indicus

The order Coliiformes consists of only six birds, all in the family Coliidae. They have been classified as a separate order because zoologists have so far failed to find a satisfactory interrelation with any other group. Some of their anatomical features point to the parrots, and their behaviour in using the beak to help with climbing; on the other hand there are anatomical features that bear no relationship to parrots.

Order COLIIFORMES

colius (New L) derived from *kolios* (Gr) the green woodpecker, but there seems to be no good reason for the name.

Family COLIIDAE 6 species

Red-faced Mousebird *Colius indicus*
Indicus (L) of India; the name is misleading as it does not live in India;

the six mousebirds are found only in Africa; this one inhabits the Congo River area, southern Tanzania, and ranging south. The name mousebird has been given because they creep along branches of trees with the body horizontal and close to the branch; in fact like a mouse. 'Red-faced' is an allusion to the bright red band surrounding the eye and extending to the top of the bill.

White-headed Mousebird *C. leucocephalus*
leukos (Gr) white   *kephalē* (Gr) the head. Inhabiting Africa south of the Sahara.

Blue-naped Mousebird *C. macrourus*
makros (Gr) long   *oura* (Gr) the tail; the mousebirds have long tails and this species has a bright blue patch on the nape. Ranging from Senegal in the west to Somalia in the east and south to Tanzania.

30 Trogons TROGONIFORMES

Collared Trogon
Trogon collaris

The order Trogoniformes consists of only one family and all the members are much alike in body form. Like the birds in the order Coliiformes they are classified as a separate group as they appear to have no near relatives. The Resplendent Quetzal *Pharomachrus mocino* is the national bird of Guatemala; a coin named the quetzal is the unit of currency and the bird is pictured on the coin, on the stamps, and on the flag. It is a colourful spectacular bird with a long train.

Order TROGONIFORMES

trōgō (Gr) I gnaw   *trōgōn* (Gr) gnawing   cf *trōglē* (Gr) a hole made by gnawing; trogons nest in old tree trunks in holes which they enlarge by gnawing; they also excavate holes in termite's nests. The trogon's beak is small and not particularly strong, so they have to choose dead and partly rotting trees.

Family TROGONIDAE   36 species

Resplendent Quetzal   *Pharomachrus mocino*
pharos (Gr) a mantle, a cloak   *makros* (Gr) long; a reference to the

long trailing tail: named after Dr J. M. Mocino (1757-1819), a Mexican naturalist. Quetzal is derived from *quetzalli*, an Aztec word for the bird's long tail feathers; it lives in the mountain forests of Central America, ranging from southern Mexico to Costa Rica and Panama. (See introductory notes, above.)

Eared Trogon   *Euptilotis neoxenus*
eu- (Gr) prefix meaning well, nicely   *ptilon* (Gr) feathers   *ous* (Gr), genitive *ōtis*, the ear; 'well-feathered ears'; it has tufts of feathers that look like ears   *neos* (Gr) new, recent   *xenos* (Gr) a stranger; probably so named because it was a newly discovered species in an unusual locality; more northern than other trogons. Inhabiting Central America.

Collared or Red-bellied Trogon   *Trogon collaris*
collum (L) the neck   *-aris* (L) suffix meaning belonging to; it has a white bar across the upper part of the breast, and a red belly. Inhabiting Central America and ranging south to northern Bolivia, Brazil, the western part of Colombia and Ecuador, and Trinidad and Tobago.

Mountain Trogon   *T. mexicanus*
-anus (L) suffix meaning belonging to; 'of Mexico'. Inhabiting the mountains of Mexico and Central America.

White-tailed Trogon   *T. viridis*
viridis (L) green; the upper parts are bronze green and the outer tail feathers are black with white tips. Inhabiting Panama and ranging south to north-west Bolivia and Brazil, the western part of Colombia and Ecuador, and Trinidad.

Narina's Trogon   *Apaloderma narina*
hapalos (Gr) soft, tender   *derma* (Gr) the skin; taxidermists have found this bird to be a problem as the delicate skin easily breaks and the feathers are liable to fall out; all trogons are alike in this respect: named after a Hottentot girl, Narina, who lived in the Knysna District of Cape Province about the years 1765 to 1782; little is known about her but she evidently died young. This trogon is widespread in Africa south of the Sahara.

Scarlet-rumped Trogon   *Harpactes duvauceli*
harpaktēs (Gr) a robber; it robs the nests of wasps and termites and then uses the nest as its own: named after A. Duvaucel (1796-1824)

a French naturalist who was at one time collecting in Sumatra. This trogon has a scarlet belly; it lives in the Burma to Vietnam area, and Malaysia including Sumatra and Borneo.

Red-headed Trogon   *H. erythrocephalus*
eruthros (Gr) red   *kephalē* (Gr) the head. Inhabiting India and ranging through Burma to Vietnam and Malaysia.

31 Kingfishers, Bee-eaters, Rollers, Hornbills and their kin CORACIIFORMES

Hoopoe
Upupa epops

The order Coraciiformes includes the kingfishers, todies, motmots, bee-eaters, rollers, hoopoes and hornbills. They all have hooked or slightly curved beaks except the kingfishers whose beaks are straight, large and pointed, and all are adapted for digging nesting holes in the banks of rivers or enlarging holes in trees. They are all carnivorous, and the diet may include small mammals and birds, fish, crustaceans, and insects; motmots, wood-hoopoes and hornbills also eat some fruit and berries.

There are strange legends about the kingfishers; the ancient Greeks thought they conceived at sea and built floating nests, and so at this time the gods favoured them and kept the sea calm. The Greek word for kingfisher, *alkuon*, is derived from *hals* (Gr) of the sea, and *kuō* (Gr) I conceive, hence 'halcyon days', calm days, kingfisher days.

Order CORACIIFORMES

korax (Gr) a crow or raven; also anything hooked like a raven's beak (see notes above).

Family ALCEDINIDAE 90 species
alcedo (L) a kingfisher.

Pied Kingfisher *Ceryle rudis*
kērulos (Gr) a sea bird, the halcyon; it is not really a sea bird (see notes above) *rudis* (L) a foil; a reference to the long sharp beak. Inhabiting southern Europe, Africa south of the Sahara, southern Asia including the Oriental region. Known as the Pied Kingfisher for its entirely black and white plumage.

Amazon Kingfisher *Chloroceryle amazona*
khloros (Gr) green *ceryle*, see above: inhabiting Central America as well as the Amazon basin in South America.

Green Kingfisher *C. americana*
Inhabiting Texas and ranging to Argentina.

Common Kingfisher *Alcedo atthis*
alcedo (L) the kingfisher *Atthis* (L) Athenian. Widespread in Europe including the British Isles, southern Asia, Africa, the Oriental region including India, the Burma-Cambodia area, Malaysia, New Guinea and the Pacific Islands.

Three-toed Kingfisher *Ceyx erithacus*
keux (Gr) a seagull; another reference to the kingfisher as though it is a sea bird, which it is not *erithakos* (Gr) the name of a solitary bird which can be taught to speak; this translation is given in Liddell and Scott's Greek lexicon; it is true that the kingfisher is a solitary bird, or sometimes in pairs, but there is no known case of one being taught to speak. All kingfishers in the genus *Ceyx* are three-toed; this species inhabits the Oriental region ranging from India to Malaysia.

Kookaburra or Laughing Jackass *Dacelo gigas*
(or *D. novaeguineae*)
Dacelo is simply an anagram of *alcedo* (L) a kingfisher *gigas* (L) a giant; this is a large bird and may measure up to 46 cm (18 in) in length. Sometimes known as the Forest Kingfisher, it does not need to live near water and fish is probably not included in its normal diet of small reptiles, crabs, frogs and insects; originally found only in south-eastern Australia it has been introduced to western areas and Tasmania and New Zealand. *Kookaburra* is a native Australian name and people living in Australia are familiar with its terrible cackling laughter, said to be rather like a donkey braying.

Blue-winged Kookaburra *D. leachii*
Named after Dr W. E. Leach (1790-1836), zoologist at the British Museum (Natural History). Inhabiting Australia and New Guinea.

Shovel-billed Kingfisher *Clytoceyx rex*
klutos (Gr) famous, glorious *keux* (Gr) a seagull; another reference to the kingfisher as though it is a sea bird, which it is not *rex* (L) a king; 'the king of seagulls'; it is certainly one of the largest kingfishers and like the kookaburra may measure up to 46 cm (18 in) in length. The large shovel-shaped bill is used for digging up earth-worms; apparently its food consists largely of earth-worms, which is unusual for a kingfisher. It is found only in the mountain forests of New Guinea.

White-backed Kingfisher *Halcyon albonotata*
alkuōn (Gr) the kingfisher; see introductory notes about derivation on p. 185 *albus* (L) white *nōtos* (Gr) the back *-atus* (L) suffix meaning provided with; 'having a white back'. Inhabiting New Britain.

Chestnut-bellied Kingfisher *H. farquhari*
Named after Admiral Sir A. M. Farquhar (1855-1937); the name was given in 1899 after his voyage to the New Hebrides in 1894, where this kingfisher lives. The New Hebrides is a group of islands lying to the east of the Coral Sea, eastern Australia.

Grey-headed Kingfisher *H. leucocephala*
leukos (Gr) grey or white *kephalē* (Gr) the head. Inhabiting most of Africa south of the Sahara and southern Arabia.

Forest Kingfisher *H. macleayii*
Named after Alexander Macleay (1767-1848), the Scottish zoologist who was Secretary of the Linnaean Society of London from 1798 to 1825; he then went to Australia where he was Colonial Secretary of New South Wales. This Forest Kingfisher does not need to live near water; it inhabits New Guinea and Australia.

Brown-backed Paradise Kingfisher *Tanysiptera danae*
tanusipteros = tanupteros (Gr) long-winged *pteron* (Gr) wings, can mean feathers; this refers to the long tail feathers which form a train: the bird is named after Danae of Greek mythology; in the legend she was the mother of Perseus; it inhabits New Guinea.

Family TODIDAE 5 species
todus (L) name of a small bird, a tody.

Narrow-billed Tody *Todus angustirostris*
angustus (L) narrow   *rostrum* (L) the beak. Inhabiting the eastern part of the Dominican Republic on the Island of Hispaniola, in the West Indies.

Puerto Rican Tody *T. mexicanus*
Although named from Mexico it is found only on the Island of Puerto Rico, West Indies.

Jamaican Tody *T. todus*
Found only on the Island of Jamaica.

Family   MOMOTIDAE   8 species
momot (New L) from American-Spanish *motmot*, supposed to be an imitation of the birds call.

Tody Motmot *Hylomanes momotula*
hulē (Gr) a wood, forest   *mania* (Gr) madness; as a suffix it is used to mean 'mad on'; 'mad about forests'   *-ulus* (L) diminutive suffix; it is the smallest motmot: it inhabits the forests of Mexico and Central America.

Broad-billed Motmot *Elektron platyrhynchum*
ēlektron (Gr) amber; sometimes used to mean bright, gleaming; in this sense 'brightly coloured motmot'   *platus* (Gr) wide, broad   *rhunkhos* (Gr) snout, beak. Inhabiting Central and South America.

Turquoise-browed Motmot *Eumomota superciliosa*
eu- (Gr) prefix meaning well, nicely; in this case probably means 'nicely coloured motmot'   *supercilium* (L) eyebrow   *superciliosus* (L) in this case meant to mean 'much eyebrow' though the Latin word really means haughty, supercilious. Inhabiting Mexico and ranging south to Costa Rica, Central America.

Rufous Motmot *Baryphthengus ruficapillus*
barus (Gr) deep   *phthongos* (Gr) the voice, a sound   *baruphthongos* (Gr) deep-voiced; they utter a 'ghostly hoot'   *rufus* (L) reddish   *capillus* (L) hair. Inhabiting Central America from Nicaragua ranging south to Columbia and on the east of the Andes to Paraguay and Argentina.

Blue-crowned Motmot *Momotus momota*
Momotus, see above under Family: the crown and throat are light blue. Inhabiting Central and northern South America on both sides of the Andes; also Trinidad and Tobago.

Family MEROPIDAE   23 species
merops (Gr) a bird, the bee-eater.

Celebes Bearded Bee-eater   *Meropogon forsteni*
merops (Gr) a bird, the bee-eater   *pōgōn* (Gr) the beard: named after Dr E. A. Forsten (1811-1843), a naturalist from Java, in the Dutch East Indes; he was Director of the Natural History Museum in Batavia in 1839. It inhabits Celebes.

European or Common Bee-eater   *Merops apiaster*
apis (L) a bee   *-aster* (L) a suffix sometimes used to denote the diminutive; 'a small bee-eater'. It is widespread in Europe and sometimes seen in the British Isles in summer; it also inhabits parts of Asia and northern Africa, migrating south to Arabia and the whole of Africa.

Red-throated Bee-eater   *M. bulocki*
bulocki is a mis-spelling; the bird is named after William Bullock (1775-c. 1840), an English traveller, naturalist, and mine owner; he founded the Bullock Museum in 1799. Inhabiting western Africa to Uganda.

Carmine Bee-eater   *M. nubicus*
-icus (L) suffix meaning belonging to; Nubia is a tract of country with no precise limits in north-eastern Africa, to the south of Egypt; this bee-eater inhabits a belt of country stretching from Senegal in the west to Somalia in the east, and migrating south to Kenya, Zaire, and Tanzania. A very beautiful bird, mostly carmine, with other parts blue-green and pale blue.

Rainbow Bee-eater   *M. ornatus*
ornatus (L) dress, ornament; another beautiful and brightly-coloured bird, mostly a brilliant light green with bands of black, orange and blue on the throat and face and pale blue underparts. Inhabiting Celebes, New Guinea, some Pacific islands, and Australia.

Family LEPTOSOMATIDAE   1 species
Although in appearance and behaviour it is like the true rollers, it differs anatomically in several respects which places it in a family and genus on its own   *leptos* (Gr) slender, small   *sōma* (Gr) body, genitive *somatos*.

Cuckoo Roller or Courol   *Leptosomus discolor*
discolor (L) of different colours; the male is a metallic green above with

grey to light grey underparts. The name roller refers to its undulating and spectacular aerial manoeuvres; it is not related to the cuckoos; *courol* is probably a native Malagasy name. It is found only in Madagascar and Comoro Islands.

Family   CORACIIDAE   16 species
korax (Gr), genitive *korakos*, a crow or raven; anything hooked like a raven's beak. (See introductory notes on p. 185.)

Pitta-like Ground Roller   *Atelornis pittoides*
a- (Gr) not   *teleios* (Gr) complete   *ornis* (Gr) a bird; a reference to the unusually short primary feathers of the wing: *pitta* (Telugu or Tamil; these are Dravidian languages of India) a small bird   *-oides* (New L) from *eidos* (Gr) apparent shape, form, resemblance; the Pittidae form a complete family (see p. 219). Confined to the island of Madagascar.

Short-legged Ground Roller   *Brachypteracias leptosomus*
brakhus (Gr) short   *pteron* (Gr) feathers; can mean wings; it has unusually short wings, and short legs   *-acias* (New L) a suffix derived from Latin meaning tendency   *leptos* (Gr) slender, small   *sōma* (Gr) the body: like the Cuckoo Roller, above, the birds in this family are known as rollers because of the undulating and aerobatic flight behaviour, and the five species of ground rollers because they are usually seen on the ground and run for cover when alarmed. Like other ground rollers this species is confined to Madagascar.

Indian Roller   *Coracias benghalensis*
korakias (Gr) like a raven or crow; from *korax* (Gr), genitive *korakos*, a raven or crow; it is not really like a crow, being much smaller, about 30 cm (12 in) compared to the crow at about 46 cm (18 in); it is not black, but brightly coloured like all rollers   *-ensis* (L) suffix meaning belonging to; named from the Bengal area of India, it is also known in Iran and other parts of eastern Arabia, and in Burma and Thailand.

Blue-bellied Roller   *C. cyanogaster*
kuaneos (Gr) dark blue   *gaster* (Gr) the belly. Inhabiting Africa.

European Roller   *C. garrulus*
garrulus (L) talkative; the male and female have been seen to perch together calling to each other alternately and continuously in a sort of

conversation. Inhabiting central Europe and ranging east to the Caspian area; most of the Mediterranean area including north-west Africa and ranging east to Turkestan; they nearly all migrate to East Africa in winter.

Broad-billed Roller or Dollar Bird   *Eurystomus orientalis*
eurus (Gr) wide   *stoma* (Gr) the mouth   *-alis* (L) suffix meaning relating to; 'of the Orient'; sometimes called Dollar Bird because of the white circular patches on the open wings. Ranging from northern India to Manchuria and Japan; the Solomon Islands; the Burma-Thailand-Vietnam area; Malaysia, New Guinea, and Australia.

Family UPUPIDAE   1 species
upupa (L) a hoopoe; supposed to be an imitation of the bird's cry.

Hoopoe   *Upupa epops*
epops (Gr) a hoopoe. Closely related to the wood-hoopoes, although there are some slight anatomical differences; some authorities consider they belong in the same family. Inhabiting central and southern Europe, and has been seen in England and Iceland; Africa except central areas, Madagascar, central and southern Asia as far east as Japan and ranging south to India, Sri Lanka, and Malaysia.

Family PHOENICULIDAE   8 species
phoinix (Gr), genitive *phoinikos*, purple-red, crimson   *-culus* (L) diminutive suffix; can mean somewhat, e.g. 'purplish'; the plumage of these birds is usually blackish with a metallic gloss of blue, green or purple.

Black Wood-Hoopoe   *Phoeniculus aterrimus*
ater (L) black   *aterrimus* (L) very black; it has a metallic gloss. Inhabiting tropical Africa.

White-headed Wood-Hoopoe   *P. bollei*
Named after Dr C. A. Bolle (1821-1909) a German zoologist; he was in the Canary Islands in 1852 and 1856. The head is really a very pale buff colour, and the body has a metallic gloss of blue, green and purple. Inhabiting the tropical forests of Africa.

Green Wood-Hoopoe   *P. purpureus*
purpureus (L) usually purple-coloured, but can mean shining, and

various colours such as reddish, violet, brownish, blackish; the general colour is blackish glossed with green and violet or blue, and a bright red bill. Inhabiting Africa south of the Sahara.

Family BUCEROTIDAE 44 species
boukerōs (Gr) horned like an ox; a reference to the large bill, and the horny casque which some species have on the base of the bill and the head.

Crowned Hornbill *Tockus alboterminatus*
Tockus is derived from a Portuguese imitation of the bird's cry 'toco-toco-tock' *albus* (L) white *terminus* (L) limit, boundary, end -*atus* (L) suffix meaning provided with, 'having a white end'; a reference to the white tips of the outer tail feathers. It does not have the horny casque on the bill but there is a small crest of feathers on the head. It inhabits the eastern part of Africa from Somalia south to Mozambique (formerly Portuguese) and ranging west to Zambia and south-east Congo.

Van der Decken's Hornbill *T. deckeni*
Named after Baron Van der K. C. Decken (1833-1865), a Dutch naturalist; he was exploring in East Africa from 1857 to 1865. Similar to *T. alboterminatus* but paler head and all white outer tail feathers. Inhabiting Ethiopia and southern Somalia and south through Kenya to northern Tanzania.

Malabar Grey Hornbill *T. griseus*
griseus (New L) grey. Named from the Malabar Coast which is the western coast from Goa to the southern tip; this hornbill inhabits that part of India.

White-throated Brown Hornbill *Ptilolaemus tickelli*
ptilon (Gr) feathers *laimos* (Gr) the throat. Named after Col S. R. Tickell (1811-1875) a British Army officer and naturalist who was stationed in India and Burma from 1834 to 1865. Inhabiting Assam and the Burma-Thailand area.

Rufous-necked Hornbill *Aceros nipalensis*
a- (Gr) prefix meaning not, or there is not *keras* (Gr) the horn of an animal *akerōs = akeratos* (Gr) hornless; this hornbill does not have the horny casque on the bill, though some in this genus do -*ensis* (L) suffix meaning belonging to; 'of Nepal'; Nepal is a small country on the north-east border of India bounded on the north by the Himalayas.

Blyth's Hornbill   *A. plicatus*
plicatus (L) braided, folded; the male has 4 to 8 folds in the casque, the female rather less: named after E. Blyth (1810-1873), a zoologist who was Curator of the Natural History Museum in Calcutta from 1842 to 1864. Inhabiting the Burma-Thailand area, Malaysia, New Guinea, the Solomon Islands and other Pacific islands in that area.

Narcondam Hornbill   *A. narcondami*
Some authorities include this species with *A. undulatus* (below). Narcondam is a small rocky island of the Andaman group of islands in the Bay of Bengal; it is too small to be named in ordinary maps, and this hornbill is considered to be confined to this island and not found anywhere else in the world. It is a typical fairly large hornbill with marked ridges across the casque like the Indian Pied Hornbill *Anthracoceros malabaricus* (below).

Wreathed Hornbill   *A. undulatus*
undulatus (L) undulated, having waves; this, and the name 'wreathed', refers to the ridges across the casque. Inhabiting India, the Burma-Thailand area, and Malaysia.

Indian Pied Hornbill   *Anthracoceros malabaricus*
anthrax (Gr), genitive *anthrakos*, coal or charcoal   *keras* (Gr) the horn of an animal; this suggests a black horn, but the bill and the casque in this species is pale yellow; it is probably a reference to the plumage which is generally black with a green or dark blue sheen; there is some white on the wings and a white belly, giving the pied appearance when in flight: named from the Malabar Coast   *-icus* (L) a suffix meaning belonging to; the Malabar Coast of India is the south-western coast from Goa to the southern tip. This hornbill also inhabits Burma and south-east China.

Trumpeter Hornbill   *Bycanistes bucinator*
bukanē (Gr) a trumpet   *-istēs* (Gr) suffix of agent, one who acts, hence *bukanistēs* (Gr) a trumpeter   *bucina* (L) a curved trumpet   *bucinator* (L) a trumpeter; most hornbills make loud and sometimes raucous noises. Inhabiting East Africa; although many different species live in Africa they are not known in Madagascar.

Rhinoceros Hornbill   *Buceros rhinoceros*
boukerōs (Gr) big-horned, horned like an ox   *rhis* (Gr), genitive *rhinos*, the nose   *keras* (Gr) the horn of an animal   *rhinokerōs* (Gr) a nose-horn; a reference to the prominent upcurved casque on the top

of the bill. A very large hornbill, about 127 cm (50 in), living in the Thailand area and Malaysia.

Abyssinian Ground Hornbill   *Bucorvus abyssinicus*
bou- (Gr) a prefix often used to mean something huge, as in *boukerōs* (above)   *corvus* (L) a raven or rook; 'a huge raven'; it is all black except for some white on the primary wing feathers, usually only noticeable during flight   *-icus* (L) a suffix meaning belonging to; from Ethiopia (formerly Abyssinia) it ranges south to Kenya and west across Africa to the Senegal area keeping north of Congo forests. Known as a Ground Hornbill because it rarely flies, and may walk a long distance searching for insects and small reptiles. There is only one other Ground Hornbill, *B. cafer*, which inhabits the southern half of Africa, and is very similar to *B. abyssinicus*.

32 Jacamars, Honeyguides, Toucans, Woodpeckers and their kin PICIFORMES

Spot-billed Toucanet
Selenidera maculirostris

This group of birds, of the order Piciformes, range in size from about 9 to 61 cm ($3\frac{1}{2}$ to 24 in), say from a sparrow to a large raven. They are not well known except for the toucans, of Central and South America, on account of the enormous and colourful bill, and the woodpeckers which have an almost world-wide distribution except for Madagascar and Australasia. They are all related for anatomical reasons, and all are insect eaters, though some, for instance the barbets and the woodpeckers, also eat seeds and fruit. The toucans also eat small reptiles, mammals, and nestlings, and the honeyguides eat honey, beexwax, grubs and the bees.

Not so well known are the 15 species of jacamars of tropical America, some of which are very colourful with a brilliant metallic sheen of bronze or green, their close relatives the 32 species of puffbirds, also from tropical America, so called because of the habit of 'puffing out' the loosely packed feathers round the head and neck, and the 78 species of barbets of tropical America, Africa, and the Oriental region. The puffbirds are not so brightly coloured as the jacamars, and some species could be described as dowdy, and their behaviour when not flying is lethargic and evidently appears foolish, which has earned them a local native name that translated means 'Silly John'.

Order PICIFORMES

picus (L) a woodpecker; according to a legend Picus, son of Saturn, was changed by Circe into a woodpecker.

Family GALBULIDAE 15 species

galbula (L) diminutive of *galbina* (L) a small bird, perhaps a species of thrush, the yellow thrush, or the yellow oriole cf *galbinus* (L) greenish-yellow. The birds in this family and in the order Piciformes are not related to the thrushes; the name probably originates from the colour as several jacamars are a metallic green or metallic golden green.

White-eared Jacamar *Galbalcyrhynchus leucotis*
galbula (L) a small bird *alkuōn* (Gr) the kingfisher *rhunkhos* (Gr) a beak, a bill; the heavy beak and short tail give it the appearance of a kingfisher *leukos* (Gr) white *ous* (Gr), genitive *ōtos*, the ear. Ranging from southern Mexico to southern Brazil but mainly in the Amazon region. The name jacamar is from a Tupi native name *jacama-ciri*.

Pale-headed Jacamar *Brachygalba goeringi*
brakhus (Gr) short *galba*, a shortened form of *galbina* (L) a small bird, probably meant to emphasize the smallness of the bird; it is about the size of a sparrow: named after Prof Anton Goering (1836-1905) a German naturalist and artist; he was in Venezuela from 1866 to 1872 collecting for the Zoological Society of London. It inhabits Panama and ranges south to Peru and Bolivia.

Three-toed Jacamar *Jacamaralcyon tridactyla*
alkuōn (Gr) the kingfisher; jacamars are similar to kingfishers in colour, shape of beak, and behaviour *tria* (Gr) three *daktulos* (Gr) a finger or toe; it has two toes directed forward but only one backward; other jacamars have two directed forward and two backward. Inhabiting south-eastern Brazil.

Yellow-billed Jacamar *Galbula albirostris*
galbula (L) diminutive of *galbina* (L) a small bird; see notes above

under Family *albus* (L) white *rostrum* (L) the snout, the beak; in spite of this name 'white-beaked' the beak is mainly yellow. Inhabiting the Guyanas, Venezuela, the eastern side of the Andes in Columbia, Ecuador, and Peru, and the Amazon area in Brazil.

Rufous-tailed Jacamar *G. ruficauda*
rufus (L) red, ruddy *cauda* (L) the tail; the underparts including the tail are red or bright chestnut. A very common jacamar in Central America and the northern part of South America including Colombia, Ecuador, Brazil and south to Paraguay and Argentina; also Trinidad and Tobago.

Great Jacamar *Jacamerops aurea*
merops (L) a bee-eater 'a jacamar-bee-eater'; jacamars do eat bees and usually their diet consists entirely of insects *aureus* (L) golden; it has a brilliant metallic golden green head and most of the body. This is the largest jacamar, measuring some 30 to 36 cm (12 to 14 in) in length; it inhabits Central and northern South America from Costa Rica to Brazil.

Family BUCCONIDAE 32 species
bucco (L), genitive *bucconis*, a babbler, a fool, derived from *bucca* (L) the cheek, specially when puffed out in speaking, hence the English name 'puff-bird'; the plumage on the head and neck is easily puffed out giving an enlarged appearance.

Chestnut-capped Puffbird *Bucco macrodactylus*
makros (Gr) large *daktulos* (Gr) a finger or toe; it has relatively large feet for a small bird of about 13 cm (5 in) in length. The head is capped by chestnut-brown plumage. Inhabiting southern Venezuela and the Andes in Colombia, ranging south to eastern Peru, the western part of the Amazon basin in Brazil, and northern Bolivia.

Spot-backed Puffbird *Nystalus maculatus*
nustaleos (Gr) drowsy; a reference to their lethargic behaviour when not flying (see introductory notes on p. 195) *macula* (L) a mark, a spot *-atus* (L) suffix meaning provided with. Inhabiting South America, mostly north-western area.

White-whiskered Puffbird or Softwing *Malacoptila panamensis*
malakos (Gr) soft *ptilon* (Gr) a feather; properly the soft feathers or down of a bird; the feathers are unusually soft, hence the English

name 'softwing'   -*ensis* (L) suffix meaning belonging to, particularly a locality, 'of Panama'. Inhabiting southern Mexico and Central America and ranging south to Colombia and western Ecuador. 'White-whiskered' refers to the tufts of white feathers on the cheeks.

Lance-billed Monklet   *Micromonacha lanceolata*
mikros (Gr) small   *monakhos* (Gr) a monk; 'a small monk', hence monklet; the name refers to the sombre dark brown colour; it is the smallest puffbird, about 13 cm (5 in) or less   *lanceolatus* (L) armed with a small lance or spike; a reference to the small pointed beak. Inhabiting Costa Rica in Central America and ranging south to the Amazon area in Brazil, South America.

Grey-cheeked or Red-capped Nunlet   *Nonnula ruficapilla*
nonna (Gr) a nun   -*ulus* (L) diminutive suffix, 'a nunlet'; it is one of the smallest puffbirds, about 15 cm (6 in) long, and the name refers to the rather drab brown colour   *rufus* (L) red   *capillus* (L) the hair of men, usually the hair of the head; can mean the hair of animals, in this case it means the plumage of the head, which is reddish brown; the cheeks are grey. Inhabiting Panama to northern Colombia, eastern Peru and western Brazil.

Yellow-billed Nunbird   *Monasa flavirostris*
Monasa is evidently a coined word from *monakhos* (Gr) a monk, and the name alludes to the mostly black colour; the beak is yellowish   *flavus* (L) yellow   *rostrum* (L) the snout, the beak. Inhabiting Colombia and the eastern side of the Andes to eastern Peru and the western part of the Amazon basin in Brazil.

Swallow-Wing   *Chelidoptera tenebrosa*
khelidōn (Gr) a swallow   *pteron* (Gr) feathers, wings; usually in the plural; can mean a bird's wing, usually wings; it has long swallow-like wings, white underneath   *tenebrosus* (L) dark, gloomy; usually means darkness but in this case refers to the dark plumage which is almost black. Inhabiting the northern part of South America east of the Andes including Brazil and northern Bolivia.

Family   CAPITONIDAE   78 species
capito (L), genitive *capitonis*, one that has a large head, big-headed; these birds, the barbets, have a large head and rather thick heavy bill.

Black-spotted Barbet   *Capito niger*
niger (L) black; the male has black upperparts and tail; the female has

the throat, breast and flanks spotted with dark brown. Inhabiting Venezuela south of the River Orinocco, Colombia, Peru and Bolivia east of the Andes, and the western part of the Amazon basin in Brazil.

Red-headed Barbet *Eubucco bourcierii*
eu (Gr) a prefix meaning well, nicely *bucco* (L) a babbler, derived from *bucca* (L) the cheek, specially when puffed out in speaking; a hybrid word of Greek and Latin, could means 'fat-cheeked', alluding to the size of the head: named after Jules Bourcier (1797-1873), a French naturalist who was the French Consul General in Ecuador from 1849 to 1850. The male has a scarlet head and throat, but the female has a yellow and black head with blue cheeks. The English name barbet, or 'little beard', is from *barbe* (Fr) and alludes to the hair-like bristles that surround the rather large head and throat and on the chin. Inhabiting Costa Rica and Panama and ranging south to Colombia, Ecuador, and north-eastern Peru.

Prongbilled Barbet *Semnornis frantzii*
semnos (Gr) grand, fine *ornis* (Gr) a bird: named after Dr A. von Frantzius (1821-1877), a German naturalist who was in Brazil from 1849 to 1853, and Costa Rica from 1853 to 1868. This barbet has two sharp prongs on the tip of the lower mandible and one on the tip of the upper mandible which fits between them when the bill is closed; a good weapon for securing wriggling insects; it inhabits Costa Rica and Panama in Central America.

Golden-whiskered Barbet *Megalaima chrysopogon*
megas (Gr) big, wide *laimos* (Gr) the throat; barbets are stout-bodied with big heads and thick necks *khrusos* (Gr) gold *pōgōn* (Gr) the beard: inhabiting Sumatra and Borneo.

Red-vented Barbet *M. lagrandieri*
Named after Vice Admiral P. P. de Lagrandiere (1807-1876); in 1865 he was Governor of what was then known as French Cochin-China, now Vietnam. This barbet, which has red underparts, inhabits the Burma-Thailand-Vietnam area.

Naked-faced Barbet *Gymnobucco calvus*
gumnos (Gr) naked *bucco* (L), see under Red-headed Barbet above *calvus* (L) bald. Inhabiting Africa.

Golden-rumped Tinkerbird *Pogoniulus bilineatus*
pōgōn (Gr) the beard *-ulus* (L) diminutive suffix, 'the little bearded

one'; it is only about 10 cm (4 in) overall *bilineatus* (L) having two lines; it has a white line above and below the eye, the plumage is glossy black above with a golden yellow rump. The Tinkerbirds, of which there are 10 species in the genus *Pogoniulus*, get this name from their monotonous call which is a continuous bell-like 'tink', sounding like a metal hammer on an anvil and this can go on for hours. Inhabiting Uganda and Kenya and ranging south through East Africa to Natal.

Pied Barbet *Lybius leucomelas* (formerly *Tricholaema*)
A mis-spelling of Libya, although this barbet does not live there; named in 1783, in those days Libya had a very wide African connotation *leukos* (Gr) white *melas* (Gr) black; a black and white barbet with a red forehead. Distribution is widespread in southern Africa.

Black-breasted Barbet *L. rolleti*
Named after Brun Rollet (1810-1855) a French elephant hunter in the White Nile area in Sudan, and in Ethiopia, from 1831 to 1851. Inhabiting Africa south of the Sahara.

D'Arnaud's Barbet *Trachyphonus darnaudii*
trakhus (Gr) rough *phōnē* (Gr) a sound, the voice of men or animals: named after D'Arnaud (initials and dates not recorded) a French explorer and elephant hunter in the Blue Nile area and Ethiopia from 1839 to 1843. Inhabiting Sudan and ranging across to the Horn of Africa and south to Tanzania.

Levaillant's Barbet *T. vaillantii*
Named after F. Levaillant (1753-1824), a French naturalist and explorer in South Africa from 1781 to 1784. This barbet is found in the southern part of Africa from Angola across to Tanzania and ranging south to eastern South Africa.

Family INDICATORIDAE   14 species
indico (L) I show, I point out; indicator, one who points out; there are many stories about these birds leading animals, and men, to bees' nests, hence the English name 'honeyguide'. For many years naturalists dismissed them as 'tall stories' but it is now accepted that some species, particularly the Greater Honeyguide *Indicator indicator*, do lead people and animals to bees' nests by continually calling, a churring

sound, and then moving on until the man or animal follows; the ratel or honeybadger is known to follow in this way. The bird is not strong enough to break into the nest but the ratel, with its powerful claws, breaks it open and takes its fill, and the honeyguide then takes its share of the honey, the bees, their grubs, and even the wax; this latter is another puzzle for zoologists as wax is virtually indigestible by any animal except the honeyguides.

Wahlberg's Honeybird *Prodotiscus regulus*
prodo (L) I disclose, I show; can mean I make known, I report *-iscus* (L) diminutive suffix; 'a little reporter' *rex* (L), genitive *regis*, a king diminutive *regulus* (L) a little king; named after J. A. Wahlberg (1810–1856) a Swedish traveller and naturalist. One of the smallest honeyguides, only about 10 cm (4 in) long, it inhabits Africa south of the Sahara.

Greater or Black-throated Honeyguide *Indicator indicator*
indico (L) I show, I point out; see notes under Family, above. One of the largest honeyguides, about 20 cm (8 in) long, and best known for its habit of leading men and animals to bees' nests; the male has a black patch on the throat. Wide distribution in Africa but not seen in the West African rain forests, the Sahara, or the Kalahari Desert.

Lesser Honeyguide *I. minor*
minor (L) lesser, smaller; it is about 14 cm ($5\frac{1}{2}$ in) long. This species is not known to be one of those that guide men and animals to bees' nests though it does eat bees' wax, grubs, and other insects. Distribution similar to *I. indicator*, above.

Indian or Orange-rumped Honeyguide *I. xanthonotus*
xanthos (Gr) various shades of yellow including golden, orange, and even reddish *nōtos* (Gr) the back; mostly yellow in colour with a large orange-yellow patch on the rump. Inhabiting India, the Himalayan forests, and the Burma-Thailand-Vietnam area.

Lyre-tailed Honeyguide *Melichneutes robustus*
meli (Gr) honey *ikhneutēs* (Gr) a tracker, a hunter *robustus* (L) strong, robust. The central tail feathers are elongated and lyre-shaped; distribution is widespread in Africa and similar to *I. indicator*.

Family RAMPHASTIDAE 38 species
rhamphos (Gr) a beak *-astus* (Gr) augmentative suffix, 'a huge beak'.

Emerald Toucanet *Aulacorhynchus prasinus*
aulax (Gr), genitive *aulakos*, a furrow   *rhunkhos* (Gr) the beak; it has grooved mandibles   *prason* (Gr) a leek   *prasinos* (Gr) of a leek-green; the plumage is almost entirely shades of green, some quite bright. Inhabiting Mexico and ranging south through Central America to northern Venezuela, Colombia, eastern Ecuador and eastern Peru, in mountain forests from 900 to 3,000 m (3,000 to 10,000 ft).

Brown-mandibled Araçari   *Pteroglossus mariae*
pteron (Gr) feathers or wings   *glossa* (Gr) the tongue; the long tongue is fringed, probably to assist in catching and dealing with insects: named in honour of Max J. Beauharnais (1817-1852), a prince distinguished for his love and support of science, 3rd Prince of Eichstadt and Duke of Leuchtenberg, and particularly in honour of his wife The Duchess Marie Beauharnais (1819-1876), Duchess of Leuchtenberg. Inhabiting the upper Amazon basin, including the eastern parts of Colombia, Ecuador, and Peru, and the western part of Brazil. Araçari is a Portuguese name for the 11 toucans in this genus; it is derived from the Tupi language.

Many-banded Araçari   *P. pluricinctus*
plus (L), genitive *pluris*, more   *pluri-* as a prefix usually means several, but although the English name is 'many-banded' there are in fact only two bands   *cinctus* (L) a girdle; there are two black bands across the reddish-yellow underparts. Inhabiting Venezuela and nearby north-western Brazil, eastern Colombia and ranging south to north-eastern Peru.

Spot-billed Toucanet   *Selenidera maculirostris*
selēnē (Gr) the moon   *selēnion* (Gr) any small moon-shaped object   *derē* (Gr) the neck, throat; in allusion to the crescent-shaped golden-yellow collar round the hind neck   *macula* (L) a mark, a spot   *rostrum* (L) the beak, snout. Inhabiting Brazil.

Black-billed Mountain Toucan   *Andigena nigrirostris*
andinus (New L) Andean, of the Andes   *genus* (L) a race, a kind   *niger* (L) black   *rostrum* (L) the beak, snout.

Plate-billed Mountain Toucan   *A. laminirostris*
andinus (New L) Andean, of the Andes   *genus* (L) a race, a kind   *lamina* (L) a plate or thin piece of metal or other material   *rostrum* (L) the beak, the bill; it has plates on the sides of the bill. Inhabiting the Andes Mountains in Ecuador and Peru.

Orange-billed Toucan *Ramphastos aurantiirostris*
rhamphos (Gr) a beak or bill   *-astus* (Gr) augmentative suffix, 'a huge beak'   *aurantium* (New L) an orange, derived from *aurum* (L) gold *aureus* (L) golden   *rostrum* (L) the beak, bill. Inhabiting northern South America.

Chestnut-mandibled Toucan   *R. swainsonii*
Named after W. Swainson, FRS (1789-1855), a much travelled zoologist, artist and taxidermist; he was in South America from 1816 to 1818 and he also worked in Africa and New Zealand. Inhabiting the Panama area and particularly Barro Colorado Island; this island is in the Gatun Lake in the Panama Canal Zone.

Family   PICIDAE   206 species
picus (L) the woodpecker.

Red-breasted Wryneck   *Jynx ruficollis*
iugx (or *iunx*) (Gr) the wryneck   *rufus* (L) red, reddish   *collum* (L) the neck; it has a reddish-brown collar. Inhabiting Africa from Cameroun in the west across to Ethiopia in the east and ranging south to The Cape, but not known in South-West Africa. The wryneck is related to the woodpeckers in several aspects of its anatomy but it does not have the strong beak and is not able to excavate holes in trees; it has a habit of twisting its neck into peculiar contortions, particularly when disturbed, hence the name 'wryneck'.

Wryneck   *J. torquilla*
torqueo (L) I twist   *-illus* (L) diminutive suffix; 'little twister' (see above). Inhabiting Europe, including southern Scandinavia, Great Britain, where it is now seldom seen, Africa north of the equator, and ranging across Asia to Japan.

Olivaceous Piculet   *Picumnus olivaceus*
Picumnus and Pilumnus were two brother deities of the Romans; Picumnus was a personification of the woodpecker   *oliva* (L) an olive *-aceus* (L) suffix meaning similar to, like; olive coloured. Inhabiting Central and South America. A piculet is a small woodpecker, this one is tiny, no bigger than a blue tit; it has olive-green upperparts and upper breast.

White-bellied Piculet   *P. spilogaster*
spilos (Gr) a spot, a blemish   *gaster* (Gr) the belly; the belly is white

with black markings. Inhabiting Venezuela, Guyana, Surinam, and ranging south into Brazil.

Antillean Piculet *Nesoctites micromegas*
nēsos (Gr) an island   *ktites* = *ktistes* (Gr) an inhabitant; Antilles is the name applied to the group of islands, including Cuba, that lie to the north of the Caribbean Sea   *mikros* (Gr) small   *megas* (Gr) big; 'a small big one'; the piculets are the small woodpeckers.

Ground Woodpecker *Geocolaptes olivaceus*
gē (Gr) the earth   *kolaptō* (Gr) I cut, chisel   *kolaptēs* (Gr) a cutter, a chiseller   *oliva* (L) an olive   *-aceus* (L) suffix meaning like; in this case olive coloured. This woodpecker spends almost its entire life on the ground, only occasionally seen in trees, in which case it climbs there; the upperparts are olive brown. It is confined to south-east and southern South Africa.

Yellow-shafted Flicker *Colaptes auratus*
Colaptes, see above   *auratus* (L) golden, adorned with gold; the upperparts are not golden but there are yellow shafts to the flight feathers and the underwings and undertail are bright yellow; this gives it the English name. Inhabiting Alaska, Canada, Newfoundland, and ranging south to Florida; it keeps to the eastern side of the Rocky Mountains.

Golden-green Woodpecker *Piculus chrysochloros*
picus (L) the woodpecker   *-ulus* (L) diminutive suffix, 'a little woodpecker'; woodpeckers range in size from 9 to 61 cm ($3\frac{1}{2}$ to 24 in); this is one of the small ones, about 15 cm (6 in) long   *khrusos* (Gr) gold   *khloros* (Gr) green. Inhabiting Central America.

Golden-tailed Woodpecker *Campethera abingoni*
kampē (Gr) a caterpillar   *thēraō* (Gr) I hunt, chase, wild animals; can mean I take, catch, wild animals; it feeds on various insects and grubs including caterpillars and ants: named after M. Abingdon, the 5th Earl of Abingdon (1784-1854), an English naturalist; this is a misspelling of Abingdon, but as the name was established and universally recognised in 1836 it cannot now be changed although recently certain exceptions to this rule have been allowed in cases of mistakes in spelling. Inhabiting the Senegal area in West Africa and ranging across to Sudan, and from Central and East Africa and Somalia south to Natal.

Fine-spotted Woodpecker *C. punctuligera*
punctus (L) a puncture *punctatus* (L) spotted as with punctures *-ulus* (L) diminutive suffix *gero* (L) I bear, carry; 'bearing small spots'; the upperparts are finely spotted with white, and the underparts pale with small dark spots. Inhabiting the Senegal area, northern Zaire and southern Sudan.

Chestnut Woodpecker *Celeus elegans*
keleos (Gr) the green woodpecker *elegans* (L) neat, elegant; the plumage is mainly a chestnut colour. Inhabiting Venezuela, Colombia east of the Andes, ranging south to the Amazon basin and northern Bolivia; also Trinidad.

Grey-headed Woodpecker *Picus canus*
picus (L) the woodpecker; see notes under Order Piciformes on p. 196 *canus* (L) white, hoary; often used to mean the grey hair of the aged. Inhabiting Eurasia from southern Scandinavia and France ranging east to Japan and south-east to Sumatra and also the Himalayas.

Green Woodpecker *P. viridis*
viridis (L) green. Inhabiting a similar area to *P. canus* above, but not extending as far as Sumatra.

Lineated Woodpecker *Dryocopus lineatus*
drus (Gr), genitive *druos*, a tree *kopos* (Gr) striking, beating; 'tree striking' *lineatus* (L) lined. Inhabiting Central and South America.

Black and White Woodpecker *Phloeoceastes melanoleucos*
phloios (Gr) peel or bark of trees *keazō* (Gr) I cleave, I split wood *-istes* (Gr) suffix meaning one who acts; 'a cleaver of bark' *melas* (Gr), genitive *melanos*, black *leukos* (Gr) white; the colour is mostly black with white patches and white lines down the neck, and underparts dull white and black. Inhabiting Central America, Trinidad, South America on the eastern side of the Andes ranging south to northern Argentina.

Acorn Woodpecker *Melanerpes formicivorus* (formerly *Centurus*)
melas (Gr), genitive *melanos*, black *herpēs* (Gr) a creeper, one that moves slowly, 'a black creeper'; a reference to the way a woodpecker creeps slowly up the trunk of a tree searching for insects and grubs; this woodpecker has a glossy black back, wings and tail but it does not follow that all species in this genus are black, though a number of them are; the generic name is simply a label and they are grouped

together because of similarities in their anatomy and not because of the colour of the plumage   *formica* (L) an ant   *voro* (L) I devour; although ants form an important part of the diet, this woodpecker is well known as a lover of acorns; groups of five or six will live together and spend hours drilling thousands of holes in the trunk of a tree, and into each hole an acorn is inserted as a reserve food for times when insects are scarce. Inhabiting coastal areas on the western side of the USA from Oregon ranging south through Central America to Colombia.

Red-crowned Woodpecker   *M. rubricapillus*
rubor (L) redness   *capillus* (L) hair, usually the hair of the head, can mean the hair of animals; the crown and nape of the neck are crimson. Inhabiting Panama and Costa Rica and ranging south to Venezuela and Colombia; also Tobago.

Red-breasted Sapsucker   *Sphyrapicus ruber*
sphura (Gr) a hammer   *picus* (L) the woodpecker   *ruber* (L) red; it hammers on tree trunks and other objects, even metal, in a fast and then slow rhythm. The English name comes from its liking for sap; it drills many small holes usually in deciduous trees and drinks the sap, however its main food is insects and these are attracted by the sap oozing from the holes. Inhabiting the western part of Canada and the USA.

Arabian Woodpecker   *Picoides dorae*   (formerly *Dendrocopos*)
picus (L) the woodpecker   *-oides* (New L) from *eidos* (Gr) shape, form, resemblance: the specific name is in honour of Mrs H. Dora Philby (1888-1957), the wife of J. B. H. Philby, a naturalist and explorer who led the British political mission to central Arabia in 1917 and 1918 and later explored the southern province of Nejd in 1920. This woodpecker inhabits Arabia and Egypt.

Great Spotted Woodpecker   *P. major*
major = *maior* (L) greater; woodpeckers range in size from about 9 to 61 cm ($3\frac{1}{2}$ to 24 in); this is not one of the biggest, being about 23 cm (9 in), but the comparison is with the Middle and Lesser Spotted Woodpeckers; the plumage is predominately black with white spots and bars. Inhabiting Europe including Great Britain, but not Ireland, ranging south to north-west Africa, Asia and east to Japan.

Middle Spotted Woodpecker   *P. medius*
medius (L) middle. The range is similar to *P. major*, above, but not in

the British Isles and not ranging so far north or south in Asia.

Lesser Spotted Woodpecker   *P. minor*
minor (L) lesser. Inhabiting Europe including the southern part of Great Britain, north-west Africa, Turkey, and Asia ranging east to Japan. One of the smaller woodpeckers, about 15 cm (6 in) long.

Brown-backed Woodpecker   *P. stricklandi*
Named after H. E. Strickland, FRS (1811-1853) an English zoologist. Inhabiting Mexico.

Three-toed Woodpecker   *P. tridactylus*
treis (Gr) = *tri* (L) three   *daktulos* (Gr) a finger, or a toe; it has two toes pointing forwards and one pointing backwards, though most woodpeckers are zygodactyl, i.e. having two forwards and two backwards; there are other three-toed woodpeckers. Distribution is widespread and includes North America, Eurasia, ranging south to India and the Burma-Thailand-Vietnam area.

Cuban Green Woodpecker   *Xiphidiopicus percussus*
xiphos (Gr) a sword   *xiphidion* (Gr) a small sword   *picus* (L) the woodpecker   *percussus* (L) a knocking, striking; references to its sharp beak and habit of hammering on trees in search of insects. Inhabiting Cuba.

Lesser Bay Woodpecker   *Blythipicus rubiginosus*
Named after E. Blyth (1810-1873) a zoologist and Curator of the Calcutta Museum from 1842 to 1864   *picus* (L) the woodpecker *ruber* (L) red   *rubigo* (L), genitive *rubiginis*, rust   *-osus* (L) suffix meaning full of   *rubiginosus*, rusty, rust-coloured. Inhabiting the Burma-Thailand-Vietnam area and Malaysia.

Crimson-backed Woodpecker   *Chrysocolaptes lucidus*
khrusos (Gr) gold   *kolapto* (Gr) I cut, chisel   *kolaptēs* (Gr) a cutter, a chiseller   *lucidus* (L) bright, shining; a reference to the bright crimson crest, crown and back. Inhabiting India including Ceylon, the Burma-Thailand-Vietnam area, and Malaysia.

Magellanic Woodpecker   *Campephilus magellanicus*
kampē (Gr) a caterpillar   *philos* (Gr) dear, pleasing   *-icus* (L) prefix meaning belonging to, 'of Magellan's Strait'. Inhabiting the southern tip of Chile, Patagonia, and the island Tierra del Fuego; Magellan's Strait separates this island from the mainland.

33 Perching Birds PASSERIFORMES

White-throated Seedeater
Sporophila albogularis

Order   PASSERIFORMES

passer (L) a sparrow, or any small bird   *forma* (L) form, shape; can mean sort, kind, so not necessarily referring to the actual shape; the birds in this very big order are by no means all 'sparrow-like' but they do have certain anatomical features in common, e.g. regarding the claws, there are three toes in front and one behind; they are sometimes referred to as 'perching birds'.

Family   EURYLAIMIDAE   14 species
eurus (Gr) wide   *laimos* (Gr) the throat; the birds in this family have a broad flat head and a wide bill, hence the English name broadbill.

Rufous-sided Broadbill   *Smithornis rufolateralis*
Named after Sir Andrew Smith (1797-1872), an army surgeon who was a pioneer in scientific research in southern Africa   *ornis* (Gr) a bird   *rufus* (L) red, ruddy   *latus* (L), genitive *lateris*, side, flank -*alis* (L) suffix meaning relating to. Inhabiting West and Central Africa; it has prominent reddish-brown patches on the sides of the chest.

Grauer's or African Green Broadbill   *Pseudocalyptomena graueri*
pseudēs (Gr) false   *kaluptos* (Gr) covered, wrapped round; the bill is covered at the base with a tuft of green feathers; this bird was first

discovered by a collector named Grauer in Tanzania (then known as Tanganyika) and later in 1909 was described by Lord Rothschild and given the name *Pseudocalyptomena graueri*, 'false' because at that time Green Broadbills of the genus *Calyptomena* were not considered to be African birds, and only known in the Malaysian area. The specific name refers to Rudolph Grauer (1871-1927), an Australian ornithologist who was collecting in Africa from 1904 to 1911. The bird is very rare, and seldom seen, and then only in two areas; one in eastern Zaire and the other in southern Uganda.

Dusky Broadbill   *Corydon sumatranus*
Corydon is taken from *Korudōn*, the name of a well-known Greek shepherd   -*anus* (L) suffix meaning belonging to; the name is taken from Sumatra but it also inhabits other parts of south-eastern Asia and Malaysia. The plumage is very dark, almost black, hence 'dusky'.

Black and Yellow Broadbill   *Eurylaimus ochromalus*
Eurylaimus, see notes under Family, above   *ōkhros* (Gr) pale yellow   *malus* (L) derived from *melas* (Gr) black; it is a black bird with parts of the wings and back yellow. Inhabiting the Burma-Thailand-Vietnam area and Malaysia.

Long-tailed Broadbill   *Psarisomus dalhousiae*
psaros (Gr) speckled, like a starling   *soma* (Gr) the body: named after Countess C. Dalhousie (1786-1839), the wife of the Governor General of India in 1829. Inhabiting India and ranging east to Malaysia.

Lesser Green Broadbill   *Calyptomena viridis*
kaluptos (Gr) covered, wrapped round; the bill is covered at the base with a tuft of green feathers   *viridis* (L) green. This is the smallest of the four Green Broadbills, about 15 cm (6 in) long; the range is Burma, Malaysia, Indonesia including Borneo.

Family   DENDROCOLAPTIDAE   50 species
dendron (Gr) a tree   *kolaptēr* (Gr) a chisel   *kolaptēs* (Gr) a chiseller, of birds a pecker.

Plain Brown Woodcreeper   *Dendrocincla fuliginosa*
dendron (Gr) a tree   *kinklos* (Gr) a bird, a kind of wagtail   *fuligo* (L), genitive *fuliginis*, soot   -*osus* (L) suffix mean full of, prone to, 'very sooty'; a reference to the rather dull brown plumage. Inhabiting Central America and ranging south to Brazil.

Olivaceous Woodcreeper *Sittasomus griseicapillus*
sittē (Gr) a kind of woodpecker *soma* (Gr) the body *griseus* (New L) derived from *greis* (G) grey *capillus* (L) the hair of men, usually the hair of the head, can mean the hair of animals; the plumage is mainly olive-coloured. Inhabiting Central America and ranging south to southern Brazil.

Wedge-billed Woodcreeper *Glyphorynchus spirurus*
gluphō (Gr) I carve, cut *rhunkhos* (Gr) the bill *speiroō* (Gr) I wrap round *oura* (Gr) the tail; probably a reference to the way the tail spreads when used as a support for climbing vertical tree trunks. The bill is short and the upper mandible flattened, hence 'wedge-billed'; woodcreepers do not actually cut into the tree like woodpeckers but prize off the bark with their strong bills, searching for insects, grubs, and spiders. Inhabiting Central America and South America on the eastern side of the Andes, south as far as Bolivia and Brazil.

Cinnamon-throated Woodcreeper *Dendrexetastes rufigula*
dendron (Gr) a tree *exetastēs* (Gr) one who searches out, examines; alluding to the bird's search for insects under the bark *rufus* (L) red, reddish *gula* (L) the throat. Inhabiting South America, from Colombia to Brazil.

Red-billed Woodcreeper *Hylexetastes perrotii*
hulē (Gr) a wood, forest *exetastēs*, see above: named after Jean Perrot (1790-1858), a French taxidermist; he worked for the Paris Museum in 1820. Inhabiting South America.

White-throated Woodcreeper *Xiphocolaptes albicollis*
xiphos (Gr) a sword *kolaptēr* (Gr) a chisel *kolaptēs* (Gr) a chiseller *albus* (L) white *collum* (L) the neck; see notes above under *Glyphorynchus spirurus*. Inhabiting Venezuela, Brazil and Peru.

Barred Woodcreeper *Dendrocolaptes certhia*
dendron (Gr) a tree *colaptes*, see above *kerthios* (Gr) a little bird, a treecreeper. Inhabiting Central and South America.

Buff-throated Woodcreeper *Xiphorhynchus guttatus*
xiphos (Gr) a sword *rhunkhos* (Gr) the beak, bill; it has a powerful beak, slightly curved, 25 to 38 mm (1 to $1\frac{1}{2}$ in) long *gutta* (L) a drop, of a fluid *guttatus* (L) spotted, speckled; it has very noticeable pale spots and speckles on the buff plumage of the head and back of neck. Inhabiting Central America from Guatemala to Panama, and South

America in Trinidad and Tobago, ranging south on the eastern side of the Andes to Bolivia and the Amazon area.

Spix's Woodcreeper   *X. spixii*
Named after Dr J. B. von Spix (1781-1826), a German Professor of Zoology at the Munich Museum; he was in Brazil from 1817 to 1820. Inhabiting northern South America to the Amazon area.

Narrow-billed Woodcreeper   *Lepidocolaptes angustirostris*
lepidus (L) neat, graceful   *kolaptēr* (Gr) a chisel   *kolaptēs* (Gr) a chiseller   *angustus* (L) narrow   *rostrum* (L) a beak, bill. Inhabiting Brazil and Argentina.

Streak-headed Woodcreeper   *L. souleyetii*
Named after F. L. A. Souleyet (1811-1852), a French naval surgeon and naturalist; he was in Peru in 1836. There are pale buff streaks on the head and the back of the neck; it inhabits Central and South America.

Black-billed Scythebill   *Campylorhamphus falcularius*
kampulos (Gr) bent, curved   *rhamphos* (Gr) a beak, bill, specially the crooked beak of birds   *falx* (L) a sickle, genitive *falcis*   *-ulus* (L) diminutive suffix   *-arius* (L) suffix meaning belonging to; by comparison with the beak of other woodcreepers the five scythebills in the genus *Campylorhamphus* are quite remarkable; they are long, slender and curved, a 7·5-cm (3-in) beak on a 25·5-cm (10-in) bird. Inhabiting Brazil, Paraguay, and Argentina.

Family   FURNARIIDAE   217 species
furnus (L) an oven   *furnarius* (L) a baker. The birds in the genus *Furnarius* build a nest of mud that resembles an oven, and this has given them the name Ovenbirds and the family as a whole the Latin name Furnariidae, but it is a very big group with a wide variation of nest-building and a number of different local and English names such as Miner, Earthcreeper, Hornero, and Spinetail. They are small brown forest birds living in Central and South America and ranging from Mexico to southern Argentina.

Common Miner   *Geositta cunicularia*
ge (Gr) the ground, earth   *sittē* (Gr) a kind of woodpecker   *cuniculum* (L) an underground passage, a cavity; spending all its time on the ground, it burrows deep into a sandy bank for the nest, hence the English name 'miner'. Inhabiting southern South America.

Rufous Hornero or Ovenbird   *Furnarius rufus*
furnus (L) an oven   *furnarius* (L) a baker   *rufus* (L) red, ruddy. The name Hornero is from the Spanish   *hornero* (Sp) a baker. It inhabits the southern part of South America.

Curve-billed Reedhaunter   *Limnornis curvirostris*
limnē (Gr) a marsh, pond   *ornis* (Gr) a bird   *curvus* (L) curved   *rostrum* (L) the beak, bill; it searches among reeds for small crustaceans and other small water animals. Inhabiting South America.

Grey-flanked Shaketail   *Cinclodes oustaleti*
kinklos (Gr) a bird, perhaps the water ouzel   *-odes* = *-oides* (New L) from *eidos* (Gr) shape, form, resemblance; it is rather like the dipper, or water ouzel, it lives near water, and has the habit of flicking its tail up and down like the wagtail: named after Dr J. F. E. Oustalet (1844-1905), a French Professor of Zoology; he was Curator of Mammals at the Natural History Museum in Paris from 1900 to 1905. Inhabiting southern South America.

Rush-loving Spinetail   *Phleocryptes melanops*
phleōs (Gr) a water plant, a rush   *kruptos* (Gr) hidden, secret; 'hidden among rushes'   *melas* (Gr), genitive *melanos*, black   *ops* from *opsis* (Gr) aspect, appearance. Known as a 'spinetail' because the tail feathers end in bare spines. Inhabiting South America.

Pale-breasted Spinetail   *Synallaxis albescens*
sunallaxis (Gr) exchange; a reference to the loud calls a pair make to each other while foraging in the undergrowth, so establishing the pair bond   *albus* (L) white   *-escens* (L) suffix meaning beginning to, tendency; 'whitish'; it is chestnut coloured above with a pale buff breast; 'spinetail', see above. Inhabiting Central and South America from southern Mexico to southern Argentina.

Straight-billed Reedhaunter   *Limnoctites rectirostris*
limnē (Gr) a marsh, pond   *ktitēs* (Gr) an inhabitant   *rectus* (L) straight   *rostrum* (L) the beak, bill. Inhabiting South America.

Pearled Treerunner   *Margarornis squamiger*
margarōdēs (Gr) pearl-like   *ornis* (Gr) a bird   *squama* (L) a scale   *gero* (L) I bear, carry; the breast is covered with pearl-like marking with black edges, giving the appearance of scales. Inhabiting Venezuela and Colombia and ranging south to Peru and Bolivia.

Riker's Palmcreeper *Berlepschia rikeri*
Named after H. Graf. von Berlepsch (1850-1915), a German zoologist who collected many thousands of specimens in South America, and C. B. Riker (1863-1947), a zoologist who was in Brazil from 1884 to 1887. This bird, living in the Amazon area, spends almost its entire life in the palm trees.

Red-fronted Thornbird *Phacellodomus rufifrons*
phakelos (Gr) a bundle; sometimes written in Greek as *phakellos*, but this is incorrect   *domos* (Gr) a house, structure; the nest is built with bundles of sticks round the drooping limb of a tree, forming a column sometimes 1·5 or 2 m (5 or 6 ft) high; several birds help to build the structure which contains six or seven compartments, but probably only one pair use it for breeding   *rufus* (L) red   *frons* (L) brow, forehead. Widespread in the northern half of South America on the western side.

Spotted Barbtail *Premnoplex brunnescens*
premnon (Gr) the trunk of a tree   *plexus* (L) a knitting, interweaving; a reference to the form of nest-building, though the nests are usually woven round an overhanging bough, or higher up in a fork; this bird sometimes builds a globular structure   *brunneus* (New L) brown   *-escens* (L) suffix meaning beginning to, tendency, 'brownish'. Inhabiting southern Mexico to Bolivia.

Streak-breasted Treehunter *Thripadectes rufobrunneus*
thrips (Gr) a woodworm   *dēktēs* (Gr) a biter   *rufus* (L) red   *brunneus* (New L) brown. Inhabiting Central America.

Streak-capped Treehunter *T. virgaticeps*
virga (L) a twig   *virgatus* (L) made of twigs; can mean striped   *ceps* (New L) from *caput* (L) the head. Inhabiting western Venezuela, Colombia, and Ecuador.

Plain Xenops *Xenops minutus*
xenos (Gr) a stranger, foreigner   *ops* (Gr) the eye, face; a newly discovered bird and named in 1811; there are only four in this genus; *minutus* (L) small, minute; at 13 cm (5 in) long it is one of the smallest in this family which range from 13 to 28 cm (5 to 11 in). Inhabiting Mexico to South America east of the Andes, including Bolivia, Paraguay, northern Argentina, and on the west of the Andes to Ecuador.

Tawny-throated Leafscraper *Sclerurus mexicanus*
sklēros (Gr) hard, stiff   *oura* (Gr) the tail; the tail feathers have stiff spines to help support the bird when climbing vertical tree trunks *-anus* (L) suffix meaning belonging to; inhabiting Mexico and ranging south through Central America to South America.

Streamcreeper *Lochmias nematura*
lokhmē (Gr) a thicket, bush, specially one serving as a lair for an animal *lokhmaios* (Gr) belonging to a bush; the name is probably misleading as apparently the nest is usually a hole in a bank   *nēma* (Gr), genitive *nēmatos*, thread   *oura* (Gr) the tail; a reference to the tail feathers which end in bare spines. Sometimes known as the Sharptailed Streamcreeper, it lives near mountain streams in eastern Panama, ranging south through Central America and South America to northern Argentina.

Family   FORMICARIIDAE   230 species
formica (L) an ant   *-arius* (L) suffix meaning belonging to; they probably do not eat ants (see below). The antbirds, which have been given various names such as antshrike, antwren, and antthrush, form a large group of about 230 species. The English names, and the Latin name for the family, are misleading; it is not possible to say that they never eat ants, but ants do not form part of their normal diet. However they are sometimes seen following columns of army ants in order to feed on the insects and small animals that are disturbed and are escaping from the ants; this seems to be the reason for the name. Some species also eat fruit and berries and some of the larger species are known to eat very small snakes and lizards.

The birds range in size from about 7·5 to 18 cm (3 to 14 in), and although related to the ovenbirds they are more colourful, especially the males. Living in the dense forests of tropical Central and South America they are not easily seen, and taken as a whole very little accurate information about their habits is available.

Fasciated Antshrike *Cymbilaimus lineatus*
kumbē (Gr) a cup, bowl; can mean a kind of bird, perhaps a tumbler pigeon   *laimos* (Gr) the throat   *linea* (L) a line   *lineatus* (L) lined; most of the plumage is marked with conspicuous pale or dark lines or bands. Living on the eastern side of the Andes ranging south to Peru, Bolivia, and the Amazon area. They have been given the English

name antshrike because the bill is hooked at the tip like that of the shrike, and used for killing and eating small animals.

Black-headed Antshrike *Thamnophilus nigriceps*
thamnos (Gr) a bush, shrub   *philos* (Gr) loved, pleasing; some of the species in this genus come out of the dense forest and live in the bushes and bamboo thickets near human habitations   *niger* (L) black   *ceps* (New L) from *caput* (L) the head; for the name 'shrike' see above. Inhabiting Central and South America.

White-flanked Antwren *Myrmotherula axillaris*
murmēx (Gr) the ant   *thēraō* (Gr) I hunt wild beasts; can mean I catch wild beasts   *-ulus* (L) diminutive suffix; 'catch small wild beasts'; as explained above in the notes under Family, the antwren does not eat ants   *axilla* (L) the armpit   *-aris* (L) suffix meaning belonging to; the male has a white patch of feathers under the wings which are exposed in courtship display or anger. It is a small wren-like bird only about 10 cm (4 in) long living in the forest undergrowth of Central and South America.

Klages's Antwren *M. klagesi*
Named after S. M. Klages (fl 1900), a devoted and untiring naturalist and collector who sent many thousands of skins to the Carnegie Museum in Pittsburg; he was in Venezuela from 1898 to 1913 and Brazil in 1922. This antwren inhabits the forests in the northern part of South America.

Black-bellied Antwren *Formicivora melanogaster*
formica (L) an ant   *voro* (L) I eat; the antwrens do not eat ants, as explained in the notes under Family opposite   *melas* (Gr), genitive *melanos*, black   *gastēr* (Gr) the belly. A small antbird resembling a wren, living in Brazil and Bolivia.

Striated Antbird *Drymophila devillei*
drumos (Gr) a forest   *philos* (Gr) loved, pleasing: named after E. Deville (1824-1853), a French naturalist and taxidermist at the Natural History Museum in Paris; he was in South America from 1843 to 1847. Inhabiting South America.

Jet Antbird *Cercomacra nigricans*
kerkos (Gr) the tail of an animal   *makros* (Gr) long   *nigricans* (L) swarthy, black; 'black as jet'; a black antbird with a long tail living in the forests of South America.

White-backed Fire-eye   *Pyriglena leuconota*
pyr (Gr) fire   *glēnē* (Gr) the eyeball   *leukos* (Gr) white   *nōtos* (Gr) the back. Inhabiting Colombia and Argentina.

Goeldi's Antbird   *Myrmeciza goeldii*
murmēx (Gr) the ant   *murmēkizō* (Gr) I feel as if ants were creeping about me; can mean I creep like ants: named after Dr E. A. Goeldi (1859-1917), a Spanish-American zoologist who founded the Goeldi Museum in Paraguay; he lived in Brazil from 1894 to 1905. This antbird inhabits the northern half of South America.

Black-headed Antthrush   *Formicarius nigricapillus*
formica (L) an ant   *-arius* (L) suffix meaning belonging to; they do not eat ants, as explained in the notes under Family on p. 214   *niger* (L) black   *capillus* (L) the hair of men, usually of the head; can mean the hair of animals. Inhabiting Central America and ranging south through Venezuela and Colombia to Bolivia and Brazil. The antthrushes have rather big thrush-like heads.

Wing-banded Antbird   *Myrmornis torquata*
murmex = *murmos* (Gr) the ant   *ornis* (Gr) a bird; antbirds do not eat ants (see above)   *torquatus* (L) wearing a twisted collar or necklace; it has a collar of zig-zag white lines round the neck. Inhabiting Central America and the northern part of South America.

Black-crowned Antpitta   *Pittasoma michleri*
pitta (Telugu or Tamil; these are Dravidian languages of India) a small bird   *soma* (Gr) the body: named after Brig Gen N. Michler (1827-1881) who did a survey in Panama during the years 1857 to 1861. The English name antpitta has been given because these birds are similar to the pittas in the family Pittidae; this one lives in the Panama area of Central America and ranges south to the northern part of South America.

Rusty-breasted Antpitta   *Grallaricula ferrugineipectus*
grallae (L) stilts   *-arius* (L) suffix meaning belonging to   *-culus* (L) diminutive suffix; 'of small stilts'; the antpittas and their close relatives, for example *Grallaria*, are mostly terrestrial and have longer legs than the other antbirds, however this particular species is not often seen on the ground   *ferrugo* (L) rust, of iron   *ferrugineus* (L) rust-coloured   *pectus* (L) the breast. Inhabiting northern Venezuela, Colombia, and northern Peru.

Great Antpitta *Grallaria excelsa*
grallae (L) stilts   *-arius* (L) suffix meaning belonging to; it has long legs (see above)   *excelsus* (L) high, elevated; a reference to its habitat which is high up in the Andes in north-western South America. One of the larger antbirds, it is about 25·5 cm (10 in) long.

Brown-banded Antpitta   *G. milleri*
Named after Leo E. Miller (fl 1910), he was in South America with Dr F. M. Chapman, the well known ornithologist who wrote several books about South Africa. They were there from 1910 to 1917; in 1918 Miller published his book *In the Wilds of South America*. This antpitta lives in the northern part of South America.

Chestnut Crowned Antpitta   *G. ruficapilla*
rufus (L) red, ruddy   *capillus* (L) the hair of men, usually the hair of the head; can mean the hair of animals. This is one of the large ground-loving antbirds inhabiting the forests of the northern part of South America.

Family   CONOPOPHAGIDAE   8 species
kōnōps (Gr), genitive *kōnōpos*, a gnat, mosquito   *phagein* (Gr) to eat. The Gnat-eaters, as both their Latin and English names imply, are insectivorous, their diet probably consisting entirely of small insects. Related to, and in some respects resembling, the two previous families, they are small ground-loving birds about 13 cm (5 in) long.

D'Orbigny's Gnat-eater   *Conopophaga ardesiaca*
Conopophaga, see above   *ardesco* (L) I gleam, glitter; possibly *-acus* (L) relating to; this is a coined name and not to be taken too literally; the plumage is brown above and grey below. The bird is named after Prof A. D. d'Orbigny (1803-1857), a French zoologist who was Professor at the Museum of Natural History in Paris in 1854. He was in South America from 1826 to 1833. It inhabits Bolivia and Peru.

Black-bellied Gnat-eater   *C. melanogaster*
melas (Gr), genitive *melanos*, black   *gaster* (Gr) the belly; the male has a black cap on the head and black breast and underparts. Inhabiting Bolivia and the Amazon area of Brazil.

Robert's Gnat-eater   *C. roberti*
Named after Alphonse Robert (fl 1900), a French naturalist and collector; in 1901 he was in Brazil collecting for the Tring Zoological

Museum; this Gnat-eater was named after him in 1905. Inhabiting the northern part of South America.

Family RHINOCRYPTIDAE 29 species
rhis (Gr), genitive *rhinos*, the nose   *kruptos* (Gr) hidden, covered; a reference to a peculiar anatomical feature of this family; they have a moveable flap to cover each nostril, thought to be a protection against dust or sand. They are ground-loving birds and similar to the Conopophagidae (above), ranging from 10 to 25.5 cm (4½ to 10 in) long. They have been given a variety of English names but the one most used is *Tapaculo*, a native name of Spanish origin, and often used by the native people with an amusing meaning which is 'Cover your bottom!'; this is a reference to their habit of strutting about with the tail cocked up and their rear end exposed. They spend almost their entire life on the ground, scratching about like domestic hens looking for insects and seeds; this has given them another English name, Gallito, derived from the Spanish and meaning a cockerel.

Black-throated Huet-huet   *Pteroptochos tarnii*
pteron (Gr) a wing   *ptōkhos* (Gr) one who crouches or cringes; 'a winged croucher'; these birds have been described as 'skulking about in the undergrowth'. They have secretive habits and are seldom seen though often heard: named after J. Tarn (1794-1877), a naturalist, and surgeon on H.M.S. *Adventure*, South America, from 1825 to 1830. It inhabits the forest undergrowth in south-western South America, most common in Chile and Patagonia; the name 'huet-huet' is an imitation of the call.

White-throated Tapaculo   *Scelorchilus albicollis*
skelos (Gr) the leg   *orkhilos* (Gr) a bird, probably a wren; perhaps 'a leggy wren'; with their cocked up tails they resemble wrens but have much longer and stouter legs   *albus* (L) white   *collum* (L) the neck. Inhabiting the western part of South America. For tapaculo see notes under Family, above.

Grey Gallito   *Rhinocrypta lanceolata*
rhis (Gr), genitive *rhinos*, the nose   *kruptos* (Gr) hidden, covered; see notes under Family, above   *lancea* (L) a light spear or lance   *lanceola*, a small lance   *lanceolatus* (L) armed with a small lance; a reference to the pointed rather slender bill. Inhabiting Chile, Argentina, Paraguay, and Uruguay. For Gallito see notes under Family, above.

Sandy Gallito *Teledromas fuscus*
tēle (Gr) far   *dromos* (Gr) running, escape; 'far-running'; when disturbed, like all members of the family it prefers running to flying; the legs are long for a bird of this size, with a body of about 18 cm (7 in), and it takes long strides; the flight muscles are weak and the leg muscles strong   *fuscus* (L) dark, dark coloured; it is a sandy brown colour. Most common in Argentina.

Andean Tapaculo *Scytalopus magellanicus*
skutalē (Gr) a thick stick, a cudgel   *pous* (Gr) the foot; 'thick-footed'; a reference to the comparatively heavy legs and feet common in this family, see above: named from the Strait of Magellan, which separates the island of Tierra del Fuego from the mainland of Patagonia; however it is by no means confined to this area and ranges from northwest Venezuela through Colombia and along the line of the Andes to Peru, Bolivia, Chile, Argentina to Cape Horn and the Falkland Islands; in the Andes it is known to live as high as 4,000 m (13,000 ft).

Pale-throated Tapaculo *S. panamensis*
One of the few that are found as far north as Central America, it ranges from the mountains of Panama south to Colombia and Ecuador   *-ensis* (L) suffix meaning belonging to, usually applying to a locality.

Family   PITTIDAE   26 species
pitta is a name derived from a language spoken in Telingana, India, which lies roughly north from Madras to the border of Orissa; it means 'a small bird'. The fact that this little family are all in the same genus, *Pitta*, tells us that their anatomy, habits, and diet, are all very similar; minor differences are indicated by the specific name. They are colourful birds, ranging in size from about 15 to 28 cm (6 to 11 in) long, including a very short tail; the diet is varied, and includes insects, worms, fruit and berries, and very small reptiles.

African Pitta *Pitta angolensis*
Pitta, see above   *-ensis* (L) suffix meaning belonging to, usually applying to a locality; named from Angola, it is also found in Congo, Zaire, Tanzania, and ranging south to Transvaal.

Blue-winged Pitta *P. brachyura*
brakhus (Gr) short   *oura* (Gr) the tail; the tail is so short that it is almost non-existent; the family as a whole have short tails. Widespread in south-eastern Asia and India, the Burma-Thailand-

Vietnam area, Malaysia, and ranging further east to Korea and Japan. A gaily-coloured bird with bright blue wings.

Red-breasted Pitta *P. erythrogaster*
eruthros (Gr) red   *gaster* (Gr) the belly; actually the breast is partly green but the underparts or belly are bright red. Inhabiting the Philippines, and ranging south through Celebes, New Guinea and northern Australia.

Koch's Pitta *P. kochi*
Named after Dr G. von Koch (1849-1914), a German zoologist and taxidermist; he was a Professor at the Darmstadt Museum in 1875. A rare pitta, and confined to certain areas in the mountains of Luzon.

Rainbow Pitta *P. iris*
iris (Gr), genitive *iridos*, the rainbow; from *iridos* we get the English word iridescent; this is a brilliantly coloured bird with an iridescent plumage. Inhabiting Australia.

Phayre's Pitta *P. phayrei*
Named after Lt Gen Sir A. P. Phayre (1812-1885), a naturalist who was in the Indian Army in 1828 and Commander of the British in Burma from 1862 to 1867. This pitta inhabits the Burma to Vietnam area.

Family PHILEPITTIDAE 4 species
phileō (Gr) I love   *pitta*, a native name for a small bird (see notes under Family on p. 219). They have a superficial resemblance to pittas, of the family Pittidae; the Latin name for this family is taken to mean 'like a pitta'.

Velvet Asity *Philepitta castanea*
castaneus (New L) chestnut-coloured, derived from *kastanos* (Gr) the chestnut tree; the male is black but in fresh plumage the feathers are tipped with yellow giving the appearance of chestnut-colour; as the tips wear off it becomes a rich black with a slight purple sheen that has been described as a 'velvety black'; the females are more green with some yellow. The asities and false-sunbirds are found only in Madagascar, and this one lives on the eastern side; they total only four species and range from 10 to 15 cm (4 to 6 in) in length; they eat insects, fruit and berries and some like nectar. Asity is the local native name.

Wattled False Sunbird *Neodrepanis coruscans*
neos (Gr) new, recent *drepanē* (Gr) a sickle *drepanis* (Gr) a kind of bird; a reference to its sickle-shaped bill; originally classified as a sunbird in the family Nectariniidae, it has recently been established for various anatomical reasons that this was wrong, hence 'recent' and now known as 'false sunbird' *coruscus* (L) glittering, gleaming; a reference to the iridescent blue plumage: it has a large wattle around the eye though not present in the female. Confined to the forests of Madagascar.

Small-billed False Sunbird *N. hypoxantha*
hupo (Gr) under, beneath, less than usual *xanthos* (Gr) yellow; the breast and the underparts are yellow: it has a small sickle-shaped bill. Inhabiting forests in eastern Madagascar, it is very rare and may now be extinct due to the almost complete destruction of its forest habitat.

Family ACANTHISITTIDAE 3 species
akanthis (Gr) a small bird; this is given in different translations as a goldfinch, a linnet, and a siskin, but the New Zealand Wrens do not appear to have any special relationship with these birds which are all in the family Fringillidae *sittē* (Gr) (Lat *sitta*) a woodpecker, and sometimes translated as a nuthatch; however regardless of these translations *sitte* or *sitta* is frequently used for small creeping birds like nuthatches, e.g. Sittidae. The small family Acanthisittidae has been variously placed taxonomically by different authors and some believe they have a relationship with the Thornbill *Acanthiza*, of Australia. They are small insect-eating birds only about 7·5 to 10 cm (3 to 4 in) long.

Rock Wren *Xenicus gilviventris*
xenos (Gr) a foreigner, a stranger *-icus* (L) suffix meaning belonging to; 'of foreign places'; at the time when this name was given New Zealand would have seemed a very 'far-away' place *gilvus* (L) pale yellow *venter* (L), genitive *ventris*, the belly, stomach; the underparts are a pale grey-brown with some yellow on the flanks. This bird will sometimes eat the fruit of alpine plants in addition to insects; it inhabits the slopes of mountains, and is confined to South Island, New Zealand.

Bush Wren *X. longipes*
longus (L) long *pes* (L) the foot; the feet are large for a bird of this size, particularly the hind toe and claw, which is useful for a bird that

spends a lot of its time climbing up and down trees searching for insects. Inhabiting both North and South Islands, New Zealand.

Rifleman *Acanthisitta chloris*
Acanthisitta, see notes under Family, above   *khloros* (Gr) green or greenish yellow; the upperparts are greenish yellow and the flanks yellow. It has become known as a 'rifleman' because of the peculiar call that sounds like 'zing', and is similar to the sound of someone firing a rifle. It inhabits both Islands of New Zealand and some of the offshore islands, but not the northern part of North Island.

Family   TYRANNIDAE   362 species
tyrannus (L) a monarch, a ruler, particularly a severe and cruel ruler; the tyrant flycatchers have earned this name because of the aggressive behaviour of many of the species, small birds attacking and harassing bigger birds such as birds of prey by diving at their backs. This behaviour is particularly noticeable in the kingbirds of the genus *Tyrannus*, but others in this group are equally aggressive when defending their territories.

This very large family, although similar in general appearance and feeding behaviour to the Old World flycatchers of the family Muscicapidae, anatomically they are different and not considered to be closely related. As their name implies they are insect eaters but the diet is by no means confined to insects; many species will also take fruit, small mammals, reptiles and amphibians; they range in size from about 7·5 to 36 cm (3 to 14 in) and are only found in the Americas, particularly South America.

White-tailed Shrike-Tyrant *Agriornis albicauda*
ager (L), genitive *agri*; a field, open country   or *agrios* (Gr) living in the fields, of animals can mean wild, savage   *ornis* (Gr) a bird, an aggressive bird as the English name shrike-tyrant suggests; the shrike is also known as the butcher bird   *albus* (L) white   *cauda* (L) the tail of an animal. Inhabiting South America.

Spot-billed Ground-Tyrant *Muscisaxicola maculirostris*
musca (L) a fly   *saxum* (L) a large stone or rock   *colo* (L) I inhabit; 'a rock-dwelling flycatcher'   *macula* (L) a mark, a spot   *rostrum* (L) the beak. Inhabiting western South America.

Say's Phoebe *Sayornis saya*
Named by Charles L. Bonaparte in honour of Thomas Say (1787-

1834), the famous American entomologist   *ornis* (Gr) a bird: it is unusual to have a personal name twice in the Latin name and is caused by a change of the generic name. It is said that phoebe, sometimes phebe, is an alteration of pewee influenced by the name Phoebe; pewee is a name used for birds in the genus *Contopus* (see p. 224), and is an imitation of their cry. Inhabiting North America and Mexico.

Vermilion Flycatcher   *Pyrocephalus rubinus*
pyr (Gr), genitive *pyros*, fire   *kephalē* (Gr) the head   *ruber* (L) red *-inus* (L) suffix meaning like; the male has a bright red head and underparts. Inhabiting the southern part of the USA and ranging south through Central America to Argentina.

Cattle Tyrant   *Machetornis rixosus*
makhē (Gr) battle, combat   *makhētēs* (Gr) a fighter   *ornis* (Gr) a bird *rixa* (L) a fight, quarrel   *-osus* (L) suffix meaning full of, prone to; quarrelsome; although this is one of the aggressive tyrants it is best known for its habit of riding on the backs of cattle, sometimes for many miles, searching for insects or hopping to the ground for insects disturbed by the animal. It ranges from Colombia and Venezuela south to Argentina.

Fork-tailed Flycatcher   *Muscivora tyrannus*
musca (L) a fly   *voro* (L) I devour   *tyrannus* (L) a monarch, a ruler, particularly a severe and cruel ruler. An aggressive bird, widespread and ranging from southern Mexico south to Venezuela, Colombia and Brazil; a southern race (i.e. a sub-species) inhabits Paraguay, Argentina, and Uruguay, and in winter moves north as far as the islands of Trinidad and Curacao.

Thick-billed Kingbird   *Tyrannus crassirostris*
Tyrannus, see above   *crassus* (L) thick   *rostrum* (L) the beak; an aggressive bird inhabiting North and Central America. The name kingbird derives from the Latin *tyrannus*, a monarch.

Eastern Kingbird   *T. tyrannus*
One of the most aggressive of the tyrant flycatchers, it must not be thought that this has any connection with the tautonymous name, which could be translated as 'a tyrannical tyrant'; it is true, however, that the two authors, who gave each name separately, were doubtless influenced by the bird's behaviour; the fact that they are now in juxtaposition is because there has been a change in classification (see

p. 13 regarding tautonyms). Widespread, including southern Canada and south to Florida, along the Gulf Coast to Texas, New Mexico, Costa Rica, east to the Guyanas and south through western Brazil to Peru, Bolivia, and northern Argentina.

Grey-capped Flycatcher   *Myiozetetes granadensis*
myia (Gr) a fly   *zēteō* (Gr) I seek, search   *zētētēs* (Gr) a seeker, a searcher   *-ensis* (L) suffix meaning belonging to; named from Granada, in Nicaragua, Central America, it is not confined to that area and ranges south into northern South America.

Boat-billed Flycatcher   *Megarynchus pitangua*
megas (Gr) big   *rhunkhos* (Gr) the beak; it has a long heavy bill hooked at the tip: *pitangus* is a native South American name (Tupi language) for this large-billed flycatcher, inhabiting Mexico and ranging south through most of South America.

Cocos Island Flycatcher   *Nesotriccus ridgwayi*
nēsos (Gr) an island   *trikkos* (Gr) a small bird: named after R. Ridgway (1850-1929), an American ornithologist; he was Curator of Birds at the Smithsonian Institute in Washington from 1880 to 1929. Cocos is an island belonging to Costa Rica and lying just to the south in the Pacific Ocean.

Tropical Pewee   *Contopus cinereus*
kontos (Gr) short   *pous* (Gr) the foot   *cinereus* (L) ash-coloured, grey. Wide distribution in Central and South America including the West Indies and Trinidad; it is named from its call which is a distinct 'pee-wee'.

Eastern Wood Pewee   *C. virens*
virens (L) becoming green, greenish; in Canada it inhabits Manitoba, Ontario, Nova Scotia, and ranges south through eastern USA to Florida, west along the Gulf Coast to Texas, Costa Rica in Central America and south to Colombia and Peru in South America.

Yellow-bellied Flycatcher   *Empidonax flaviventris*
empis (Gr), genitive *empidos*, a gnat, mosquito   *onax = anax* (Gr) a king, lord or master   *flavus* (L) yellow   *venter* (L), genitive *ventris*, the belly; the diet is mostly insects, particularly mosquitos, and they are very skilled at taking them on the wing. Widespread in eastern Canada and ranging south through eastern USA, migrating in winter to Mexico and Panama.

Traill's Flycatcher *E. traillii*
Named by Audubon in honour of Dr Thomas S. Traill (1781-1862), a Scottish doctor and Professor of Medicine at Edinburgh University in 1832; he edited the 8th edition of *The Encyclopaedia Britannica*. This flycatcher is widespread in Alaska and Canada and the USA though not in the south-east; also in Mexico and ranging south to Panama.

Golden-crowned Spadebill *Platyrinchus coronatus*
platus (Gr) flat, wide *rhunkhos* (Gr) the beak, snout; a mis-spelling; it is usually spelt *rhynchus* in a Latin name; the bill is flattened and spade-like *corona* (L) a crown *coronatus* (L) crowned. Inhabiting Central and South America.

Black-headed Tody-Flycatcher *Todirostrum nigriceps*
todus (L) a small bird *rostrum* (L) the beak, snout; 'tody-beaked'; a comparison with the real tody of the family Todidae, a small brightly-coloured insectivorous bird rather like the smaller flycatchers; they are not closely related *niger* (L) black *ceps* (New L) from *caput* (L) the head. Inhabiting Costa Rica to northern South America.

Boat-billed Tody-Tyrant *Microcochlearius josephinae*
mikros (Gr) small *coclearum* (L) a spoon; a reference to the small spoonshaped bill: named after Josephine V. McConnell (born 1906) in 1914, when she was only eight years of age; the daughter of F. V. McConnell (1868-1914), the zoologist, she married Paul L. de Laszlo.

Short-tailed Pygmy-Tyrant *Myiornis ecaudatus*
muia (Gr) a fly *ornis* (Gr) a bird; a reference to its insect-eating habits *ecaudis* (L) without a tail *-atus* (L) provided with; 'not provided with a tail'; a very small almost tailless flycatcher inhabiting Central and South America.

Sharp-tailed Tyrant *Culicivora caudacuta*
culex (L), genitive *culicis*, a gnat, midge *voro* (L) I devour *cauda* (L) the tail *acutus* (L) sharp, pointed. An insect-eating tyrant flycatcher inhabiting South America.

Torrent Tyrannulet *Serpophaga cinerea*
serphos (Gr) a small insect, a gnat *phagein* (Gr) to eat *serpo-* is a mis-spelling of the Greek word *serphos* *cinereus* (L) ash-coloured, grey; a small tyrant flycatcher living near mountain streams in Central and South America.

Mountain Elaenia *Elaenia frantzii*
elaenia (New L) from *elainos* (Gr) of the olive tree, olive-coloured; a reference to the colour of the plumage: named after Dr A. von Frantzius (1821–1877), a German naturalist who was in Brazil from 1849 to 1853, and Costa Rica from 1853 to 1868. Inhabiting mountainous areas in Central and South America.

Bolivian Tyrannulet *Tyranniscus bolivianus*
-iscus (New L) from *-iskos* (Gr) diminutive suffix; 'a small tyrant' *-anus* (L) suffix meaning belonging to; inhabiting Bolivia.

Family OXYRUNCIDAE 1 species
oxus (Gr) sharp, pointed *rhunkhos* (Gr) beak, bill; usually spelt *rhynchus* in a Latin name; it has a strong pointed bill hence the English name is also sharpbill. The classification of this bird has never been satisfactorily settled as it appears to have no close relatives, but the Tyrannidae seem to be the nearest and it has usually been placed in that family; however some ornithologists now prefer to give it a family on its own as in several ways it differs from the tyrant flycatchers, for instance it does not eat insects and the diet seems to consist of fruit and berries.

Sharpbill *Oxyruncus cristatus*
Oxyruncus, see above *cristatus* (L) crested; it has a yellow to scarlet crest, sometimes described as orange. It inhabits Costa Rica and Panama and ranges south through Amazonian Brazil and Paraguay, but the distribution is not necessarily continuous.

Family PIPRIDAE 53 species
pipra (Gr) a bird; some say possibly a woodpecker but these birds, known as manakins, are not closely related to woodpeckers and are not noticeably like them in habits and behaviour. The males are brightly coloured and take part in spectacular aerobatic courtship displays; the diet consists of insects and berries and sometimes small invertebrates.

Golden-headed Manakin *Pipra erythrocephala*
eruthros (Gr) red *kephalē* (Gr) the head; the male has a golden-orange crown; it inhabits Central America and the northern part of South America. The English name manakin is from the Dutch *manneken*, meaning a small man, a dwarf; they are very small birds, about the size of the titmouse.

Red-headed Manakin *P. rubrocapilla*
ruber (L) red *capillus* (L) hair of men, usually the hair of the head, can mean the hair of animals. Inhabiting Peru, Bolivia and Brazil.

Wire-tailed Manakin *Teleonema filicauda*
teleos (Gr) entire, perfect *nēma* (Gr) a thread *filum* (L) a thread *cauda* (L) the tail; a reference to the unusual tail which appears to consist of two long wires or threads as long as the whole body. Inhabiting South America.

White-throated Manakin *Corapipo gutturalis*
korē (Gr) a maiden, a girl; can mean a puppet, a doll *pipō* (Gr) a bird, possibly the woodpecker *pipō* = *pipra* (see notes under Family opposite) a 'puppet-bird' a 'manikin-bird' *guttur* (L) the throat *-alis* (L) suffix meaning relating to; a reference to the white throat. Inhabiting northern South America.

White-bearded Manakin *Manacus manacus*
manacus (New L) from *manneken* (Du) a small man, a dwarf; the white throat gives it the name 'bearded', and this is prominent during the courtship display dance when the white feathers are puffed out. Widely distributed in the north-western part of South America as far south as northern Argentina; also known in Trinidad.

Grey-headed Manakin *Piprites griseiceps*
pipra (Gr) a bird (see notes under Family opposite) *-ites* (Gr) suffix denoting a group, belonging to a group *griseus* (New L) from *greis* (Ger) grey *ceps* (New L) from *caput* (L) the head. Inhabiting Central America.

Thrush-like Manakin *Schiffornis turdinus*
ornis (Gr) a bird; named after Dr M. Schiff (1823-1896), a German zoologist; he was Curator of Birds at the Senckenberg Museum from 1844 to 1853 *turdus* (L) a thrush *-inus* (L) suffix meaning like; a reddish-brown bird about the size of a thrush, it is widespread in Central and South America from Mexico south to Brazil.

Family COTINGIDAE 79 species
cotinga is a name of Tupi origin, a language spoken by South American Indians of the Amazon area; it is derived from two words *coting* (Tupi) wash, and *tinga* (Tupi) white; however the birds in this family are by no means all white, and the name probably originates from the White Bellbird, *Procnias alba*. In fact it is a very varied group with all

kinds of different colours, unusual decorations, and sizes, ranging from about 10 to 46 cm (4 to 18 in); they eat insects, fruit and berries, and nearly all of them live in Central and South America.

Andean Cock-of-the-Rock *Rupicola peruviana*
rupes (L), genitive *rupis*, a rock, cliff *colo* (L) I inhabit, dwell in *-anus* (L) suffix meaning belonging to, 'of Peru'. A spectacular bird with a brilliant orange to red 'cape' surrounding the head and shoulders and a bushy crest. Ground-loving amongst rocks it lives in north-western South America, ranging through Venezuela, Columbia, Ecuador, Peru, and Bolivia.

Guianan Cock-of-the-Rock *R. rupicola*
Another brightly coloured bird with a crest similar to above; it is not confined to the Guianas and is also known in adjacent areas of Brazil and southern Venezuela.

Black-headed Berry-eater *Carpornis melanocephalus*
karpos (Gr) fruit *ornis* (Gr) a bird; a reference to its fondness of fruit and berries *melas* (Gr), genitive *melanos*, black *kephalē* (Gr) the head. Inhabiting south-east Brazil.

Purple-throated Cotinga *Porphyrolaema porphyrolaema*
porphuris (Gr) purple *laimos* (Gr) the throat. Inhabiting the northern part of South America.

Lovely Cotinga *Cotinga amabilis*
Cotinga, see notes under Family, above *amabilis* (L) lovely; a brightly coloured bird inhabiting Central America.

Pompadour Cotinga *Xipholena punicea*
xiphos (Gr) a sword *ōlenē* (Gr) an arm; can mean an armful, a bundle; probably a reference to the peculiarly twisted wing coverts *puniceus* (L) reddish, purple-coloured. Living in Venezuela and ranging south to the Amazon area. The male has brilliant ornamental plumage, and for this reason has been given the name Pompadour Cotinga after Madame de Pompadour, the famous French courtesan.

Yellow-billed Cotinga *Carpodectes antoniae*
karpos (Gr) fruit *dēktēs* (Gr) a biter: named in honour of Antonia Ridgway in 1884, the daughter of R. Ridgway (1850-1929), the Curator of Birds at the Smithsonian Institute in Washington. It inhabits Central America.

COTINGIDAE

Green and Black Fruiteater *Pipreola riefferii*
pipra (Gr) a bird   *-olus* (L) diminutive suffix: named after Rieffer in 1840, his initials and dates do not appear to be recorded; he formed a collection from Bogata, Texas, in 1840. This fruiteater inhabits the northern part of South America.

Red-crested Fruiteater *Ampelion rubrocristatus*
ampelos (Gr) a vine, hence *ampeliōn* (Gr) a singing bird that frequents vines   *ruber* (L) red   *cristatus* (L) crested. This bird, partial to grapes, inhabits the northern part of South America.

Scaled Fruiteater *Ampelioides tschudii*
ampelos (Gr) see above   *-oides* (New L) from *eidos* (Gr) apparent shape, resemblance: named after J. J. Baron von Tschudi (1818–1889), a Swiss ornithologist who was collecting in Peru from 1838 to 1842. Inhabiting the northern part of South America.

Black-capped Becard *Pachyramphus marginatus*
pakhus (Gr) thick, can mean great, large   *rhamphos* (Gr) a beak, specially a hooked beak as in birds of prey; a reference to the large beak, hooked at the tip, which is useful for an insectivorous bird eating large insects; this bird eats grasshoppers and beetles and similar insects, rather than fruit   *margo* (L), genitive *marginis*, border, margin   *marginatus* (L) having a margin; a reference to the white-tipped tail and the feathers tipped with iridescent blue; the female has tawny margins on the wings. Becard is a name derived from *bécarde* (Fr) from *bec* (Fr) a beak; it is usually applied to all the 15 species in the genus *Pachyramphus* which are big-billed birds. They live in the northern part of South America and in some cases also Central America.

Black-tailed Tityra *Tityra cayana*
Tityrus (L) was the name of a shepherd in the 1st Eclogue of Virgil   *cayana* refers to Cayenne, in French Guiana, a name given by Linnaeus in 1766. It ranges from Guyana, Venezuela, and Colombia in the north, southwards through Peru, part of Brazil, and Bolivia and Paraguay.

Long-wattled Umbrellabird *Cephalopterus penduliger*
kephalē (Gr) the head   *pteron* (Gr) feathers; 'head-feathers'; it has a spectacular canopy of feathers on the head which resembles a kind of umbrella   *pendulus* (L) hanging down   *gero* (L) I carry; a reference to the pendulus feathered wattle hanging from under the neck which

can be up to 46 cm (18 in) long; the length of the whole bird ranges from 41 to 48 cm (16 to 19 in). Inhabiting the western slopes of the Andes in Columbia and Ecuador.

Capuchin Monkbird *Perissocephalus tricolor*
perissos (Gr) odd; in addition to meaning odd numbers it can also mean strange, remarkable   *kephalē* (Gr) the head; a reference to the naked head above a collar of feathers resembling a monk, hence Capuchin Monkbird   *tricolor* (L) three colours; the plumage is brown with a naked blue and grey head. Inhabiting the north-western part of South America.

White Bellbird *Procnias alba*
According to the Greek legend Proknē, daughter of Pandion, was transformed by the gods into a swallow, but this does not mean that this bird is closely related to the swallows or resembles them; in the eighteenth and nineteenth centuries a number of names taken from classical mythology were used for scientific names without any particular significance for the animal concerned   *albus* (L) white. Inhabiting the north-eastern part of South America, from the Guyanas to Amazonia.

Three-wattled Bellbird *P. tricarunculata*
tri- (L) three   *caruncula* (L) a small piece of flesh, a wattle   *-atus* (L) suffix meaning provided with; it has three remarkable long thin wattles growing round the mouth. Inhabiting most of Central America.

Family PHYTOTOMIDAE 3 species
phuton (Gr) a plant, tree   *tomos* (Gr) a cut, a piece cut off. This small family, all in the same genus, are closely related to the Cotingidae; they have a wasteful habit of cutting leaves, buds, fruit and twigs from trees or plants most of which remains uneaten, and to aid this habit they have a powerful finch-like beak with serrated edges; naturally they are unpopular with farmers and gardeners. Colourful birds with a harsh call, their length is about 18 cm (7 in).

Peruvian Plantcutter *Phytotoma raimondii*
Named after Prof A. Raimondi (1825-1890), an Italian zoologist and explorer who lived in Peru from 1850 to 1870; he was appointed a Director of the Lima Museum in 1877. This plantcutter inhabits Peru.

Reddish Plantcutter *P. rutila*
rutilus (L) red, ruddy; a fairly common and colourful bird inhabiting Argentina and Patagonia.

Family MENURIDAE 2 species
mēnē (Gr) the moon   *oura* (Gr) the tail; the elaborate lyre-shaped tail is formed by the outer pair of feathers, about 50 cm (20 in) long, forming the frame of the lyre; these feathers, a light brown, are decorated with golden bars shaped like crescent moons. Superficially rather like pheasants, the lyrebirds appear to have no really close relatives, but can be connected in some respects with the scrub-birds (below); their diet is mostly insects and worms, but may include crustaceans and molluscs. Famous in Australia, where they live, they appear on one of the Australian postage stamps.

Albert's Lyrebird *Menura alberti*
Named in honour of Prince Albert (1819-1861), Prince Consort of Queen Victoria. It inhabits the forests of south-eastern Australia.

Superb Lyrebird *M. novaehollandiae*
novaehollandiae (New L) New Holland; this is a name that has occasionally been used for Java since the Dutch arrived there in 1596. In 1769 Australia, undiscovered by the Western World, was known as Terra Australis Incognitis based on reports from Marco Polo, the Venetian traveller (1254-1324). Later certain areas and possibly the whole continent, including Tasmania, became known as New Holland.

Family ATRICHORNITHIDAE 2 species
atrikhos (Gr) hairless; a reference to the absence of bristles round the gape   *ornis* (Gr), genitive *ornithos*, a bird. Known as Scrub-Birds because they live mostly on the ground among the stunted bushes and brushwood where they hunt for insects, worms, crustaceans and seeds.

Noisy Scrub-Bird *Atrichornis clamosus*
clamo (L) I cry out, I shout aloud   *clamosus* (L) full of clamour, noisy; as the name suggests, the call is loud and penetrating. Very rare, and possibly extinct, it inhabits south-western Australia.

Rufous Scrub-Bird *A. rufescens*
rufus (L) red, ruddy   *-escens* (L) suffix denoting somewhat; reddish; the plumage is mostly rufous and pale brown. Inhabiting south-eastern Queensland and north-eastern New South Wales, Australia.

Family ALAUDIDAE 76 species
alauda (L) the lark. This is a family of rather inconspicuous almost drab brownish birds ranging from 12·5 to 23 cm (5 to 9 in) long; they have become famous because of their sweet song, particularly the skylark, which sings while hovering some 9 to 12 m (30 to 40 ft) above the ground. The distribution is almost world-wide, although only two species are known in America and two in Australia; their diet consists of insects, worms, small crustaceans and occasionally berries.

Rufous-naped Lark *Mirafra africana*
mirus (L) wonderful; African 'wonder-bird'. Inhabiting Africa south of the Sahara, particularly the east and southern parts; not often seen to the west of Cameroon.

Singing Bush-lark *M. javanica*
Named from Java, it is widespread including Africa and ranging through India, Burma, Malaysia, New Guinea, and Australia.

Desert Lark *Ammomanes deserti*
ammos (Gr) sand, a sandy place   *manēs* (Gr) a type of cup; a reference to the form of the nest which is a cup scraped in the ground   *desertus* (L) a solitary place, the desert. Ranging from the Sahara in Africa to Afghanistan, southern Eurasia, and India.

Thick-billed Lark *Rhamphocoris clot-bey*
rhamphos (Gr) a beak, bill   *corium* (L) leather; 'leather-billed': named after Dr A. Clot Bey (1795-1868) in 1850; he was an author and zoologist who spent some time in Egypt. A recent ruling states that hyphens may not be used in scientific names but this one will probably remain unchanged. This lark inhabits southern Eurasia including part of North Africa.

Calandra Lark *Melanocorypha calandra*
melas (Gr), genitive *melanos*, black   *koruphos* (Gr) a small bird   *kalandra* (Gr) a kind of lark. Inhabiting Europe and Asia, and northern Africa.

Short-toed Lark *Calandrella cinerea*
-ellus (L) diminutive suffix; 'a small lark'; one of the smaller larks, being only about 12·5 cm (5 in) in length   *cinereus* (L) ash-coloured; the plumage is usually pale brown with dark marking but there can be a variation with some grey, making it more ash-coloured. The birds in this genus have a shorter hind toe than other larks. This species is

widespread, ranging from Spain and North Africa east to Mongolia; South Africa on eastern side including Uganda, Ethiopia, part of Arabia; winter range can be the Sahara, Sudan, and east to India.

Stark's Short-toed Lark *C. starki*
Named in 1902 after Dr A. C. Stark (1846-1899), a naturalist and author who was in South Africa from 1886 to 1899. This species inhabits Africa.

Dupont's Lark *Chersophilus duponti*
khersos (Gr) dry land, barren land *philos* (Gr) loved, pleasing; 'desert-loving': named after L. Dupont (c. 1820-1846), a French naturalist, collector, and dealer in animals. It inhabits arid areas of northern Africa.

Crested Lark *Galerida cristata*
galerum (L) a helmet-like cap for the head *galerita avis* (L) the crested lark *cristatus* (L) crested; it has a prominent crest of brownish feathers. Widespread, ranging from Europe (though not Great Britain) east to Korea and south to the Himalayas and Arabia, northern Africa, Sudan, and east to Guinea.

Thekla's Lark *G. theklae*
Named in memory of Thekla Brehm in 1858, who died that year at the age of 26; she was the daughter of Dr Christian Ludwig Brehm (1787-1864), the German zoologist. Inhabiting Spain, the Balearic Islands, North African coast, up the Nile to the mountains of Ethiopia, Somaliland and Kenya.

Wood Lark *Lullula arborea*
Lullula is a coined word and said to be derived from the bird's call, which sounds like 'lu-lu-lu', a familiar phrase in the song *arbor* (L) a tree *arboreus* (L) pertaining to trees; this does not seem to be a suitable name for this bird, which nests on the ground, feeds on the ground, and prefers to live on hillsides where there are few trees, and other bare areas; however it frequents the edges of woods at times and has been seen to perch in the trees. It inhabits Europe, including Britain and Scandinavia, and ranges east to the Ural Mountains and south to Spain, Italy, and North Africa.

Skylark *Alauda arvensis*
alauda (L) the lark *arvum* (L) a field, cultivated land *-ensis* (L) suffix meaning belonging to. Inhabiting Europe except the extreme

north and ranging from Britain across Asia to Japan and the Bering Straits, south to North Africa and ranges east, south of the Caspian Sea to Sinkiang. It has been introduced to other parts of the world.

Horned Lark   *Eremophila alpestris*
eremos (Gr) a desolate place, a wilderness   *philos* (Gr) loved, pleasing *alpestris* (New L) pertaining to the Alps, high mountains; it frequents desert areas and rocky alpine slopes up to 5,180 m (17,000 ft). It has two tufts of black feathers that look like horns. The only lark in America apart from the Skylark which has been introduced, it also inhabits Eurasia from Scandinavia ranging east to Siberia, North Africa east through to Middle East to mountain ranges of southern Asia including the Himalayas, India, and Burma.

Family   HIRUNDINIDAE   74 species
hirundo (L) a swallow; genitive *hirundinis*. Superficially the swallows resemble the swifts, both in appearance and manner of flying, but they are not closely related; the swallows and martins, however, are in the same family, and there is very little difference between them; there is one martin in Britain that is called a swallow in America. The House Martin can be distinguished from the swallows by its white rump and the tail which is less forked. A very widespread family known almost throughout the world, though not in New Zealand. They eat insects, which they catch on the wing, and they only come down to the ground to collect mud for their nests.

African River Martin   *Pseudochelidon eurystomina*
pseudēs (Gr) false, deceptive   *khelidōn* (Gr) a swallow   *eurus* (Gr) wide *stoma* (Gr) the mouth   *-inus* (L) suffix meaning like, converting noun to adjective; 'wide-mouthed'; it flies with a wide gape to assist in catching flying insects. This swallow-like bird has been a problem for ornithologists with regard to its place in classification, and at one time it was placed with the wood swallows in the family Artamidae; some authors give it a family on its own, Pseudochelidonidae, but recent opinion seems to favour putting it with the true swallows, as it is given here; because of this problem its Latin name was given as *Pseudochelidon*, 'deceptive swallow'. As recently as 1968 another species has been found in Thailand. The African species frequents the banks of the Lower Congo and Ubangi Rivers in West Africa.

White-eyed River Martin   *Ps. sirintarae*
This rare river martin was discovered in 1968 by the late Kitti Thon-

glongya (died 1974), who also discovered the Hog-nosed Bat *Craseonycteris thonglongyai* and named in his honour by his friend J. Edwards Hill of the British Museum (Natural History). The river-martin was found in a marsh in the same area, Nakhon Sawan, in central Thailand, and named by Dr Boonsong Lekagul in honour of HRH Princess Sirindhorn Thepratanasuda, a daughter of King Bhumibol Adulyadej—'for her very keen interest in natural history'.

Tree Swallow *Tachycineta bicolor*
takhus (Gr) fast, swift *kineō* (Gr) I move *kinētēs* (Gr) a mover; strictly, one that sets going a movement *bicolor* (L) of two colours; the upper parts are blue and bronze-green. It frequents open wooded country and usually nests in tree hollows. It inhabits North America and ranges north as far as Alaska, and south to Panama and Cuba.

Caribbean Martin *Progne dominicensis*
Prognē = *Proknē* (Gr); according to a legend, Proknē, daughter of Pandion, was transformed by the gods into a swallow *-ensis* (L) suffix meaning belonging to, usually a locality; named from the Dominican Republic, it inhabits the Caribbean area and Central America.

Blue and White Swallow *Notiochelidon cyanoleuca*
notios (Gr) southern *khelidōn* (Gr) the swallow *kuaneos* (Gr) blue *leukos* (Gr) white. Inhabiting Central and South America.

African Sand Martin *Riparia paludicola*
ripa (L) the bank of a stream or river *riparius* (L) one that frequents the banks of streams *palus* (L), genitive *paludis*, a marsh, swamp *colo* (L) I inhabit; it makes its nest by tunnelling into the banks of streams or other sandbanks. Inhabiting Africa south of Sudan and Ethiopia, but not Zaire; Madagascar, southern India, the Burma-Vietnam area, Malaysia, and the Philippines.

Sand Martin *R. riparia*
In the USA this bird is known as the Bank Swallow, which confuses the problem about the difference between a martin and a swallow (see notes under Family opposite). Inhabiting North, Central, and South America, Eurasia including the British Isles, Africa and Madagascar, India, the Burma-Vietnam area, Malaysia and Japan.

Crag Martin *Hirundo rupestris*
hirundo (L) a swallow *rupes* (L) a rock, cliff *rupestris* (New L) living

among rocks. Inhabiting southern Europe, Mediterranean islands, the northern part of Africa, Asia Minor and ranging east to western China and southern India.

Common or Barn Swallow *H. rustica*
rusticus (L) belonging to the country, rural. Probably the best known swallow with an almost world-wide distribution: North, Central and South America, Eurasia including Great Britain, Africa, India, Burma to Vietnam, Malaysia, New Guinea, and northern Australia.

Cliff Swallow *Petrochelidon pyrrhonota*
petra (Gr) a rock   *khelidōn* (Gr) a swallow   *purrhos* = *purros* (Gr) red, flame-coloured   *noton* (Gr) the back; a reference to the upper tail coverts which are reddish. Although by nature it originally built the nest on rock and cliff faces, nowadays many cliff swallows prefer to build under the eaves of houses and barns. Inhabiting North, Central, and South America.

House Martin *Delichon urbica*
Delichon is simply an anagram of *chelidon* (= *khelidōn* Gr) a swallow *urbicus* (L) pertaining to a city; it builds the nest under eaves of houses, on bridges, on sea cliffs, or inland cliffs. Inhabiting Eurasia including Great Britain, and Spain; ranging south to northern Africa, east to Asia Minor and the Himalayas, and the Thailand-Vietnam area.

Blue Rough-winged Swallow *Psalidoprocne pristoptera*
psalis (Gr), genitive *psalidos*, a single bladed knife or razor, but can mean a pair of shears; a reference to the forked tail   *Prognē* = *Proknē* (Gr); according to a legend, Proknē, daughter of Pandion, was transformed by the gods into a swallow   *pristēs* (Gr) a saw or file   *pteron* (Gr) feathers, can mean wings; a reference to the serrated outer primary feathers on the wings; hence 'rough-winged' swallow; this is thought to assist the bird when clinging to vertical walls or cliffs. Inhabiting Eritrea and Ethiopia.

Family MOTACILLIDAE 54 species
The family name, which is derived from the generic name *Motacilla*, is misleading; *Motacilla* does not mean wagtail, from *motator* (L) a mover, and *cilla*, a tail, because *cilla* does not mean a tail, and in fact there is no such word. There is a very rare word *cillo* (L) I move, but this would not make sense; Varro would not use a name that meant 'moving mover'. *Motacilla* is a coined word, using *-illa* (L) a diminu-

tive suffix, and means 'little mover'; when Varro explained this name he said '*Quod semper movet caudam*', when he might have been expected to say '*Quod semper movet cillam*', but he did not. This wrong interpretation probably started as long ago as the fourteenth century, and still persists today among some ornithologists; for example we are quite happy to interpret *Haliaeetus albicilla* as the White-tailed Eagle, and in fact the specific name was supposed to mean 'white-tailed', but it does not. Marcus Terentius Varro (116-27 B.C.) was a Roman scholar and author of a great number of books; a genus of American tropical shrubs, *Varronia*, is named after him.

The wagtails and pipits comprise a widespread family ranging from the Americas through Eurasia and Africa to Australia. Sparrow-sized birds, some with tails nearly as long as the body, their diet is varied and consists mostly of insects but may include worms, small crustaceans and some seeds.

Forest Wagtail   *Dendronanthus indicus*   (or *Motacilla*)
dendron (Gr) a tree   *anthos* (Gr) a small bird like the yellow wagtail -*icus* (L) suffix meaning belonging to, Indian; although named from India, it also inhabits Siberia, Manchuria, Korea, northern China, and Assam. The only wagtail that wags its tail sideways instead of up and down.

White Wagtail   *Motacilla alba alba*
Motacilla, see notes under Family, above   *albus* (L) white: the forehead, sides of the head, and underparts are white, the upperparts are grey with a black crown, wings and tail. Widespread in Eurasia including Iceland and Great Britain, and ranging east to Japan; the northern part of Africa, India, Burma to Malaysia.

Pied Wagtail   *M. a. yarrellii*
This sub-species, and *M. a. alba*, above, are very similar; the Pied Wagtail can be distinguished from the White Wagtail by its black back: it is named after William Yarrell (1784-1856), the English ornithologist and author; he wrote *The History of British Birds* which was published in 1843. Distribution similar to White Wagtail.

Grey Wagtail   *M. cinerea*
cinereus (L) ash-coloured; although known as the Grey Wagtail it has distinctly yellow underparts rather like the Yellow Wagtail, so it can be mistaken for this bird, but the back is darker and the male has a black throat. Inhabiting Eurasia including the British Isles but not

Iceland or northern Scandinavia; ranging east to Kamchatka and Japan and migrating south to northern Africa, the Burma-Vietnam area, Malaysia, Indonesia, and New Guinea.

Mountain Wagtail *M. clara*
clarus (L) bright, shining. Inhabiting the mountains of Africa.

Yellow Wagtail *M. flava*
flavus (L) yellow. Widespread in Eurasia including England and Wales but not Ireland, Scotland, Iceland, and northern Siberia; ranging east to the oriental region, Malaysia, Indonesia, and migrating south to northern Africa.

Rosy-breasted Longclaw *Macronyx ameliae*
makros (Gr) long   *onux* (Gr) a claw; all birds in the family Motacillidae have a rather long hind claw, but those in the genus *Macronyx* have this claw unusually long: named in honour of Amélie, the Marquise de Tarragon (fl 1840); she married the Marquis Leone de Tarragon (1813-1896), a French zoologist. It inhabits East Africa ranging from Kenya through Tanzania to southern Natal.

Yellow-throated Longclaw *M. croceus*
croceus (L) pertaining to saffron; can mean saffron-coloured, yellow, golden; the chin and throat are bright yellow, and the hind toe is exceptionally long, more than 4 cm ($1\frac{1}{2}$ in). Widespread in Africa, from Senegal and Angola in the west, and south to Natal.

Tawny Pipit *Anthus campestris*
anthos (Gr) a small bird like the yellow wagtail   *campus* (L) open level land, a plain   *campestris* (L) pertaining to a plain, a field. The pipits in this genus also have long hind claws, like those in the genus *Macronyx*, above, but not so long as the latter. Living in open, dry and sandy country it inhabits Eurasia, but not Great Britain, Scandinavia and other northern parts; ranging south to Africa, and east to India and the Burma-Vietnam area.

Richard's or New Zealand Pipit *A. novaeseelandiae*
novaeseelandiae (New L) New Zealand. The name probably refers to A. Richard (1794-1852) a botanist, and son of the famous botanist Prof L. C. M. Richard. Inhabiting eastern Eurasia, from Siberia south through India, Malaysia, New Guinea, Australia, Tasmania and New Zealand; also widespread in Africa.

Sprague's Pipit *A. spragueii*
Named after I. Sprague (1811-1895) who also has the botanical genus *Spraguea* named after him; he was an American botanist and worked at the New York Botanical Gardens. Inhabiting North and Central America.

Family CAMPEPHAGIDAE 72 species
kampē (Gr) a caterpillar *phagein* (Gr) to eat; the Cuckoo-Shrikes are largely insect eaters, but they will also take berries and fruit, and have been known to eat small lizards. Although in some respects they resemble cuckoos and also shrikes they are not closely related to either; varying in size from 12·5 to 30 cm (5 to 12 in), they inhabit tropical areas but not the Americas.

Ground Cuckoo-Shrike *Pteropodocys maxima*
pteron (Gr) a wing *pous* (Gr), genitive *podos*, a foot *oxus* (Gr) sharp, pointed; can mean quick, swift; 'swift on wing and foot'; largely ground-living, where they hunt amongst the undergrowth for insects, they also fly well and roost high in the trees *maximus* (L) the largest; it is the largest bird in the family, and may measure more than 30 cm (12 in). Inhabiting Australia, but not in the north-western parts.

White-rumped Cuckoo-Shrike *Coracina leucopygia*
korax (Gr), genitive *korakos*, a raven or crow; anything hooked like a raven's beak *-inus* (L) suffix meaning like; 'raven-like', a reference to the hooked bill, similar to the hooked bill of the shrike, in the family Laniidae *leukos* (Gr) white *pugē* (Gr) the rump, buttocks. Inhabiting Celebes.

Black-faced Cuckoo-Shrike *C. novaehollandiae*
novaehollandiae (New L) New Holland; it was named from Tasmania (see p. 231). This cuckoo-shrike has a black forehead, face, and throat. Widespread in the oriental area, ranging from India to New Guinea, some Pacific islands, Australia, Tasmania, and sometimes seen in New Zealand.

Long-billed Greybird *C. tenuirostris*
tenuis (L) thin, slender *rostrum* (L) the beak, bill. The name Greybird is used for some of the cuckoo-shrikes because of their rather dull grey, black, and white plumage. Inhabiting New Guinea, the Solomon Islands, and Australia.

Black-and-White Triller *Lalage melanoleuca*
Lalage (L) the name of a girl, possibly from *lallo* (L) I sing a lullaby; this name and the English name Triller is a reference to the melodious song *melas* (Gr) black *leukos* (Gr) white. Inhabiting part of the Philippines.

White-winged Triller *L. sueurii*
Named after C. A. Le Sueur (1778-1846), a French zoologist; he was a Director of the Natural History Museum in Le Havre. This triller inhabits the Lesser Sundas, New Guinea, and Australia.

Black Cuckoo-Shrike *Campephaga flava*
kampē (Gr) a caterpillar *phagein* (Gr) to eat *flavus* (L) yellow; the male is black and sometimes has some yellow plumage on the shoulders; the female is olive-brown relieved with yellow margins on the wings and tail and black and yellow bars on the underparts. Inhabiting Sudan, Ethiopia, and Somalia and ranging south to Angola.

Red-shouldered Cuckoo-Shrike *C. phoenicea*
phoinix (Gr), genitive *phoinikos*, purple-red, crimson; the male is blue-black with bright red shoulders. Widespread in Africa particularly Congo.

Wattled Cuckoo-Shrike *C. lobata*
lobos (Gr) a lobe *lobatus* (New L) lobed; it has wattles consisting of yellow lobes under the eyes. A rare and unusual cuckoo-shrike of tropical Africa.

Short-billed Minivet *Pericrocotus brevirostris*
peri (Gr) around, roundabout: hence *peri-* (New L) all around *crocota* (L) a saffron-coloured court dress *brevis* (L) short *rostrum* (L) the beak, bill; the birds in this genus are not all yellow. The origin of the name Minivet is obscure, but certainly it suggests something small, and these birds are the smaller ones in the family. This one breeds in the Himalayas and ranges south to India and the Burma-Vietnam area.

Scarlet Minivet *P. flammeus*
flammeus (L) flaming; can mean flame coloured, fiery red; the male and female make a very colourful pair; the male with a black head and upperparts and a bright red chest and belly, and the female with a grey crown and upperparts and a bright yellow breast and belly.

Inhabiting southern India and Sri Lanka, Bangladesh, and the Burma-Vietnam area, and Malaysia.

Common Wood Shrike *Tephrodornis pondicerianus*
tephrōdēs (Gr) ash-coloured   *ornis* (Gr) a bird   *-anus* (L) suffix meaning belonging to; named from Pondicherry in south-east India, it also inhabits the Burma-Vietnam area and southern China.

Family   PYCNONOTIDAE   118 species
puknos (Gr) compact; of plumage thick, close   *nōton* (Gr) the back; the birds in this family, known as Bulbuls, have thick sometimes tangled-looking plumage on the back, but typically rather sparse on the nape of the neck where there are hair-like feathers. They are smallish birds, varying from the size of a sparrow to that of a blackbird, with a rather sombre plumage occasionally relieved by patches of white, yellow or red; the diet consists of insects, fruit and berries. The name bulbul is considered to be of Persian and Arabic origin and may be imitative, though the song is pleasant and in some cases melodious.

Finch-billed Bulbul *Spizixos canifrons*
spiza (Gr) a finch   *ixos* (Gr) mistletoe; can mean the mistletoe berry *canus* (L) white, hoary   *frons* (L) forehead, brow. Inhabiting Assam, the Burma-Vietnam area and southern China.

Slender-billed Greenbul *Andropadus gracilirostris*
anēr (Gr), genitive *andros*, a man, as opposed to a woman; however can be used to mean everyman, everyone   *pados* (Gr) a tree; 'man of the trees'   *gracilis* (L) slender, thin   *rostrum* (L) the beak, bill. Inhabiting Africa.

Red-eyed Bulbul *Pycnonotus nigricans*
Pycnonotus, see above, under Family   *nigricans* (L) blackish, swarthy; the upperparts are sooty brown with a blackish head and throat; the red eye stands out clearly against this background. Inhabiting the western part of southern Africa but not along the southern coastal belt.

Yellow-throated Bulbul *P. xantholaemus*
xanthos (Gr) yellow   *laimos* (Gr) the throat. Inhabiting southern India.

Joyful Greenbul *Chlorocichla laetissima*
khloros (Gr) green   *kikhlē* (Gr) a bird like the thrush   *laeto* (L) I make

joyful, I gladden; *laetissima*, very joyful; a reference to the melodious song; most bulbuls are good singers, and for that reason are popular garden birds in Africa and the East, although they can be destructive. Inhabiting Africa.

Yellow-striped Greenbul   *Phyllastrephus flavostriatus*
phullon (Gr) a leaf   *strephō* (Gr) I twist; an obscure name, and not explained in the ornithological records in the British Museum (Natural History)   *flavus* (L) yellow   *stria* (L) a furrow, channel   *striatus* (New L) striped. Inhabiting the central parts of Africa.

Terrestrial Bulbul or Brownbul   *P. terrestris*
terra (L) earth, ground   *terrestris* (L) belonging to the land; unlike the behaviour of bulbuls as a whole, it frequently descends to the ground in search of insects and grubs. Inhabiting south-eastern Africa.

Dwarf Bearded Bulbul   *Criniger finschi*
crinis (L) hair   *gero* (Gr) I bear, I carry; it has bristles under the chin and on the nape of the neck there are sparse hair-like feathers: named after Dr F. H. O. Finsch (1839-1917), a Dutch zoologist who worked in the Natural History Museum in Leyden from 1897 to 1904; he was in New Guinea from 1879 to 1882. This is a very small bulbul inhabiting Sumatra and Borneo.

Oriental Brown-eared Bulbul   *Hypsipetes flavala*
hupsipetēs (Gr) high-flying, soaring   *flavus* (L) yellow   *ala* (L) a wing; the upper parts including the crest are brown and there is a yellow patch on the wing. Inhabiting the Himalayas and ranging east to Yunnan and south through the Burma-Vietnam area to Malaysia.

McClelland's Bulbul   *H. mcclellandii*
Named after Dr J. McClelland (1805-1875), a Scottish zoologist who collected and studied in India. This bulbul inhabits the Burma-Vietnam area.

Family   IRENIDAE   14 species
named after Eirēnē, the goddess of peace, derived from *eirēnē* (Gr) peace, a time of peace. These birds are variously known as Ioras, Leafbirds, and Fairy Bluebirds; they are colourful birds of the oriental forests, the predominant colour being blue. The size ranges from 12·5 to 27 cm (5 to 10½ in) and the diet is mostly fruit and berries but also some insects and nectar.

Common Iora *Aegithina tiphia*
aigithos (Gr) a hedge sparrow   *-inus* (L) suffix meaning like; the four birds in this genus are small, about the size of a hedge sparrow, say 15 cm (6 in), but they are certainly more colourful   *tiphē* (Gr) an insect, perhaps a kind of beetle. The origin of the name Iora is obscure, but doubtless a local oriental native name. Inhabiting India, the Burma-Vietnam area, and Malaysia.

Golden-fronted Leafbird *Chloropsis aurifrons*
khloros (Gr) green   *opsis* (Gr) appearance, aspect; the predominant colour is green   *aurum* (L) gold   *aureus* (L) golden, colour of gold   *frons* (L) forehead, brow; it has a bright orange-yellow patch on the forehead. Inhabiting the Himalayan foothills, the southern part of India including Sri Lanka, the Burma-Vietnam area and Malaysia.

Blue-winged Leafbird *C. cochinchinensis*
-ensis (L) suffix meaning belonging to, usually a locality; what was known as Cochinchina in the seventeenth century is now the central and southern part of Vietnam; although named from that area it ranges from India through the Burma-Vietnam area to Sumatra.

Fairy Bluebird *Irena puella*
Named after Eirēnē, the goddess of peace, derived from *eirēnē* (Gr) peace, a time of peace   *puella* (L) a girl, a maiden; in this case used to suggest something pretty. A beautiful bird, as the English name suggests, and one of the largest in the family, at about 25·5 to 28 cm (10 to 11 in); it is widespread in the Oriental region ranging from India to Malaysia.

Family PRIONOPIDAE 9 species
priōn (Gr) a saw   *ops*, from *opsis* (Gr) appearance; a reference to those in the genus *Prionops* which have a serrated edge to the bill, like a saw. Some authors include this group, the Helmet Shrikes, with the Shrikes or Butcher Birds in the family Laniidae, and there remains some controversy among ornithologists as to how to place the shrikes taxonomically. A third group, the Vanga Shrikes in the family Vangidae, are restricted to Madagascar.

They are all rather like small birds of prey, ranging from 15 to 36 cm (6 to 14 in) long, with the typical hooked beak, and they are all carnivorous, the diet including insects, small reptiles, small mammals and birds. Some are known as Butcher Birds on account of their habit of impaling their prey on a suitable spike or thorn which they will return to later, and which also acts as a vice to hold the animal while they dismember it for eating.

Rüppell's White-crowned Shrike *Eurocephalus rueppelli*
euros (Gr) width, breadth   *kephalē* (Gr) the head; a reference to the rather thick neck and head, the latter having a white crown: named after Dr W. P. E. S. Rüppell (1794-1884), a zoologist who was in North Africa from 1822 to 1827, and in Abyssinia (now Ethiopia) from 1830 to 1834; he collected for the Senckenberg Museum. Inhabiting the eastern part of Africa.

Yellow-crested Helmet Shrike *Prionops alberti*
priōn (Gr) a saw   *ops*, from *opsis* (Gr) appearance; a reference to the serrated edge of the bill, like a saw: named after King Albert (1875-1934), King of the Belgians from 1909 to 1934. Inhabiting Africa. The name 'helmet' refers to the colouring of the head and neck.

Long-crested Helmet Shrike *P. plumata*
pluma (L) a small soft feather   *plumatus* (L) feathered; a reference to the white forward-pointing crest on the head. Widespread in Africa as far south as Angola, Zimbabwe, and Mozambique.

Family   LANIIDAE   70 species
lanio (L) I tear, I rend in pieces   *lanius* (L) a butcher; a reference to their unpleasant habit of impaling their prey on a spike or thorn, even while still alive, to hold it while they dismember it for eating; this has led to the name Butcher Bird which is sometimes used.

Pringle's Puff-back *Dryoscopus pringlii*
drus (Gr), genitive *druos*, a tree   *skopeō* (Gr) I look; a reference to its habit of hunting for larvae among the trees. Named after Col Sir J. W. Pringle (1863-1938), who was Chief Inspector of Railways in Uganda in 1891 and 1892. Inhabiting eastern Africa. It has a soft downy rump and back and these feathers can be 'puffed out' by the male when excited.

Boubou *Laniarius aethiopicus*
laniarius (L) pertaining to a butcher; (see notes under Family above) *-icus* (L) suffix meaning belonging to; although named from Ethiopia it is widespread almost throughout Africa. The origin of the name Boubou is obscure as it does not seem to be imitative and it is not known to be a native name.

Fulleborn's Black Boubou   *L. fulleborni*
Named after Dr F. Fulleborn (1866-1933), a German zoologist. He was in German East Africa from 1896 to 1900 and a Professor at Hamburg University in 1919. Inhabiting Africa.

Fiery-breasted Bush Shrike   *Malaconotus cruentus*
malakos (Gr) soft   *nōton* (Gr) the back; a reference to the soft downy rump and back   *cruentus* (L) spotted or stained with blood; it has a bright red breast and throat. Inhabiting Africa.

Lagden's Bush Shrike   *M. lagdeni*
Named after Sir G. Y. Lagden (1851-1934), an English naturalist who was in the Gold Coast in 1883 and Commissioner in Basutoland from 1893 to 1901; at that time a British Colony, it is now known as Lesotho and is an independent nation of South Africa. This Bush Shrike inhabits eastern Zaire.

Red-backed Shrike   *Lanius collurio*
lanius (L) a butcher (see notes under Family opposite)   *kolluriōn* (Gr) a bird, possibly a thrush; the shrikes are not closely related to the thrushes, in the subfamily Turdinae, but could be similar in appearance in some cases. This is one of the shrikes that keeps a 'larder' by impaling its prey on spikes or thorns, which it can return to later; it is widespread in Eurasia, ranging from Scandinavia and Russia south to northern Spain, the Mediterranean area, and east through Asia Minor, Palestine, Iran, to Siberia, Mongolia, Manchuria to western China; some species migrate to Africa, Arabia, and India.

Northern Shrike   *L. excubitor*
excubitor (L) one who keeps watch, a sentinel; a reference to its habit of sitting on a post or branch of a tree making no effort to be concealed, and watching for possible prey or for an intruder on its territory, which it would immediately attack and drive off; other shrikes show similar behaviour. Widespread in both Old and New Worlds; Alaska, Hudson Bay, Quebec, migrating south to California, and Texas; Eurasia from Spain east through Siberia to Kamchatka, south to Iran, Arabia and India, Eurasian birds winter in Mediterranean area and northern Africa.

Tibetan or Grey-backed Shrike   *L. tephronotus*
tephros (Gr) ash-coloured   *nōton* (Gr) the back. Named from Tibet, it also inhabits Kashmir ranging east to Yunnan in China and south to south-east Asia.

Bornean Bristle-head   *Pityriasis gymnocephala*
pityriasis (New L) from *pituron* (Gr) a skin disease of the head; a reference to some warts on the bare head   *gumnos* (Gr) naked   *kephalē* (Gr) the head; the head is partly bare and has a patch of bristles, and warts. Confined to Borneo, little is known about this curious bird, and its proper place in classification has not been finally decided by ornithologists.

Family   VANGIDAE   13 species
vanga (L) a mattock; this is a short pickaxe-like implement with a curved blade or spike; a reference to the beak of the vanga shrikes which is strong, slightly curved, and in some cases hooked at the tip.

Hookbilled Vanga   *Vanga curvirostris*
vanga (L) a mattock; see above   *curvus* (L) curved   *rostrum* (L) the beak. The Vanga Shrikes are confined to Madagascar; they are related to the other shrikes and their diet is similar, namely insects and small reptiles, amphibians, and possibly small mammals.

Pollen's Vanga   *Xenopirostris polleni*
xenos (Gr) a stranger   *opsis* (Gr) appearance   *rostrum* (L) the beak; 'strange looking beak'; a reference to the heavy compressed and hooked beak with an uptilted lower manbible: named after F. P. L. Pollen (1842-1886), a naturalist and author who was in Madagascar from 1863 to 1866.

Blue Vanga   *Leptopterus madagascarinus*
leptos (Gr) slender   *pteron* (Gr) feathers, can mean wings and usually in plural   *-inus* (L) suffix meaning belonging to; like all vangas it is found only in Madagascar.

Coral-billed Nuthatch   *Hypositta corallirostris*
hupo (Gr) under, less than usual; here used to mean 'not quite like' *sittē* (Gr) (= *sitta*, Lat) a kind of woodpecker; has been translated as a nuthatch   *corallinus* (L) coral-red (from *korallion* (Gr) coral, especially red coral)   *rostrum* (L) the beak. Inhabiting forests of eastern Madagascar, up to 1,500 m (5,000 ft) in mountains.

Family   PTILOGONATIDAE   8 species
ptilon (Gr) a feather or wing; properly the soft feathers or down   *gonu* (Gr), genitive *gonatos*, the knee; a reference to the soft feathers of the underparts covering the knee; strictly speaking this is not the knee, as

it is the joint between the tibia and the tarsus, so anatomically speaking this is the ankle. This small family consists of the Silky Flycatchers, the Waxwings, and the strange Hypocolius; some authors put them in a family under the name Bombycillidae. They are smallish birds ranging from about 15 to 23 cm (6 to 9 in) long, having a mixed diet consisting of insects and fruit, and the Hypocolius probably only fruit.

Cedar Waxwing   *Bombycilla cedrorum*
bombyx (L), genitive *bombycis*, the silkworm   *bombycinus* (L) of silk, silky   *cilla* (New L) the tail; there is some doubt about this translation, see p. 236 under Family   *kedros* (Gr) the cedar tree   *-orum* (L) genitive plural ending; 'of cedar trees'; it inhabits open areas where there are scattered trees, but is not known to favour the cedar more than other kinds. The secondary feathers carry waxy red spangles, often plainly visible, hence the name waxwing. Inhabiting Quebec, Ontario and British Columbia, and ranging south to Georgia and California, migrating south in winter to West Indies and Panama.

Grey Silky Flycatcher   *Ptilogonys cinereus*
Ptilogonys, see notes under Family, above   *cinis* (L), genitive *cineris*, ashes   *cinereus* (L) ash-coloured; the plumage is soft and silky, similar to that of the waxwings. Inhabiting Mexico and Guatemala.

Phainopepla   *Phainopepla nitens*
phainō (Gr) I show   *phanos* (Gr) light, bright   *pepla* (Gr) a robe, a coat   *niteo* (L) I shine   *nitens* (L) shining; the male has glossy black plumage from the tall crest on the head to the long tail. Inhabiting California and Mexico and migrating south in winter to southern Mexico.

Black-and-Yellow Silky Flycatcher   *Phainoptila melanoxantha*
phainō, see above   *ptilon* (Gr) a feather or wing; properly the soft feathers or down   *melas* (Gr), genitive *melanos*, black   *xanthos* (Gr) yellow; the upperparts are a glossy black with a blue-green sheen, and the sides, flank, and rump are yellow. Inhabiting Costa Rica and western Panama.

Hypocolius   *Hypocolius ampelinus*
hupo (Gr) under, beneath   *colius* (New L) generic name for the coly, or mousebird; indicating that it somewhat resembles the African Coly   *ampelos* (Gr) a vine. Ampelis was the name of a singing bird in the satire *The Birds* by Aristophanes, and before about 1910 *Ampelis* was

in use for the waxwings, so *ampelinus* means waxwing-like; the behaviour is similar to the waxwings. The classification of this strange bird has been a problem for ornithologists; it inhabits an area around the Persian Gulf, including Afghanistan, Iraq, Iran, and Arabia.

Family DULIDAE 1 species

doulos (Gr) a slave; apparently the name was given to this rather unusual bird because Hispaniola Island had a reputation in the past as a place for slave trading. The Palm Chat, a starling-sized bird that probably only eats berries and some flowers, has been given a family on its own as there does not seem to be any certain relationship with other groups, although in some respects it resembles the waxwings, the silky flycatchers, and the hypocolius. The English name refers to its liking for the palm trees found in its natural habitat, and its habit of gathering in flocks that keep up a constant noisy chatter.

Palmchat   *Dulus dominicus*

dulus (Gr) a slave; see above; *dominicus* refers to the Dominican Republic occupying the eastern part of the island of Hispaniola in the West Indies, the western part being Haiti; the palm chat is found only on this island and the nearby Gonave Island.

Family CINCLIDAE   4 species

kinklos (Gr) a kind of wagtail or water ouzel. These rather unusual birds, the only ones in the order Passeriformes that can swim and dive, are able to do this without the help of webbed feet; if they had webbed feet they could not be classified as 'perching birds', i.e. passerines. Known as Dippers, and sometimes Water Ouzels, the names are apt, as they live close to fast-flowing mountain streams and obtain most of their food from under the water; caddis flies, insect larvae, water beetles, snails and similar small water animals and they are known to catch very small fish like minnows.

Dipper   *Cinclus cinclus*

Cinclus from *kinklos*, see above. Inhabiting mountain streams of Europe, including the British Isles, in the Atlas Mountains of northern Africa, in Asia Minor and Central Asia; they have been seen as high as 5,180 m (17,000 ft) in the mountains of Tibet.

American Dipper   *C. mexicanus*

Named from Mexico, it has a large range from the Aleutian Islands and Alaska south to Guatemala and Panama and east to Dakota.

Family TROGLODYTIDAE 59 species

trōglē (Gr) a hole, a hollow   *dutēs* (Gr) a burrower   *trōglodutēs* (Gr) one who creeps into holes; the name refers to the form of the nest which is dome-shaped with an entrance hole, but not all wrens in this family build that type of nest; some build cup-shaped nests in holes and crevices or in bushes. They range in size from the little wren we know in Britain, about 9 cm (3½ in) long, to as much as 20 cm (8 in); there is only one wren living in Britain and Eurasia, *Troglodytes troglodytes*, all the others living in America, and mostly South America. They eat all kinds of insects and this is probably their only food.

Cactus Wren   *Campylorhynchus brunneicapillus*
kampulos (Gr) bent, curved   *rhunkhos* (Gr) the snout, beak; it has a fairly long slightly curved beak   *brunneus* (New L) brown   *capillus* (L) the hair of men, usually of the head; can mean the hair of animals; the predominant colour is brown. Known as the cactus wren because it usually builds the nest in a cactus or thorny bush and inhabits the cactus desert. Ranging from California, Utah and Texas south to Mexico.

Tooth-billed Wren   *Odontorchilus cinereus*
odous (Gr), genitive *odontos*, a tooth   *kheilos* (Gr) a lip, rim; of humans the lip, of birds the beak, bill; a reference to the serrated edge of the beak   *cinis* (L), genitive *cineris*, ashes   *cinereus* (L) ash-coloured. Inhabiting South America.

Canyon Wren   *Salpinctes mexicanus*
salpinx (Gr) a war trumpet   *salpinktēs* (Gr) a trumpeter; a reference to its loud call; although wrens, both male and female, have pleasant songs, a defiant male has a very loud call when proclaiming its territory. Named from Mexico, it ranges north, and south to Central America.

Sepia-Brown Wren   *Cinnycerthia peruana*
kinnuris (Gr) a small bird   *kerthios* (Gr) a little bird, perhaps a tree-creeper   *-anus* (L) suffix meaning belonging to; inhabiting Peru.

Zapata Wren   *Ferminia cerverai*
Named after Fermin Z. Cervera (dates not recorded), a naturalist who was in Cuba in 1926 when this wren was first discovered and named; it is very unusual for a bird to bear both the first name and the surname of a naturalist. It is confined to a marsh in southern Cuba on the Zapata Peninsula.

Black-throated Wren *Thryothorus atrogularis*
thruon (Gr) a rush, a reed   *thouros* (Gr) rushing, impetuous; the male has a habit of building quite a number of nests that are never used, and seems to do this with a sense of urgency; one ornithologist described it as 'The male's frantic nest building'. Eventually the female chooses one of the nests and the male may use another one for roosting; they are often built in thick clumps of reeds   *ater* (L) black   *gula* (L) the throat   *-aris* (L) suffix meaning pertaining to. Inhabiting Central America.

Spot-breasted Wren *T. maculipectus*
macula (L) a mark, a spot   *pectus* (L) the breast; the white or pale underparts are heavily spotted and barred with black. Inhabiting Mexico and Central America.

House Wren *Troglodytes aedon*
Troglodytes, see notes under Family on p. 249   *aēdōn* (Gr) properly a songstress, but has been used to mean the nightingale; many wrens, both male and female, have a melodious song, and have been compared to the nightingale. Inhabiting North, Central, and South America.

Common Wren *T. troglodytes troglodytes*
Often known in Britain as the 'Jenny Wren', the Latin name unfortunately has become something of a joke; it is the Nominate Subspecies, so it has been saddled with the name *Troglodytes troglodytes troglodytes*. For an explanation of how this extraordinary name has come about see Chapter 1, Page 13, under Tautonyms; there are other cases in which an animal has what could be called a 'tautonymous trinomial name'. It is widespread in the western part of Europe, northern Africa, and ranging east through Asia Minor, to eastern China, Japan, and the Kuril and Aleutian Islands; it is also widespread in North America. It is the only true wren known that is not confined to the New World.

Shetland Islands Wren *T. t. zetlandicus*
More than 30 subspecies of the Common Wren are known; they seem able to colonise quite remote islands and become resident, and thus form a quite distinct subspecies; *zetland* (New L) Shetland   *-icus* (L) suffix meaning belonging to; as the name tells us, it lives on the Shetland Islands.

Chestnut-breasted Wren *Cyphorhinus thoracicus*
kuphos (Gr) curved   *rhis* (Gr), genitive *rhinos*, the nose; a reference to the slightly curved beak   *thorax* (Gr), genitive *thorakos*, the breast *-icus* (L) suffix meaning pertaining to; the throat and breast are rufous chestnut in colour. Inhabiting Colombia, mostly west of the Andes, and south to Ecuador and Peru.

Family   MIMIDAE   30 species
mimus (L) a mimic actor; the name has been given because of their ability to mimic the songs of other birds, which of course accounts for the English name Mocking Birds. They range in size from about 20 to 30 cm (8 to 12 in), and are similar in several ways to the thrushes, to which they are related, and they are also related to the wrens. Inhabiting the New World from Canada to South America, the diet is probably mostly insects but they also take some fruit and berries, and seeds.

Grey Catbird   *Dumetella carolinensis*
dumetum (L) a thorn brake, a thicket   *-ellus* (L) diminutive suffix; they inhabit dense scrub and thorn bushes, usually near water: named from Carolina, their range is widespread from southern Canada to Florida, and west to Texas and New Mexico, migrating south in winter to Cuba and Panama. The name catbird refers to one of the calls which is a catlike mewing sound.

Brown-backed Mockingbird   *Mimus dorsalis*
mimus (L) a mimic actor   *dorsum* (L) the back   *-alis* (L) suffix meaning relating to; a reference to the brown back. Inhabiting Bolivia and Argentina.

Mockingbird   *M. polyglottos*
polus (Gr) many   *glōssa* = *glōtta* (Attic) the tongue; 'many voiced'; mocking birds have a variety of songs, many quite melodious; some ornithologists consider they are their own songs which happen to be similar to other birds' songs, and this has given rise to the idea that they are miming. Widespread in the USA from Wyoming east to Ohio and Maryland, and from California south to the West Indies and Mexico, and in some cases to Central and northern South America.

Galapagos Mockingbird   *Nesomimus trifasciatus*
nesos (Gr) an island   *mimus* (Gr) a mimic actor   *tria* (L) three *fascia* (L) a band, girdle   *-atus* (L) suffix meaning provided with; a

reference to the white margins of the wing coverts which can be seen as three white bands. There are several different races of the mockingbird confined to the Galapagos group of islands.

Curve-billed Thrasher *Toxostoma curvirostre*
toxon (Gr) a bow for use with arrows; can mean anything bowed or arched *stoma* (Gr) the mouth *curvus* (L) curved *rostrum* (L) the beak: in both names a reference to the slightly curved bill. Inhabiting Texas, New Mexico and Arizona and ranging south to Mexico. The English name thrasher is said to derive from thrush, but this has not been properly confirmed and it remains somewhat obscure; they are thrush-like birds, with a melodious song, and are certainly related to the thrushes.

Le Conte's Thrasher *T. lecontei*
Named in honour of Dr John Lawrence Le Conte (1825-1883), an eminent zoologist; although he took a great interest in birds he made his name as an entomologist. This thrasher inhabits a similar area to the curve-billed thrasher, above, keeping mostly to arid parts.

Brown Thrasher *T. rufum*
rufus (L) red, ruddy; the upperparts are reddish brown from the crown to the long tail. This thrasher often repeats a short phrase, like the Song Thrush *Turdus philomelos*. It inhabits a wide area from southern Canada south to Florida, the coast of the Gulf of Mexico, and Texas.

Brown Trembler *Cinclocerthia ruficauda*
kinklos (Gr) a kind of wagtail *kerthios* (Gr) a little bird, a treecreeper; an apparently meaningless name as it is neither a wagtail nor a treecreeper, and it is not closely related to either *rufus* (L) red, ruddy *cauda* (L) the tail of an animal: the English name has been given because of its peculiar habit of violent trembling. It is found only in the West Indies, Central America.

Pearly-eyed Thrasher *Margarops fuscatus*
margaritēs (Gr) a pearl *ops*, from *opsis* (Gr) aspect, appearance, also *ops* (Gr) the eye, face *fuscus* (L) dark *fuscatus* (L) dark-coloured. Inhabiting the West Indies.

Family PRUNELLIDAE 13 species
prunus (L) a plum tree *brunus* (New L) brown *prunelle* (Fr) a sloe, from its dark colour; it is the fruit of the blackthorn; possibly with

-ellus (L) diminutive suffix. There is disagreement among authors about the origin of the name *Prunella* for the accentors, but it seems to be generally agreed that it refers to their brown colour; the one that is familiar to us in Britain, the Dunnock, is almost certainly named from its dun colour. *Accentor* is a Latin word, and means one who sings with another; it is a good songster but tends to be a soloist and is not reputed, as are some birds, to sing 'a duet' with its mate. They are sparrow-sized birds, or slightly larger, but the beak is thin and pointed, and the diet consists of insects, with more seeds and berries in the winter.

Alpine Accentor *Prunella collaris*
Prunella, see above *collum* (L) the neck *collaris* (L) pertaining to the neck; it has a grey collar which shows against the background of brown. It inhabits Spain and northern Africa and ranges through the alpine areas of southern Europe and Asia to Japan, and is known to breed in alpine meadows and scrub from 1,500 to about 5,200 m (5,000 to about 17,000 ft).

Dunnock *P. modularis*
modulator (L) one who measures, a director of music; can mean a musician; a reference to its high-pitched warble. Sometimes known as the hedge sparrow, it is not a sparrow, but is superficially somewhat like a sparrow and often builds its nest in hedges, particularly hawthorn hedges; common in Britain, it is widespread in Europe though not in southern Russia and the Balkans; it is seen in Asia Minor and Iran, and winters in Israel, Greece, southern Italy, Egypt and northern Africa.

Family MUSCICAPIDAE 1,300 species
musca (L) a fly *capio* (L) I take, seize. Under this main family heading, the thrushes and their kin number about 1,300 species, so it is usual to divide them into 11 subfamily groups; these are now almost universally recognised though authors may vary to some extent regarding the subfamily names and the grouping. With such a large number of species it is not really possible to make any general remarks with regard to size, diet, and habits; anything of special interest will be mentioned under each subfamily heading. The reader should be reminded, as first mentioned in Chapter 4, that the suffix *-idae* denotes a family, and *-inae* a subfamily.

Subfamily TURDINAE 304 species
turdus (L) a thrush. This group includes a tremendous variety of

thrushes and their close relatives such as the wheatears, the robins, the redstarts, the nightingales, and the blackbirds; they are mostly insectivorous but also eat fruit and berries and some will take worms and snails when available. The group includes some of the finest songsters.

Forest Robin   *Stiphrornis erythrothorax*
stiphros (Gr) firm, sturdy   *ornis* (Gr) a bird   *eruthros* (Gr) red   *thorax* (Gr) the breast; not to be confused with the robin we know in the British Isles, *Erithacus rubecula*, it is a bigger bird, though they are related; it inhabits Africa, from Cameroon to Uganda.

Rusty-bellied Shortwing   *Brachypteryx hyperythra*
brakhus (Gr) short   *pterux* (Gr) a wing   *hupo* (Gr) under, beneath   *eruthros* (Gr) red. This shortwing inhabits India; there are five others, mostly oriental.

Wren-Thrush   *Zeledonia coronata*
Named after J. C. Zeledon (1846-1923), a naturalist from Costa Rica   *corona* (L) a crown   *coronata* (L) wearing a crown; a reference to the tawny crown edged with black. Inhabiting Costa Rica and Panama.

Bearded Scrub Robin   *Cercotrichas barbata*
kerkos (Gr) the tail of an animal   *trikhas* (Gr) a thrush or field-fare; 'thrush-tailed'   *barba* (L) a beard   *barbata* (L) bearded. The English names are misleading because names such as robin, thrush, wheatear, chat and others are rather indiscriminately used in this large group. This scrub robin inhabits Africa.

Sooty Rock Chat   *Pinarornis plumosus*
pinaros (Gr) dirty   *ornis* (Gr) a bird; this name, and the English name 'sooty', indicate the rather drab grey plumage   *pluma* (L) a small soft feather   *-osus* (L) suffix meaning full of; known as a 'rock chat' from the habitat and the continuous chattering call. Inhabiting Africa.

Southern Scrub Robin   *Drymodes brunneopygia*
drumōdēs (Gr) of the woods   *brunneus* (New L) brown   *pugē* (Gr) the rump; a reference to the buff underparts. Inhabiting the interior part of south and south-west Australia.

Eurasian Robin   *Erithacus rubecula*
erithakos (Gr) a solitary bird; has been translated as the red-breast   *ruber* (L) red   *-culus* (L) diminutive suffix; 'the little red one'. This is the robin that we know in the British Isles; it is confined to Europe and neighbouring countries such as Siberia, Asia Minor, part of

north-west Africa, the Canaries and Azores.

Thrush Nightingale   *Luscinia luscinia*
luscinius (L) a nightingale: this small bird is said to resemble *Erithacus rubecula*, above; it has a fine song considered to be more powerful than the nightingale *megarhynchos*, with pure bell-like notes. Inhabiting Eurasia from Denmark and Sweden to the River Ob area in Russia and ranging south to the Black Sea; it winters in the eastern part of Africa mostly south of the equator.

Nightingale   *L. megarhynchos*
megas (Gr) big, wide   *rhunkhos* (Gr) the beak; it would be difficult to discern that the beak is any bigger than other birds in the family. This is the nightingale that we know in Britain; it ranges across Eurasia and south to Africa.

Cape Robin   *Cossypha caffra*
kossuphos (Gr) a singing bird, like the blackbird   *caffra* is a coined name, from Kaffraria; this was a name applied to a large area in eastern South Africa, but is now obsolete. Inhabiting East Africa and ranging south through Tanzania to South Africa.

Redstart   *Phoenicurus phoenicurus*
phoinix (Gr), genitive *phoinikos*, red, dark, red   *oura* (Gr) the tail; a reference to the orange-chestnut coloured tail. This is the redstart well known in Britain, though it is not found in Ireland; it is widespread in Eurasia including Asia Minor and Iran, but local in north-west Africa and wintering south of the Sahara to the equator.

Eastern Bluebird   *Sialia sialis*
sialis (Gr) a kind of bird; a spectacular bright blue bird living in America; it ranges from eastern Canada south to Florida, the coast of the Gulf of Mexico, Texas, Mexico, and south to Honduras.

Townsend's Solitaire   *Myadestes townsendi*
muia (Gr) a fly   *edestēs* (Gr) an eater: named after John Kirk Townsend (1809-1851), an American ornithologist and author. The name solitaire has been given because it is a shy bird and tends to keep to itself; it inhabits the mountains of western North America and Alaska and winters south to Mexico.

Black-tailed Chat   *Cercomela melanura*
kerkos (Gr) the tail of an animal   *melas* (Gr) black   *oura* (Gr) the tail; inhabiting Arabia and Africa.

Stonechat *Saxicola torquata*
saxum (L) a stone *colo* (L) I inhabit; it lives in open country, heaths, moors, alpine meadows and mountains up to 3,600 m (12,000 ft); it has been said the name is taken from its alarm call which sounds like two stones being knocked together, and does not refer to a stony or rocky habitat *torquatus* (L) wearing a collar made of twisted material; it has a partial white collar merging into a chestnut breast. It inhabits the south-western part of Europe including Denmark and the British Isles, East Africa and Madagascar; it ranges east through Asia Minor to China, Korea, and Japan.

Sooty Chat *Myrmecocichla nigra*
murmēx (Gr), genitive *murmēkos*, an ant *kikhlē* (Gr) a bird like a thrush; it has a thrush-like song but it is not known to eat ants; it often inhabits places where there are termite hills *niger* (L) black; the male is a glossy black and the female a sooty brown. It is widely distributed in the central and western parts of Africa including Sudan, Cameroon, Zaire, Angola, and parts of East Africa.

Mountain Wheatear *Oenanthe monticola*
oinē (Gr) poetic name for the vine *oinanthē* (Gr) the first shoot of the vine; can mean a bird, one that appears in Greece at the same time as the first shoot of the vine, some say the wheatear *mons* (L), genitive *montis*, a mountain *colo* (L) I inhabit; it usually lives in rocky and stony areas but not always in the mountains. Inhabiting south-west Africa.

Wheatear *O. oenanthe*
This is the most far-ranging of the wheatears, inhabiting most of Eurasia except the extreme north in Siberia; it is found in Alaska and Iceland and winters in tropical Africa and southern Arabia. It is the only wheatear that regularly inhabits the British Isles.

Short-toed Rock Thrush *Monticola brevipes*
mons (L), genitive *montis*, a mountain *colo* (L) I inhabit *brevis* (L) short *pes* (L) the foot. Inhabiting mountainous areas of Transvaal in South Africa.

Rock Thrush *M. saxatilis*
saxum (L) a stone *saxatilis* (L) one that dwells among rocks; the English and the Latin names must leave little doubt that it inhabits mountains; this is so and it also favours boulder-strewn rocky hillsides. It lives in southern Europe, Spain, part of north-west Africa, Asia

Minor and the mountains of south-west Asia; it winters in tropical Africa.

Ashy Ground Thrush   *Zoothera cinerea*
zōos (Gr) alive   *thērao* (Gr) I hunt, can mean I catch; a reference to the diet of snails, worms, and grubs for which it hunts on the ground *cinereus* (L) ash-coloured. Inhabiting Philippines.

Wood Thrush   *Hylocichla mustelina*
hulē (Gr) a wood, forest   *kikhlē* (Gr) a bird like a thrush   *mustela* (L) a weasel   *mustelinus* (L) weasel-coloured; this is a reference to the chestnut-brown plumage with white underparts. It inhabits the central and eastern parts of the USA ranging south to Florida, Texas, and in winter Mexico and Panama.

White-collared Blackbird   *Turdus albocinctus*
turdus (L) a thrush   *albus* (L) white   *cinctus* (L) a girding; can mean a girdle. Inhabiting India and the Burma-Vietnam area, Tibet and China.

Blackbird   *T. merula*
merula (L) the European blackbird. Inhabiting nearly the whole of Europe including the British Isles, and part of northern Africa, and ranging east through Asia Minor, the Caucasus, the mountains of southern Asia to southern China.

American Robin   *T. migratorius*
migrator (L), genitive *migratoris*, a wanderer; a reference to its rare visits to western Europe in the autumn and winter; quite unlike the Eurasian Robin *Erithacus rubecula* which we know in Britain, it is much bigger, about 25 cm (10 in) long compared to 14 cm ($5\frac{1}{2}$ in); it is more like and closely related to the blackbird *T. merula*, above, and it is only the chestnut red breast that has given rise to the name 'robin'. It inhabits Alaska, most of Canada, and ranges south to Mexico and Guatemala.

Olive Thrush   *T. olivaceus*
oliva (L) an olive   *olivaceus*, like an olive; a reference to the dark olive-coloured plumage, both upper and underparts. Inhabiting open hillsides and mountains and has been seen as high as 3,000 m (10,000 ft) on Kilimanjaro; widespread in most of Africa.

Song Thrush   *T. philomelos*
philos (Gr) beloved, dear   *melos* (Gr) a song; 'a song-lover'; there

could be a connection with the Greek legend in which Philomela was changed by the gods into a nightingale, another bird with a fine song. Widespread in Europe including the British Isles and ranging east through Asia Minor to the Lake Baikal area; it winters in southern Europe, northern Africa and Arabia.

Fieldfare *T. pilaris*
pilus (L) a hair *-aris* (L) suffix meaning pertaining to; apparently this was a translation from the Greek *thrix*, genitive *trikhos*, hair, but this was a mistake because the word used was *trikhas* (Gr) a kind of thrush, the fieldfare. Inhabiting Europe including the British Isles and Iceland and ranging east into Asia to the Lake Baikal area, and south to Arabia in winter. Fieldfare is from an Old English word meaning 'field-dweller', or 'fell-dweller'.

Mountain Blackbird *T. poliocephalus*
polios (Gr) hoary, grey *kephalē* (Gr) the head; this grey-headed thrush lives in the mountainous areas of Malaysia, Indonesia, New Guinea, and the neighbouring Pacific Islands.

Ring Ouzel *T. torquatus*
torquatus (L) wearing a necklace made of twisted material; a reference to the white breast-band which is prominent in the male. Inhabiting southern Europe and isolated parts in northern Scandinavia and northern Britain, and wintering in Africa and Asia Minor. Ouzel is from an Old English word *osle*, the blackbird.

Mistle Thrush *T. viscivorus*
viscum (L) the mistletoe *voro* (L) I devour; Aristotle recorded that it was fond of mistletoe berries; in addition to fruit and berries it will also take earthworms and insects. Widespread in Europe including the British Isles but not the northern part of Scandinavia, ranging east through Asia Minor and the mountains of south-west Asia and up to 3,350 m (11,000 ft) in the Himalayas; some migration in winter to Mediterranean areas.

Subfamily ORTHONYCHINAE 20 species
orthos (Gr) straight *onux* (Gr) a claw, genitive *onukhos*; Prof Temminck (1778–1858), the Dutch zoologist, says so named from the straightness of its claws. This group includes the Logrunners, Whipbirds, Quail-Thrushes, and their kin; they eat a variety of insects and some will also take worms, fruit, and berries. They all live in the Oriental and Australasian regions.

Northern Logrunner *Orthonyx spaldingi*
Named after E. Spalding (fl 1867-1894), a naturalist and taxidermist of Australia; he worked at the Queensland Museum from 1880 to 1894. It spends a lot of its time on the ground, running about over fallen tree trunks and forest debris hunting for insects; it also eats berries. Inhabiting forests along the coast of northern Queensland in Australia.

Eastern Whip-bird *Psophodes olivaceus*
psophōdēs (Gr) noisy   *oliva* (L) an olive   *olivaceus* (L) similar to, olive-coloured; a reference to the dark olive-green upperparts; a noisy bird, it has a long, loud whistling call which increases in strength to finish with a sort of 'whip-crack'. Inhabiting eastern Australia from northern Queensland south through New South Wales to Victoria.

Cinnamon Quail-Thrush *Cinclosoma cinnamomeum*
kinklos (Gr) a kind of ouzel, or thrush   *soma* (Gr) the body; 'thrush-bodied'; it is about the size and colour of the song thrush *Turdus philomelos*; *cinnamomeum* (L) cinnamon; a reference to the chestnut brown upperparts. Inhabits arid stony deserts of south-western Australia.

Malay Rail Babbler *Eupetes macrocercus*
eu- (Gr) a prefix meaning well, nicely   *petes* (New L) a flier, derived from *petomai* (Gr) I fly; 'flying well'   *makros* (Gr) long   *kerkos* (Gr) the tail of an animal; a reference to the unusually long tail. Inhabiting Malaysia and Borneo.

Subfamily TIMALIINAE   252 species
timalia (New L) a bird name, probably from an Indian native name. The correct classification of some of the birds in this large subfamily has been a problem for ornithologists; they range in size from about 10 to 46 cm (4 to 18 in), they range in colour from rather drab to very colourful; as a general rule they have rather short rounded wings, longish tails, and a bill like that of a thrush, and the diet may be insectivorous or vegetarian. They are mostly known as Babblers on account of their continuous loud chattering and calling.

Ashy-headed Babbler *Trichastoma cinereiceps*
trikhas (Gr) a kind of thrush, or fieldfare   *stoma* (Gr) the mouth; 'thrush-billed'   *cinereus* (L) ash-coloured   *ceps* (New L) from *caput* (L) the head. Inhabiting Malaysia.

Tickell's Babbler *T. tickelli*
Named after Col S. R. Tickell (1811-1875), a naturalist who was in

India and Burma from 1834 to 1865. This babbler inhabits India and ranges east through Burma to Philippines.

White-throated Babbler　*Malacopteron albogulare*
malakos (Gr) soft　*pteron* (Gr) feathers, wings　*albus* (L) white　*gula* (L) the throat. Inhabiting Malaysia.

Rusty-cheeked Scimitar Babbler　*Pomatorhinus erythrogenys*
pōma (Gr), genitive *pōmatos*, a lid, a cover　*rhis* (Gr), genitive *rhinos*, the nose; a reference to the corneous covering of the nares which is one of the distinguishing features of this genus　*eruthros* (Gr) red　*genus* (Gr) the jaw, the cheek. Inhabiting the Himalayas and ranging east from Bangladesh to southern China and Taiwan. It has a long curved bill, hence 'scimitar' babbler.

Black-throated Wren-Babbler　*Napothera atrigularis*
napē (Gr) a woody dell　*thēraō* (Gr) I hunt, I catch; 'a hunter in woods'　*ater* (L) black　*gula* (L) the throat　*-aris* (L) suffix meaning pertaining to. Inhabiting Borneo. The name 'wren' refers to the size, one of the smallest babblers.

Barred-Wing Wren-Babbler　*Spelaeornis troglodytoides*
spēlaios (Gr) a grotto, a cave　*ornis* (Gr) a bird; a reference to the form of the nest which is dome-shaped with an entrance hole at the side　*trōglē* (Gr) a hole, a hollow　*trōglodutēs* (Gr) one who creeps into holes　*-oides* (New L) from *eidos* (Gr) apparent shape, resemblance; a reference to it being somewhat like the Common Wren *Troglodytes troglodytes*, hence the English name Wren-Babbler; the wren itself takes its Latin name from the form of its nest. Inhabiting the Himalayas and the northern part of India and ranging south and east to the Burma-Vietnam area.

Wedge-billed Wren-Babbler　*Sphenocichla humei*
sphen (Gr) a wedge　*kikhlē* (Gr) a bird like a thrush: named after A. O. Hume (1829-1912), a naturalist and author who was in India in 1873. This wren-babbler lives in Assam and Burma.

Deignan's Babbler　*Stachyris rodolphei*
Stachyris (New L) spike-like, from *stakhuēros* (Gr) with ears of corn; a reference to the short spiky bill. Named after Rodolph M. de Schauensee (born 1901), an American zoologist and author of Philadelphia who specialised in taxonomy; he was in Siam (now Thailand) from 1932 to 1938; and H. G. Deignan (born 1906), a zoologist and author

who was also in Siam from 1928 to 1937. This babbler inhabits Thailand and neighbouring countries.

Red-capped Babbler   *Timalia pileata*
timalia (New L) a bird name, probably from an Indian native name *pileus* = *pilleus* (L) a felt cap   *pilleatus* (L) wearing the *pilleus*; a reference to the red plumage on the crown. Inhabiting India, the Burma-Vietnam area and Java.

Wren-Tit   *Chamaea fasciata*
khamai (Gr) on the earth, on the ground; it spends most of its time in thick cover hopping about looking for insects, and rarely flying   *fascia* (L) a band or girdle   *fasciata* (L) banded, can mean striped; a reference to the buff brown underparts marked with long dark streaks. Inhabiting Oregon, California and south to Lower California.

Arrow-marked Babbler   *Turdoides jardinei*
turdus (L) a thrush   *-oides* (New L) from *eidos* (Gr) apparent shape, resemblance; at 24 cm ($9\frac{1}{2}$ in) it is about the same size as a thrush but the plumage is darker; some of the birds in this genus, comprising 26 species, are thrush-like in colour, others less so; this one is flecked with small white sharp-pointed marks, hence 'arrow-marked': named after Sir W. Jardine (1800-1874), an English naturalist and author. It is widespread in Africa, particularly central areas centred on Zaire and Kenya.

Spiny Babbler   *T. nipalensis*
-ensis (L) suffix meaning belonging to, usually of places; it inhabits Nepal, north-east India, and surrounding areas. It has spiny shaft tips to its feathers, hence 'spiny babbler'.

White-crested Laughing Thrush   *Garrulax leucolophus*
garrulus (L) talkative   *-ax* (L) suffix denoting an aggressive tendency; the 44 species in this large genus are known for their loud cackling sort of 'laughter', and they seem to attempt to outdo each other, each one calling louder than the one before   *leukos* (Gr) white   *lophos* (Gr) a crest. Widespread in the Oriental Region from India to Malaysia.

Collared Laughing Thrush   *G. yersini*
Named after Dr A. E. J. Yersin (1863-1943), a Swiss-French bacteriologist and Director of the Pasteur Institute of Indo-China in 1919; this country has now been broken up and in 1951 became Laos, Cambodia, and Vietnam. This laughing thrush inhabits Annam.

Peking Robin *Leiothrix lutea*
leios (Gr) smooth, soft *thrix* (Gr) hair, in this case taken to mean feathers *luteus* (L) golden-yellow; the throat is yellow merging into an orange coloured breast; this also gives it the English name 'robin'. From the southern Himalayas it ranges east across northern Burma to China, remaining south of the Yangtze River.

Chestnut-headed Tit-Babbler *Alcippe castaneceps*
Alkippē was the daughter of Ares, a Greek god of war; there is probably no special connection with Alkippē; a number of generic and specific names have been given that were taken from classical mythology without any particular reason *castaneus* (New L) chestnut-coloured, from *kastanos* (Gr) the chestnut tree *ceps* (New L) from *caput* (L) the head. Inhabiting the Himalayas and ranging south through India and Burma to Malaysia, Indonesia, and the Philippines.

Chapin's Flycatcher-Babbler *Lioptilus chapini*
leios (Gr) smooth, soft *ptilon* (Gr) a feather or a wing, but usually means the soft feathers or down of a bird: named after Dr J. P. Chapin (1889-1964), an American ornithologist and author who spent many years in the Belgian Congo, now Zaire, and collected for the American Museum of Natural History. Inhabiting Zaire.

Bare-headed Rockfowl *Picathartes gymnocephalus*
pica (L) a magpie *kathartēs* (Gr) a cleanser, a purifier *Cathartes* the Turkey Vulture; a combination of *pica* and *cathartēs*; it is partly corvine (resembling a crow) and bald like a vulture *gumnos* (Gr) naked *kephalē* (Gr) the head; the front of the head and the cheeks are naked and the skin is bright yellow. During the past 100 years, since the bird was first discovered, there has been continuous discussion among ornithologists about the taxonomic position; the consensus of opinion now seems to be that its nearest relative is the babbler. It is confined to some small areas in Sierra Leone and Ghana, western Africa.

Subfamily PARADOXORNITHINAE 19 species
paradoxos (Gr) contrary to opinion, strange *ornis* (Gr), genitive *ornithos*, a bird; like the Bare-headed Rockfowl, above, this small group of birds has been a puzzle for the ornithologists. The beak is heavy and rounded, like that of a parrot, which has given rise to the name Parrotbill, but they are not closely related to the parrots; it has been suggested that they are related to the babblers, and also to the

titmice, and this problem gave them the name *Paradoxornis*, 'strange bird'. They vary in length from about 12·5 to 30 cm (5 to 12 in), and their food is mainly insects, but they will take seeds and other vegetarian food when necessary.

Bearded Tit or Reedling *Panurus biarmicus*
panu (Gr) all, altogether   *oura* (Gr) the tail; in this case meant to stress the length of the tail; this bird is about 16·5 cm (6½ in) long of which 7·5 cm (3 in) is tail; *biarmicus* (obscure); a name given by Linnaeus who often failed to give explanations of his names: 'Perhaps a corruption of *beardmanica* ("bearded manikin"), the barbarous name invented by Albin and referred to by Linnaeus with reference to the male's black moustache.' (Macleod). E. Albin (fl 1713-1759) was an English artist and author of *The Natural History of Birds*. The male has a black stripe on either side of the bill that gives the appearance of drooping moustaches. The main distribution is in the Black Sea area and it inhabits the reeds around lakes and swamps, hence 'reedling'; it ranges east to the River Ob, and west to England and Spain.

Ashy-throated Parrotbill *Paradoxornis alphonsianus*
Paradoxornis, see notes above under Subfamily; named after Prof Alphonse Milne-Edwards (1835-1900), a French zoologist who was a Professor at the Paris Museum of Natural History in 1876 and a Director from 1891 to 1900. This parrotbill inhabits the southern part of Eurasia including part of the Oriental Region.

Greater Red-headed Parrotbill *P. ruficeps*
rufus (L) red   *ceps* (New L) from *caput* (L) the head. Inhabiting India and the Burma-Vietnam area.

Subfamily SYLVIINAE   339 species
sylva = *silva* (L) a wood, a forest. The members of this very big subfamily are known as Old World Warblers, nearly all living in Eurasia and Africa and ranging south-east to Australasia; a small group of about 12 species known as Gnatcatchers live in the Americas, ranging from the USA to Brazil. They are mostly smallish birds ranging from about 9 to 20 cm (3½ to 8 in), though some are a bit larger; the diet is mostly insects but they will also take worms and other invertebrates and some fruit and berries when necessary. Many are very good and melodious songsters which has given them the popular name Warblers.

Blue-grey Gnatcatcher *Polioptila caerulea*
polios (Gr) hoary, grey   *ptilon* (Gr) a feather or wing   *caeruleus* (L) blue. Inhabiting the southern part of the USA and wintering in Mexico, Guatemala, Cuba and Bahamas.

Cetti's Warbler *Cettia cetti*
There are 12 species in the genus *Cettia*, named after François Cetti (1726-1780); he was an Italian Jesuit, and a zoologist and author, and published a book *The Natural History of Sardinia* in 1774. This warbler inhabits south-western Europe including Corsica and Sardinia and other Mediterranean islands, and the northern coastal strip of Africa; recently it has been known to visit England; it ranges east through Asia Minor, Iraq, to Pakistan.

Knysna Scrub Warbler *Bradypterus sylvaticus*
bradus (Gr) slow   *pteron* (Gr) wings; a reference to the mode of flight *sylvaticus* = *silvaticus* (L) belonging to a wood, or trees. Inhabiting dense scrub and bramble thickets at the forest edge, it is named from the town of Knysna on the south coast of South Africa, and is found only in the extreme south ranging from Table Mountain east to Natal.

Chinese Bush Warbler *B. tacsanowskius*
Named after Dr W. Taczanowski (1819-1890), a Polish zoologist and author who worked at the Zoological Museum in Warsaw from 1855 to 1890. It inhabits China, India, and the Burma-Vietnam area.

Grasshopper Warbler *Locustella naevia*
locusta (L) a locust, a grasshopper   *-ellus* (L) diminutive suffix; grasshoppers probably form part of the diet, but it has been suggested that the high-pitched rasping call, very like the sound of a stridulating grasshopper, has given rise to the English name   *naevus* (L) a mole or wart on the body; can mean a spot, a blemish; the pale buff throat and underparts are usually marked with spots and streaks. Inhabiting western Europe including the British Isles but not northern Scandinavia; it winters in southern Europe, northern Africa, and ranges east to India.

Great Reed Warbler *Acrocephalus arundinaceus*
akron (Gr) a point, top   *kephalē* (Gr) the head; the crown of the head is more pointed than in other Sylviinae   *arundo* = *harundo* (L) the reed, cane   *harundinaceus* (L) like a reed, pertaining to reeds. One of the largest birds in this subfamily, about 19 cm ($7\frac{1}{2}$ in) long, it builds its nest in the reeds. Widespread in Europe but not Britain or Sweden

and Norway, it ranges east through southern Eurasia to Burma and western China, and south to Africa.

Sedge Warbler   *A. schoenobaenus*
skhoinos (Gr) the reed, rush   *bainō* (Gr) I walk, step; can also mean to stand, to be in a place. Inhabiting Europe including the British Isles but not Spain; east to India and western China, and wintering in Africa as far south as Natal.

Melodious Warbler   *Hippolais polyglotta*
hippolais (New L) from *hupolais* (Gr) a small bird; the Liddell and Scott Lexicon gives the Chiffchaff or 'the singing hedge-sparrow' *polus* (Gr) many   *glōtta* = *glōssa* (Gr) the tongue; 'many voiced'; it has a variety of musical songs and is sometimes imitative. Inhabiting France, Spain, Italy and the northern part of Africa.

Blackcap   *Sylvia atricapilla*
sylva = *silva* (L) a wood, a forest   *ater* (L) black   *capillus* (L) the hair of men, usually the hair of the head; can mean the hair of animals; the male has a sharply defined black crown and the female a reddish brown crown. Widespread in Eurasia including the British Isles, south to northern Africa, east to Asia Minor and part of Arabia, and western Siberia.

Whitethroat   *S. communis*
communis (L) common, general: widespread in Europe including the British Isles but not northern Scandinavia; ranging south to northern Africa, and east to Arabia, south-west Asia and India. The white throat is very noticeable against the brown of the head and upperparts.

Sardinian Warbler   *S. melanocephala*
melas (Gr), genitive *melanos*, black   *kephalē* (Gr) the head; unlike the blackcap (above) the head is entirely black to below the eye. Named from Sardinia it is widespread in the Mediterranean region in a wide belt all round the coast, including northern Africa; it ranges east through Asia Minor, part of Arabia, the Persian Gulf, and probably somewhat further east.

Chiffchaff   *Phylloscopus collybita*
phullon (Gr) a leaf   *skopos* (Gr) a watchman, a lookout man   *skopeō* (Gr) I see; a reference to its habit of searching amongst foliage for insects: *collybita* is probably a corruption of *kollubistēs* (Gr) a money-

changer, as the monotonous song is said to resemble the jingle of coins being counted; in France the bird is sometimes known as *Compteur d'Argent* (MacLeod). Inhabiting Eurasia including the British Isles, parts of northern Africa, Asia Minor, Arabia, and ranging east to India and Burma.

Wood Warbler *P. sibilatrix*
sibilator (L) a whistler *-atrix* (L) suffix meaning feminine; a reference to the song which is a series of notes, often given in flight, and repeated at a gradually increasing rate. Inhabiting Europe including England and Scotland but not Ireland or Spain, and ranging east to the Black Sea area and the Ural Mountains.

Goldcrest *Regulus regulus*
rex (L), genitive *regis*, a king *regulus* (L) a little king; in ancient times it was called 'king of the birds', probably by Aristotle, because of the golden stripe on the crown, and hence 'goldcrest'. Widespread in Eurasia, including the British Isles, Spain, and also northern Africa; ranging east to Black Sea area, Iran, Turkestan, Himalayas and Tibet.

Golden-crowned Kinglet *R. satrapa*
satrapa (L) a wealthy ruler, a governor of a Persian province. Inhabiting North America from Alaska and in the east from Nova Scotia ranging south through Mexico to Guatemala.

Brown Emu-tail *Dromaeocercus brunneus*
dromaios (Gr) swift, running at full speed; giving rise to the Latin name of the emu *Dromaius*, on account of this bird being a very fast runner *kerkos* (Gr) the tail of an animal; 'emu-tailed' *brunneus* (New L) brown. Inhabiting Africa.

Black-throated Prinia *Prinia atrogularis*
prinya (Javanese) a bird, probably this particular warbler as they are found in Java *ater* (L) black *gula* (L) the throat *gularis*, pertaining to the throat. Inhabiting southern Asia and the Oriental Region to Malaysia and Indonesia.

Red-winged Warbler *P. erythroptera*
eruthros (Gr) red *pteron* (Gr) feathers, wings. Inhabiting Africa.

Carruthers' Cisticola *Cisticola carruthersi*
cista (L) a wooden box or basket, often woven of twigs *colo* (L) I inhabit, I dwell in; a reference to the nest, which is a ball of twisted grass with a side entrance, sometimes with leaves stitched in; has been

called a 'purse nest': named after A. Douglas M. Carruthers (1882-1962), a naturalist who was exploring in Uganda in 1906. This warbler lives in Africa.

Golden-headed Cisticola *C. exilis*
exilis (L) thin, small; one of the smallest warblers, it is only about 9 cm (3½ in) long: the male has a golden crown during the breeding season. Inhabiting the Indian subcontinent, China, the Burma-Vietnam area, ranging south through Indonesia to the northern and eastern parts of Australia, and north-eastern Tasmania.

Common Tailorbird *Orthotomus sutorius*
orthos (Gr) straight   *tomē* (Gr) a cutting off; a reference to the cutting of the fibres that are used to sew the nest together   *sutilis* (L) sewed together   *sutor* (L) a shoemaker   *sutorius* (L) actually means 'belonging to a shoemaker'; it is intended as a reference to the nest which is a remarkable structure made of a leaf folded over or leaves sewn together, the nest itself being made inside this 'purse'. Widespread in the Oriental region including Sri Lanka and southern China.

Bar-throated Apalis *Apalis thoracica*
Apalis, an obscure name, probably from an African native name; it is not given in reference books, and not explained in the ornithological records in the British Museum (Natural History)   *thōrax* (Gr), genitive *thōrakos*, the chest   *-icus* (L) suffix meaning belonging to; it has a black bar across the throat at the top part of the chest. Inhabiting eastern and southern Africa south of the Equator but not found in coastal areas.

Yellow-backed Eremomela *Eremomela icteropygialis*
erēmos (Gr) lonely, solitary; of places, a wilderness, desert   *melos* (Gr) a song; a 'desert songster'; a reference to its habitat which is dry open bush and desert areas   *ikteros* (Gr) the jaundice; also a bird of a yellowish green colour, by looking at which a jaundiced person was cured—the bird died!   *pugē* (Gr) the rump, buttocks   *-alis* (L) suffix meaning relating to. Inhabiting Africa south of the Sahara and ranging south through eastern Africa to south Africa but not in the eastern and most southern coastal areas.

Long-billed Crombec *Sylvietta rufescens*
sylva = *silva* (L) a wood, a forest   *-etta*, a diminutive suffix   *rufus* (L) red, ruddy   *-escens* (L) suffix meaning beginning to, approaching, i.e. 'reddish'; the predominant colour of the plumage is a reddish

brown: the name Crombec comes from the Old English word *crump*, or *crumb*, meaning crooked, and *bec*, a beak; a reference to the beak which is long and curved. Inhabiting south-eastern Zaire, Zambia, and Malawi and ranging south to South Africa.

Spinifex Bird *Eremiornis carteri*
erēmos (Gr) lonely, solitary; of places, a wilderness, desert *ornis* (Gr) a bird; an allusion to its habitat which is arid and often desert country with low scrub: named after T. C. Carter (1863-1931), an English naturalist who explored and collected specimens in Australia. The English name derives from a type of Australian grass known as spinifex. This warbler inhabits Australia from central Queensland ranging west through Northern Territory to part of Western Australia, and also Barrow Island.

Fernbird *Bowdleria punctata*
Named after Dr R. Bowdler Sharp (1847-1909), an English zoologist and author who worked in the Bird Room at the British Museum (Natural History) from 1872 to 1909 *punctum* (L) a hole, a puncture *punctatus*, spotted as with punctures; a reference to the spotted dark brown throat and breast. The English name refers to the habitat which is wasteland and ferny scrub; it inhabits New Zealand and nearby islands.

Subfamily   MALURINAE   29 species
malos (Gr) has various meanings, and some consider it is the same as *malakos* (Gr) soft; here it is taken to mean slender *oura* (Gr) the tail; a reference to the long slender tail.

This group of small birds about 10 to 16·5 cm (4 to $6\frac{1}{2}$ in) long, mainly insectivorous, have been given various English names such as Wren, Wren-Warbler, and Grass-Wren; they live in Australia and some neighbouring islands.

Superb Wren-Warbler   *Malurus cyaneus*
kuaneos (Gr) dark blue, glossy blue; of the swallow; it is not entirely blue, but the head and shoulders are blue, with the hind neck, the throat, and the lower back black, making a striking contrast. Inhabiting eastern and southern Australia, Tasmania, and some islands in the Bass Strait.

Red-backed Wren-Warbler   *M. melanocephalus*
melas (Gr), genitive *melanos*, black   *kephalē* (Gr) the head; the head and neck are glossy black and the back is red. Inhabiting western part

of Australia and ranging east to northern Queensland and south to New South Wales.

Blue Wren-Warbler *Todopsis cyanocephala*
todus (L) a small bird, a tody   *opsis* (Gr) aspect, appearance; indicating that it is rather like a tody, of the family Todidae, a small brightly coloured insectivorous bird   *kuaneos* (Gr) dark blue, glossy blue *kephalē* (Gr) the head. Inhabiting New Guinea.

Black Grass-Wren *Amytornis housei*
Named after Amytis, daughter of Astyages, the last king of the Median Empire   *ornis* (Gr) a bird; and Dr F. M. House (1865-1936), a zoologist and sheep breeder from Western Australia. During a long period in which this bird was not seen by any observers it was found again in the Kimberley district of Western Australia in 1968. The plumage is mainly black; habitat woodland and probably spinifex grass.

Striated Grass-Wren *A. striatus*
stria (L) a furrow, a channel   *striatus* (New L) striped. Inhabiting Australia.

Subfamily ACANTHIZINAE 59 species
akantha (Gr) a thorn   *-iza* is a mutilated form of *spiza* (Gr) a finch or any small bird, derived from *spizō* (Gr) I pipe, I chirp, from the shrill note of small birds; the name is an allusion to the short fine bill, hence the English name 'thornbill'.
  This group of Australasian Warblers have been given various names such as Thornbill, Bristle-Bird, and Gerygone; they are small, from about 9 to 18 cm ($3\frac{1}{2}$ to 7 in) long, and mainly insectivorous.

Bristle-Bird *Dasyornis broadbenti*
dasus (Gr) hairy, shaggy   *ornis* (Gr) a bird; a reference to the rictal bristles: named after Kendall Broadbent (1837-1911) a naturalist and specially a taxidermist who worked at the Queensland Museum. Inhabiting Australia.

Brown Weebill *Smicrornis brevirostris*
smikros (Gr) an Ionic form of *mikros* (Gr) small   *ornis* (Gr) a bird; an allusion to the size of this tiny bird, about 9 cm ($3\frac{1}{2}$ in) long   *brevis* (L) short   *rostrum* (L) the beak; a reference to the small beak, hence also 'weebill'. Inhabiting Queensland and Victoria and ranging across southern Australia to Western Australia.

Yellow-tailed Thornbill *Acanthiza chrysorrhoa*
Acanthiza, see notes under Subfamily, above *khrusos* (Gr) gold *orhos* (Gr) the rump, bottom; a reference to the rump and adjacent part of the tail which is yellow. Inhabiting Australia.

Pilot-Bird *Pycnoptilus floccosus*
puknos (Gr) thick, compact; of a bird's plumage thick, close *ptilon* (Gr) a feather or wing; properly the soft feathers or down of a bird *floccus* (L) a flock of wool *floccosus* (L) full of flocks of wool; very woolly; a reference to the thick plumage. The name 'pilot bird' has been given because it has a reputation for guiding the Superb Lyrebird *Menura novaehollandiae* to food, but it is also said that it is the Lyrebird that is the 'pilot'. Inhabiting the mountains of the south-eastern part of Australia.

Chestnut-tailed Ground-Wren *Hylacola pyrrhopygia*
hula (Doric) = *hulē* (Gr) a wood, a forest *colo* (L) I inhabit *purros* (Gr) red; flame-coloured *pugē* (Gr) the rump, buttocks. Inhabiting south-eastern Australia.

White-throated Gerygone Warbler *Gerygone olivacea*
gērugonē (Gr) born of sound; an echo; the name is from *The Idylls of Theocritus*, poems of idealised rustic life; a reference to the sweet song of these warblers, 'a distinctive and beautiful warble' *olivaceus* (L) like an olive, olive coloured; the upperparts are ashy-brown to olive, and the chin and throat are white. Inhabiting the northern part of Western Australia, ranging east to Queensland and south to Victoria; also found in New Guinea.

Yellow-breasted Gerygone Warbler *G. sulphurea*
sulfur (L) brimstone, sulphur *sulfureus* (L) like sulphur; a reference to the yellow breast. Inhabiting the Burma-Vietnam area and Malaysia.

Spotted Scrub-Wren *Sericornis maculatus*
sērikos (Gr) silken *ornis* (Gr) a bird *macula* (L) a mark, a spot *maculatus*, spotted; a reference to the black marks on the white throat and breast. Inhabiting south-western Australia and some neighbouring islands.

Black-and-Green Sericornis *S. nigroviridis*
niger (L) black *viridis* (L) green. Inhabiting New Guinea.

Rufous Songlark *Cinclorhamphus mathewsi*
kinklos (Gr) a small bird, probably a water ouzel or dipper *rhamphos* (Gr) the crooked beak of birds; a reference to the slightly curved beak: named after G. M. Mathews (1876-1949), an Australian naturalist and author; he founded the Mathews Ornithological Library and published his book *The Birds of Australia* in 1910. Widespread on the Australian mainland apart from Cape York Peninsula in Queensland.

Subfamily MUSCICAPINAE 134 species
musca (L) a fly *capio* (L) I take, seize. This subfamily, known as Old World Flycatchers, is widespread in Europe, Africa, southern Asia, and ranging east to Australasia; as the name tells us, they are not known in the New World, i.e. the Americas, and it also suggests, correctly, that their main food is insects.

Pale Flycatcher *Bradornis pallidus*
bradus (Gr) slow *ornis* (Gr) a bird *pallidus* (L) pale; the throat, belly and underparts are pale brown to white, the upperparts darker. Widespread through most of Africa.

South African Black Flycatcher *Melaenornis pannelaina*
melas (Gr), genitive *melanos*, black *ornis* (Gr) a bird *panu* (Gr) altogether; can mean very, exceedingly *elaia* (Gr) an olive *elainos* (Gr) of the olive tree; the plumage is entirely black with a bluish-green gloss. Inhabiting Kenya and ranging south to South Africa and across to West Africa south of Congo.

White-browed Forest Flycatcher *Fraseria cinerascens*
Named after Louis Fraser (fl 1819-1866) of the Zoological Society of London; he went on an expedition to Niger during 1841 and 1842 *cinereus* (L) ash-coloured *-ascens* = *-escens* (L) suffix meaning beginning to, approaching, greyish. Inhabiting Africa.

Pied Flycatcher *Ficedula hypoleuca*
ficedula (=*ficecula* and *ficetula*) (L) a garden warbler or similar small bird, a *biccafico* (It) from *biccare*, to peck, and *fica*, a fig, 'a fig pecker'; they are not known to eat figs but might have been seen pecking insects from figs; insects, larvae, and spiders are their main food *hupo* (Gr) under, less than usual *leukos* (Gr) white; the underparts are a dullish white, 'off white'. Inhabiting large areas of Europe including western Britain, parts of Spain, and northern Africa, ranging east to

Siberia and south to Asia Minor; wintering in Africa, south to Tanzania.

Palawan Flycatcher *F. platenae*
Named after Dr Margarete Platen, wife of Dr C. C. Platen (1843-1899); they were in the Celebes and Philippines from 1878 to 1894. The English name refers to Palawan Island in the Philippines where the bird was found.

Brown Flycatcher *Muscicapa latirostris*
musca (L) a fly *capio* (L) I take, seize; the diet consists of various types of insects including beetles and grasshoppers *latus* (L) wide *rostrum* (L) the beak; a reference to the unusually broad bill: the upperparts are a blackish brown. Inhabiting eastern Siberia and ranging south to Manchuria and Korea, parts of India south-east through Burma to Indonesia and the Philippines.

Spotted Flycatcher *M. striata*
stria (L) a furrow *striatus* (New L) striped; it has dark stripes on the forehead and breast, but on the forehead these appear like broken lines, hence spotted. Widespread in Europe including the British Isles, and part of northern Africa, ranging east into Asia to the borders of Manchuria, and wintering in north-west India and Africa.

Grey Tit-Flycatcher *Myioparus plumbeus*
muia (Gr) a fly *parus* (L) a titmouse *plumbum* (L) lead *plumbeus* (L) leaden, lead-coloured. Inhabiting Africa.

Southern Yellow Robin *Eopsaltria australis*
ēōs (Gr) dawn, the red colour at dawn; can mean the east *psaltria* (Gr) a harpist; 'a harp-player from the east' *auster* (L) the south *australis* (L) southern; it does not necessarily mean Australia. Inhabiting the eastern part of Australia.

Yellow-bellied Robin *E. flaviventris*
flavus (L) yellow *venter* (L), genitive *ventris*, the belly. 'Robin' is a local name; although related to the robins it is not a true robin, as in the subfamily Turdinae. Inhabiting the Pacific Islands to the east of New Guinea.

White-faced Robin *Tregallasia leucops*
Named after T. H. Tregallas (1864-1938), an Australian ornithologist from Victoria *leukos* (Gr) white *ops* (Gr) the eye, the face. Inhabiting Australia and New Guinea.

Rock Robin Flycatcher   *Petroica archboldi*
petra (Gr) a rock   *-icus* (L) suffix meaning belonging to: named after R. Archbold (born 1907); an American zoologist who worked in the Mammals Department at the American Museum of Natural History; he was in New Guinea in 1933 and 1934. This flycatcher lives in Papua New Guinea.

Red-capped Robin Flycatcher   *P. goodenovii*
Named after Bishop Samuel Goodenough (1743-1829), an English naturalist who was at one time Vice-President of the Linnean Society of London. Widespread in Australia although not found in desert areas or humid forests.

Grey-headed Flycatcher   *Culicicapa ceylonensis*
culex (L), genitive *culicis*, a gnat, a fly   *capio* (L) I take, seize   *-ensis* (L) suffix meaning belonging to, usually of places; 'of Ceylon', now known as Sri Lanka. From India it ranges east through the Oriental area to Malaysia and Indonesia.

Subfamily   RHIPIDURINAE   38 species
rhipis (Gr), genitive *rhipidos*, a fan   *oura* (Gr) the tail; the birds in this subfamily have fan-shaped tails that can be spread into quite a large fan which they can also wave up and down, which accounts for the English name Fantail Flycatcher.

Grey Fantail   *Rhipidura fuliginosa*
fuligo (L), genitive *fuliginis*, soot   *-osus* (L) suffix meaning full of, prone to; 'very sooty'; a reference to the plumage which is mainly grey. Widespread in Australia, also found in Tasmania, New Zealand, New Caledonia, New Guinea; and also occurs on some Pacific islands.

Red-backed Fantail Flycatcher   *R. opistherythra*
opisthe (Gr) behind   *eruthros* (Gr) red. Inhabiting New Guinea.

Red-tailed Fantail   *R. phoenicura*
phoinix (Gr), genitive *phoinikos*, red   *oura* (Gr) the tail. Inhabiting the Indonesian area in the Oriental region.

Rufous-fronted Fantail   *R. rufifrons*
rufus (L) red   *frons* (L) forehead, brow. Inhabiting Celebes and ranging east to New Guinea, Solomon and other Pacific islands, and Australia.

Subfamily MONARCHINAE 133 species
monarkhos (Gr) a monarch, a king; the describers N. A. Vigors and Dr T. Horsfield wrongly supposed that these birds were allied to the Kingbirds of the family Tyrannidae, genus *Tyrannus*, named from their aggressive behaviour (see notes under Family on p. 222). N. A. Vigors, FRS (1785-1840) was Editor of the *Zoological Journal* from 1827 to 1834; Dr T. Horsfield (1773-1859) was a scientist who was in Sumatra from 1796 to 1818; he named many mammals and birds in the East.

Cape Flycatcher *Batis capensis*
batis (Gr) a ray or skate; can also mean a bird that frequents bushes; living in woodland areas it builds its nest in trees and bushes   *-ensis* (L) suffix meaning belonging to, usually of a place; from the Cape of Good Hope, South Africa; it ranges through the Cape Province as far north as Natal.

Little Yellow Flycatcher *Erythrocercus holochlorus*
eruthros (Gr) red   *kerkos* (Gr) the tail of an animal   *holos* (Gr) whole, entire; can mean on the whole, in general   *khloros* (Gr) green; can also mean honey-coloured, yellow. Inhabiting Africa.

Black Paradise Flycatcher *Terpsiphone atrocaudata*
terpsis (Gr) enjoyment, delight   *phōnē* (Gr) a sound, the voice, of men or animals; a reference to the joyful song, although some of the birds in this genus are rather indifferent songsters   *ater* (L) black   *cauda* (L) a tail   *caudata* (L) having a tail; the black tail may be as much as 25 cm (10 in) long. Inhabiting southern Asia and ranging south through Burma to Malaysia and Indonesia.

Seychelles Paradise Flycatcher   *T. corvina*
corvus (L) a rook   *-inus* (L) suffix meaning like; it is not as big as a rook, the body, without tail, being about 20 cm (8 in), but the colour is a glossy blue-black; the central tail feathers may be 25 to 30 cm (10 to 12 in) long. It is confined to a small island in the east of the Seychelles group known as La Digue.

African Paradise Flycatcher   *T. viridis*
viridis (L) green; the head neck and breast is a metallic blue-green. Widespread in Africa extending to south-western Arabia, but not known in Madagascar.

Black Myiagra Flycatcher   *Myiagra atra*
muia (Gr) a fly   *agra* (Gr) a catching, a hunting; can mean that which

is taken in hunting, the prey   *ater* (L) black. Inhabiting New Guinea.

Restless Flycatcher   *M. inquieta*   (formerly *Seisura*)
inquietus (L) restless, unquiet; a reference to the bird's habit of making constant small movements, as though nervous. Inhabiting northern Australia and ranging along the coastal area to the north-east and the east; it is also known in the south-west.

Yap Island Monarch   *Monarcha godeffroyi*
Monarcha, see notes under subfamily opposite: J. C. Godeffroy (1813-1885) was a German zoologist; he founded the Godeffroy Museum in Hamburg and organised various collectors who went to the South Pacific. Yap Island, a small Pacific island, lies about 1,288 km (800 miles) north of New Guinea in the group known as the Caroline Islands.

Black-faced Monarch Flycatcher   *M. melanopsis*
melas (Gr), genitive *melanos*, black   *opsis* (Gr) appearance, face; the colour is mainly grey, with a sharply defined black throat and forehead which surround the beak. Inhabiting Timor, New Guinea, and the coastal belt in eastern Australia from Cape York south to Victoria.

Versicolour Flycatcher   *Mayrornis versicolor*
Mayr + *ornis* (Gr) a bird; the name refers to Dr Ernst Mayr (born 1904), a Professor of Zoology at Harvard University, and a Director of the Museum of Comparative Zoology; he has written several authoritative books on birds   *versicolor* (L) of various colours, partly coloured. Inhabiting the islands of the South Pacific.

Subfamily   PACHYCEPHALINAE   48 species
pakhus (Gr) thick, stout   *kephalē* (Gr) the head; sometimes known by the name Thickheads, on account of the large head and rather shrike-like bills; they are also known as Whistlers, a reference to the pleasant call notes, and also sometimes called Shrike-Thrushes. They range in size from 15 to about 30 cm (6 to about 12 in), and the diet is mainly insects though some berries may also be taken.

Crested Bellbird   *Oreoica gutturalis*
oros (Gr), genitive *oreos*, a mountain   *-icus* (L) suffix meaning belonging to   *guttur* (L) the throat   *-alis* (L) suffix meaning relating to; a reference to the black gorget round the white face and throat; it has a black crest on the forehead and the name 'bellbird' refers to the bell-like note heard at the end of the song. Widespread in Australia but mostly away from coastal areas.

Golden-faced Pachycare *Pachycare flavogrisea*
pakhus (Gr) thick, stout   *karē* (Gr) the head; see above under Subfamily   *flavus* (L) yellow, golden   *griseus* (New L) grey. Inhabiting New Guinea.

Lorentz's Whistler   *Pachycephala lorentzi*
Named after Dr H. A. Lorentz (1871-1944), a zoologist who was exploring in New Guinea during the years 1903 to 1910, and later was appointed as Dutch Consul in South Africa. The birds in this genus are usually known as Whistlers on account of the pleasant whistling call notes. Inhabiting New Guinea.

Golden Whistler   *P. pectoralis*
pectus (L), genitive *pectoris*, the breast   -*alis* (L) suffix meaning relating to; a reference to the prominent band of black across the golden breast and the white throat which makes a contrast. It is widespread in the Australasian area, from Indonesia to the Bismarck Archipelago, and Fiji, and along the southern part of Australia including Tasmania.

Rufous Shrike-Thrush   *Colluricincla megarhyncha*
kolluriōn (Gr) a bird like a thrush   *kinklos* (Gr) a bird, perhaps the water ouzel; this bird in the genus *Cinclus* is considered by some to be related to the thrushes; it is more often known as a Dipper   *megas* (Gr) big   *rhunkhos* (Gr) the beak; a reference to the shrike-like beak. Inhabiting Indonesia and Australia.

Family AEGITHALIDAE   7 species
aigithalos (Gr) the tit, titmouse; sometimes classified as one of three subfamilies under Paridae, in which case the name becomes Aegithalinae; the other two are Parinae and Remizinae. This little group are known as Long-tailed Tits.

Long-tailed Tit   *Aegithalos caudatus*
cauda (L) the tail of an animal   -*atus* (L) suffix meaning provided with; a reference to the tail which may be even longer than the body, the whole bird being about 12·5 to 15 cm (5 to 6 in). Widespread in Europe including the British Isles, ranging east through Asia Minor, Iran, and the Caucasus to Kamchatka, Japan, and China.

White-cheeked Long-tailed Tit   *A. leucogenys*
leukos (Gr) white   *genus* (Gr) the cheek, the chin. Inhabiting southern Asia.

Common Bush Tit *Psaltriparus minimus*
psaltria (Gr) a female harpist *parus* (L) a titmouse, or tit; a reference to the high-pitched buzzing notes of the call *minimus* (L) smallest; it is only 11·5 cm (4½ in) long. Inhabiting the western part of North America, and Mexico.

Family REMIZIDAE 9 species
remiz is probably a Polish name for these birds; its use as a generic name was given by Dr F. P. Jarocki in an obscure Warsaw periodical in 1819; it replaced the former name *Anthoscopus*. Sometimes classified as a subfamily, see above under Family Aegithalidae; they are generally known as Penduline Tits.

Mouse-coloured Penduline Tit *Remiz musculus*
mus (L) a mouse, diminutive *musculus*, a small mouse; in this case taken to mean like a mouse; the name penduline is from the Latin *pendulus*, hanging, pendent, and refers to the type of nest which is built suspended from twigs of willow or other trees and usually hanging over water. Inhabiting Africa.

Penduline Tit *R. pendulinus*
Inhabiting the central part of Europe and ranging east across Eurasia, and south to southern France, Italy, Greece, Asia Minor to China.

Verdin *Auriparus flaviceps*
aurum (L) gold *parus* (L) a tit *flavus* (L) yellow, golden *ceps* (New L) from *caput* (L) the head; the head, face, and throat are golden yellow *verdin* is a French word for a bird, usually used to mean the yellowhammer. Inhabiting the south-western part of the USA and northern Mexico.

Fire-capped Tit *Cephalopyrus flammiceps*
kephalē (Gr) the head *pur* (Gr), genitive *puros*, fire *flamma* (L) a blaze, a flame *ceps* (New L) from *caput* (L) the head. The range is from India to China.

Family PARIDAE 46 species
parus (L) a titmouse, a tomtit. Sometimes classified as a subfamily; see under Family Aegithalidae opposite. These small birds, variously known as tits, tomtits, titmice, and chickadees, are popular wherever they come in contact with humans and are regular visitors to the garden bird table. Mainly insectivorous, they can manage on

other foods when necessary, and will take bread and other scraps put out in the garden, and of course nuts; this can be a real life-saver for them during a hard winter.

Coal Tit *Parus ater*
parus (L) a titmouse   *ater* (L) black; not entirely black, the colour is mostly grey, and the black head has a white patch on the back of the neck and the cheeks. Inhabiting Eurasia including the British Isles, Africa north of the Sahara, and ranging east to Kamchakta to Japan.

Black-capped Chickadee *P. atricapillus*
ater (L) black   *capillus* (L) the hair of men, usually the hair of the head; can mean the hair of animals: 'chickadee' is imitative of the call. Inhabiting Canada, the USA, and ranging south to Texas and northern Mexico.

Blue Tit *P. caeruleus*
caeruleus (L) blue; this particularly refers to the blue cap. Widespread in the western part of Eurasia including the British Isles, Africa north of the Sahara, ranging east through Asia Minor, to Caucasus, and Iran.

Crested Tit *P. cristatus*
crista (L) usually means a tuft on the head of animals   *cristatus* (L) crested. Inhabiting Europe but not the British Isles except northern Scotland, and not Italy, but ranging east to western Siberia.

Elegant Titmouse *P. elegans*
elegans (L) neat, elegant. Inhabiting the Philippines.

Great Tit *P. major*
major (L) greatest; one of the largest tits at about 14 cm ($5\frac{1}{2}$ in). Inhabiting Eurasia including the British Isles, Africa north of the Sahara, and ranging east to India, the Burma-Vietnam area, Malaysia, Indonesia and China.

Willow Tit *P. montanus*
mons (L), genitive *montis*, a mountain   *-anus* (L) suffix meaning belonging to; it is known to inhabit mountain shrubs at 2,133 m (7,000 ft) altitude in Asia: although it often breeds in marshy areas it does not have a special liking for willow trees. It is widespread in Eurasia including the southern half of Britain, but not Spain or Africa, and ranges east to Siberia, Kamchatka, and Japan.

Marsh Tit *P. palustris*
palus (L) a swamp, a marsh   *palustria* (L) swampy or marshy places; a misleading name as it does not usually frequent marshy places. Inhabiting Europe including England and Wales but not Ireland and Scotland, and not northern Scandinavia or Spain. A separate population inhabits eastern Asia.

Chestnut-backed Chickadee *P. rufescens*
rufus (L) red, ruddy   *-escens* (L) suffix meaning approaching, beginning to; i.e. 'reddish': the name 'chickadee' is imitative of the call. Inhabiting North America.

Sultan Tit *Melanochlora sultanea*
melas (Gr), genitive *melanos*, black   *khloros* (Gr) green, can mean honey-coloured, yellow   *sultaneus* (New L) like a sultan, from the colourful exotic plumage; mainly black offset by a bright golden-yellow crest, chest, and underparts. Probably the largest tit with a length up to 20 cm (8 in), inhabiting the eastern Himalayas from Nepal south to Burma and Malaysia.

Family SITTIDAE   21 species
sittē (Gr) a kind of woodpecker; also used to mean the nuthatch. The Nuthatches are small insectivorous birds closely related to the tits and often seen with them in parties hunting for insects and spiders; they will also take seeds and nuts, wedging a nut into a crevice and hammering at it with their strong beaks like a woodpecker; they walk about tree trunks, up, down, and across just as though they were on the ground.

Red-breasted Nuthatch *Sitta canadensis*
sittē (Gr) = *sitta* (New L) the nuthatch   *-ensis* (L) suffix meaning belonging to, usually of a place; it is not confined to Canada, and ranges from Alaska to Newfoundland and south to California, Florida, and northern Mexico.

Nuthatch *S. europaea*
Widespread in Europe including the southern half of Britain and the southern half of Scandinavia, ranging east to include Asia Minor, the Caucasus, Iran, Siberia, Japan, India, China and the Burma area.

Corsican Nuthatch *S. whiteheadi*
Named after John Whitehead (1860-1899), an English explorer and

naturalist who made an expedition to Corsica, and later to Borneo in 1885, and the Philippines in 1893.

Pink-faced Nuthatch   *Daphoenositta miranda*
daphoinos (Gr) has been used to mean, of wild beasts, blood-reeking, bloody; probably more correctly of their colour, red, tawny   *sittē* (Gr) = *sitta* (New L) the nuthatch; a reference to the colour of the face   *miror* (L) I wonder, I admire   *mirandus* (L) wonderful, marvellous. Inhabiting Papua New Guinea.

Wall Creeper   *Tichodroma murina*
teikhos (Gr) a wall   *dromos* (Gr) running about   *murus* (L) a wall *-inus* (L) suffix meaning belonging to; a reference to its habit of climbing about on rocks looking for insects, but it also frequents trees. Inhabiting mountains in Spain, northern Africa, in the Alps and other European ranges, Asia Minor, the Caucasus, Iran, and east through the Himalayas to north-west China; in inhabited areas it climbs about on walls.

Family   CERTHIIDAE   6 species
kerthios (Gr) a little bird, a treecreeper. These small birds, known as Treecreepers, are related to the Nuthatches; as the name suggests, they spend a lot of their time creeping about on trees looking for small invertebrate animals and often in parties with tits or nuthatches; unlike the latter which have soft tails, they have stiff tails that they use for support when climbing. Although essentially they are birds of the Old World, it will be seen that one species has managed to establish itself in America.

Short-toed Treecreeper   *Certhia brachydactyla*
brakhus (Gr) short   *daktulos* (Gr) a finger, can mean a toe; a name which tells us that the toes are short compared to other creepers which all have longish toes and claws. Widespread in Europe but not known in the British Isles or Scandinavia; it ranges south to the northern part of Africa and east to parts of Asia.

Common Treecreeper   *C. familiaris*
familiaris (L) a servant; can mean familiar, habitual. Very widespread in both America and Eurasia; it ranges from Alaska south to Nicaragua in Central America, and northern Siberia south to parts of China, the Himalayas and Japan; in Europe it is well known in the British Isles, the southern part of Scandinavia, but not Spain or the northern part of Africa.

Spotted Creeper *Salpornis spilonota*
salpinx (Gr) a war trumpet   *ornis* (Gr) a bird; an allusion to the shrill call note   *spilos* (Gr) a blemish, a spot   *nōton* (Gr) the back; the plumage is mainly brown, the upperparts and back being liberally spotted with white. Inhabiting most of Africa ranging south to Zambia and Zimbabwe, and northern South Africa; also the Himalayan foothills and India.

Family RHABDORNITHIDAE   only 2 species
rhabdos (Gr) a rod or stick   *rhabdōtos* (Gr) striped; of animals streaked   *ornis* (Gr), genitive *ornithos*, a bird; a reference to the striped head. Closely related to the Certhiidae, above, these two birds known as Philippine Creepers are confined to some of the Philippine Islands.

Plain-headed Creeper *Rhabdornis inornatus*
inornatus (L) undecorated, plain; a reference to the absence of the stripes on the head. Found only in the Philippine Islands.

Stripe-headed Creeper *R. mystacalis*
mustax (Gr), genitive *mustakos*, a moustache   *-alis* (L) suffix meaning relating to, like; a reference to the white stripes on the head and above the beak which give the appearance of a moustache. Like the Plain-headed Creeper, above, it is found only in the Philippine Islands.

Family CLIMACTERIDAE   6 species
klimaktēr (Gr) the rung of a ladder; a reference to their manner of climbing trees as though on a ladder.

White-throated Treecreeper *Climacteris leucophaea*
leukos (Gr) white   *phaios* (Gr) dark, grey; a reference to the white throat which is in contrast to the mainly grey plumage. Eating mainly insects and spiders, the treecreepers work their way up tree trunks in a spiral climb searching for their prey. Inhabiting Australia and New Guinea.

Black-tailed Treecreeper *C. melanura*
melas (Gr), genitive *melanos*, black   *oura* (Gr) the tail. Inhabiting Australia.

Family DICAEIDAE   58 species
dicaeum (New L) a coined name meaning the flowerpecker. They do not actually eat flowers but they take nectar from flowers with a

specially shaped tongue; they also eat berries and some species are particularly fond of mistletoe berries; probably all species also eat insects and spiders.

Olive-backed Flowerpecker *Prionochilus olivaceus*
prion (Gr) a saw   *kheilos* (Gr) a lip, rim; of humans the lip, of birds the beak; a reference to the serrated or saw-like edge of the beak *oliva* (L) an olive   *olivaceus* (L) similar to, olive-coloured. Inhabiting the Philippines.

Anna's Flowerpecker *Dicaeum annae*
dicaeum (New L) a coined name meaning the flowerpecker: named after Dr Anna A. Weber-Van Bosse (1852-1942), a Dutch botanist who was in New Guinea from 1888 to 1890; she was the wife of Prof M. W. C. Weber, the Dutch zoologist. This flowerpecker lives in Sumbalra and Flores.

Scarlet-backed Flowerpecker *D. cruentatum*
cruento (L) I make bloody   *cruentatum*, stained with blood, red. Inhabiting India, the Burma-Vietnam area, Sumatra and Borneo.

Nehrkorn's Flowerpecker *D. nehrkorni*
Named after Adolf Nehrkorn (1841-1916), a German ornithologist who collected for the Berlin and Brunswick museums. Inhabiting the mountains of Celebes.

Crested Berrypecker *Paramythia montium*
paramuthia (Gr) encouragement, exhortation; a reference to the behaviour of the male during nest-building; he takes no part in the work but accompanies the female while she is collecting the material and building, as though to give encouragement   *mons* (L), genitive *montis*, a mountain; it inhabits the mountains and forests of New Guinea and is one of the flowerpeckers that is fond of the mistletoe berries.

Spotted Pardalote *Pardalotus punctatus*
pardalōtus (Gr) spotted like a leopard   *punctus* (L) a puncture   *punctatus* (L) spotted as with punctures; these flowerpeckers have come to be known as 'pardalotes' on account of their spotted plumage. Inhabiting the eastern and southern part of Australia and Tasmania.

Forty-spotted Pardalote *P. quadrigintus*
quadriginta (L) forty. Inhabiting Tasmania and Banks Island.

Family NECTARINIIDAE 118 species
nektar (Gr) nectar; in Greek mythology the drink of the gods; also *nectar* (L) nectar *-inus* (L) a suffix meaning belonging to; a reference to their liking for the honey from the glands of plants. This family, known as Sunbirds, have a similar diet to the Flowerpeckers, and in addition to nectar they eat insects and spiders, and in some cases berries.

Violet-backed Sunbird *Anthreptes longuemarei*
anthos (Gr) a flower   *threptēr* (Gr) a feeder, a rearer; a reference to their habit of taking nectar from flowers; named after G. de Longuemare (fl 1831-1841), a French amateur collector. Inhabiting Africa.

Blue-headed Sunbird *Nectarinia alinae*
Named in honour of Lady Aline Jackson, the wife of Sir F. J. Jackson (1860-1929), naturalist and author; he was Governor of Uganda from 1911 to 1917. Inhabiting East Africa.

Sumba Sunbird *N. buettikoferi*
Named after Dr J. Büttikofer (1850-1927), a Dutch zoologist who was Director of the Zoological Gardens in Rotterdam from 1897 to 1924. Sumba is one of the chain of islands in Indonesia that lie to the east of Java.

Malachite Sunbird *N. famosa*
famosus (L) famous, much talked of: malachite is a mineral from which a green pigment is made; this refers to the upperparts, including the head and neck, which are a metallic green. Inhabiting Sudan, Ethiopia, and ranging south through East Africa to South Africa.

Loten's Sunbird *N. lotenia*
Named after J. G. Loten, FRS (1710-1789), a British naturalist who was Governor of Ceylon (now known as Sri Lanka) from 1752 to 1757. This sunbird inhabits India and Sri Lanka.

Beautiful Sunbird *N. pulchella*
pulcher (L) beautiful *-ellus* (L) diminutive suffix; 'a little beauty'; most sunbirds are small, less than $12\frac{1}{2}$ cm (5 in) including the tail, and have spectacular colouring with a metallic sheen; they can be compared to the humming birds of South America but they are not related. Inhabiting Senegal and Sierra Leone in the western part of Africa, Sudan to Somalia in the east, and south to Tanzania.

Mrs Gould's Sunbird *Aethopyga gouldiae*
aithos (Gr) burnt; can mean a red-brown colour *pugē* (Gr) the rump; a reference to the dark colour of the plumage under the tail: named after Mrs E. Gould (1804-1841) a bird artist, and the wife of J. Gould, FRS (1804-1881) an English zoologist. Inhabiting southern Asia, India, the Burma-Vietnam area and China.

Streaked Spider Hunter *Arachnothera magna*
arakhnēs (Gr) a spider   *thēraō* (Gr) I hunt, chase, wild beasts; can mean I catch wild beasts; it has been seen to hover and pick a spider out of its web, but like other birds in this family it also takes insects, nectar, and mistletoe berries   *magnus* (L) great; it is one of the largest species, measuring 21·5 cm (8½ in) from the beak to the tip of the tail; the beak itself may be 5 cm (2 in) long. The English name refers to the colour of the upperparts which are olive to yellow and streaked with black. Inhabiting the Himalayan area, Sikkim, Assam, and the Burma-Vietnam area.

Family   ZOSTEROPIDAE   79 species
zōstēr (Gr) a girdle, a band   *ops* (Gr) the eye; a reference to the white ring round the eye, and they are usually known as White-Eyes. Almost without exception the birds in this family have a white ring round the eye; they are small birds, from 10 to 12·5 cm (4 to 5 in) long, and related to the Sunbirds; the diet is similar consisting of nectar, insects and berries.

Mangrove White-Eye   *Zosterops chloris*
khloros (Gr) green; a yellowish green plumage is predominant in this family, and nearly all have the white ring round the eye. Inhabiting Indonesia, Papua New Guinea, and Australia.

Pale White-Eye   *Z. pallida*
pallidus (L) pale, pallid; as the English and Latin names suggest, the plumage is pale, with more yellow than other species. Inhabiting Ethiopia, Kenya, Tanzania, and South Africa.

Oriental White-Eye   *Z. palpebrosa*
palpebra (L) the eyelid; can mean the eyelashes   *-osus* (L) suffix meaning prone to, full of; 'prominent eyelashes'; a reference to the ring of small white feathers round the eye. Inhabiting south-eastern Asia, including Afghanistan, India, the Burma-Vietnam area, south-western China, and Indonesia.

African Yellow White-Eye *Z. senegalensis*
-ensis (L) suffix meaning belonging to, usually a place; in addition to Senegal it ranges south through East and Central Africa to Mozambique and South Africa. The plumage is mainly yellow; the name does not refer to the ring round the eye, but see *Z. wallacei*, below.

Yellow-spectacled or Wallace's White-Eye *Z. wallacei*
The only species known that has a yellow eye-ring instead of white: named after Dr Alfred R. Wallace, FRS (1823-1913), the British zoologist, who was in Malaysia from 1848 to 1852; he is well known for establishing the Wallace Line, an imaginary line separating Bali, Borneo, and Mindanao, from Lombok, Celebes, and Talaut Island, and this is zoologically important. This white-eye inhabits the Lesser Sundas.

Woodford's White-Eye *Woodfordia superciliosa*
Named after C. M. Woodford (1852-1927), the Resident Commissioner in the Solomons Protectorate from 1897 to 1915 *supercilium* (L) the eyebrow *-osus* (L) suffix meaning prone to, full of; 'prominent eyebrows'; a reference to the ring of feathers round the eye. Inhabiting the Solomon Islands.

Javan Crested White-Eye *Lophozosterops javanica*
lophos (Gr) a crest, the crest of birds *-icus* (L) belonging to, 'of Java'; inhabiting Java and neighbouring islands.

Black-capped Speirops *Speirops lugubris*
speira (Gr) anything wound or wrapped round a thing *ops* (Gr) the eye; a reference to the ring of small white feathers that surround the eye *lugubris* (L) of or belonging to mourning, mourning apparel; a reference to the black cap. Inhabiting Cameroon.

Family EPTHIANURIDAE 5 species
phthinas (Gr) decreasing, wasting *oura* (Gr) the tail; *Epthianura* is a coined name and supposed to mean 'decreased tail', a reference to the unusually small tail. This small family are known as Australian Chats, the diet is insects hunted on the ground though they will take nectar if available.

White-fronted Chat *Epthianura albifrons*
albus (L) white *frons* (L) forehead. Inhabiting Queensland, New South Wales, Victoria, and ranging west along the southern part of Australia.

Crimson Chat *E. tricolor*
tricolor (New L) of three colours; it has a bright plumage consisting of crimson, brown, and white. Inhabiting western and southern parts of Australia and partly central.

Gibber-bird *Ashbyia lovensis*
Named after Edwin Ashby (1861-1941), an Australian ornithologist; he was President of the Royal Australian Ornithologists Union in 1926   *-ensis* (L) suffix meaning belonging to; named from Love's Creek, near Alice Springs in central Australia. Gibber is a native name for the desert stones and pebbles polished by sandblast; this chat lives in desert areas of central Australia.

Family   MELIPHAGIDAE   169 species
meli (Gr) honey   *phagein* (Gr) to eat. Known in general as Honey-eaters, they have a tongue that is semi-tubular and bristle-tipped; adaptations for feeding on nectar from flowers, but they also take insects, fruit, and berries. Ranging in size from 10 to 36 cm (4 to 14 in), they show a great diversity of structure and habits, but the one thing they all have in common is the specially adapted tongue.

Long-billed Honeyeater   *Melilestes megarhynchus*
meli (Gr) honey   *lēstēs* (Gr) a robber; 'a honey robber'   *megas* (Gr) big   *rhunkhos* (Gr) the beak, bill. Inhabiting New Guinea.

Slaty-chinned Longbill   *Toxorhamphus poliopterus*
toxon (Gr) a bow for use with arrows; can mean anything bowed or arched   *rhamphos* (Gr) a beak, bill, specially the curved beak of birds; a reference to the long downward curved bill   *polios* (Gr) hoary, grey, usually of hair   *pteron* (Gr) feathers; a reference to the slate-coloured plumage. Inhabiting New Guinea.

Brown Honeyeater   *Lichmera indistincta*
lichmērēs (Gr) playing with the tongue, licking, as of snakes; the tongue is specially shaped and bristled-tipped for taking nectar and insects from flowers   *indistinctus* (L) unpretentious, indistinct; a reference to the sombre brown plumage. Inhabiting Australia and ranging west to Bali and north to New Guinea.

Red-headed Honeyeater   *Myzomela erythrocephala*
muzō (Gr) I suck in   *meli* (Gr) honey   *eruthros* (Gr) red   *kephalē* (Gr) the head. One of the smallest birds in this family, only $12\frac{1}{2}$ cm (5 in) long, it lives in the mangrove swamps of Australia.

Dainty Honeyeater *M. pulchella*
pulcher (L) beautiful *-ellus* (L) diminutive suffix, 'a little beauty'.
Inhabiting New Ireland.

Yellow-faced Honeyeater *Meliphaga chrysops*
meli (Gr) honey *phagein* (Gr) to eat *khrusos* (Gr) gold *khruseos* (Gr) gold-coloured, golden-yellow *ops* (Gr) the eye, also the face. Inhabiting Australia from northern Queensland and ranging along the coastal belt to the southern parts.

Lewin's Honeyeater *M. lewini*
Named after J. W. Lewin (1770-1819), a naturalist, author, and artist, of New South Wales; he wrote and published the book *Birds of New Holland*. Inhabiting eastern Australia.

White-eared Mountain Meliphaga *M. montana*
mons (L), genitive *montis*, a mountain *montanus* (L) of a mountain. In some cases honeyeaters are known as meliphagas; this one lives in the mountains of New Guinea.

Orange-cheeked Honeyeater *Oreornis chrysogenys*
oros (Gr), genitive *oreos*, a mountain *ornis* (Gr) a bird *khrusos* (Gr) gold *khruseos* (Gr) gold-coloured, golden-yellow *genus* (Gr) the jaw, cheek. Another honeyeater inhabiting the mountains of New Guinea.

White-throated Honeyeater *Melithreptus albogularis*
meli (Gr) honey *threptos* (Gr) fed, brought up *albus* (L) white *gula* (L) the throat *-aris* (L) suffix meaning pertaining to. Inhabiting Australia and New Guinea.

Strong-billed Honeyeater *M. validirostris*
validus (L) strong *rostrum* (L) the beak. Inhabiting Tasmania.

White-fronted Melidectes *Melidectes leucostephes*
meli (Gr) honey *dektēs* (Gr) a beggar, a receiver *leukos* (Gr) white *stephos* (Gr) a crown, a garland. Inhabiting New Guinea.

Bar-breasted Honeyeater *Ramsayornis fasciatus*
Named after Dr E. P. Ramsay (1842-1916), an Australian zoologist; he was Curator of the Australian Museum in Sydney from 1874 to 1894 *ornis* (Gr) a bird *fascia* (L) a band or girdle *fasciatus* (L) banded, can mean striped; a reference to the stripes across the breast. Inhabiting Australia.

Rufous-throated Honeyeater *Conopophila rufogularis*
kōnōps (Gr), genitive *kōnōpos*, a gnat, a mosquito *philos* (Gr) loved, pleasing; in addition to nectar the honeyeaters like the insects that are attracted by the nectar, and the specially adapted and bristle-tipped tongue assists in their collection; it is also thought that the birds help with the pollination of the flowers *rufus* (L) red *gularis* (L) pertaining to the throat. Inhabiting northern Australia.

Eastern Spinebill *Acanthorhynchus tenuirostris*
akantha (Gr) a thorn, a prickle *rhunkhos* (Gr) the beak *tenuis* (L) thin, slender *rostrum* (L) the beak; these are references to the unusually long spinelike bill. Ranging from northern Queensland to southern Australia, including Kangaroo Island and Tasmania.

Bellbird *Anthornis melanura*
anthos (Gr) a flower, a blossom *ornis* (Gr) a bird; a reference to its fondness of flowers where it can obtain nectar *melas* (Gr) black *oura* (Gr) the tail; the tail is really dark brown but it varies and is occasionally almost black. These birds sometimes sing in chorus and it sounds like the pealing of bells; they are confined to New Zealand and neighbouring islands.

Tui or Parson Bird *Prosthemadera novaeseelandiae*
prosthema (Gr) an addition, an appendage *deirē* (Gr) the neck, throat; a reference to the two white tufts of feathers on each side of the throat which resemble the two white 'lapels' sometimes worn by clergymen, and this has given rise to the name 'parson bird'; it also has a white lacy collar *novaeseelandiae* (New L) New Zealand. *Tui* is a Maori name for the bird which is confined to New Zealand and neighbouring islands.

Cape Sugarbird *Promerops cafer*
pro- (L) for *merops* (L) a bird, the bee-eater; *promerops* is a coined name, and the reason for the Latin prefix is obscure; the bee-eater, in the genus *Merops*, eats bees but does not eat honey, whereas the sugarbird of South Africa does eat honey; why there are two species of *Promerops* living in Africa, a long way from the other honeyeaters of the east, is something of a mystery, and may be an example of convergent evolution *kafir* (Ar) the name of a South African people. Inhabiting the southern part of South Africa.

Family EMBERIZIDAE
emberiza (New L) from Swiss-German *emmeritz*, a bunting or yellow

hammer. This very big group of about 550 species can be divided into 5 subfamilies: the Emberizinae (the Buntings and American Sparrows), the Catamblyrhynchinae (the Plush-capped Finch), the Cardinalinae (the Cardinal-Grosbeaks), the Thraupinae (the Tanagers and Honeycreepers) and the Tersinae (the Swallow-Tanager).

Ornithologists have various opinions about the divisions, and the naming of the subfamilies, as correct anatomical distinctions are by no means obvious; this book follows the system used by E. S. Gruson in his book *A Checklist of the Birds of the World*.

They range in size from 8 to about 30 cm (3 to about 12 in), and their general appearance and beak structure is very varied; the food is mainly insects, berries, seeds and fruit, and the honeycreepers also take nectar.

Subfamily EMBERIZINAE 281 species
Crested Bunting *Melophus lathami*
melas (Gr) black *lophos* (Gr) a crest; the upperparts are a glossy black including the pointed crest: named after Dr J. Latham, FRS (1740–1837) an English zoologist and author. Inhabiting the Himalayas, Yunnan, and Burma.

Yellow Bunting or Yellowhammer *Emberiza citrinella*
Emberiza, see above under Subfamily *citrus* (L) the citron-tree *citrinus* (New L) citron or lemon-coloured *-ellus* (L) diminutive suffix. Inhabiting Europe including the British Isles and ranging east through Eurasia to the Sea of Okhotsk.

Golden-breasted Bunting *E. flaviventris*
flavus (L) yellow, golden *venter* (L), genitive *ventris*, the belly, stomach; the yellow plumage extends up the breast to the throat. Inhabiting Africa from Nigeria to Ethiopia and ranging south to South Africa.

Black-headed Bunting *E. melanocephala*
melas (Gr), genitive *melanos*, black *kephalē* (Gr) the head. Inhabiting south-eastern Europe, Asia Minor, Georgia, the Caucasus, Iran, and the mountains of Turkestan.

Reed Bunting *E. schoeniclus*
skhoinos (Gr) a rush, or reed *skhoiniklos* (Gr) a water-bird, a name used by Aristotle, probably to mean the white water-wagtail; it is not related to the White Wagtail *Motacilla alba* and in this case is only used to indicate its habitat among the reeds. Wide distribution throughout

Europe and Central Asia, but not Iceland; it includes northern Africa and Asia Minor and extends east along a narrower band to Kamchatka and northern Japan.

Socotra Mountain Bunting *E. socotrana*
-anus (L) suffix meaning belonging to; Socotra is an island in the Indian Ocean lying about 322 km (200 miles) to the east of the Horn of Africa; the Horn of Africa is not marked in maps; it is the northeastern part of Somalia.

Lapland Bunting or Longspur *Calcarius lapponicus*
calcar (L), genitive *calcaris*, a spur   *-icus* (L) belonging to; 'of Lapland'; the generic name refers to the unusually long hind toe and claw. Inhabiting the northern coasts of Eurasia from Norway to America and Greenland but not Iceland, and migrating south in winter.

Snow Bunting *Plectrophenax nivalis*
plēktron (Gr) a cock's spur   *phenax* (Gr) a cheat, an impostor; for technical reasons the name was changed by Dr Stejneger from *Plectrophanes*, 'spur-showing', to *Plectrophenax*, but the name does not seem to have any meaning except that it took the place of *Plectrophanes*, i.e. 'an impostor'; it does have a long hind claw   *nix* (L), genitive *nivis*, snow   *nivalis* (L) of snow, snowy. Inhabiting northern American and Eurasian coasts and arctic islands, ranging south to the British Isles and parts of Eurasia as far east as Kamchatka.

American Tree Sparrow *Spizella arborea*
spiza (Gr) a finch   *-ellus* (L) diminutive suffix   *arbor* (L) a tree   *arboreus* (L) pertaining to a tree: the Greek word *spiza*, a finch, 'a small piping bird', is fairly widely used for small birds; the American sparrows are not related to the sparrows of the Old World (Family Ploceidae). This tree sparrow inhabits North America ranging from Alaska, northern Canada, and Newfoundland, to southern USA.

Patagonian Sierra-Finch *Phrygilus patagonicus*
phrugilos (Gr) a bird, perhaps a finch   *-icus* (L) suffix meaning belonging to, 'of Patagonia'; this is the southern part of Argentina, South America   *sierra* is Spanish for a ridge of mountains.

White-throated Seedeater *Sporophila albogularis*
spora (Gr) seed   *philos* (Gr) loved, pleasing   *albus* (L) white   *gula* (L) the throat   *-aris* (L) suffix meaning pertaining to. Inhabiting Brazil.

Slate-coloured Seedeater *S. schistacea*
skhistos (Gr) divided, cleft, as a piece of slate; hence *schist* (New L) slate, and *schistaceus* (New L) slaty, slate-coloured. Inhabiting Central and South America.

Blue Seedeater *Amaurospiza concolor*
amauros (Gr) dark *spiza* (Gr) a finch, 'a small piping bird'; a reference to the blue plumage *concolor* (L) similar in colour, of one colour. Inhabiting Central and South America.

Cuban Bullfinch *Melopyrrha nigra*
melas (Gr) black *purrhos* (Gr) red, flame-coloured; a reference to the black plumage with the flame-coloured breast; it is not related to the Old World bullfinches in the family Fringillidae. Inhabiting Cuba and nearby islands.

St Lucia Black Finch *Melanospiza richardsoni*
melas (Gr) black *spiza* (Gr) 'a small piping bird', a finch: named after W. B. Richardson (fl 1919), an American naturalist and author; he was in Central America on several expeditions during the period 1887 to 1917. St Lucia Island is one of the group known as the Windward Islands in the Caribbean Sea.

Large Ground Finch *Geospiza magnirostris*
gē (Gr) the earth, ground *spiza* (Gr) 'a small piping bird', a finch *magnus* (L) great *rostrum* (L) the beak; one of the larger ground finches with a big strong beak. This is one of a number of finches that are confined to the Galapagos Islands, and are known as Darwin's Finches; C. R. Darwin, FRS (1809-1882) was the zoologist who became famous for his work on the theory of evolution by natural selection, which was based on the Galapagos finches.

Cocos Island Finch *Pinaroloxias inornata*
pinaros (Gr) dirty *loxos* (Gr) crosswise; *Loxia* was used for the crossbills but later was used for other finch-like birds; *pinaros* indicates the dull plumage; cf. Sooty Rock Chat *Pinarornis plumosus* *inornatus* (L) plain, unadorned; another reference to the rather drab greyish-brown plumage. It is confined to Cocos Island, some 966 km (600 miles) to the north-east of Galapagos, where all the other Darwin finches live (see above and page 19).

Rufous-sided Towhee *Pipilo erythrophthalmus*
pipio (L) a young piping or chirping bird *pipilo* (L) I chirp *erythros*

(Gr) red   *ophthalmos* (Gr) the eye; they have a bright red eye and rufous plumage on the flanks. Inhabiting Canada and ranging through most of the USA to northern Mexico. The name towhee is imitative of the two-note call which sounds like to-whee.

Pectoral Sparrow   *Arremon taciturnus*
arrhēmōn (Gr) silent, without speech   *taciturnus* (L) not talkative, quiet; a reference to the absence of a song; it only makes a repeated high call: 'pectoral' from *pectus* (L) the breast; refers to a black patch on each side of the breast. Inhabiting Venezuela and Colombia.

Black-headed Brush-Finch   *Atlapetes atricapillus*
Atlapetes, obscure, possibly a corruption of *altus* (L) high + *petes* (New L) a flier, from *petomai* (Gr) to fly, of birds, bees etc.; the name is not explained in the ornithological records in the British Museum (Natural History)   *ater* (L) black   *capillus* (L) the hair, usually the hair of the head, can mean the hair of animals. Inhabiting Central and South America.

Rufous-capped Brush-Finch   *A. pileatus*
pileus = *pilleus* (L) a felt cap   *pilleatus* (L) wearing a felt cap. Inhabiting southern Mexico.

Subfamily   CATAMBLYRHYNCHINAE   1 species
katamblunō (Gr) I make blunt   *rhunkhos* (Gr) the beak; an allusion to the stubby beak. Little is known about this unusual finch-like bird and so for the present it is placed in a family on its own.

Plush-capped Finch   *Catamblyrhynchus diadema*
diadema (Gr) a band or fillet, usually worn round the head; a reference to the golden brown forecrown which is erect and plush-like to the touch. Inhabiting Venezuela and Colombia and ranging south through Ecuador and Peru to Bolivia.

Subfamily   CARDINALINAE   37 species
cardinalis (L) a chief, a principal; here taken to mean red on account of the red robes worn by cardinals; although all the birds in this subfamily are not red, the name is an allusion to the red plumage of the birds in the genus *Cardinalis* from which the subfamily takes its name.

Cardinal   *Cardinalis cardinalis*   (formerly *Pyrrhuloxia*)
Inhabiting southern Canada and ranging south through the USA to Florida, the Gulf Coast, Mexico, and part of Central America.

Yellow-shouldered Grosbeak *Caryothraustes humeralis*
karuon (Gr) a nut, can be almost any kind of nut   *thrauō* (Gr) I break in pieces   *thraustos* (Gr) broken; a reference to its ability to break open the toughest nuts   *humerus* = *umerus* (L) the upper arm   *umerale* (L) a cape for the shoulders; a reference to the yellow plumage on the 'shoulders': the name grosbeak has been given because of the large, powerful, conical bill. Inhabiting South America.

Blue Grosbeak   *Passerina caerulea*
passer (L) a sparrow, or other small bird   *-inus* (L) suffix meaning like; it is similar to a sparrow in size and shape, but not in colour   *caeruleus* (L) dark blue. Inhabiting North and Central America.

Painted Bunting   *P. ciris*
keiris (Gr) a bird mentioned in Greek mythology: 'painted' is a suitable name for this bird with a plumage of gaudy colours including blue, green, yellow, and various shades of red in a distinct pattern. Inhabiting southern USA, Mexico, and Panama.

Subfamily   THRAUPINAE   233 species
thraupis (Gr) a little bird. This large group consists of smallish birds measuring from 10 to 20 cm (4 to 8 in); the diet is varied and may include seeds, fruit, insects, and in some cases honey. They are mostly known as Tanagers and Honeycreepers though some unusual names are used such as Euphonias and Flower-Piercers.

Yellow-green Bush Tanager   *Chlorospingus flavovirens*
khloros (Gr) green, pale green, to yellow   *spingos* = *spinos* (Gr) a small bird   *flavus* (L) yellow   *virens* (L) becoming green, or green. Inhabiting Ecuador.

Grey-capped Hemispingus   *Hemispingus reyi*
hēmi- (Gr) prefix meaning half   *spingos* = *spinos* (Gr) a small bird; in this case *hēmi-* is taken to mean like, rather than half, and as spinos has been used to mean a finch, the name would mean 'like a finch': named after Dr J. G. C. E. Rey (1838-1909), a German zoologist who made a special study of oology, i.e. birds' eggs. This tanager lives in South America.

Summer Tanager   *Piranga rubra*
piranga (New L) from a native name for this bird   *rubra* (L) red; it is almost entirely rosy red. Fairly widespread in certain parts of the USA from Wisconsin south to Florida and west to New Mexico and

California, in summer, hence the name Summer Tanager; in winter migrating south to Mexico, through Central America, to Peru.

Azure-shouldered Tanager *Thraupis cyanoptera*
thraupis (Gr) a little bird, sometimes taken to mean a goldfinch *kuaneos* (Gr) glossy blue *pteron* (Gr) feathers, can mean wings. Inhabiting South America.

Golden-crowned Tanager *Iridosornis rufivertex*
iris (Gr), genitive *iridos*, the rainbow; can mean any bright-coloured circle, as a halo; a reference to the circular golden patch on the top of the black head *ornis* (Gr) a bird *rufus* (L) red *vertex* (L) a top, a summit; a misleading name as the crown is usually golden, but it can vary in different localities. Inhabiting Venezuela, Colombia, and Ecuador.

Thick-billed Euphonia *Euphonia laniirostris*
euphonia (Gr) goodness of voice; indicating a rather better song than other tanagers which taken as a whole are poor songsters *lanius* (L) a butcher *rostrum* (L) the beak; 'butcher-beaked'; a reference to the powerful beak. Inhabiting Central America and north-western South America, ranging from Costa Rica south to Bolivia and neighbouring parts of Brazil.

Glistening-green Tanager *Chlorochrysa phoenicotis*
khlōros (Gr) green *khruseos* (Gr) golden-yellow *phoinix* (Gr), genitive *phoinikos*, purple-red, crimson *ous* (Gr), genitive *ōtos*, the ear; an allusion to the small blue and red patches just above the ear coverts. Inhabiting the western part of Pacific Colombia and north-western Ecuador.

Black-headed Tanager *Tangara cyanoptera*
Tangara is a Tupi native name for a brightly-coloured bird *kuaneos* (Gr) glossy blue *pteron* (Gr) feathers, can mean wings; it has a black head and the wings are black with blue flight feathers. Inhabiting Guyana, Venezuela, north-eastern Colombia, and northern Brazil.

Black and Green Tanager *T. nigroviridis*
niger (L) black *viridis* (L) green; the plumage appears to be alternate streaks of black and green, with the green changing almost to blue in certain parts and with changing light. Inhabiting the mountains of Venezuela, Colombia, and Ecuador, and ranging south to the northern part of Bolivia.

Purple Honeycreeper *Cyanerpes caeruleus*
kuaneos (Gr) dark blue, glossy blue *herpēstēs* (Gr) a creeping thing *caeruleus* (L) dark blue; the plumage of the male is generally purple and black, while the female is quite different being olive green. In addition to insects and fruit the honeycreepers take nectar. Inhabiting Trinidad and the north-western part of South America including the Amazon Basin.

Bluish Flowerpiercer *Diglossa caerulescens*
di- (Gr) a prefix meaning two, double *glōssa* (Gr) the tongue; the tip of the tongue is divided and has feather-like ends to facilitate taking the nectar, and the beak is specially adapted to actually pierce the corolla of the flower *caeruleus* (L) dark blue *-escens* (L) suffix meaning approaching, beginning to be, i.e. bluish; the plumage is rather a nondescript greyish blue. Inhabiting the Andes Mountains in Colombia, Ecuador, Peru, and northern Bolivia.

Subfamily TERSININAE 1 species

Swallow-Tanager *Tersina viridis*
Tersina, a name coined by Vieillot, evidently from the French vernacular name *La Tersine*; further information is not given in Vieillot's description in the ornithological records in the British Museum (Natural History) *viridis* (L) green; the plumage of the male is really a torquoise blue but this changes to an emerald green, according to changes of light; the female is bright green. Inhabiting Trinidad and most of the northern half of South America, ranging from Panama in Central America to northern Argentina including Brazil and Peru. The Swallow-Tanager is difficult to classify and so has been given a subfamily on its own; some authors give it a family. Anatomically it is very different from a tanager and is not related to the swallows, but it has a swallow-like bill and catches flying insects in a similar manner to swallows. L. J. P. Vieillot (1748-1831) was a well-known French zoologist and author.

Family PARULIDAE 120 species
parula (New L) from *parus* (L) a titmouse *-ulus* (L) diminutive suffix; a misleading name as this family consists of birds that are mostly larger than the tits, ranging from 10 to 18 cm (4 to 7 in), whereas the tits are mostly about 10 to $12\frac{1}{2}$ cm (4 to 5 in). Known as Wood Warblers or American Warblers they are not related to the Old World Warblers

in the subfamily Sylviinae; the diet is mostly insects and fruit though some will take nectar.

Blue-winged Warbler   *Vermivora pinus*
vermis (L) a worm   *voro* (L) I devour; it may include worms in the diet but insects are the main source of food   *pinus* (L) a pine; it is known to frequent pine forests but this is not the only habitat. The plumage is mostly yellow with blue wings; it inhabits the central and eastern USA ranging south to Georgia and wintering further south to Nicaragua.

Virginia's Warbler   *V. virginiae*
Named in honour of Mrs M. Virginia C. Anderson, the wife of Dr W. W. Anderson (1824-1901), a surgeon in the United States Army from 1849 to 1861. The range is western USA and Mexico.

Northern Parula   *Parula americana*
Parula, see under Family, above: a small greyish blue warbler that inhabits the eastern part of North America.

Yellow-throated Warbler   *Dendroica dominica*
dendron (Gr) a tree   *-icus* (L) suffix meaning belonging to; it favours mature woodland areas: named after the Dominican Republic, one of the islands in the West Indies, it is fairly widespread in the USA and ranges south to Central America in winter.

Kirtland's Warbler   *D. kirtlandii*
Named after Dr J. P. Kirtland (1793-1877), an American zoologist from Ohio. A very rare warbler, it is restricted apparently by choice to an area of pine forest in north central Michigan, but migrates south in winter.

Ovenbird   *Seiurus aurocapillus*
seiō (Gr) I shake, I move to and fro   *oura* (Gr) the tail; it does not actually wag the tail but raises it when walking over a pile of leaves and then lowers it again   *aurum* (L) gold   *aureus* (L) golden, colour of gold   *capillus* (L) the hair of men, usually the hair of the head, can mean the hair of animals; it has a reddish-gold stripe on the crown. The name ovenbird comes from the form of the nest, a domed structure with an entrance at the side. Inhabiting Canada and the USA and ranging south in winter to the Gulf Coast, the Lesser Antilles, and Mexico to Colombia, South America.

Worm-eating Warbler　*Helmitheros vermivorus*
helmins (Gr) a worm　*thēraō* (Gr) I hunt, I take; it eats various small invertebrates　*vermis* (L) a worm　*voro* (L) I devour. Inhabiting the USA and moving south in winter to the Bahamas, the West Indies, and Central America as far as Panama.

Prothonotary Warbler　*Protonotaria citrea*
protos (Gr) first　*notarius* (L) a secretary; this refers to the Chief Secretary of the Chancery at Rome, who wears yellow robes　*kitrea* (Gr) the citron tree; indicating the yellow plumage of the bird. Inhabiting the south-eastern part of the USA, Central America, and the northern part of South America.

Grey-crowned Yellowthroat　*Geothlypis poliocephala*
gē (Gr) the earth, ground　*thlupis* (Gr) a small bird; an obscure Greek word probably used to mean a finch　*polios* (Gr) hoary, grey　*kephalē* (Gr) the head; the birds in this genus usually have yellow plumage on the throat and upper breast. Inhabiting North and Central America.

Canada Warbler　*Wilsonia canadensis*
Named after Alexander Wilson (1766-1813), a Scottish ornithologist who settled in the USA and became known as the 'Father of American Ornithology'; a number of other birds bear his name　*-ensis* (L) suffix meaning belonging to; it is not confined to Canada, and ranges south in eastern USA, and winters in Guatemala, Central America, south to Ecuador and Peru in South America.

Golden-fronted Redstart　*Myioborus ornatus*
muia (Gr) a fly　*boros* (Gr) devouring　*ornatus* (L) decorated, adorned; a reference to the brilliant golden face and breast in contrast to the dark olive-grey upperparts. Inhabiting the eastern Andes in Venezuela and Colombia, South America.

Golden-crowned Warbler　*Basileuterus culicivorus*
basileutōr = *basileus* (Gr) a king　*culex* (L), genitive *culicis*, a gnat, a midge　*voro* (L) I devour. Inhabiting Central and South America.

Rufous-capped Warbler　*B. rufifrons*
rufus (L) red　*frons* (L) forehead, brow; the crown and ear-coverts are chestnut-coloured. Inhabiting Mexico and Central America and ranging south to Colombia and Venezuela.

White-eared Conebill *Conirostrum leucogenys*
conus (L) a cone   *rostrum* (L) the beak; a reference to the cone-shaped bill   *leukos* (Gr) white   *genus* (Gr) the cheek. Inhabiting Central and South America.

Bananaquit *Coereba flaveola*
coereba (Braz) a small bird   *flavus* (L) yellow   *-olus* (L) diminutive suffix; 'small and yellow': it is not known specially to favour bananas but is fond of various fruits and nectar. Inhabiting Central America and the West Indies, Peru, Bolivia, Paraguay, Brazil and Argentina.

Family DREPANIDIDAE   15 species
drepanon (Gr) a sickle; a reference to the sickle-shaped bill, though some species have a short parrot-like bill. Usually known as Hawaiian Honeycreepers they are confined to the Hawaiian Islands.

Crested Honeycreeper *Palmeria dolei*
Named after Henry C. Palmer (fl 1890); he collected for Rothschild's Tring Museum on Laysan, one of the islands in the Hawaiian group, from 1890 to 1893: also S. B. Dole (1844-1926), a judge in Hawaii and President of the Hawaiian Republic from 1894 to 1900.

Iiwi *Vestiaria coccinea*
vestis (L) clothing, a covering   *-arius* (L) suffix meaning pertaining to   *coccinus* (L) scarlet garments   *coccineus* (L) scarlet coloured; a reference to the brilliant red plumage which covers most of the body, and which was at one time used to make feather cloaks. *Iiwi* is a Hawaiian native name.

Amakihi *Viridonia virens*
viridis (L) green   *virens* (L) becoming green; referring to the bright green plumage. *Amakihi* is a Hawaiian native name.

Akepa *Loxops coccinea*
loxos (Gr) cross-wise   *ops* (Gr) the eye, face; can also mean aspect, appearance; it refers to the beak which has the tips of the lower and upper mandibles slightly crossed   *coccineus* (L) scarlet coloured; the plumage is more a bright orange colour than scarlet. *Akepa* is a Hawaiian native name.

Parrotbill *Psittirostra psittacea*
psittakos (Gr) a parrot   or *psittacus* (L) a parrot   *rostrum* (L) the beak   *-aceus* (L) suffix meaning similar to, like; this is one of the Drepani-

didae that has a bill more like that of a parrot, not long and curved like a scimitar. Inhabiting the Hawaiian Islands.

Family VIREONIDAE 39 species
vireo (L), genitive *vireonis*, a kind of bird, according to some the greenfinch; they are similar in size and colour to the greenfinch, but are only distantly related. Usually known as Vireos and Greenlets, the diet consists of insects and fruit.

Bell's Vireo *Vireo belli*
Named after J. G. Bell (1812-1899); an American naturalist and taxidermist of New York. Inhabiting North America and Central America.

Red-eyed Vireo *V. olivaceus*
oliva (L) an olive *olivaceus* (L) similar to; 'olive-coloured'; it is olive-green above and whitish below. One of the best known Vireos it ranges from Canada, south through the USA but mostly in the west central part, to the Gulf of Mexico and south to Brazil.

Golden-fronted Greenlet *Hylophilus aurantifrons*
hulē (Gr) a wood, forest *philos* (Gr) beloved, dear; a reference to the habitat which is mostly forest and woodland areas *aurum* (L) gold *auratus* (L) golden *aurantium* (New L) an orange *frons* (L) the forehead; the crown is bright orange. Inhabiting Central and South America.

Tawny-crowned Greenlet *H. ochraceiceps*
ōkhra (Gr) yellow-coloured earth, yellow-ochre *ochraceus* (New L) like ochre, pale yellow *ceps* (New L) from *caput* (L) the head; it has a yellowish to orange crown. Inhabiting Central America, the Guyanas, Venezuela, Brazil, Colombia, Ecuador and Bolivia.

Family ICTERIDAE 92 species
ikteros (Gr) the jaundice; also a bird of a yellowish-green colour, by looking at which a jaundiced person was cured; the bird then died! In this group there is great diversity of feeding habits, nest building, mating behaviour, and size, which ranges from about 18 to 53 cm (7 to 21 in) in length.

Dusky-green Oropendola *Psarocolius atrovirens*
psar (Gr), genitive *psaros*, a starling *kolios* (Gr) a kind of woodpecker. Wagler does not fully explain the name; the Icteridae are analagous

to the Old World starlings and one species is known as the Military Starling, but they are not starlings and they are not woodpeckers (see Misleading Names p. 16)   *ater* (L) black   *virens* (L) becoming green. The name *Oropendola* is derived from *oro* (Sp) gold, and *pendola* (Sp) a feather, a plume; the wings have bright yellow outer feathers. Inhabiting the forests of the northern part of South America. Dr Joannes G. Wagler (1800-1832) was a German naturalist and Professor of Zoology at Munich University from 1827 to 1832.

Green Oropendola   *Ps. viridis*
viridis (L) green. Inhabiting the northern tropical areas of South America.

Chestnut-headed Oropendola   *Ps. wagleri*
Named after Dr J. G. Wagler (see above). Inhabiting the forests of Central America and the northern part of South America.

Scarlet-rumped Cacique   *Cacicus uropygialis*
cacicus (New L) from cacique, a native Indian chief, particularly in areas where there is a Spanish culture, as in the West Indies and Central and South America   *oura* (Gr) the tail   *pugē* (Gr) the rump, buttocks   *-alis* (L) suffix meaning relating to; a reference to the red plumage of the tail and rump. Inhabiting the West Indies, Central America, and northern South America.

Northern Oriole   *Icterus galbula*
Icterus, see under Family, above   *galbina* (L) diminutive *galbula*, a small bird, probably an oriole; also *galbina* (L) pale green garments; the male is a glossy black with some orange parts, but the female is olive yellow above with yellow underparts and tail. Inhabiting Canada including Nova Scotia, and ranging south through eastern USA to Georgia and Texas.

White-edged Oriole   *I. graceannae*
Named after Grace Anna Lewis (1821-1912), an American naturalist, specially a botanist, and teacher of biology. This oriole inhabits the western tropical area of South America; these orioles must not be confused with the Old World Orioles of the family Oriolidae, and they are not closely related.

Jamaican Blackbird   *Nesopsar nigerrimus*
nesos (Gr) an island   *psar* (Gr) a starling   *niger* (L) black   *nigerrimus*, very black. The American Blackbirds must not be confused

with our blackbirds in the family Muscicapidae, and they are not closely related; this one lives on the island of Jamaica.

Oriole Blackbird   *Gymnomystax mexicanus*
gumnos (Gr) naked   *mustax* (Gr) the upper lip; there is a patch of bluish white bare skin at the base of the bill and on the cheeks   *-anus* (L) suffix meaning belonging to; although named from Mexico by Linnaeus, this was an error; it inhabits north-western South America. It is one of the largest birds in this family, the male being up to 48 cm (19 in) long.

Yellow-headed Blackbird   *Xanthocephalus xanthocephalus*
xanthos (Gr) yellow   *kephalē* (Gr) the head; the head, neck, and upper breast are bright yellow, making a remarkable contrast with the rather drab colour of the body. Inhabiting the southern part of western Canada, the western USA, and ranging south in winter to southern Mexico.

Red-winged Blackbird   *Agelaius phoenicus*
agelaios (Gr) gregarious; a gregarious bird, breeding socially in groups, though sometimes only in scattered pairs   *phoinix* (Gr), genitive *phoinikos*, purple red, crimson; there is a red patch on the upper part of the wing. Inhabiting southern Canada, widespread in the USA, and ranging south in winter to southern Mexico.

Eastern Meadowlark   *Sturnella magna*
sturnus (L) a starling   *-ellus* (L) diminutive suffix; it is bigger than a starling but is one of the smaller birds in this family   *magnus* (L) large; this only indicates that it is bigger than the other birds in the genus *Sturnella*. Inhabiting Canada and ranging south through the eastern part of the USA to Florida, west to Mexico, Central America, Colombia and Venezuela.

Western Meadowlark   *S. neglecta*
neglectus (L) a neglecting, neglect; this species is so like *S. magna*, above, that for nearly 100 years it was thought to be the same bird; when ornithologists discovered and agreed that it was a separate species it was given the specific name *neglecta*, and the new name has been internationally recognised since 1844. Although the two species often live in overlapping territories they do not hybridise; how do they know? The two quite different songs are thought to be the answer. Inhabiting south-western Canada and ranging south through the western half of the USA to Mexico.

Greater Antillean Grackle *Quiscalus niger*
quiscalus (New L) a quail; they do not look like quails and are not related to them, but the flight may be similar; their close relatives the Meadowlarks, above, are noted for their quail-like flight   *niger* (L) black; the plumage is black with a glossy sheen of steel blue. Inhabiting the Greater Antilles; this is the group of islands that includes Cuba, Jamaica, and the Haiti and Dominican Republics.

Brown-headed Cowbird *Molothrus ater*
molobros (Gr) a greedy beggar, a lazy fellow; in this case intended to mean a parasite; *molothros* is not a Greek word, it is a mistake and should be *molobros*. Cowbirds are parasitic, but not in the same way as the cuckoo; they lay several eggs, each one in a different nest, and a great variety of different species; the host's eggs or nestlings are not thrown out and may grow up quite amicably with the intruder. In ancient times when bison were abundant cowbirds followed them to feed on the insects on their backs or those flushed from the grass by the trampling feet, now they follow the herds of cattle which has given rise to the name 'cowbirds'   *ater* (L) black; the plumage is dark glossy blue-black with brown head and neck. Inhabiting southern Canada, widespread in the USA and ranging south to southern Mexico.

Family   FRINGILLIDAE
Subfamily   FRINGILLINAE   3 species
fringilla (L) a small bird, according to some the chaffinch.

Chaffinch *Fringilla coelebs*
coelebs = *caelebs* (L) unmarried, single, whether of a bachelor or a widower; sometimes chaffinches gather in flocks of one sex only, and at one time it was thought that the females migrated south leaving the males behind, and they became known as 'bachelor birds'. Widespread in Europe including Scandinavia and the British Isles, ranging east through the central part of Asia to the western half of Mongolia; also northern Africa, Asia Minor, the Middle East, the Canary Islands and the Azores.

Brambling *F. montifringilla*
mons (L), genitive *montis*, a mountain; it breeds mainly in the mountains of northern Europe and northern Asia. The distribution is similar to *F. coelebs*, above, but extending into more northern areas and to the east as far as Kamchatka and south to Japan.

Subfamily CARDUELINAE 122 species
carduus (L) the wild thistle   *carduelis* (L) the thistle-finch, goldfinch; a reference to their liking for seeding thistle heads but they will take other seeds and occasionally insects on the ground.

Canary   *Serinus canaria*
serinus (New L) pertaining to the bird known as the serin; also *serin* (Fr) the canary: the name canary is said to originate from *canis* (L) a dog, because of the large dogs that were kept on one of the islands in Roman times, and was called Canaria; eventually the name was used for the whole group of islands. Wild canaries live in the Canary Islands, the Azores, and Madeira; they are greenish yellow streaked with brown and black, but the pure yellow ones seen in captivity are the result of selective breeding.

Yellow Canary   *S. flaviventris*
flavus (L) yellow   *venter* (L), genitive *ventris*, the belly; the upperparts are olive green with dark streaks and the forehead, breast and belly a bright yellow. Inhabiting the western part of southern Africa.

Serin   *S. serinus*
See above under Canary. Inhabiting western Europe but only recently seen in southern Sweden and Britain; north-western Africa and up to 2,450 m (8,000 ft) in the Atlas Mountains, Asia Minor and Palestine.

Eurasian Goldfinch   *Carduelis carduelis*
See above under Subfamily. Inhabiting Eurasia including southern Scandinavia, the British Isles, northern Africa, Asia Minor, and ranging east to western Mongolia and western Tibet; it is found also in the Canary Islands and the Azores, and has been introduced to New Zealand and the USA.

Greenfinch   *C. chloris*
khlōros (Gr) green; the plumage is generally a fairly dark olive green with bright yellow patches on the wings and tail. Widespread in Europe including southern Scandinavia, the British Isles, northern Africa, the Azores, Asia Minor, and northern Iran.

Eurasian Siskin   *C. spinus*
spingos = *spinos* (Gr) a small bird, probably a kind of finch. Inhabiting Europe including the British Isles and the southern half of Scandinavia, and ranging east to China, Korea and Japan.

Linnet *Acanthis cannabina*
akanthis (Gr) a bird fond of thistles, the siskin, or the linnet   *cannabis* (L) hemp   *cannabinus* (L) pertaining to hemp; a reference to its liking for the seeds of the hemp plant, but it also eats other seeds, specially thistles, and some insects. Widespread in Europe including southern Scandinavia, the British Isles, the Canary Islands and Africa north of the Sahara, Asia Minor, ranging east to Kazakhstan and south to parts of the Oriental Region.

Redpoll   *A. flammea*
flammeus (L) flaming, fiery; can mean fiery-red, a reference to the red forehead. Inhabiting the northern part of Europe including the British Isles, and north to Baffin Land, Greenland, and Siberia; introduced to New Zealand.

House Finch   *Carpodacus mexicanus*
karpos (Gr) fruit   *daknō* (Gr) I bite   *dakos* (Gr) a biting animal; a 'fruit-biter'; the Greek word *dakos* really means a poisonous biting animal such as a snake   *-anus* (L) a suffix meaning belonging to; named from Mexico, it ranges from British Columbia in Canada south through the western part of the USA to southern Mexico.

Red-mantled Rosefinch   *C. rhodochlamys*
rhodon (Gr) a rose   *rhodoeis* (Gr) rose-coloured   *khlamus* (Gr) a short cloak. Inhabiting Asia including India and the Burma-Vietnam area.

Pine Grosbeak   *Pinicola enucleator*
pinus (L) a pine-tree or fir-tree   *colo* (L) I inhabit, dwell in; a reference to one of their favourite trees   *enucleo* (L) I take out the kernel; with its powerful beak it can dig into the hard cones of pine trees. The name grosbeak indicates 'big-beak'. Inhabiting the northern part of North America, Scandinavia, and Asia, and ranging south to the Burma-Vietnam area.

Red Crossbill   *Loxia curvirostra*
loxos (Gr) cross-wise   *curvus* (L) curved   *rostrum* (L) the beak; the plainly curved and rather parrot-like bill is crossed at the tip though this is not always easily seen; the male is red to orange-red but the female is a yellowish green. Widespread along the coastal part of North America from Alaska south to Panama in Central America, ranging east in Canada to Newfoundland; fairly widespread in certain areas of Eurasia including Britain, Spain, northern Africa, Asia

Minor, and east to Manchuria and Japan and south to India, Burma, the Philippines and Indonesia.

Bullfinch *Pyrrhula pyrrhula*
purrhos = *purros* (Gr) red, flame-coloured *purroulas* (Gr) a red-coloured bird, perhaps the bullfinch; the cheeks and the underparts are red, with upperparts grey, black, and white markings. Inhabiting Eurasia including the Azores, northern Spain, the British Isles, northern Asia Minor, and ranging east to Kamchatka and Japan.

Hawfinch *Coccothraustes coccothraustes*
kokkos (Gr) a kernel *thrauō* (Gr) I break in pieces *-istes* (Gr) suffix meaning the one who acts; 'kernel breaker'; a reference to the powerful beak which can actually crack open a cherry stone. Inhabiting Europe including the southernmost part of Scandinavia, and England and Wales and northernmost part of Africa, ranging east across Asia to the Pacific, Japan, and south to India.

Family ESTRILDIDAE 124 species
estrilda (New L) from *astrild*, an Afrikaans name for this bird; it is also known in South Africa by the Afrikaans name *Rooibekkie*; the usual English name is Waxbill.

Red-headed Blue-bill *Spermophaga ruficapilla*
sperma (Gr) seed *phagein* (Gr) to eat; it is mostly a seed-eater but also takes insects *rufus* (L) red *capillus* (L) hair of men, usually the hair of the head, can mean the hair of animals. Inhabiting Africa.

African Firefinch *Lagonosticta rubricata*
lagōn (Gr), genitive *lagonos*, the flank, of men or animals *stiktos* (Gr) dotted, dappled; a reference to white spots on the side of the breast *rubrica* (L) red ochre *-atus* (L) suffix meaning provided with; the plumage is red becoming brown to grey towards the tail. Northern part of western Africa ranging east to Ethiopia, and south on the eastern side to South Africa.

Blue-breasted Waxbill or Angolan Cordon-Bleu *Uraeginthus angolensis*
oura (Gr) the tail *aeginthus* (New L) derived from *aigithos* (Gr) a hedge-sparrow; 'sparrow-tailed'; the bird is similar in size and shape to the Cape Sparrow of Africa *-ensis* (L) suffix meaning belonging to; named from Angola it is also found in the eastern part of South Africa specially the Kruger Park.

Waxbill *Estrilda astrild*
estrilada see Family, p. 305. Most of the waxbills have a pink or red bill with a waxy appearance suggesting sealing wax which has given rise to the English name. This waxbill is fairly common and widespread in Africa south of the Sahara.

Black-cheeked Waxbill *E. erythronotos*
eruthros (Gr) red *noton* (Gr) the back; the plumage is black on the sides of the face, and red on the back and underparts. Inhabiting Africa south of the Sahara but not further south than the Orange River in South Africa.

Avadavat (or Amadavat) *Amandava amandava*
Avadavat and *Amandava* are corruptions of the name of the Indian city Ahmadabad, in the province of Bombay; it was from here that the first of these birds were sent to Europe. A small red to orange bird no bigger than a wren, with a typical waxy-looking red bill, it is much favoured as a cage bird. Inhabiting India, the Burma-Vietnam area, Malaysia, and Indonesia.

Zebra Waxbill *A. subflava*
sub (L) under, below *flavus* (L) yellow; a reference to the yellow throat which merges into scarlet, and the sides of the body have yellow bars which gives rise to the English name Zebra Waxbill. Inhabiting Africa south of the Sahara.

Black Chinned Quail-Finch *Ortygospiza atricollis*
ortux (Gr), genitive *ortugos*, the quail *spiza* (Gr) a finch; an allusion to the quail-like flight, rising steeply with whirring wings and then dropping to cover *ater* (L) black *collum* (L) the neck; the cheeks and throat are black. Inhabiting the Senegal area and ranging east to Ethiopia and south through the eastern part of Africa to South Africa.

Zebra Finch *Poephila guttata*
poa (Gr) grass, can mean a grassy place, a meadow; becomes *poē* when used in compounds *philos* (Gr) loved, pleasing; the habitat is usually riverside grasslands *guttatus* (L) spotted, speckled; it also has bands of black and white which gives it the English name. Common in Australia it also inhabits Lesser Sundas and Moluccas.

Green-faced Parrot-Finch *Erythrura viridifacies*
eruthros (Gr) red *oura* (Gr) the tail; a reference to the crimson tail *viridis* (L) green *facies* (L) form, face; not necessarily meaning only

the face as the plumage is mostly grass-green. Known only from Luzon.

Gouldian Finch *Chloebia gouldiae*
khloē (Gr) the shoots of young green plants, grass   *bios* (Gr) living, manner or means of living; this finch and its relatives are sometimes known as grassfinches, and although they have a finch-like bill they are not true finches; they seldom come to the ground but climb about on the stems of tall grasses and eat the seeds and insects they find there. This finch is named in honour of Mrs E. Gould (1804-1841), a bird artist and the wife of J. Gould, FRS, a zoologist and the author of books on birds. Inhabiting northern areas of Australia and sometimes migrating south to breed.

Chestnut-breasted Finch *Lonchura castaneothorax*
lonkhē (Gr) a spear-head   *oura* (Gr) the tail; a reference to the pointed tail   *castanea* (L) the chestnut tree   *castaneus* (New L) chestnut-coloured   *thōrax* (Gr) the breast. Inhabiting northern Australia to New South Wales, also New Guinea.

Java Sparrow *Padda oryzivora*
The generic name *Padda* is a reference to the paddy fields where they find rice, their favourite food   *oruza* (Gr) rice   *voro* (L) I eat; a hybrid word formed from Greek and Latin; they will also take other seeds but can become quite a pest in the rice fields. Inhabiting Burma ranging south to Malaysia and Indonesia.

Family PLOCEIDAE   150 species
plokē (Gr) a twining, a weaving   *plokeus* (Gr) a plaiter, a weaver; a reference to the form of the nest, which in some cases is a huge complicated woven nest, a communal place housing many birds.

Subfamily VIDUINAE   9 species
The generic name *Vidua* is derived from Whydah (sometimes Ouidah) a small town on the coast of Dahomey in western Africa where these birds were first discovered. They are parasitic, and choose certain species of birds where the eggs are laid, and only one in each nest; the stranger does not throw out the host's eggs or fledglings as does the cuckoo. They are seed-eaters and also take insects.

Pintailed Whydah *Vidua macroura*
Vidua, see above   *makros* (Gr) long   *oura* (Gr) the tail; the very long tail can be up to about 20 cm (8 in) which looks strange on a bird with

a body of 11·5 to 12·75 cm (4½ to 5 in). Widespread in Africa south of the Sahara including South Africa.

Paradise Whydah *V. paradisea*
paradeisos (Gr) a park or pleasure ground, often used to mean a garden; an Oriental word meaning the garden of Eden; the name is probably used for this whydah on account of the quite remarkable and spectacular tail which is lyre-shaped in flight. Only the males have the long tail and in some species even the male does not have it and may look similar to the female. Widespread in Africa south of the Sahara.

Subfamily PLOCEINAE 141 species
plokeus (Gr) see under Family, p. 307.

Donaldson Smith's Sparrow Weaver *Plocepasser donaldsoni*
plokeus (Gr) a weaver; a reference to the form of the nest *passer* (L) a sparrow; the sparrows in this family are true sparrows and include our House Sparrow: named after Dr A. Donaldson Smith (1864–1939), an American zoologist who was in East Africa in 1894 and 1895. Inhabiting Africa south of the Sahara.

Social Weaver *Philetairus socius*
philos (Gr) loved, pleasing *etairos* (Gr) a companion *socius* (L) sharing, joining in; this species is famous for the enormous communal nests which they all help to build, woven from grasses to make a structure that can accommodate two or three hundred pairs, each in its own compartment. Inhabiting the western and central part of southern Africa.

House Sparrow *Passer domesticus domesticus*
passer (L) a sparrow *domus* (L) a house *domesticus* (L) belonging to the house, familiar, domestic. Sometimes known as the English Sparrow, it is widespread in Europe, parts of northern Africa, southwestern Asia, India, Burma, and east to Manchuria, but it has been introduced to so many other countries that its original range is hard to define; for example introduced to Canada, the USA, West Indies, parts of South America, Australia, Tasmania, and New Zealand.

Italian Sparrow *P.d. italiae*
This subspecies is similar to the House Sparrow, having a brown cap and a small black bib. It is not known except in Italy and Corsica. (For notes about subspecies, see Chapter 2, page 18).

PLOCEINAE

Cape Sparrow   *P. melanurus*
melas (Gr), genitive *melanos*, black   *oura* (Gr) the tail; it has black tail feathers with buff margins. Common in Cape Town and the western part of southern Africa.

Tree Sparrow   *P. montanus*
montanus (L) belonging to a mountain; it is not restricted to mountainous areas and inhabits Europe, including the British Isles, Asia, including India, and south to the Burma-Vietnam area, Indonesia, and east to Japan. The appearance is similar to the House Sparrow though it is slightly smaller; it has been introduced to North America, Australia, and New Zealand.

Swahili Sparrow   *P. suahelicus*
-icus (L) suffix meaning belonging to; there is no such place as Swahili; it is a language originally from Zanzibar, and now spoken and used as a common tongue by many tribes in large areas of East Africa and Zaire.

Rock Sparrow   *Petronia petronia*
petra (L) a rock, a crag   *petronius* (L) of a rock, or crag; a reference to the habitat of dry rocky slopes with grass and low scrub. Inhabiting the Canary Islands and the Mediterranean area and ranging east through Asia Minor to the mountains and desert areas of south-west Asia to Tibet and China.

Snow Finch   *Montifringilla nivalis*
mons (L), genitive *montis*, a mountain   *fringilla* (L) a small bird, according to some authorities the chaffinch   *nix* (L), genitive *nivis*, snow   *nivalis* (L) of snow, snowy; a reference to the habitat of rocky slopes and screes, high mountains and borders of glaciers at 6,000 m (20,000 ft) or more in the Alps. Inhabiting the mountains, though not all, ranging from the Pyrenees to the Altai, and some of the mountains of Tibet.

Golden Palm-Weaver   *Ploceus bojeri*
plokeus (Gr) a weaver; a reference to the form of the nest: named after Wenzel Bojer (1800-1856), a Czechoslovakian naturalist from Prague; he collected in Madagascar and Zanzibar and was at one time Curator of the Mauritius Museum. The males in the genus *Ploceus* are golden yellow and the woven nests are frequently hung in palm trees. Inhabiting Somalia and Kenya.

Black-headed Weaver *P. cucullatus*
cucullus (L) a hood   *cucullatus* (L) hooded; a reference to the black head and neck which gives the impression that it is wearing a hood. Widespread in Africa except the south-western part and The Cape.

Baya Weaver   *P. philippinus*
-inus (L) suffix meaning belonging to; named from the Philippines, it inhabits India, the Burma-Vietnam area, Malaysia, Indonesia, and the Philippines. *Bayā* is a Hindi word of East India for the weaver.

Red-billed Quelea   *Quelea quelea*
quelea (New L) derived from an African native name; it has a striking red bill. Inhabiting a part of the west coast of Africa south of the Sahara and ranging east along a belt of country to Sudan and Ethiopia, and south through eastern Africa to northern South Africa.

Yellow-shouldered Widow Bird   *Euplectes macrourus*
eu- (Gr) prefix meaning well, nicely   *plektos* (Gr) plaited, twisted; 'well plaited'; a reference to the nest which is made of woven grasses. The range is very similar to the Red-billed Quelea, above, but only extending south as far as Mozambique, Malawi, and Angola.

Family STURNIDAE   106 species
sturnus (L) a starling; some of the birds in this group are known as Mynahs, and have become familiar to us because they are often kept as cage birds on account of their clever imitation of the human voice; they are, however, true starlings, and some other starlings are clever imitators.

Glossy Starling   *Aplonis metallicus*
Aplonis, obscure, but may have some connection with Apollo, the Greek sun-god, i.e. 'shining'. H. Wolstenhome, BA, of Wahroonga, Sydney, in the Official Checklist of the Birds of Australia, referred to the MS of Dr Herbert Langton (deceased), expert on the derivation of bird names; he says: 'Like myself he could not find the origin of certain obscure names, such as *Aplonis*, *Biziura*, and *Epthianura*'   *metallicus* (L) belonging to metal, metallic; a reference to the shining plumage, and hence the English name. Inhabiting the southern Pacific on the many small islands, and Papua New Guinea, and Australia.

Burchell's Glossy Starling   *Lamprotornis australis*
lamprotēs (Gr) brilliance   *ornis* (Gr) a bird; a reference to the metallic

green plumage with a purple sheen   *australis* (L) southern; this does not mean Australia, it means the southern part of Africa: named after Dr W. J. Burchell (1782-1863), a naturalist and author who explored South Africa in 1811; he is better known through having Burchell's Zebra named after him. This starling inhabits much of southern Africa particularly Angola and Botswana.

Wattled Starling   *Creatophora cinerea*
kreas (Gr), genitive *kreatos*, a piece of flesh   *phoreō* (Gr) I bear, I have: a reference to the black wattles which grow on the side of the face and under the beak in the breeding season   *cinis* (L), genitive *cineris*, ashes   *cinereus*, ash-coloured; the plumage is mostly grey with some black on the flight and tail feathers that have a greenish gloss. Inhabiting south-western Arabia, Somalia, and ranging west to Zaire, Angola, and south to The Cape.

Rose-coloured Starling   *Sturnus roseus*
sturnus (L) a starling   *roseus* (L) red, rose-coloured; the colour of the body is rose pink. Inhabiting south-eastern Europe, Asia Minor, Iran, Turkestan, the Caspian region and Altai, and migrating south to India in winter.

Common Starling   *S. vulgaris*
vulgaris (L) ordinary, commonplace. Known now in many parts of the world, it inhabits Iceland and most of Europe except Spain and southern France; ranging east across western and central Asia. It has been introduced to North America, South Africa, Australia and New Zealand.

Rothschild's Mynah   *Leucopsar rothschildi*
leukos (Gr) white   *psar* (Gr) a starling; a remarkable starling almost entirely white except for some bare skin on the face which is blue: named after Lionel Walter, Baron Rothschild, FRS (1868-1937), a zoologist and author; he founded the Tring Museum in 1889. It is very rare, and confined to the island of Bali, Indonesia.

Chinese Mynah   *Acridotheres cristatellus*
akris (Gr), genitive *akridos*, a locust   *thēraō* (Gr) I hunt, I catch; it will take insects other than locusts, and also eats fruit and grain   *crista* (L) a crest, usually means a tuft on the head of animals   *cristatus* (L) crested   *-ellus* (L) diminutive suffix; it has a small tuft of rather ragged feathers on the head just behind the bill. Inhabiting southern China south of the Yangtze River, and Burma.

Common Mynah   *A. tristis*
tristis (L) sad, gloomy; here used to mean dull colouring compared to other mynahs; although glossy the plumage is mostly black with some brown. Inhabiting Kazakhstan in the USSR and ranging south to Iran, Afghanistan, India, the Burma-Vietnam area, and Indonesia; it has been introduced to South Africa, the Seychelles, Mauritius, Australia, Tasmania, and New Zealand.

Golden-crested Mynah   *Mino coronatus*
mino (New L) from *myna* = mynah, from the Hindi *mainā*   *corona* (L) a crown   *coronatus*, having a crown; it has a yellow head and a long yellow crest lying flat on the head. Inhabiting India and the Burma-Vietnam area.

Yellow-billed Oxpecker   *Buphagus africanus*
bous (Gr) an ox, a bull   *phagein* (Gr) to eat; a reference to its habit of clinging to the backs of large animals like buffalo, rhino, and antelopes, where they climb about searching for ticks, flies, and other insects on which they feed   *africanus* (L) of Africa. Inhabiting Eritrea and ranging south to South Africa, though not eastern Kenya and Tanzania; it tends to keep to the areas that are the habitat of the host animals.

Red-billed Oxpecker   *B. erythrorhynchus*
eruthros (Gr) red   *rhunkhos* (Gr) the snout, beak. The range is very similar to *B. africanus*, above, and this bird has been seen at about 2,437 m (8,000 ft) in Kenya.

Family ORIOLIDAE   28 species
oriolus (New L) from *aureolus*, the diminutive of *aureus* (L) of gold, golden; the name originates from the Golden Oriole which has a brilliant golden head and upper part of the body with black wings and tail. The diet is insects and fruit, and they range in size from about 18 to 30.5 cm (7 to 12 in); known as Old World Orioles, they must not be confused with the American orioles of the genus *Icterus*, family Icteridae, to which they are not closely related.

Crimson-breasted Oriole   *Oriolus cruentus*
Oriolus, see above   *cruentus* (L) spotted or stained with blood; a reference to the red breast. Inhabiting Malaysia and Indonesia.

Golden Oriole   *O. oriolus*
Oriolus, see above; this oriole is said to have a rather musical call that

sounds like 'ori-ole'. Inhabiting north-western Africa, Iberia, widespread across most of Eurasia but not the northern part, east as far as Tibet and India.

Yellow Figbird *Sphecotheres flaviventris*
sphēx (Gr), genitive *sphekos*, a wasp   *thērao* (Gr) I hunt, can mean I catch, wild beasts; it is not recorded that they eat wasps, but certainly various large insects such as cockchafers and grasshoppers, and also fruit especially wild figs *flavus* (L) yellow   *venter* (L), genitive *ventris*, the belly; a reference to the bright yellow underparts. Inhabiting the northern coastal area of Australia.

Figbird *S. vieilloti*
Named after L. J. P. Vieillot (1748-1831), the well-known French zoologist and author. Inhabiting Papua New Guinea, and Australia as above.

Family   DICRURIDAE   20 species
dikroos = dikros (Gr) forked   *oura* (Gr) the tail; nearly all species in this family have a forked tail. Usually known as Drongos, they range in length from about 18 to 38 cm (7 to 15 in), though including the very long tail of the Racket-tailed Drongos this could be 63 cm (25 in); the diet consists of insects and small frogs and lizards, and sometimes nectar.

Mountain Drongo   *Chaetorhynchus papuensis*
khaitē (Gr) long flowing hair, giving rise to *chaeta* (New L) a bristle *rhunkhos* (Gr) the beak; all drongos have rictal bristles around the beak but in this case the bristles are longer than the beak   *-ensis* (L) suffix meaning belonging to; named from the then Territory of Papua, it inhabits the mountain forests of Papua New Guinea.

New Ireland Drongo   *Dicrurus megarhynchus*
Dicrurus, see above   *megas* (Gr) big, wide   *rhunkhos* (Gr) the beak; a reference to the big strong beak. It is named from New Ireland, one of the islands of the Bismarck Archipelago, lying to the north-east of Papua New Guinea.

Square-tailed Drongo   *D. ludwigii*
Named after C. F. H. Baron von Ludwig (1784-1847), a South African botanist from Cape Town. One of the drongos, which usually have forked tails, that has a square tail. Inhabiting the southern part of South Africa. *Drongo* is a native name in Madagascar.

Greater Racket-tailed Drongo *D. paradiseus*
paradeisos (Gr) a park; the specific name in this case refers to the similarity of the bird to the Birds of Paradise, on account of the long ornamental tail; in this bird the tail consists of two long shafts devoid of feathers and ending with two small 'flags' or 'rackets'. Inhabiting India, the Burma-Vietnam area, and Malaysia.

Family CALLAEIDAE 3 species
kallaion (Gr) a cock's comb; can mean wattles; a reference to the brightly coloured fleshy wattle on each side of the lower mandible. Usually known as Wattlebirds, the smallest is about 25 cm (10 in) and the largest 50 cm (20 in) long; the diet is mainly vegetable food but sometimes they also take insects and nectar.

Kokako *Callaeas cinerea*
cinerea (L) ash-coloured; the plumage is mostly a bluish-grey. Kokako is a Maori name for this bird; confined to the South Island of New Zealand, it has bright blue and yellow wattles; although widespread it is very rare.

Saddleback Wattlebird *Creadion carunculatus*
kreas (Gr) flesh, a piece of meat   *kreadion* (Gr diminutive) a small piece of meat   *caruncula* (L) a small piece of flesh   *-atus* (L) suffix meaning provided with; a reference to the small orange-coloured wattles on each side of the lower mandible. The name 'saddleback' refers to the wide brown band across the glossy black back. It is now found only on Hen Island, off the North Island of New Zealand, and three small islands to the south-west of Stewart Island at the southern end of South Island, New Zealand.

Family GRALLINIDAE 4 species
grallae (L) stilts   *-inus* (L) suffix meaning like, belonging to; a reference to the legs which are long for a bird of this size, about 25 cm (10 in), and influenced by it often being seen walking about in shallow water, thus keeping the body dry. This small family have been given various names such as chough and magpie-lark, but they are not closely related to any of these birds. The diet consists of insects and small invertebrates found in or near water such as worms and snails.

Magpie-Lark *Grallina cyanoleuca*
Grallina, see above   *kyaneos* (Gr) dark blue   *leukos* (Gr) white; the plumage is a piebald mixture of black and white, rather than dark

blue. Widespread in Australia, but not Tasmania; usually seen near water.

White-winged Chough *Corcorax melanorhamphos*
corvus (L) a crow *korax* (Gr) a crow: it is not a chough or a crow though the appearance is similar, and it is about the same size as a rook or a carrion crow, namely 46 cm (18 in) *melas* (Gr), genitive *melanos*, black *rhamphos* (Gr) a beak, bill, especially a crooked beak as in birds of prey; it has a black curved beak and the plumage is black except for a white patch on the wings. Inhabiting Australia in the eastern part from southern Queensland to New South Wales, and much of the southern region.

Family ARTAMIDAE 10 species
artamos (Gr) a butcher; known as Wood-Swallows, these birds were originally confused with the shrikes, sometimes known as Butcher-birds, in the genus *Lanius* (L) a butcher; Linnaeus described the first known species as a shrike in 1771. Many of the shrikes were well known to have the habit of impaling their prey on any convenient spikes, where they could remain as though in a larder until required for eating. The wood-swallows feed mostly on insects of various kinds, some being hawked in the air.

White-breasted Wood-Swallow *Artamus leucorhynchus*
Artamus, see above *leukos* (Gr) white *rhunkhos* (Gr) the snout, beak; the beak is white, tinged with very pale blue, and the breast and underparts are white. The birds in this small family are swallow-like in some respects but are not closely related. Inhabiting Indonesia, the Philippines, New Guinea, and ranging east to the Fiji Islands; in Australia the northern coastal region and in the east ranging south to New South Wales.

White-browed Wood-Swallow *A. superciliosus*
super (L) over, above *cilium* (L) the eyelid, giving rise to *cilia* (New L) a hair *ciliosus* (New L) full of hairs; it has a prominent white eyebrow. Widespread in Australia in eastern areas.

Family CRACTICIDAE 11 species
kraktikos (Gr) noisy; an allusion to the strident alarm call but they do have a pleasant song. Known variously as Butcherbirds, Bell Magpies, and Currawongs, they have the same trick as the shrikes, in the genus *Lanius*, of impaling their prey on a suitable spike (see above, under Family Artamidae).

Grey Butcherbird *Cracticus torquatus*
Cracticus, see above   *torquatus* (L) wearing a collar; a reference to the white band round the neck; the plumage of the upper parts is grey. Fairly widespread in Australia except the northern coastal region.

Pied Currawong *Strepera graculina*
strepo (L) I make a noise   *streperus* (New L) noisy; a reference to the strident alarm call which sounds like a loud 'currawong', and no doubt this has given rise to the Australian native name   *graculus* (L) a jackdaw   *-inus* (L) suffix meaning like; the Latin word originates from the jackdaw's call, which is supposed to sound like 'gra gra', though some consider it is 'jack jack'; the currawongs are not closely related to the jackdaw. The Pied Currawong is mostly black with some white on the wings, rump, and tail; it inhabits the eastern coastal area of Australia, and Lord Howe Island which lies about 805 km (500 miles) to the east of the mainland.

Family   PTILONORHYNCHIDAE   17 species
ptilon (Gr) a feather   *rhunkhos* (Gr) the snout, beak; a reference to the feathers that partly cover the beak. Known as Bowerbirds from their habit of building an elaborate bower of grasses, sometimes roofed over like a sort of wigwam, and sometimes just an avenue; in front there is a circular court carefully decorated with coloured stones and other coloured objects, and some species even paint the interior, making their own paint with a mixture of saliva and the juice of berries, and apply this with a 'brush' consisting of a piece of fibrous bark; however some species do not build a bower. The diet consists of fruit, insects, worms, and other small invertebrates.

Tooth-billed Bowerbird *Scenopoeetes dentirostris*
skēnē (Gr) a covered or sheltered place   *poiētēs* (Gr) one who makes, a maker; a perfect description of the male bird and his bower   *dens* (L), genitive *dentis*, a tooth   *rostrum* (L) the beak; an allusion to the serrated edges of the beak used by the male for cutting the leaves to decorate his bower. Inhabiting the north-eastern part of Australia.

Archbold's Bowerbird *Archboldia papuensis*
Named after R. Archbold (born 1907), a zoologist who was in the Mammals Department of the American Museum of Natural History, and was in New Guinea in 1933 and 1934   *-ensis* (L) suffix meaning belonging to; named from Papua New Guinea, where it lives.

New Guinea Regent Bowerbird *Sericulus bakeri*
sērikos (Gr) silken   *-culus* (L) diminutive suffix, here taken to mean somewhat; a reference to the glossy plumage (cf Satin Bowerbird, below): named after G. F. Baker, junior (1878-1937), a naturalist and a New York banker; he was a Trustee of the American Museum of Natural History. Inhabiting Papua New Guinea.

Satin Bowerbird *Ptilonorhynchus violaceus*
ptilon (Gr) a feather   *rhunkhos* (Gr) the beak; a reference to the feathers that partly cover the beak   *violaceus* (L) violet-coloured; the plumage of the male is a silky black, the feathers having specially formed edges that give a glossy violet blue effect in sunlight. Inhabiting eastern Australia from Queensland south to Victoria.

Spotted Bowerbird *Chlamydera maculata*
khlamus (Gr) a short cloak, or mantle   *derē = deirē* (Gr) the neck, throat; a reference to the mantle or neck frill that can be raised or lowered   *macula* (L) a mark, a spot   *maculatus*, spotted; the brownish plumage is mottled with golden buff spots. Inhabiting eastern Australia from Queensland south to northern Victoria.

Family   PARADISAEIDAE   40 species
paradeisos (Gr) a park, a garden; in a legendary sense it has come to mean a garden as in Heaven. The Birds of Paradise first became known to the western world in the sixteenth century when a ship from the Spanish fleet, the *Vittoria*, returned to Spain from the Molucca Islands bringing a gift of some of the skins of these birds from a sultan in the Moluccas to the King of Spain; the feathers and plumes were so beautiful and spectacular that the Spaniards said they must be from paradise, and so gave them the name Birds of Paradise. Closely related to the Bowerbirds, they also have a spectacular mating display; the diet is similar.

Multi-crested Bird of Paradise   *Cnemophilus macgregorii*
knemos (Gr) the shoulder of a mountain, can mean the lower part of a mountain   *philos* (Gr) loved, pleasing: named after Sir W. Macgregor (1846-1919), Governor of Queensland, Australia, from 1909 to 1914; he was in New Guinea for several years about 1890. This bird lives on the lower slopes of the mountains of Papua New Guinea.

Paradise Crow   *Lycocorax pyrrhopterus*
lukos (Gr) a daw or a chough; a daw is a kind of crow, cf. jackdaw

korax (Gr) a raven or crow; the birds of paradise are similar to crows in some respects and are closely related to them   *purros* (Gr) red *pteron* (Gr) wings; a reference to the wings, although they are usually a light brown rather than red. Inhabiting the Molucca Islands.

Curl-breasted Manucode   *Manucodia comrii*
Manucodia from *manucodiata* (New L) derived from a Malay name for the bird, *manuqdewata*, literally 'a bird of the gods': named after Dr P. Comrie (1832–1882), a Naval Surgeon on *HMS Basilisk* from 1871 to 1874: the English name is an allusion to the crinkled feathers of the body which finish as a 'topknot' on the head; it is sometimes known as the Curl-crested Manucode. It lives on the Trobriand and D'Entrecasteaux Islands which lie just to the east of Papua New Guinea.

Victoria Riflebird   *Ptiloris victoriae*
ptilon (Gr) a wing or feather   *os* (L), genitive *oris*, the mouth, pertaining to the mouth; a reference to the feathers that extend over the base of the upper mandible: named in honour of Queen Victoria (1819–1901), Queen of Great Britain and Ireland from 1837 to 1901. The Riflebirds derive their English name from the high-pitched call which is said to resemble the whine or whistle of a rifle bullet. Inhabiting the Cape York Peninsula of Australia.

Twelve-wired Bird of Paradise   *Seleucides melanoleuca*
seleukos (Gr), genitive *seleukidos*, a bird that eats locusts; this is a reference to its liking for insects, which would probably include locusts   *melas* (Gr), genitive *melanos*, black   *leukos* (Gr) white, can mean grey; the plumage of the male is black and the underparts are pale but not white, and usually a pale lemon-yellow. The English name refers to six plumes that grow from each flank and terminate with thin shafts up to $30\frac{1}{2}$ cm (12 in) long that resemble wires. It lives in central and western Papua New Guinea.

Black-billed Sicklebill Bird of Paradise   *Drepanornis albertisii*
drepanon (Gr) a curved sword, a sickle   *ornis* (Gr) a bird: named after Luigi M. d'Albertis (1841–1901), an Italian zoological-ethnologist; he was in New Guinea from 1871 to 1877. It inhabits the high mountains of Papua New Guinea.

Princess Stephanie's Bird of Paradise   *Astrapia stephaniae*
astrapē (Gr) lightning, can mean the brightness of flowers; a reference

to the brightly coloured iridescent plumage: named in honour of Princess Stephanie (1864-1945) of Belgium. Inhabiting Papua New Guinea.

Queen Carola's Parotia   *Parotia carolae*
parōtis (Gr) a gland beside the ear; can also mean a lock of hair beside the ear; a reference to the crest on the head which extends down beside the ear; in this species the crest is kept constantly on the move: named in honour of Queen Carola of Saxony (born 1833), the wife of King Albert of Saxony (1828-1902); he was the King of Saxony from 1873 until his death in 1902. Inhabiting Papua New Guinea.

King of Saxony Bird of Paradise   *Pteridophora alberti*
pteris (Gr), genitive *pteridon*, a kind of fern, so called from its feathery leaves; a reference to the plumes of feathers on the crown that may reach a length of 46 cm (18 in)   *phoreō* (Gr) I have, I bear: named in honour of King Albert of Saxony (see above). Inhabiting the mountains of Papua New Guinea.

King Bird of Paradise   *Cicinnurus regius*
kikinnos (Gr) a curled lock of hair, a ringlet   *oura* (Gr) the tail; an allusion to the two wirelike central tail feathers which have tips consisting of green circular feathers   *rex* (L), genitive *regis*, a king; although named a 'king bird' it is the smallest member of the family, being only about 15 cm (6 in) long, but the extraordinary tail feathers of the male may increase this by another 18 cm (7 in). Inhabiting Papua New Guinea and the Kepulaun Aru Islands.

Greater Bird of Paradise   *Paradisaea apoda*
Paradisaea (see under Family on p. 317)   *a-* (Gr) prefix meaning not, without   *pous* (Gr), genitive *podos*, a foot; 'without feet'; the name was given by the first European naturalists to see the skins of these birds, who found that they had no legs, as they had been cut off during the process of preparing the skins for shipping. Without more careful examination they assumed that the birds had no legs, and never came down to land, and they thought up all kinds of bizarre explanations about their mode of living, including a hollow in the back of the male where the egg was deposited in flight, and the female remaining sitting on it during this 'airborne incubation'! One of the largest birds of paradise, it inhabits southern Papua New Guinea and the Kepulauan Aru Islands, which lie to the south-west.

Family CORVIDAE 103 species
corvus (L) a raven; this family consists of the Jays, Magpies, Ravens, and Crows, and of course the Rook, which is a type of crow, in the same way that the Jackdaw is a type of crow. There are some big birds in this family, for instance the raven *Corvus corax* can be as much as 61 cm (24 in) long; they eat a great variety of different foods including carrion, vegetable matter, insects, the eggs of birds and reptiles, and even small reptiles.

Steller's Jay *Cyanocitta stelleri*
kuaneos (Gr) dark blue, glossy blue   *kitta* (Gr) a jay; the front part of the body is black, the wings and tail a purplish blue, and altogether less colourful than some of the other jays: named after G. W. Steller (1709-1769), a German zoologist and explorer, particularly of northern areas such as Alaska and Siberia; several other birds have been named in his honour. This jay ranges over a large area of North America from southern Alaska, south on the western side, to Nicaragua in Central America.

Scrub Jay *Aphelocoma coerulescens*
aphelēs (Gr) smooth   *komē* (Gr) the hair, usually of the head; an allusion to the sleek plumage   *caeruleus* (L) dark blue   *-escens* (L) suffix meaning approaching, beginning to, i.e. 'almost dark blue'; the colour of the feathers is a blend of light blue and dark blue, the hind parts and tail being light blue. The range is across the USA from Washington to the coast of the Pacific and south to southern Mexico; there is also an isolated race in Florida. It is known as the Scrub Jay from its habitat, the dense scrub of oaks, sand pines, and similar forest trees.

Azure-hooded Jay *Cyanolyca cucullata*
kuaneos (Gr) dark blue, glossy blue   *lukos* (Gr) a kind of chough   *cucullus* (L) a hood   *cucullatus* (L) hooded. Inhabiting Central America.

Purplish Jay *Cyanocorax cyanomelas*
kuaneos (Gr) dark blue, glossy blue   *korax* (Gr) a raven or crow   *melas* (Gr) black; a mixture of blue and black to suggest purple. Inhabiting central South America.

Eurasian Jay *Garrulus glandarius*
garrulus (L) talkative; although shy and usually remaining hidden it has a great variety of cries and calls and is a good mimic   *glans* (L),

genitive *glandis*, an acorn   *glandarius* (L) of or belonging to acorns; the diet is very varied but in autumn they eat a lot of acorns and also bury them in the ground for future use. Inhabiting Europe, including the British Isles, but not northern Scandinavia or northern Russia; north-west Africa, Asia Minor, and ranging east to Manchuria, Japan, China, and northern Laos and Vietnam.

Green Magpie   *Cissa chinensis*
kissa (also Attic *kitta*) (Gr) a chattering greedy bird, like a jay   *-ensis* (L) suffix meaning belonging to, 'of China'; in addition to China it inhabits large areas of south-eastern Asia including the Burma-Vietnam area, the Malay Peninsula, Sumatra and Borneo. The colour is mostly a bright blue-green.

Azure-winged Magpie   *Cyanopica cyanus*
kuaneos (Gr) dark blue, glossy blue   *pica* (L) a magpie; a hybrid word of Greek and Latin; the wings and the long tail feathers are blue. One group inhabits a large area of south-western Spain and Portugal, but the main population is in China, Korea, and Japan.

Andaman Treepie   *Dendrocitta bayleyi*
dendron (Gr) a tree   *kitta* (Attic) = *kissa* (Gr) a chattering greedy bird like a jay: named after Sir E. C. Bayley (1821-1894), an English statesman and an archeologist, he was in India from 1842 to 1878. Inhabiting the Andaman Islands which lie to the south of Burma in the Bay of Bengal; there are nine magpies that are known as treepies.

Common Magpie   *Pica pica*
pica (L) a magpie. Very widespread in the Northern Hemisphere, from Alaska, Canada, the western USA, to northern Africa, Eurasia including the British Isles, Asia Minor, southern China and Japan.

Abyssinian or Stresemann's Bush-Crow   *Zavattariornis stresemanni*
Named in 1938 by Dr Moltoni for Prof E. Zavattari (born 1883), an Italian Professor of Zoology in Pavia, northern Italy   *ornis* (Gr) a bird: 'Zavattari's bird'; also Prof Dr E. Stresemann (born 1889), a German zoologist and Director of Ornithology at the Zoological Museum of Berlin in 1921. It is unusual for both the generic and specific names to refer to zoologists. Dr E. Moltoni (born 1896), was an Italian ornithologist of Milan, and author of the book *Birds of Italian Somaliland*. This rare bush-crow was discovered in southern Abyssinia, now known as Ethiopia. It is not recorded elsewhere as yet.

Clark's Nutcracker   *Nucifraga columbiana*
nux (L), genitive *nucis*, a nut   *frango* (L) I break, I dash to pieces; part of the diet consists of pine seeds and acorns which it extracts from the shell with great skill: named from British Columbia, it inhabits the mountains from southern Alaska through British Columbia, Alberta, South Dakota, New Mexico, and California; it has been seen as high as 3,600 m (12,000 ft) in the mountains. Named after Brigadier-General W. Clark (1770-1828), American Army; he led the Lewis-Clark River Missouri and River Columbia Expedition in 1804 to 1806; he became Governor of Missouri in 1813. Captain M. Lewis became Governor of Louisiana in 1907.

Red-billed Chough   *Pyrrhocorax pyrrhocorax*
purrhos (Gr) flame-coloured, red; a reference to the slender curved red bill and red legs and feet   *korax* (Gr) a raven or crow: it is usually found in high mountainous areas, and inhabits the western part of Scotland, Ireland, and England, mountain areas of Spain, northern Africa, Switzerland, Italy and Greece; it ranges east through Asia Minor, Iran and Tibet to north-western China and Manchuria. The Alpine Chough *Pyrrhocorax graculus* has been seen on Mount Everest at about 8,200 m (27,000 ft) which is probably as high as any bird can fly.

Raven   *Corvus corax*
corvus (L) a raven   *corax* (L) = *korax* (Gr) a raven. Widespread round the world in the Northern Hemisphere.

Carrion Crow   *C. corone corone*
korōnē (Gr) a kind of sea-bird, a sea-crow; can mean a kind of ordinary crow, a jackdaw; the second specific name, properly known as the sub-specific name, indicates that it is the nominate sub-species (see Chapter 2, p. 19); the Hooded Crow, a sub-species, is given below. The Carrion Crow is widespread in Eurasia including England and Scotland but not the northern coastal area of the USSR; it ranges east to the Pacific but probably never south of the Tropic of Cancer.

Hooded Crow   *C. c. cornix*
cornix (L) a crow; this is a sub-species of the Carrion Crow, and has a grey upperpart of the body which makes the black head and neck stand out as a 'hood'. It inhabits Scotland and Ireland and a large area of central Eurasia roughly between the River Elbe and the River Yenisei; where the area overlaps that of the Carrion Crow these two sub-species often interbreed producing a mixed race, a hybrid.

Thick-billed Raven   *C. crassirostris*
crassus (L) thick, heavy   *rostrum* (L) the beak; the ravens tend to have big heavy beaks. Inhabiting north-eastern Africa.

Rook   *C. frugilegus*
frux (L), genitive *frugis*, fruits of the earth, vegetables grown underground; can be used to mean fruits in general; it has a very mixed diet which includes earthworms, insects, fruit, and grain   *lego* (L) I gather, I collect   *frugilegus* (L) fruit-gathering. Widespread in Europe including the British Isles but only the southern part of Scandinavia; the Azores and Madeira and parts of northern Africa, and most of Asia.

Jackdaw   *C. monedula*
monedula (L) a jackdaw, a daw; daw is an English word meaning a bird of the crow kind. Widespread in Europe including the British Isles but not northern Spain, south-west France, northern Scandinavia and northern Russia; it is found in the northern part of Africa and ranges east through Asia Minor, India, the Burma-Vietnam area, part of the Himalayas, and in Mongolia.

Fish Crow   *C. ossifragus*
os (L), genitive *ossis*, a bone   *frango* (L) I break, I dash to pieces; prominent in the varied diet of this crow, as the English name suggests, are marine animals, and it is particularly fond of shellfish; the Latin name refers to its ability to break open the hard shells. It inhabits the coastal regions, rivers and lakes of the Atlantic coast from southern Massachusetts south to Florida and west along the Gulf coast to eastern Texas.

Appendix

Transliteration of Greek Alphabet

Greek		Name	Modern System	Latin System
Α	α	alpha	a	a
Β	β	bēta	b	b
Γ	γ	gamma	g	g
Δ	δ	delta	d	d
Ε	ε	epsilon	e	e
Ζ	ζ	zēta	z	z
Η	η	ēta	ē	e
Θ	θ	thēta	th	th
Ι	ι	iōta	i	i
Κ	κ	kappa	k	c
Λ	λ	lambda	l	l
Μ	μ	mū	m	m
Ν	ν	nū	n	n
Ξ	ξ	xi	x	x
Ο	ο	omicron	o	o
Π	π	pi	p	p
Ρ	ρ	rhō	r	r
Σ	σ ς	sigma	s	s
Τ	τ	tau	t	t
Υ	υ	upsilon	u	y
Φ	φ	phi	ph	ph
Χ	χ	chi	kh	ch
Ψ	ψ	psi	ps	ps
Ω	ω	ōmega	ō	o

Bibliography

In addition to the books mentioned under Acknowledgements the following may be found useful:

Synopsis of Animal Classification, R. B. Clark and A. L. Panchen, Chapman & Hall, London.
Biological Nomenclature, C. Jeffrey, Edward Arnold, London.
An Introduction to the Classification of Animals, C. J. Lerwill, Constable, London.
Mammals—Their Latin Names Explained, A. F. Gotch, Blandford Press, Poole.

General Index

This index includes only technical terms, names of zoologists and animals other than those birds included in Chapters 6 to 33. Some individual species of animals are listed with their Latin name in *italics*; Phyla, Subphyla and Classes are indicated THUS.

Abdim, Bey al-Arnaut 72
Abingdon, M. 204
ACANTHOCEPHALA 24
Acorn Worm 21, 26
ACRANIA 26
Adams, E. 52
AGNATHA 27
Albertis, C. L. M. d' 170, 318
Albert, King of the Belgians 244
Albert, King of Saxony 319
Albert, Prince 231
Albin, E. 263
Alcedo 16, *186*
Amélie, Marquise de Tarragon 250
Amherst, Earl W. P. 114
Amherst, Lady Sarah 16, 114
Amoeba 22
AMPHIBIA 27
Amphibian 26
Anatomy 14, 19
Anderson, Dr W. W. 296
Anderson, Mrs M. V. C. 296
André, E. 175
Andrews, Dr C. W. 66
Anguis fragilis 20
Animalcules 23
Animal Kingdom 21
ANNELIDA 25
ANNULATA 25
Ant 214
Antelope 22
Anthropoidea 12
Apteryx 14
Archaeopteryx 31
Archaeornis 31, 155
Archbold, R. 170, 273, 316
Aristophanes 247
Aristotle 11, 266, 289
Arrow Worm 24
ARTHROPODA 25
Ashby, E. 286
Audubon, J. J. L. 167, 225
Autotomy 20
AVES 27, 28

Baer, K. E. V. 86
Baillon, L. A. F. 121
Baird, S. F. 133
Baker, Dr J. R. 149
Baker, Edith 121
Baker, G. F. 121, 317

Ballivian, Gen J. 110
Banks, Sir J. 58
Barbarism 15
Barrow, Sir J. 88
Bartram, W. 129
Bat, Falaba House 19
 Hog-nosed 235
Bayley, Sir E. C. 321
Beak 19
Beard Worm 24
Beauharnais, Duchess Marie 202
Beauharnais, Prince M. J. 202
Bee 189
Bell, J. G. 299
Bennett, Dr G. 44
Bensch, J. H. E. 117
Berg, Dr F. G. 141
Berlepsch, H. G. 213
Bernier, Dr J. A. 83
Bhumibol, H.M. King 235
Bilharzia 23
Billberg, G. J. 70
Binominal system 11
Bird 26, 27
Blood, temperature 30
Blyth, E. 193, 207
Boissonneau, A. 178
Bojer, W. 309
Bolle, Dr C. A. 191
Bonaparte, C. L. 222
Bonelli, Prof F. A. 100
Boonsong Lekagul, Dr 235
Bootlace Worm 23
Boucard, A. 49
Bougainville, Adm H. Y. P. Baron de 64
Bourcier, Jules 199
Bourke, Maj Gen 153
Bowdler Sharp, Dr R. 268
BRACHIATA 24
BRACHIOPODA 24
BRADYODONTI 27
BRANCHIOTREMATA 26
Brehm, Dr C. L. 233
Brehm, Thekla 233
Brewer, Dr T. M. 178
Brewer, Lucy 178
Broadbent, K. 269
Brodie, Sir B. C. 165
Bruijn, Dr J. 106
Brunnich, M. T. 143
BRYOZOA 24

Bullock, W. 189
Burchell, Dr W. J. 146, 311
Burmeister, Dr K. H. K. 124
Burrough, Dr 92
Büttikofer, Dr J. 283

Cabot, Dr S. 112
CALYSSOZOA 24
Carentan, E. Canivet de 177
Carinate 42
Carola, Queen of Saxony 319
Carruthers, A. D. M. 267
Carter, T. C. 268
Cartilage fish 27
Cat 27
CEPHALOCHORDATA 26
Cervera, F. Z. 249
Cetti, F. 264
CHAETOGNATHA 24
Chapin, Dr J. P. 262
Chapman, Dr F. M. 217
Cherrie, G. K. 175
CHONDRICHTHYES 27
CHONDROPTERYGII 27
CHORDATA 21, 26, 28, 29
Clark, Brig Gen W. 322
Class 18, 27
Classification 10
Claw 21, 100, 214
Clot Bey, Dr A. 232
CNIDARIA 22
COELENTERATA 22
Cold-blooded 30
Colenso, Rev W. 65
Comb Jelly 22
Comma Butterfly 15
Commission on Zoological Nomenclature, International 12, 15, 19
Comrie, Dr P. 318
Cook, Capt. J. 81
Cooper, W. 97
Coral 22
Cott, Dr H. 9
Coulon, Dr L. de 155
Crepuscular 168
Craseonycteris thonglongya 235
Crocodile 27
Crustacean 25
CTENOPHORA 22
Cuvier, Baron G. L. 19, 103, 10[
Cuvier, M. F. 103

GENERAL INDEX 327

Cynomys endovicianus 17

Dacelo 15
Dalhousie, Countess C. 209
D'Arnaud 200
Darwin, C. R. 19, 43, 291
Decken, Baron K. C. 192
Deignan, H. C. 260
Denham, Lt Col D. 124
Derby, 13th Earl of 107
Deville, E. 215
Dickinson, Dr J. 103
Diurnal 91
Dog 27
Dogfish 27
Dole, S. B. 298
Donaldson Smith, Dr 308
D'Orbigny, Prof A. D. 138
Duckbill 12
Duivenbode, C. W. R. 151
Duivenbode, L. D. H. A. 151
Duméril, Prof A. M. C. 165
Dumont d'Urville, J. S. C. 50
Dupont, L. 233
Duvaucel, A. 183

Earthworm 25
ECHINODERA 23
ECHINODERIDA 23
ECHINODERMATA 21, 25
ECHIURA 25
ECHIURIDA 25
ECHIUROIDEA 25
ECTOPROCTA 24
ELASMOBRANCHII 27
ELEUTHEROZOA 26
Elliot, Dr D. G. 114
Elphinstone, M. 147
Embryo 21, 29
ENDOPROCTA 24
ENTOPROCTA 24
Erinaceus europaeus 12
Euler, C. 160
Everett, A. H. 164
Eyelid 20
Eyton, T. C. 78

Family 17, 18
Farquhar, Adm Sir A. M. 187
Feathers 30
Feather Star 25
Finsch, Dr F. H. O. 242
Fischer, Dr G. A. 154
Fish 26
Flatworm 23
Fluke 23
Forsten, Dr E. A. 189
Forster, Dr J. R. 51, 141
Frantzius, Dr A. von 155, 199, 226
Fraser, L. 271
Frog 27
Fulleborn, Dr F. 245

Fytche, Maj Gen A. 112

Garnot, Dr P. 60
GASTROTRICHA 23
Gay, Dr C. 137
Generic name 11
Genus 11, 18
Gesner, Dr 129
Glands, sweat 30
Godeffroy, J. C. 275
Goeldi, Dr E. A. 216
Goering, Prof A. 196
Goodenough, Bishop S. 273
GORDIACEA 23
Gould, J. 284, 307
Gould, Mrs E. 284, 307
Gounelle, E. 177
Grauer, R. 209
Gray, G. M. 155
Greek 15
Guilding, Rev. L. 156
Gurney, J. H. 100

Haast, Sir J. von 14, 47
Hagfish 27
Halcyon days 185
Hardwicke, T. 131
Harris, C. M. 64
Harris, E. 167
Hartlaub, Dr K. J. G. 110, 158
Hedgehog 12
HEMICHORDATA 26
Hill, J. E. 235
Hodgson, B. H. 101, 111, 169
Hodgson, Mrs B. H. 111
Hoffmann, Dr C. 155
Homeothermic 30
Homonym 12
Horse 27
Horsfield, Dr T. 274
Horsehair Worm 23
House, Dr F. M. 269
Hume, A. O. 114, 260
Hume, Mrs Mary 114
Huys, E. D. de Le 113
Hyperoodon 15

Ia io 16
-idae 27
-iformes 27
Impey, Lady 112
Impey, Sir E. 112
-inae 28
Insects 25
International Commission on Zoological Nomenclature 12, 15, 19
Invertebrates 22
Iredale, T. 126

Jackson, Lady A. 283
Jackson, Sir F. J. 283

Jacquinot, Vice Adm C. H. 166
James, H. B. 75
Jardine, Sir W. 261
Jarocki, Dr F. P. 277
Jellyfish 22
Joint 29

Kalinowski, J. 49
KAMPTOZOA 24
Keel 42
Kingdom 18
King, Rear Adm P. P. 178
KINORHYNCHA 23
Kinorhynchs 23
Kirtland, Dr J. P. 296
Kittlitz, F. H. 143
Klages, S. M. 215
Koch, Dr G. von 220
Kramer, W. H. 154

La Fayette, Marquis M. J. P. 113
Lagden, Sir G. Y. 245
Lagrandiere, Vice Adm P. P. 199
Lamprey 27
Lamp Shell 24
Lancelet 21, 26
Langton, Dr H. 90, 310
Laszlo, P. L. de 225
Latham, Dr J. 106, 289
Latin names 15
Leach, Dr W. E. 187
Le Conte, Dr J. L. 252
Leech 25
LEMUROIDEA 12
LEPTOCARDII 26
Leschenault, J. B. 161
Levaillant, F. 200
Lewin, J. W. 287
Lewis, Grace A. 300
Lewis, Capt. M. 322
L'Huys, E. D. de 113
Linné, Carl von (Linnaeus) 10, 11, 14, 140, 152
Lion 22
Liver Fluke 23
Livingstone, Dr D. 159
Lizard 20, 27
Loddiges, G. 179
Longuemare, G. de 283
Lorentz, Dr H. A. 276
Loten, J. G. 283
Ludwig, Baron von 313

MacCormick, Dr R. 139
MacDougall, Dr P. 141
Macgregor, Sir W. 317
Macleay, A. 187
MAMMALIA 27
Mammals 26, 27
Man 22, 27
Mantell, W. D. B. 122
Marco Polo 231

328 GENERAL INDEX

Markham, Sir C. R. 60
Marquise de Tarragon 238
Marquis Leone de Tarragon 238
MARSIPOBRANCHII 27
Mathews, A. 178
Mathews, G. M. 271
Mayr, Dr Ernst 275
McClelland, Dr J. 242
McConnell, F. V. 225
McConnell, Josephine V. 225
Meade-Waldo, E. G. B. 146
Mechow, Major A. von 160
Meek, A. G. 152
Meiffren-Laugier, Baron 118
Meller, Dr J. C. 84
Merlin, Comtesse M. 161
MESOZOA 22
Michler, Brig Gen N. 216
Miller, L. E. 217
Milne-Edwards, A. 263
Mocino, Dr J. M. 183
MOLLUSCA 25
Molluscs 25
Moltoni, Dr E. 321
Monkey 12
Montagu, Col G. 97
Moss Animal 24
Mulsant, Mde V. 178
Muscle, flight 42
Mycetozoa 22
Mythology 152

Narina, the Hottentot girl 183
Nehrkorn, Adolph 282
NEMATA 23
NEMATODA 23
NEMATOMORPHA 23
NEMERTEA 23
Newt 27
Nomenclature, International Commission on Zoological 12, 15, 19
Nominate subspecies 19
Nordmann, A. v. 137
Notochord 21
Nuttall, T. 141, 171
Nycticeius (*Scotoecus*) *falabae* 19

Octopus 25
Orbigny, Prof A. D. d' 138, 217
Order 18
Orleans, Princess H. d' 179
Ornithorhynchus 12
OSTEICHTHYES 27
Oustalet, Dr J. F. E. 212
Owen, Sir Richard 47
Oyster 25

Pallas, Prof P. S. 146
Palmer, H. C. 298
Parasite 22
PARAZOA 22

Parkinson, S. 58
Peanut Worm 25
Pel, H. S. 165
PELMATOZOA 25
Pelzeln, A. von 55
Penis 23
Pennant, Dr T. 80
Pérouse, Capt. J. F. 106
Perrot, J. 210
Pfeiffer, Frau Ida R. 68
Phallus 23
Phayre, Lt Gen Sir A. P. 220
Philby, J. B. H. 206
Philby, Mrs H. D. 206
Phillips, E. E. Lort 110
PHORONIDA 24
PHORONIDEA 24
Phoronid 24
Phoronis 24
Phyla 12, 21
Phylum 18
PISCES 27
Platen, Dr C. C. 272
Platen, Dr Margarete 272
PLATYHELMINTHES 23
Platypus 12
POGONOPHORA 24
Poikilothermic 30
Pollen, F. P. L. 246
Polygonia c-album 15
POLYZOA 24
  ECTOPROCTA 24
  ENDOPROCTA 24
  ENTOPROCTA 24
PORIFERA 22
Prairie Dog 17
Priapos 23
PRIAPULIDA 23
Priapulids 23
Priapus 23
Prigogine, Dr A. 164
Pringle, Col Sir S. W. 244
Priority 12
Prosimii 12
PROTOZOA 22
Pucheran, Dr J. 116

Quadruped 31

Rabbit Fish 27
Race (subspecies) 18
Ragworm 25
Raimondi, Prof A. 230
Ramsay, Dr E. P. 287
Rand, Dr A. L. 117
Ratite 42
Ray 27
Reeves, J. 114
Reptiles 26, 27
REPTILIA 27
Rey, Dr J. G. C. E. 293
Rheinard, Capt 115

Ribbon Worm 23
Richard, A. 238
Richard, Prof L. C. M. 238
Richardson, W. B. 291
Ridgway, Antonia 228
Ridgway, R. 224, 228
Rieffer, Mr 229
Riker, C. B. 213
Robert, A. 217
Rollet, B. 200
Ross, J. C. Anne 159
Ross, Sir J. C. 140, 159
ROTATORIA 23
Rothschild, Baron L. W. 209, 311
ROTIFERA 23
Round Worm 23
Rüppell, Dr W. P. E. S. 244
Ruspoli, Prince E. 159

Salp 26
Salvin, O. 49
Sandwich, 4th Earl of 81
Saunders, H. 119
Savés, Théo 170
Say, Thomas 222
Schauensee, R. M. de 260
Schiff, Dr M. 227
Schütt, O. 159
Sclater, Dr P. L. 49
Scopoli, Prof J. A. 128
Sea Cucumber 26
Sea Gooseberry 22
Sea Lily 25
Sea Squirt 25
Sea Urchin 26
SELACHII 27
Sequence 22, 27
Sganzin, Capt. V. 149
Shark 27
Sharpe, Dr R. B. 137
Shaw, Dr G. 90
Simiae 12
SIPUNCULA 25
SIPUNCULOIDEA 25
Sirindhorn, H.R.H. Princess 235
Slow-worm 20
Slug 25
Smith, Sir A. 208
Snail 25
Snake 20, 27
Solander, Dr D. C. 59
Sonnerat, P. 113
Souleyet, F. L. A. 211
Spalding, E. 259
Species 11, 18
Specific name 11
Spider 25
Spiny-headed Worm 24
Spix, Dr J. B. 155, 211
Sponge 22
SPONGIDA 22
Sprague, I. 239

GENERAL INDEX

Squid 22, 25
Stanley, Hon. E. S. 107
Starfish 26
Stark, Dr A. C. 233
Steere, Prof. J. B. 162
Stejneger, Dr L. 290
Steller, G. W. 85, 320
Stephanie, Princess 319
Stock, race, or kind 21
STOMOCHORDATA 26
Stresemann, Dr E. 151, 321
Strickland, H. E. 207
Struthers, Dr J. 134
Subclass 18
Subfamily 18, 27
Subgenus 18, 19
Subkingdom 18
Suborder 18
Subphylum 18, 21
Subspecies 13, 18
Sueur, C. A. Le 240
Superclass 18
Superfamily 18
Superorder 18
Swainson, W. 93, 110, 203
Swinhoe, R. 132
Synonym 12
Systema Naturae 11
Szecheny, Count Bela 110

Taczanowski, Dr W. 264
Tarn, J. 218
Tarragon, A. Marquise de 238

Tarragon, L. Marquis de 238
Tautonym 13
Taxon 18
Taxonomy 11
Teeth 19, 155
Temminck, Prof. C. J. 112, 133, 137, 146, 258
Thomas, Oldfield 16
Thonglongya, K. 234
Tickell, Col S. R. 192, 259
Toad 27
Tortoise 27
Townsend, J. K. 175, 255
Traill, Dr T. 225
Tregallas, T. H. 272
Trinominal 18, 19
Troglodytes troglodytes troglodytes 13
Trudeau, Dr J. de B. 141
Tschudi, J. J. Baron von 229
TUNICATA 26
Turtle 27
Tweedie, Michael 13
Type-genus 28
Type-species 14

UROCHORDATA 26
Ussher, H. T. 165

Vallisnieri, Prof A. 86
Varro, M. T. 237
Vaux, W. S. 175
VERTEBRATA 21, 26, 27, 28
Vertebrates 27

Victoria, Queen 231, 318
Vieillot, L. J. P. 13, 295, 313
Vigors, N. A. 274
Vinegar Eelworms 23

Wagler, J. G. 300
Wahlberg, J. A. 201
Wallace, Dr A. R. 285
Wallace Line 285
Warm-blooded 30
Whale 27
Weber, Prof M. W. C. 282
Weber Van Bosse, Dr A. 282
Wheel Animalcules 23
Whitehead, Jeffrey 99
Whitehead, John 279
Wilson, Alexander 60, 135, 297
Wing 14, 31
Wolf, Dr T. 120
Wolstenholme, H. 90, 310
Woodford, C. M. 285
Woodford, Col. E. J. A. 166

Yarrel, W. 237
Yersin, Dr A. E. J. 261

Zavattari, Prof E. 321
Zeledon, J. C. 254
Zoological Nomenclature, International Commission on 12, 15, 19
Zyzomys 16

Index of English Names

This index contains the English names of all birds in the book. In general, the page number of the main reference is given in *italic* type, but where there are additional references of a general or less important nature, then these page numbers are also indicated.

Accentor, Alpine 253
Akepa 298
Albatross 56
   Black-browed 57
   Black-footed 57
   Grey-headed 57
   Sooty 57
   Wandering 57
Amadavat 306
Amakihi 298
Amazon 156
Anhinga 61, *65*
Ani, Groove-billed 161
   Smooth-billed 161
Antbird, Goeldi's 216
   Jet 215
   Striated 215
   Wing-banded 216
Antpitta, Black-crowned 216
   Brown-banded 217
   Chestnut-crowned 217
   Great 217
   Rusty-breasted 216
Antshrike, Black-headed 215
   Fasciated 214
Antthrush, Black-headed 216
Antwren, Black-bellied 215
   Klages's 215
   White-flanked 215
Anvilhead 71
Apalis, Brown-throated 267
Aracari, Brown-mandibled 202
   Many-banded 202
Asity, Velvet 220
Auklet, Cassin's 144
   Crested 144
Auk, Little 125
Avadavat 306
Avocet 125, *134*
   American 134

Babbler, Arrow Marked 261
   Ashy-headed 259
   Deignan's 260
   Malay Rail 259
   Red-capped 261
   Rusty-cheeked Scimitar 260
   Spiny 261
   Tickell's 259
   White-throated 260
Bananaquit 298

Barbet, Black-breasted 200
   Black-spotted 198
   D'Arnaud's 200
   Golden-whiskered 199
   Levaillant's 200
   Naked-faced 199
   Pied 200
   Prongbilled 199
   Red-headed 199
   Red-vented 199
Barbtail, Spotted 213
Becard, Black-capped 229
Bee-eater 185
   Carmine 189
   Celebes Bearded 189
   European or Common 189
   Rainbow 189
   Red-throated 189
Bellbird 288
   Crested 275
   Three-wattled (COTINGIDAE) 230
   White 230
Bird of Paradise, Black-billed Sicklebill 318
   Greater 319
   King 319
   King of Saxony 319
   Multi-crested 317
   Princess Stephanie's 318
   Twelve-wired 318
Bittern 67
   American 70
   Eurasian 71
   Least 70
   Little 70
Blackbird (ICTERIDAE) 300
   Jamaican 300
   Oriole 301
   Red-winged 301
   Yellow-headed 301
Blackbird (MUSCICAPIDAE) 257
   Mountain 258
   White-collared 257
Blackcap 265
Bluebill, Red-headed 305
Bluebird, Eastern 255
   Fairy 243
Bobwhite 105, *109*
Booby, Brown 63
   Red-footed 63
Boubou 244
   Fulleborn's Black 245

Bowerbird, Archbold's 316
   New Guinea Regent 317
   Satin 317
   Spotted 317
   Toothbilled 316
Brambling 302
Bristle-Bird 269
Bristle-head, Bornean 246
Broadbill, Black and Yellow 209
   Dusky 209
   Grauer's or African Green 208
   Lesser Green 209
   Longtailed 209
   Rufous-sided 208
Brolga 119
Bronzewing, Brush 148
Brownbird 242
Brush-Finch, Black-headed 292
   Rufous-capped 292
Brush Turkey 106
   Bruijn's 106
   Red-billed 106
Budgerigar 153
Bulbul, Dwarf Bearded 242
   Finch-billed 241
   McClelland's 242
   Oriental Brown-eared 242
   Red-eyed 241
   Terrestrial 242
   Yellow-throated 241
Bullfinch 305
   Cuban 291
Bunting, Black-headed 289
   Crested 289
   Golden-breasted 289
   Lapland or Longspur 289
   Painted 293
   Reed 289
   Snow 290
   Socotra Mountain 290
   Yellow or Yellowhammer 289
Bush-Crow, Abyssinian 321
Bush-Lark, Singing 232
Bustard, Australian 124
   Crested 124
   Denham's 124
   Little 124
Bustard-Quail 118
   Black-breasted 118
Butcherbird 243, 244, *316*
Butcherbird, Grey 316
Button-Quail, Little 118

INDEX OF ENGLISH NAMES

Buzzard, African Mountain 99
  Barred Honey 93
  Black-breasted 94
  Common 99
  Honey 93
Buzzard-Eagle, Rufous Winged 98

Cacique, Scarlet-rumped 300
Cahow 59
Canary 303
  Yellow 303
Canvasback 86
Capercaillie, Siberian or
  Black-billed 108
Caracara, Chimango 102
  Common 100
  Red-throated 100
  White-throated 100
Cardinal 292
Cassowary, Australian 44
  Bennett's 44
  One-wattled 45
Catbird, Grey 251
Chachalaca, Plain 107
Chaffinch 28, 29, *302*
Chat (EPTHIANURIDAE) 285
  Crimson 286
  White-fronted 285
Chat (MUSCICAPIDAE)
  Black-tailed 255
  Sooty 257
  Sooty Rock 254
Chickadee, Black-capped 278
  Chestnut-backed 279
Chicken, Prairie 108
Chiffchaff 265
Chough, Red-billed
  (CORVIDAE) 322
  White-winged
  (GRALLINIDAE) 315
Cisticola, Carruther's 266
  Golden-headed 267
Cockatoo, Black or
  Great Palm 151
  Sulphur-crested 152
Cock-of-the-Rock, Andean 228
  Guianan 228
Colies 180
Condor, Andean 92
  California 92
Conebill, White-eared 298
Coot 122
  Crested or knob-billed 122
  Giant 122
  Horned 122
Cordon-Bleu, Angolan 305
Corella, Little 152
Cormorant 61
  Galapagos Flightless 64
  Great 64
  Little Pied 65
  Long-tailed 64

Peruvian 64
Corncrake 121
Coronet, Chestnut-breasted 178
Cotinga, Lovely 228
  Pompadour 228
  Purple-throated 228
  Yellow-billed 228
Coua, Crested 161
  Red-capped 162
Coucal, Common 162
  Pheasant 162
  Steere's 162
  White-browed 162
Courol 189
Courser, Cream Coloured 136
  Indian 136
  Temminck's 137
Cowbird, Brown-headed 302
Crake, African Black 121
  Baillon's 121
  Carolina 121
  Spotted *119*, 121
Crane, Common 117
  Crowned 119
  Japanese 119
  Whooping 118
Creeper, Plain-headed 281
  Spotted 281
  Stripe-headed 281
  Wall 280
Crombec, Long-billed 267
Crossbill, Red 304
Crow, Carrion 322
  Fish 323
  Hooded 322
  Paradise 317
Cuckoo, Black-billed 160
  Common 157, *160*
  Emerald 160
  Golden Bronze 160
  Great Lizard 161
  Leschenault's 161
  Long-tailed 160
  Pallid 160
  Pearly-breasted 160
  Red-winged Indian 160
Cuckoo-Shrike, Black 240
  Black-faced 239
  Ground 239
  Red-shouldered 240
  Wattled 240
  White-rumped 239
Curassow, Crested or Black 107
  Helmeted 107
  Red-wattled 107
Curlew 125
  Bristle-thighed 130
  Common 14, *130*
  Eskimo 130
  Far Eastern 130
  Long-billed 130
Currawong, Pied 316

Dabchick, Red-throated 55
Darter, African 65
  Asian 65
  Australian 65
Darwin's Finches 19, *291*
Dipper 248
  American 248
Diver, Red-throated 52, 53
Diving-Petrel, Peruvian 60
  Subantarctic 60
Dollar Bird 191
Dotterel 125, *129*
  Australian 137
Dove 145
  Collared Turtle 147
  Golden 149
  Laughing 147
  Namaqua 148
  Rock 145, *147*
  Turtle 148
Dovekie 142
Dowitcher, Short-billed 132
Drongo, Greater
  Racket-tailed 314
  Mountain 313
  New Ireland 313
  Square-tailed 313
Duck 76
  Black-headed 90
  Blue-billed 89
  Common Eider 85
  Freckled 85
  Lake 89
  Mandarin 87
  Meller's 84
  Muscovy 87
  Musk 89
  Paradise 82
  Patagonian Crested 82
  Ruddy 89
  Steamer, Falkland Island
    Flightless 82
  Flying 83
  Magellan Flightless 83
  Steller's Eider 85
  Torrent 85
  Tree, Black-bellied 78
    Black-billed 78
    Eyton's 78
    Fulvous 78
    Indian 78
    Spotted 78
    Whistling 78
  Tufted 86
  White-backed 89
  White-headed 89
  Wood 87
Dunnock 253

Eagle 91
  African Fish 95
  Bald 95

INDEX OF ENGLISH NAMES

Bonelli's 100
Crowned 101
Golden 15, *100*
Grey-headed Fishing 95
Gurney's 100
Harpy 99
Long-crested 100
Monkey-eating 99
Philippine Serpent 96
Snake 96
Solitary 98
Steller's Sea 95
Tawny 100
Wedge-tailed 100
White-bellied Sea 95
White-tailed 94
Eagle-Owl, Great 164
Egret 68, 69
  Cattle 68
  Chinese 69
  Great 69
  Little 69
Elaenia, Mountain 226
Emerald, Fork-tailed 177
  Glittering-bellied 177
  Honduras 178
Emu 45
Emu-tailed, Brown 266
Eremomela, Yellow-backed 267
Euphonia, Thick-billed 294

Falcon 91, 102
  African Pygmy 102
  Grey 103
  Laughing 102
  Peregrine 14, *103*
  Prairie 103
Falconet, Pied 102
Faintail, Grey 273
  Red-tailed 273
  Rufous-fronted 273
Fernbird 268
Fieldfare 258
Figbird 313
  Yellow 313
Finch (ESTRILDIDAE) 306
  Chestnut-breasted 307
  Gouldian 307
  Zebra 306
Finch, Cocos Island
  (EMBERIZIDAE) 291
  Large Ground 291
  Plush-capped 292
  St. Lucia Black 291
Finch, House (FRINGILLIDAE) 304
Finch, Snow (PLOCEIDAE) 309
Finfoot, African 123
  Asian or Masked 123
Fireback, Crested 113
Fire-eye, White-backed 216
Firefinch, African 305
Flamingo 67, *74*

Andean 75
Greater 75
James's 75
Lesser 75
Flicker, Yellow-shafted 204
Flower-pecker, Anna's 282
  Nehrkorn's 282
  Olive-backed 282
  Scarlet-backed 282
Flower-piercer, Bluish 295
Flycatcher (MUSCICAPIDAE)
  African Paradise 274
  Black-faced Monarch 275
  Black Myiagra 274
  Black Paradise 274
  Brown 272
  Cape 274
  Grey-headed 273
  Little Yellow 274
  Palawan 272
  Pale 271
  Pied 271
  Red-backed Fantail 273
  Red-capped Robin 273
  Restless 275
  Rock Robin 273
  Seychelles Paradise 274
  South African Black 271
  Spotted 272
  Versicolour 275
  White-browed Forest 271
Flycatcher (PTILOGONATIDAE) 247
  Black and Yellow Silky 247
  Grey Silky 247
Flycatcher (TYRANNIDAE) 224
  Boat-billed 224
  Cocos Island 224
  Fork-tailed 223
  Grey-capped 224
  Traill's 225
  Vermilion 223
  Yellow-bellied 224
Flycatcher-Babbler, Chapin's 262
Forest-Falcon, Barred 102
Fowl, Ceylon Jungle 113
  Grey Jungle 113
  Red Jungle 113
Fowl, Mallee 106
Francolin, Black 110
  Hartlaub's 110
  Somali Greywing 110
  Swainson's 13, *110*
Frigatebird 61, *66*
  Ascension Island 66
  Christmas Island 66
  Greater 66
  Magnificent 66
Frogmouth 168
  Hodgson's 169
  Javan 169
  Owlet 170
  Papuan 169

Tawny 168, *169*
Fruiteater, Green and Black 229
  Red-crested 229
  Scaled 229
Fulmar, Giant 57
  Northern 58

Gadwall 84
Galah 152
Gallinule, Purple 122
Gallito, Grey 218
  Sandy 219
Gannet 61
  Common 63
Garganey 84
Geese 76, *79*
Gibber-bird 386
Gnat-catcher, Blue-grey 264
Gnat-eater, Black-billed 217
  D'Orbigny's 217
  Robert's 217
Go-away Bird 159
Godwit, Bar-tailed 130
  Black-tailed 131
Goldcrest 266
Goldeneye, Barrow's 88
Goldfinch, Eurasian 303
Goose, Andean 81
  Barnacle 80
  Bean 80
  Blue-winged 81
  Brent 80
  Canada 80
  Greylag 79
  Knob-billed 87
  Lesser White-fronted 80
  Magpie 77
  Maned 87
  Ne-ne or Hawaiian 81
  Pink-footed 79
  Red-breasted 81
  Ruddy-headed 81
  Snow 80
  Spur-winged 88
  Upland 81
  White-fronted 79
Goshawk 91, *98*
  Pale Chanting 97
  Black-mantled 98
Grackle, Greater Antillean 302
Grass-Wren, Black 269
  Striated 269
Grebe 54
  Atitlán 55
  Flightless or Short-winged 55
  Great Crested 54, 55
  Horned 54
  Little (or Red-throated
    Dabchick) 55
  Madagascar 55
  Western 55

INDEX OF ENGLISH NAMES 333

Greenbul, Joyful 241
  Slender-billed 241
  Yellow-striped 242
Greenfinch 303
Greenlet, Golden-fronted 299
  Tawny-crowned 299
Greenshank 131
Greybird, Long-billed 239
Grosbeak, Blue 293
  Pine 304
  Yellow-shouldered 293
Ground-Dove, Barred or Zebra 148
Ground-Tyrant, Spot-billed 222
Ground-Wren, Chestnut-tailed 270
Grouse 105
  Black 108
  Blue 108
  Ruffed 108
  Sage 109
  Sharp-tailed 109
  Spruce 108
  Szecheny's Pheasant 110
Guan, Crested 107
  Horned 107
Guillemot, Brunnich's 143
  Black 143
  Common Murre 143
Guinea Fowl 18, 105
  Black 115
  Helmeted 18, *115*
  Kenya Crested 116
  Tufted 115
  Vulturine 115
Gull 125
  Black-headed 140
  Common 139
  Herring 139
  Lesser Black-backed 139
  Ross's 140
Gyrfalcon 103

Harrier, Marsh 97
  Montagu's 97
  Pallid 97
Hawfinch 305
Hawk 91
  African Long-tailed 98
  Black 98
  Cooper's 97
  Galapagos 99
  Red-tailed 99
  Rough-legged 99
  Slate-coloured 98
  White 98
  White-tailed 99
Hawk-Eagle, Hodgson's 100
  Ornate 101
Hawk-Owl, Papuan 28, *166*
  Solomon Islands 166
Hemispingus, Grey-capped 293

Hen, Domestic 113
  Marianas Scrub 106
Hermit, Broad-tipped 177
  Long-tailed 177
  Pale-bellied 176
Heron 67
  Banded Tiger 70
  Black-crowned Night 69
  Boat-billed 69
  Goliath 68
  Great Blue 68
  Great White 69
  Grey 68
  Little Blue 69
  Little Green 68
  Madagascar Squacco 68
  Squacco 68
  White-backed Night 69
Hoatzin 31, *116*, 157
Hobby, African 103
Honeybird, Wahlberg's 201
Honeycreeper, Crested (DREPANIDIDAE) 298
Honeycreeper, Purple (EMBERIZIDAE) 295
Honeyeater, Bar-breasted 287
  Brown 286
  Dainty 287
  Lewin's 287
  Long-billed 286
  Orange-cheeked 287
  Red-headed 286
  Rufous-throated 288
  Strong-billed 287
  White-throated 287
  Yellow-faced 287
Honeyguide 195
  Greater or Black-throated 201
  Indian or Orange-rumped 201
  Lesser 201
  Lyre-tailed 201
Hoopoe 185, *191*
Hornbill 185
  Abyssinian Ground 194
  Blyth's 193
  Crowned 192
  Indian Pied 193
  Malaba Grey 192
  Narcondam 193
  Rhinoceros 193
  Rufous-necked 192
  Trumpeter 193
  Van der Decken's 192
  White-throated Brown 192
  Wreathed 193
Hornero, Rufous 212
Hummingbird 173
  Amethyst-throated 178
  Bee 179
  Broad-tailed 179
  Racket-tailed 179
  Rufous 179

  Sword-billed 178
  White-bellied 178
Huet-huet, Black-throated 218
Hypocolius 247

Ibis 72
  Australian White 73
  Bald 73
  Glossy 73
  Hermit 73
  Indian White 73
  Japanese 73
  Sacred 73
  Scarlet 73
  White 73
Ibisbill 134
Iiwi 298
Iora, Common 243

Jacamar 195
  Great 197
  Pale-headed 196
  Rufous-tailed 197
  Three-toed 196
  White-eared 196
  Yellow-billed 196
Jacana 125
  African 126
  American 126
  Australian 126
  Bronze-winged 126
  Pheasant-tailed 122, 126
Jackass, Laughing 186
Jackdaw 323
Jaeger, Long-tailed 138
  Pomarine 139
Jay 352
  Azure-hooded 320
  Eurasian 320
  Purplish 320
  Scrub 320
  Steller's 320

Kagu 123
Kaka 152
Kakapo 153
Kestrel, American (or American Sparrowhawk) 103
  Common 14, *104*
  Dickenson's 14, *103*
  Fox 102
Killdeer 129
Kingbird, Eastern 223
  Thick-billed 223
Kingfisher 16, *185*
  Amazon 186
  Brown-backed Paradise 187
  Chestnut-bellied 187
  Common 16, *186*
  Forest 186, *187*
  Green 186
  Grey-headed 187

334 INDEX OF ENGLISH NAMES

Pied 186
Shovel-billed 187
Three-toed 186
White-backed 187
Kinglet, Golden-crowned 266
Kite, Black 94
  Brahminy 94
  Mississippi 94
  Red 13, *94*
  Snail 93
  Square-tailed 94
  Swainson's 93
  Swallow-tailed 93
  White-tailed 93
Kittiwake, Black-legged 140
  Red-legged 139
Kiwi 14, *46*
  Common or Brown 46
  Great Spotted 14, *47*
  Little Spotted 47
Koel 160
Kokako 314
Kookaburra 15, *186*, 187
  Blue-winged 187

Lammergeier 95
Lapwing, Common 128
  Southern 127
  Spur-winged 128
Lark, Calandra 232
  Crested 233
  Desert 232
  Dupont's 233
  Horned 234
  Rufous-naped 232
  Short-toed 232
  Stark's Short-toed 233
  Thekla's 233
  Thick-billed 15, 232
  Wood 233
Laughing Thrush, Collared 261
  White-crested 261
Leafbird, Blue-winged 243
  Golden-fronted 243
Leafscraper, Tawny-throated 214
Lily-trotter 125
Limpkin 119
Linnet 304
Logrunner, Northern 259
Longbill, Slaty-chinned 286
Longclaw, Rosy-breasted 238
  Yellow-throated 238
Longspur 290
Loon 52
  Arctic (or Black-throated Diver) 53
  Yellow-billed 52
Lorikeet, Little 151
  Purple-crowned 151
  Scaly-breasted 151
Lory, Black 151
  Duivenbode's or Brown 151

Stresemann's 151
Yellow and Green 151
Lovebird, Fischer's 154
  Madagascar or Grey-headed 154
  Masked 150, *154*
Lyrebird, Albert's 231
  Superb 231

Macaw, Coulon's or Blue-headed 155
  Hyacinthine 155
  Red-and-Green 155
Magpie, Azure-winged 321
  Common 321
  Green 321
Magpie-Lark 314
Mallard 84
Manakin, Golden-headed 226
  Grey-headed 227
  Red-headed 227
  Thrush-like 227
  White-bearded 227
  White-throated 227
  Wire-tailed 227
Manucode, Curl-breasted 318
Marabou 72
Martin, African River 234
  African Sand 235
  Caribbean 235
  Crag 235
  House 236
  Sand 235
  White-eyed River 234
Meadowlark, Eastern 301
  Western 301
Melidectes, White-fronted 287
Meliphaga, White-eared Mountain 287
Merganser, Auckland Island 88
  Goosander or Common 88
  Hooded 88
  Red-breasted 89
Merlin 103
Mesite, Brown 117
  White-breasted 117
Miner, Common 211
Minivet, Scarlet 240
  Short-billed 240
Mockingbird 251
  Brown-backed 251
  Galapagos 251
Monal, Chinese 113
  Himalayan 112
Monarch, Yap Island 275
Monias, Bensch's 117
Monkbird, Capuchin 230
Monklet, Lance-billed 198
Moorhen 122
Motmot, Blue-crowned 188
  Broad-billed 188
  Rufous 188

Tody 188
Turquoise-browed 188
Mountain-Rail 120
Mousebird 180
  Blue-naped 181
  Red-faced 180
  White-headed 181
Murre, Common 143
Murrelet, Kittlitz's 143
Mynah, Chinese 311
  Common 312
  Golden-crested 312
  Rothschild's 311

New Zealand Wren (ACANTHISITTIDAE) 221
Nightingale 255
  Thrush 255
Nightjar 168
  Archbold's 170
  Common 171
  Egyptian 171
  Ladder-tailed 172
  Long-tailed 171
  Pennant-winged 172
  Rufous 171
  Spotted 171
  Standard-winged 172
  White-throated 171
Noddy, Black or Lesser Brown 142
Nunbird, Yellow-billed 198
Nunlet, Grey-cheeked or Red-capped 198
Nutcracker, Clark's 322
Nuthatch 279
  Coral-billed 246
  Corsican 279
  Pink-faced 280
  Red-breasted 279

Oilbird 169
Oriole, Crimson-breasted (ORIOLIDAE) 312
  Golden 312
  Northern (ICTERIDAE) 300
  White-edged 300
Oropendola, Chestnut-headed 300
  Dusky-green 299
  Green 300
Osprey 101
Ostrich 41, 42
Ouzel, Ring 258
Ovenbird (FURNARIIDAE) 212
Ovenbird (PARULIDAE) 297
Owl (STRIGIDAE) 164
  African Marsh 166
  African Wood 166
  Buff-fronted 167
  Crested 28, *164*
  Fearful 167
  Great Horned 165
  Hawk 163, *165*

INDEX OF ENGLISH NAMES   335

Little 166
Long-eared 167
Pel's Fishing 165
Rufous Fishing 165
Snowy 165
Tawny 166
Owl (TYTONIDAE) 166
  Barn 28, *163*
  Sooty 28, *164*
  Tanzanian Bay 28, *164*
Owlet-Nightjar, Mountain 170
  New Caledonian 170
Oxpecker, Red-billed 312
  Yellow-billed 312
Oystercatcher 125
  American 127
  Black 127
  European 127

Pachycare, Golden-faced 276
Palmchat 248
Palmcreeper, Riker's 213
Palm-weaver, Golden 309
Parakeet, Blossom-headed 154
  Golden-winged 156
  Hoffman's or
    Sulphur-winged 155
  Monk or Grey-breasted 156
  Night 153
  Red-masked 155
  Ring-necked 154
  Slender-billed 155
Pardalote, Forty-spotted 282
  Spotted 282
Parotia, Queen Carola's 319
Parrot 150
  African Grey 154
  Bourke's 153
  Geelvink Pygmy 152
  Meek's Pygmy 152
  Philippine Hanging 154
  St. Vincent 156
  Thick-billed 155
  Turquoise 153
  White-fronted 156
  Yellow-headed 156
Parrotbill (DREPANIDAE) 298
Parrotbill (MUSCICAPIDAE) 263
  Ashy-throated 263
  Greater Red-headed 263
Parrot-Finch, Green-faced 306
Parson Bird or Tui 288
Partridge, Bamboo 112
  Bearded Wood 109
  Common or Grey 111
  Madagascar 111
  Mrs Hodgson's 111
  Red-legged 110
  Tree 111
Parula, Northern 296
Peacock 115
Peafowl, Common or Blue 115

Congo 115
Peahen 115
Pelican 61
  American White 62
  Brown 62
  European White 61, 63
Penguin 50
  Adelie 50
  Emperor 51
  Galapagos 51
  Jackass 51
  King 51
  Macaroni 51
  Rockhopper 51
  Yellow-eyed 51
Petrel, Bermuda 59
  Dark-rumped 59
  Giant 57
  Parkinson's 58
  Snow 59
  Solander's 59
Pewee, Eastern Wood 224
  Tropical 224
Phainopepla 247
Phalarope, Northern 135
  Red or Grey 135
  Wilson's 135
Pheasant 105
  Argus 115
  Bronze-tailed Peacock 114
  Brown-eared 113
  Common or Ring-neck 114
  Crested Argus 115
  Elliot's Long-tailed 114
  Golden 114
  Impeyan 112
  Koklass 113
  Kalij 113
  Lady Amherst's 16, *114*
  Mrs Hume's Long-tailed 114
  Reeves's Long-tailed 114
Phoebe, Say's 222
Piculet, Antillean 204
  Olivaceous 203
  White-bellied 203
Pigeon 145
  African Green 148
  Baker's Imperial 149
  Blue or Common Ground 148
  Comoro Blue 149
  Crested 148
  Nilgiri Wood 147
  Topknot 149
  Wood 147
Pilot-Bird 270
Pintail 83
  Bahama 83
  South Georgia 84
Pipit, Richard's or
  New Zealand 238
  Sprague's 239
  Tawny 238

Pitta, African 219
  Blue-winged 219
  Koch's 220
  Phayre's 220
  Rainbow 220
  Red-breasted 220
Plains Wanderer 118
Plantain-eater, Eastern Grey 159
Plantcutter, Peruvian 230
  Reddish 231
Plover (CHARADRIIDAE) 125
  American Golden 128
  Golden 128
  Grey or Black-bellied 128
  Little Ringed 128
  Mountain 129
  Ringed 129
Plover, Crab (DROMADIDAE) 155
Plover, Egyptian
  (GLAREOLIDAE) 136
Plover, Quail (TURNICIDAE) 118
Pochard, African or Red-eyed 86
  Australian 85
  Baer's 86
  Common 86
  Red-crested 86
Poor-will 171
Potoo 168
  Common 170
  Great 170
Pratincole 137
  Black-winged 137
  White-collared 137
Prinia, Black-throated 266
Prion, Antarctic or Dove 58
Ptarmigan, Rock 108
  White-tailed 108
  Willow 108
Puffback, Pringle's 244
Puffbird, Chestnut-capped 197
  Spot-backed 197
  White-whiskered or
    Softwing 197
Puffin 144
  Horned 144
Pygmy Owl, Collared 165
Pygmy-Tyrant, Short-tailed 225

Quail, Californian
  (PHASIANIDAE) 109
  Common 14, *111*
  Manipur Bush 111
  Marbled Wood 109
  Mountain 109
  Ocellated 110
  Stripe-faced Wood 110
  Stubble 111
  Swamp 111
Quail-Finch, Black-chinned 306
Quail, Lark (TURNICIDAE) 118
  Marsh 118
Quail-Thrush, Cinnamon 259

INDEX OF ENGLISH NAMES

Quelia, Red-billed 310
Quetzal, Resplendent 182

Rail-Babbler, Malay 259
Rail, Cape 120
  Clapper 120
  Galapagos 122
  Slate-breasted 120
  Virginia 120
  Water 120
  White-striped 120
Raven 322
  Thick-billed 323
Razorbill 143
Redhead 85
Redpoll 304
Redstart, Golden-fronted
  (PARULIDAE) 297
Redstart (MUSCICAPIDAE) 255
Reedhaunter, Curve-billed 212
  Straight-billed 212
Reedling 263
Rhea 43
Rhea, Greater 43
  Lesser or Darwins 43
Riflebird, Victoria 318
Rifleman 222
Roadrunner, Greater 161
  Lesser 161
Robin, Southern Yellow
  (MUSCICAPINAE) 272
  White-faced 272
  Yellow-bellied 272
Robin, Peking (TIMALIINAE) 262
Robin, American (TURDINAE) 257
  Bearded Scrub 254
  Cape 255
  Eurasian 254
  Forest 254
  Southern Scrub 254
Rock-Chat, Sooty 254, 291
Rockfowl, Bareheaded 262
Roller, Blue-bellied (CORACIIDAE)
  186, 190
  Broad-billed 191
  European 190
  Indian 190
  Pitta-like Ground 190
  Short-legged Ground 190
Roller, Cuckoo
  (ZEPTOSOMATIDAE) 189
Rook 323
Rosefinch, Red-mantled 304
Rosella, Crimson 153
Ruff 134

Sabrewing, Lazuline 177
Sanderling 133
Sandgrouse 145
  Madagascar or Masked 147
  Namaqua 146
  Pallas's 145, *146*

Tibetan 146
Variegated 146
Sandpiper, Baird's 133
  Green 131
  Purple 133
  Solitary 131
  Spoonbilled 133
  Upland 129
  Wood 131
Sapsucker, Red-breasted 206
Scaup, New Zealand 86
Scops-Owl, Flores 164
Screamer, Horned 77
  Northern 77
  Southern 77
Screech-Owl, White-throated
  28, *164*
Scrub-Bird, Noisy 231
  Rufous 231
Scrub-Wren, Spotted 270
Scythebill, Black-billed 211
Secretary Bird 92
Seedeater, Blue 291
  Slate-coloured 291
  White-throated 290
Seedsnipe, D'Orbigny's 138
  Gay's 137
  Pygmy or Patagonian 138
Sericornis, Black and Green 270
Seriema, Burmeister's 124
  Crested 124
Serin 303
Shag, Auckland Island 65
  Blue-eyed 64
  Spotted 65
Shaketail, Grey-flanked 212
Sharpbill 226
Shearwater, Greater 58
  Short-tailed or Tasmanian 59
  Wedge-tailed 58
Sheathbill, Lesser 138
  Snowy 138
Sheld Duck 82
Shelduck 82
  Ruddy 82
Shortwing, Rusty-bellied 254
Shoveler, Northern 83
Shrike (CAMPEPHAGIDAE) 239
  Common Wood 241
Shrike (LANIIDAE) 245
  Fiery-breasted Bush 245
  Lagden's Bush 245
  Northern 245
  Red-backed 245
  Tibetan or Grey-backed 245
Shrike (PRIONOPIDAE)
  Long-crested Helmet 244
  Ruppell's White-crowned 244
  Yellow-crested Helmet 244
Shrike-Thrush, Rufous 276
Shrike-Tyrant, White-tailed 222
Sicklebill, White-tipped 177

Sierra-Finch, Patagonian 290
Siskin, Eurasian 303
Skimmer, African 142
  Black 142
  Indian 142
Skua 125
  Great 139
  MacCormick's 139
Skylark 233
Smew 88
Snipe (ROSTRATULIDAE) 125
  Painted 125, *127*
  South American Painted 127
Snipe (SCOLOPACIDAE)
  Common 14, *131*
  Jack 132
  Japanese 131
  Pintail 132
  Swinhoe's 132
Snowcock, Himalayan 110
Softwing 197
Solan Goose 63
Solitaire, Townsend's 255
Songlark, Rufous 271
Spadebill,
  Golden-crowned 225
Sparrows 308
Sparrow (EMBERIZIDAE) 290
  American Tree 290
  Pectoral 292
Sparrow (ESTRILDIDAE) 307
  Java 307
Sparrow (PLOCEIDAE) 308
  Cape 309
  House 308
  Italian 308
  Rock 309
  Swahili 309
  Tree 309
Sparrow (PRUNELLIDAE) 252
  Hedge (see Dunnock) 253
Sparrowhawk 98
  Red-thighed 98
Speirops, Black-capped 285
Spider Hunter, Streaked 284
Spinebill, Eastern 288
Spinetail, Pale-breasted 212
  Rush-loving 212
Spinifex Bird 268
Spoonbill, African 74
  Lesser 74
  Roseate 74
  Royal 74
  White 67, *74*
  Yellow-billed 74
Spur-fowl, Ceylon 112
Starling, Burchell's Glossy 310
  Common 28, *311*
  Glossy 310
  Rose-coloured 311
  Wattled 311
Steamer Duck 82

INDEX OF ENGLISH NAMES 337

Stilt, Banded 134
  Black-winged 134
Stint, Temminck's 133
Stonechat 256
Stone-Curlew 136
  Beach 136
  Southern 135
Stork (BALAENICIPITIDAE) 71
  Whale-headed or Shoe-bill 71
Stork (CICONIIDAE) Abdim's 72
  Asian Open-billed 72
  Marabou 72
  Painted 71
  Saddle-bill 72
  White 72
  Yellow-billed 71
Stork (SCOPIDAE) 71
  Hammer-head or Anvilhead 71
Storm-Petrel 60
  Markham's 60
  White-faced 60
  Wilson's 59
Streamcreeper 214
Sugarbird, Cape 288
Sunbird (NECTARINIIDAE) 283
  Beautiful 283
  Blue-headed 283
  Loten's 283
  Malachite 283
  Mrs Gould's 284
  Sumba 283
  Violet-backed 283
Sunbird (PHILEPITIDAE)
  Small-billed False 221
  Wattled False 221
Sunbittern 123
Sungrebe 123
Surfbird 133
Swallow, Blue and White 235
  Blue Rough-winged 236
  Cliff 236
  Common or Barn 236
  Tree 235
Swallow-Tanager 295
Swallow-Wing 198
Swamp Hen 122
Swan 76
  Black 76, 79
  Black-necked 79
  Coscoroba 78
  Mute 79
  Whooper or Whistling 79
Swift 173
  André's Spine-tailed 175
  Black 175
  Common 176
  Dark-backed 175
  House 176
  Pallid 176
  Palm 176
  Pygmy 176
  Spot-fronted 175

Vaux's Spine-tailed 175
  White-throated 176
Swiftlet, Giant 175
  White-bellied 174
Sylph, Long-tailed 173, *178*

Tailorbird, Common 267
Takahe 122
Tanager, Azure-shouldered 294
  Black and Green 294
  Black-headed 294
  Glistening Green 294
  Golden-crowned 294
  Summer 293
  Yellow-green Bush 293
Tapaculo, Andean 219
  Pale-throated 219
  White-throated 218
Teal, Baikal 84
  Brazilian 87
  Chestnut 83
  Madagascan 83
  South American or Speckled 84
Tern, Black 140
  Bridled 140
  Caspian 141
  Common 141
  Forster's 141
  Greater Crested 141
  Gull-billed 141
  Inca 141
  Roseate 141
  Sooty 141
  Trudeau's 141
  White 142
  White-winged Black 140
Thickhead 275
Thick-knee, Double-striped 135
  Peruvian 136
Thornbill, Yellow-tailed 270
Thornbird, Red-fronted 213
Thrasher, Brown 252
  Curve-billed 252
  Le Conte's 252
  Pearly-eyed 252
Thrush, Ashy Ground 257
  Mistle 258
  Olive 257
  Rock 256
  Short-toed Rock 256
  Song 257
  Wood 257
Thrush (TIMALIINAE) 259
  White-crested Laughing 261
  Collared Laughing 261
Tinamou 48
  Elegant-crested or Martineta 49
  Kalinowski's 49
  Slaty-breasted 49
  White-throated 48
Tinkerbird, Golden-rumped 199
Tit (AEGITHALIDAE) 276

Common Bush 277
Long-tailed 276
White-cheeked Long-tailed 276
Tit (PARADOXORNITHINAE)
  Bearded 263
Tit (PARIDAE) 277
  Blue 278
  Coal 278
  Crested 278
  Great 278
  Marsh 279
  Sultan 279
  Willow 278
Tit (REMIZIDAE)
  Fire-capped 277
  Mouse-coloured Penduline 277
  Penduline 277
Tit-Babbler, Chestnut-headed 262
Tit-Flycatcher, Grey 272
Titmouse, Elegant 278
Tityra, Black-tailed 229
Tody, Jamaican 188
  Narrow-billed 188
  Puerto Rican 188
Tody-Flycatcher 225
Tody-Tyrant, Boat-billed 225
Toucan 195
  Black-billed Mountain 202
  Chestnut-mandibled 203
  Orange-billed 203
  Plate-billed Mountain 202
Toucanet, Emerald 202
  Spot-billed 195, *202*
Towhee, Rufous-sided 291
Tragopan, Cabot's 112
  Satyr 112
  Temminck's 112
  Western 112
Trainbearer, Black-tailed 178
Treecreeper (CERTHIIDAE) 280
  Common 280
  Short-toed 280
Treecreeper (CLIMACTERIDAE) 281
  Black-tailed 281
  White-throated 281
Treehunter, Streak-breasted 213
  Streak-capped 213
Treepie, Andaman 321
Treerunner, Pearled 212
Tree Swift, Crested 174
  Whiskered 174
Trembler, Brown 252
Triller, Black and White 240
  White-winged 240
Trogon 182
  Collard or Red-bellied 183
  Eared 183
  Mountain 183
  Narina's 183
  Red-headed 184
  Scarlet-rumped 183
  White-tailed 183

INDEX OF ENGLISH NAMES

Tropicbird 61
  Red-tailed 62
  White-tailed 62
Trumpeter, Common 119
  Green-winged 120
  White-winged 120
Tui or Parson Bird 288
Tûraco 157
  Black-billed 159
  Great Blue 159
  Hartlaub's 158
  Knysna 158
  Lady Ross's 159
  Livingstone's 159
  Prince Ruspoli's 159
  White-cheeked 158
Turkey 105, *116*
  Ocellated 116
Turnstone, Black 132
  Ruddy 132
Tyrannulet, Bolivian 226
  Torrent 225
Tyrant, Cattle 223
  Sharp-tailed 225

Umbrellabird, Long-Wattled 229

Vanga, Blue 246
  Hook-billed 246
  Pollen's 246
Verdin 277
Vireo, Bell's 299
  Red-eyed 299
Vulture (ACCIPITRIDAE) 93
  Bearded 95
  Cape 96
  Indian Black 96
  Indian White-backed 96
  Palm-nut 95
  White-headed 96
Vulture (CATHARTIDAE) 92
  Black 92
  Lesser Yellow-headed 92

Wagtail, Forest 237
  Grey 237
  Mountain 238
  Pied 237
  White 237
  Yellow 238
Warbler (ACANTHIZINAE) 269
  White-throated Gerygone 270
  Yellow-breasted Gerygone 270
Warbler (PARULIDAE) 296
  Blue-winged 296
  Canada 297
  Golden-crowned 297
  Kirtland's 296
  Prothonotary 297
  Rufous-capped 297
  Virginia's 296
  Worm-eating 297
  Yellow-throated 296
Warbler (SYLVIINAE) 263
  Cetti's 264
  Chinese Bush 264
  Grasshopper 264
  Great Reed 264
  Knysna Scrub 264
  Melodious 265
  Red-winged 266
  Sardinian 265
  Sedge 265
  Wood 266
Wattlebird, Saddleback 314
Waxbill 306
  Black-cheeked 306
  Blue-breasted 305
  Zebra 306
Waxwing, Cedar 247
Weaver, Baya 310
  Black-headed 310
  Donaldson Smith's Sparrow 308
  Social 308
Weebill, Brown 269
Weka 121
Wheatear 256
  Mountain 256
Whimbrel 130
Whip-bird, Eastern 259
Whip-poor-will 171
Whistler, Golden 276
  Lorentz's 276
White-Eye, African Yellow 285
  Javan Crested 285
  Mangrove 284
  Oriental 284
  Pale 284
  Woodford's 285
  Yellow-spectacled or Wallace's 285
Whitethroat 265
Whydah, Paradise 308
  Pintailed 307
Widow Bird, Yellow-shouldered 310
Wigeon, American 83
  Eurasian 84
Woodcock, American 132
  Eurasian 132
Woodcreeper, Barred 210
  Buff-throated 210
  Cinnamon-throated 210
  Narrow-billed 211
  Olivaceous 210
  Plain Brown 209
  Red-billed 210
  Spix's 211
  Streak-headed 211
  Wedge-billed 210
  White-throated 210
Wood-Hoopoe, Black 191
  Green 191
  White-headed 191
Woodpecker 195
  Acorn 205
  Arabian 206
  Black and White 205
  Brown-backed 207
  Chestnut 205
  Crimson-backed 207
  Cuban Green 207
  Fine-spotted 205
  Golden-green 204
  Golden-tailed 204
  Great Spotted 206
  Green 205
  Grey-headed 205
  Ground 204
  Lesser Bay 207
  Lesser Spotted 207
  Lineated 205
  Magellanic 207
  Middle Spotted 207
  Red-crowned 206
  Three-toed 207
Wood-Rail, Brown 120
Woodstar, Amethyst 179
Wood-Swallow, White-breasted 315
  White-browed 315
Wren (ACANTHISITTIDAE) 221
  Bush 221
  Rock 221
Wren (TROGLODYTIDAE) 249
  Black-throated 250
  Cactus 249
  Canyon 249
  Chestnut-breasted 251
  Common 13, 250
  House 250
  Sepia-brown 249
  Shetland Islands 250
  Spot-breasted 250
  Tooth-billed 249
  Zapata 249
Wren-Babbler, Barred-wing 260
  Black-throated 260
  Wedge-billed 260
Wren-Thrush 254
Wren-Tit 261
Wren-Warbler, Blue 269
  Red-backed 268
  Superb 268
Wrybill 129
Wryneck 203
  Red-breasted 203

Xenops, Plain 213

Yellowhammer 289
Yellowshank 131
Yellowthroat, Grey-crowned 297

Index of Latin Names

This index contains the Latin names of all birds in the book. The Orders, Families and Subfamilies are indicated THUS. In general, the page number of the main reference is given in *italic* type, but where there are additional references of a general or less important nature, then these page numbers are also indicated.

Acanthis cannabina 304
  flammea 304
Acanthisitta chloris 222
ACANTHISITTIDAE 221
Acanthorhynchus tenuirostris 288
Acanthiza chrysorrhoa 221, 270
ACANTHIZINAE 269
Accipiter cooperii 97
  erythropus 98
  gentilis 91, 98
  melanochlamys 98
  nisus 98
ACCIPITRIDAE 93
Aceros narcondami 193
  nipalensis 192
  plicatus 193
  undulatus 193
Acridotheres cristatellus 311
  tristis 312
Acrocephalus arundinaceus 264
  schoenobaenus 265
Acryllium vulturinum 116
Actophilornis africanus 126
Aechmophorus occidentalis 55
AEGITHALIDAE 276, 277
Aegithalos caudatus 276
  leucogenys 276
Aegithina tiphia 243
Aegolius harrisi 167
Aegotheles albertisi 170
  cristatus 170
  savesi 170
AEGOTHELIDAE 170
Aepypodius bruijnii 106
Aeronautes saxatilis 176
Aethia cristatella 144
Aethopyga gouldiae 284
  africanus 110
Afropavo congensis 115
Agapornis cana 154
  fischeri 154
  personata 150, *154*
Agelaius phoeniceus 301
Agelastes niger 115
Aglaiocercus kingi 173, *178*
Agriocharis ocellata 116
Agriornis albicauda 222
Aix galericulata 87
  spousa 87
Ajaia ajaia 74

Alauda arvensis 233
ALAUDIDAE 232
Alca torda 143
ALCEDINIDAE 186
Alcedo atthis 16, *186*
ALCIDAE 142
Alcippe castaneceps 262
Alectoris rufa 110
Alectroenas sganzini 149
Alectura lathami 106
Alle alle 142
Amandava amandava 306
  subflava 306
Amaurospiza concolor 291
Amazelia chionogaster 178
  luciae 178
Amazona albifrons 156
  guildingii 156
  ochrocephala 156
Amazonetta brasiliensis 87
Ammomanes deserti 232
Ampelion rubrocristatus 229
Ampelioides tschudii 229
Amytornis housei 269
  striatus 269
Anarhynchus frontalis 129
Anas acuta 83
  americana 83
  bahamensis 83
  bernieri 83
  castanea 83
  clypeata 83
  flavirostris 84
  formosa 84
  georgica 84
  melleri 84
  penelope 84
  platyrhynchus 84
  querquedula 84
  strepera 84
Anastomus oscitans 72
ANATIDAE 77
Andigena laminirostris 202
  nigrirostris 202
Andropadus gracilirostris 241
Anhima cornuta 77
ANHIMIDAE 77
Anhinga anhinga 65
  melanogaster 65
  novaehollandiae 65

  rufa 65
ANHINGIDAE 65
Anodorhynchus hyacinthinus 155
Anous stolidus 142
  tenuirostris 142
Anser albifrons 79
  anser 55, 79
  brachyrhynchus 79
  caerulescens 80
  erythropus 80
  fabalis 80
Anseranas semipalmata 77
ANSERIFORMES 77
Anthornis melanura 288
Anthoscopus 277
Anthracoceros malabaricus 193
Anthreptes languemarei 283
Anthus campestris 238
  novaeseelandiae 238
  spragueii 239
Apalis thoracica 267
Apaloderma narina 183
Aphelocoma coerulescens 320
Aphriza virgata 133
Aplonis metallicus 310
APODIDAE 174
APODIFORMES 173, *174*
Aptenodytes forsteri 51
  patagonica 51
APTERIGIDAE 46
APTERIGIFORMES 46
Apteryx australis 46
  haasti 14, *47*
  oweni 47
Apus acuticaudus 175
  affinis 176
  apus 176
  pallidus 176
Aquila audax 100
  chrysaetos 15, *100*
  gurneyi 100
  rapax 100
Ara chloroptera 155
  couloni 155
Arachnothera magna 284
ARAMIDAE 119
Aramides wolfi 120
Aramus guarauna 119
Aratinga erythrogenys 155
Arborophila torqueola 111

339

INDEX OF LATIN NAMES

Archboldia papuensis 316
Ardea cinerea 68
  goliath 68
  herodias 68
ARDEIDAE 67
Ardeola idae 68
  ralloides 68
Ardeotis australis 124
Arenaria interpres 132
  melanocephala 132
Argusianus argus 115
Arremon taciturnus 292
ARTAMIDAE 234, *315*
Artamus leucorhynchus 315
  superciliosus 315
Ashbyia lovensis 286
Asio capensis 166
  otus 167
Astrapia stephaniae 318
Atelornis pittoides 190
Athene noctua 163, *166*
Atlapetes atricapillus 292
  pileatus 292
Atrichornis clamosus 231
  rufescens 231
ATRICHORNITHIDAE 231
Attagis gayi 137
Aulacorhynchus prasinus 202
Auriparus flaviceps 277
Aythya americana 85
  australis 85
  baeri 86
  ferina 86
  fuligula 86
  novaeseelandiae 86
  valisineria 86

Balaeniceps rex 71
BALAENICIPITIDAE 71
Balearica pavonina 119
Bambusicola fytchii 112
Bartramia longicauda 129
Baryphthengus ruficapillus 188
Basileuterus culicivorus 297
  rufifrons 297
Batis capensis 274
Batrachostomus hodgsoni 169
  javensis 169
Berlepschia rikeri 213
Biziura lobata 89
Blythipicus rubiginosus 207
Boissonneaua mattherosii 178
Bombycilla cedrorum 247
Bonasa umbellus 108
Botaurus lentiginosus 70
  stellaris 71
Bowdleria punctata 268
Brachygalba goeringi 196
Brachypteracias leptosomus 190
Brachypteryx hyperethra 254
Brachyramphus brevirostris 143
Bradornis pallidus 271

Bradypterus sylvaticus 264
  tacsanowskius 264
Branta bernicla 80
  canadensis 80
  leucopsis 80
  ruficollis 81
  sandvicensis 81
Brotogeris chrysopteris 156
Bubo bubo 164
  virginianus 165
Bubulcus ibis 68
Bucco macrodactylus 197
BUCCONIDAE 197
Bucephala islandica 88
Buceros rhinoceros 193
BUCEROTIDAE 192
Bucorvus abyssinicus 194
  cafer 194
Buphagus africanus 312
  erythrorhynchus 312
BURHINIDAE 135
Burhinus bistriatus 135
  magnirostris 135
  oedicnemus 136
  superciliaris 136
Butastur liventer 98
Buteo albicaudatus 99
  buteo 99
  galapagoensis 99
  jamaicensis 99
  lagopus 99
  oreophilus 99
Buteogallus anthracinus 98
Butorides virescens 68
Bycanistes bucinator 193

Cacatua galerita 152
  sanguinea 152
Cacicus uropygialis 300
Cairina moschata 87
Calandrella cinerea 232
  starki 233
Calcarius lapponicus 290
Calidris alba 133
  bairdii 133
  maritima 133
  temminckii 133
Callaeas cinerea 314
CALLAEIDAE 314
Calliphlox amethystina 179
Calyptomena viridis 209
Campephaga flava 240
  lobata 240
  phoenicea 240
CAMPEPHAGIDAE 239
Campephilus megallanicus 207
Campethera abingoni 204
  punctuligera 205
Campylopterus falcatus 177
Campylorhamphus facularius 211
Campylorhynchus brunneicaphillus 249
CAPITONIDAE 198

Capito niger 198
CAPRIMULGIDAE 168, *170*
CAPRIMULGIFORMES 168
Capromulgus aegyptius 171
  europaeus 171
  macrurus 171
  rufus 171
  vociferus 171
CARDINALINAE 292
Cardinalis cardinalis 292
CARDUELINAE 303
Carduelis carduelis 303
  chloris 303
  spinus 303
Cariama cristata 124
CARIAMIDAE 123
Carpodacus mexicanus 304
  rhodochlamys 304
Carpodectes antiniae 228
Carpornis melanocephalus 228
Caryothraustes humeralis 293
CASUARIIDAE 44
CASUARIIFORMES 44
Casuarius bennetti 44
  casuarius 44
  unappendiculatus 45
CATAMBLYRHYNCHINAE 292
Catamblyrhynchus diadema 292
Cataracta 139
Cathartes burrovianus 92
CATHARTIDAE 92
Celeus elegans 205
Centrocercus urophasianus 109
Centropelma micropterum 55
Centropus phasianinus 162
  sinensis 162
  steerei 162
  superciliosus 162
Centurus 205
Cephalopterus penduliger 229
Cephalopyrus flammiceps 277
Cepphus grylle 143
Cercococcyx mechowi 160
Cercomacra nigricans 215
Cercomela melanura 255
Cercotrichas barbata 254
Ceryle rudis 186
Ceyx erithacus 186
Certhia brachydactyla 280
  familiaris 280
CERTHIIDAE 280
Cettia cetti 264
Chaetorhynchus papuensis 313
Chaetura andrei 175
  vauxi 175
Chalcites 160
Chalcopsitta atra 151
  duivenbodei 151
Chamaea fasciata 261
CHARADRIIDAE *127*, 137
CHARADRIIFORMES 125, 126
Charadrius dubius 128

INDEX OF LATIN NAMES 341

hiaticula 129
montana 129
vociferus 129
Chauna chavaria 77
  torquata 77
Chelidoptera tenebrosa 198
Chenonetta jubata 87
Chersophilus duponti 233
CHIONIDIDAE 138
Chionis alba 138
  minor 138
Chlamydera maculata 317
Chlidonias leucoptera 140
  nigra 140
Chloebia gouldiae 307
Chloephaga melanoptera 81
  picta 81
  rubidiceps 81
Chloroceryle amazona 186
  americana 186
Chlorochrysa phoenicotis 294
Chlorocichla laetissima 241
Chloropsis aurifrons 243
  cochinchinensis 243
Chlorospingus flavovirens 293
Chlorostilbon aureoventris 177
  caniveti 177
Choriotis 124
Chrysococcyx cupreus 160
  lucidus 158, 160
Chrysocolaptes lucidus 207
Chrysolophus amherstiae 16, 114
  pictus 114
Chunga burmeisteri 124
Ciccaba woodfordii 166
Ciccinurus regius 319
Ciconia abdimii 72
  ciconia 72
CICONIIDAE 71
CICONIIFORMES 67, 75
CINCLIDAE 248
Cinclocerthia ruficauda 252
Cinclodes oustaleti 212
Cinclorhamphus mathewsi 271
Cinclosoma cinnamomeum 259
Cinclus cinclus 248
  mexicanus 248
Cinnycerthia peruana 249
Circaetus cinereus 96
Circus aeruginosus 97
  macrourus 97
  pygargus 97
Cissa chinensis 321
Cisticola carruthersi 266
  exilis 267
Cladorhynchus leucocephalus 134
Clamator coromandus 160
CLIMACTERIDAE 281
Climacteris leucophaea 281
  melanura 281
Clytoceyx rex 187

Cnemophilus macgregorii 317
Coccothraustes coccothraustes 305
Coccyzus erythropthalmus 160
  euleri 160
Cochlearius cochlearius 69
Coereba flaveola 298
Colaptes auratus 204
COLIIDAE 180
COLIIFORMES 180
Colinus virginianus 105, 109
Colius indicus 180
  leucocephalus 181
  macrourus 181
Collocalia esculenta 174
  gigas 175
Colluricincla megarhyncha 276
Columba elphinstonii 147
  livia 145, 147
  palumbus 147
COLUMBIDAE 147
COLUMBIFORMES 145, 146
Conirostrum leucogenys 298
Conopophaga ardesiaca 217
  melanogaster 217
  roberti 217
CONOPOPHAGIDAE 217
Conopophila rufogularis 288
Contopus cinereus 223, 224
  virens 224
Coracias benghalensis 190
  cyanogaster 190
  garrulus 190
CORACIIDAE 190
CORACIIFORMES 185
Coracina leucopygia 239
  novaehollandiae 239
  tenuirostris 239
Coragyps atratus 92
Corapipo gutturalis 227
Corcorax melanorhamphos 315
CORVIDAE 320
Corvus corax 320, 322
  corone corone 322
  c. cornix 322
  crassirostris 323
  frugilegus 323
  monedula 323
  ossifragus 323
Corydon sumatranus 209
Corytheola cristata 159
Corythaixoides leucogaster 159
Coscoroba coscoroba 78
Cossypha caffra 255
Cotinga amabilis 228
COTINGIDAE 227, 241
Coturnix coturnix 14, 107, 111
  novaezealandiae 111
  ypsilophorus 111
Coua cristata 161
  ruficeps 162
CRACIDAE 106
CRACTICIDAE 315

Cracticus torquatus 316
Crax alector 107
  globulosa 107
  pauxi 107
Creadion carunculatus 314
Creatophora cinerea 311
Crex crex 121
Crinifer zonurus 159
Criniger finschi 242
Crocethia 13, 133
Crossoptilon mantchuricum 113
Crotophaga ani 161
  sulcirostris 161
Crypturellus boucardi 49
CUCULIDAE 157, 160
CUCULIFORMES 157, 158
Cuculus canorus 157, 160
  pallidus 160
Culicicapa ceylonensis 273
Culicivora caudacuta 225
Cursorius coromandelicus 136
  cursor 136
  temminckii 137
Cyanerpes caeruleus 295
Cyanochen cyanoptera 81
Cyanocitta stelleri 320
Cyanocorax cyanomelas 320
Cyanolyca cucullata 320
Cyanopica cyanus 321
Cygnus atratus 79
  cygnus 79
  melanocoryphus 79
  olor 79
Cymbilaimus lineatus 214
Cyphorhinus thoracicus 251
Cypseloides cherriei 175
  niger 175
Cypsiurus parvus 176
Cyrtonyx ocellatus 110

Dacelo gigas 186
  leachii 187
  novaeguineae 186
Daphoenositta miranda 280
Daptrius americanus 101
Dasyornis broadbenti 269
Delichon urbica 236
Dendragapus canadensis 108
  obscurus 108
Dendrexetastes rufigula 210
Dendrocincla fuliginosa 209
Dendrocitta bayleyi 321
Dendrocolaptes certhia 210
DENDROCOLAPTIDAE 209
Dendrocopos 206
Dendrocygna arborea 78
  autumnalis 78
  bicolor 78
  eytoni 78
  guttata 78
  javanica 78
Dendroica dominica 296

INDEX OF LATIN NAMES

kirtlandii 296
Dendronanthus indicus 237
Dendrortyx barbatus 109
DICAEIDAE 281
Dicaeum annae 282
    cruentatum 282
    nehrkorni 282
DICRURIDAE 313
Dicrurus ludwigii 313
    megarhynchus 313
    paradiseus 314
Diglossa caerulescens 295
DIOMEDEIDAE 56
Diomedea chrysostoma 57
    exulans 57
    fusca 57
    melanophrus 57
    nigripes 56, 57
DREPANIDIDAE 298
Drepanornis albertisii 318
DROMADIDAE 135
Dromaeocercus brunneus 266
DROMAIIDAE 45
Dromaius novaehollandiae 45
Dromas ardeola 135
Drymodes brunneopygia 254
Drymophila devillei 215
Dryocopus lineatus 205
Dryoscopus pringlii 244
Ducula bakeri 149
DULIDAE 248
Dulus dominicus 248
Dumetella carolinensis 251

Edithornis sylvestris 120
Egretta alba 69
    caerulea 69
    eulophotes 69
    garzetta 69
Elaenia frantzii 226
Elanoides forficatus 93
Elanus leucurus 93
Elektron platyrhynchum 188
Emberiza citrinella 289
    flaviventris 289
    melanocephala 289
    schoeniclus 289
    socotrana 290
EMBERIZIDAE 288
EMBERIZINAE 289
Empidonax flaviventris 224
    traillii 225
Enicognathus leptorhynchus 155
Ensifera ensifera 178
Eolophus roseicapillus 152
Eopsaltria australis 272
    flaviventris 272
Ephippiorhynchus senegalensis 72
Epthianura albifrons 285
    tricolor 286
EPTHIANURIDAE 285
Eremiornis carteri 268

Eremomela icteropygialis 267
Erimophila alpestris 234
Erithacus rubecula 254, 257
Erythrocercus holochlorus 274
Erythrura viridifacies 306
Esacus magnirostris 136
Estrilda astrild 306
    erythronotos 306
ESTRILDIDAE 305
Eubucco bourcieri 199
Eudocimus albus 73
    ruber 73
Eudromia elegans 49
Eudromias morinellus 125, 129
Eudynamis scolopacea 160
Eudyptes chrysolophus 51
    crestatus 50, 51
Eumomota superciliosa 188
Eupetes macrocercus 259
Euphonia laniirostris 294
Euplectes macrourus 310
Eupodotis ruficrista 124
Euptilotis neoxenus 183
Eurocephalus ruepelli 244
Eurostopodus archboldi 170
    guttatus 171
    mystacalis 171
EURYLAIMIDAE 208
Eurylaimus ochromalus 209
Eurynorhynchus pygmeus 133
Eurypyga helias 123
EURYPYGIDAE 123
Eurystomus orientalis 191
Eutoxeres aquila 177

Falco alopex 102
    columbarius 103
    cuvieri 103
    dickensoni 14, 103
    hypoleucus 103
    mexicanus 103
    peregrinus 84. 14, 103
    rusticolus 103
    sparverius 103
    tinnunculus 14, 104
FALCONIDAE 101
FALCONIFORMES 91
Ferminia cerverai 249
Ficedula hypoleuca 271
    platenae 272
FORMICARIIDAE 214
Formicarius nigricapillus 216
Formicivora melanogaster 215
Francolinus francolinus 110
    hartlaubii 110
    lorti (or africanus) 110
    swainsoni 13, 110
Fraseria cinerascens 271
Fratercula arctica 144
    corniculata 144
Fregata andrewsi 66
    aquila 66

magnificus 66
minor 66
FREGATIDAE 66
Fringilla coelebs 29, 302
    montifringilla 302
FRINGILLIDAE 29, 221, 302
FRINGILLINAE 29, 302
Fulica atra 122
    cornuta 122
    cristata 122
    gigantea 122
Fulmarus glacialis 58
FURNARIIDAE 211
Furnarius rufus 212

Galbalcyrhynchus leucotis 196
Galbula albirostris 196
    ruficauda 197
GALBULIDAE 196
Galerida cristata 233
    theklae 233
GALLIFORMES 105, 106, 157
Gallinago gallinago 14, 131
    hardwickii 131
    megala 132
    stenura 132
Gallinula chloropus 122
Gallirallus australis 121
Galloperdix bicalcarata 112
Gallus domesticus 113
    gallus 113
    lafayettii 113
    sonneratii 113
Gampsonyx swainsonii 93
Garrulax leucolophus 261
    yersini 261
Garrulus glandarius 320
Gavia adamsii 52
    arctica 53
    stellata 53
GAVIIDAE 52
GAVIIFORMES 52
Geococcyx californianus 161
    velox 161
Geocolaptes olivaceus 204
Geopelia striata 148
Geopsittacus occidentalis 153
Geositta cunicularia 211
Geospiza magnirostris 291
Geothlypis poliocephala 297
Geronticus calvus 73
    eremita 73
Gerygone olivacea 270
    sulphurea 270
Glareola nordmanni 137
    nuchalis 137
    pratincola 137
GLAREOLIDAE 136
Glaucidium brodiei 165
Glossopsitta porphyrocephala 151
    pusilla 151
Glyphorhynchus spirurus 210

INDEX OF LATIN NAMES 343

Goura cristata 148
Grallaria excelsa 217
 milleri 217
 ruficapilla 217
Grallaricula ferrugineipectus 216
Grallina cyanoleuca 314
GRALLINIDAE 314
GRUIDAE 118
GRUIFORMES 117
Grus americana 118
 grus 117
 japonensis 119
 rubicunda 119
Guttera pucherani 116
Gygis alba 142
Gymnobucco calvus 199
Gymnomystax mexicanus 301
Gypaetus barbatus 95
Gypohierax angolensis 95
Gyps bengalensis 96
 coprotheres 96

HAEMATOPODIDAE 127
Haematopus ater 127
 ostralegus 127
 palliatus 127
Halcyon albonatata 187
 farquhari 187
 leucocephala 187
 macleayii 187
Haliaeetus albicilla 94, 97, 237
 leucocephalus 95
 leucogaster 95
 pelagicus 95
 vocifer 95
Haliastur indus 94
Hamirostra melanosternon 94
Harpactes duvauceli 183
 erythrocephalus 184
Harpia harpya 99
Harpyhaliaetus solitarius 98
Helmitheros vermivorus 297
Heliopais personata 123
Heliornis fulica 123
HELIORNITHIDAE 123
Hemiprocne longipennis 174
 mystacia 174
HEMIPROCNIDAE 174
Hemispingus reyi 293
Herpetotheres cachinnans 102
Heteronetta atricapilla 90
Hieraaetus fasciatus 100
Himantopus himantopus 134
Hippolais polyglotta 265
HIRUNDINIDAE 234
Hirundo rupestris 235
 rustica 236
Hydrobates pelagicus 60
HYDROBATIDAE 59
Hydrophasianus chirurgus 122
Hydropsalis climacocerca 172
Hylacola pyrrhopygia 270

Hylexetastes perrotii 210
Hylocichla mustelina 257
Hylomanes momotula 188
Hylophilus aurantifrons 299
 ochraceiceps 299
Hypocolius ampelinus 247
Hypositta corallirostris 246
Hypsipetes flavala 242
 mcclellandii 242

Ibidorhyncha struthersii 134
Ichthyophaga ichthyaetus 95
ICTERIDAE 299
Icterus galbula 300
 graceannae 300
Ictinia mississippiensis 94
INDICATORIDAE 200
Indicator indicator 201
 minor 201
 xanthonotus 201
Irediparra gallinacea 126
Irena puella 243
IRENIDAE 242
Iridosornis rufivertex 294
Ixobrychus exilis 70
 minutus 70

Jacamaralcyon tridactyla 196
Jacamerops aurea 197
Jacana spinosa 126
JACANIDAE 126
Jynx ruficollis 203
 torquilla 203

Kakatoe galerita 152

Lagonosticta rubricata 305
Lagopus lagopus 108
 leucurus 108
 mutus 108
Lalage melanoleuca 240
 sueurii 240
Lamporis amethystinus 178
Lamprotornis australis 310
Laniarius aethiopicus 244
 fulleborni 245
LANIIDAE 244
Lanius collurio 245
 excubitor 245
 tephronotus 245
LARIDAE 139
Larosterna inca 141
larus argentatus 139
 brevirostris 139
 canus 139
 fuscus 139
 ridibundus 140
 rosea 140
 tridactylus 140
Laterallus spilonotus 122
Leiothrix lutea 262
Leipoa ocellata 106

Lepas anatifera 81
Lepidocolaptes angustirostris 211
 souleyetii 211
Leptopterus madagascariensis 246
Leptoptilos crumeniferus 72
LEPTOSOMATIDAE 189
Leptosomus discolor 189
Lesbia victoriae 178
Leucopsar rothschildi 311
Leucopternis albicollis 98
 schistacea 98
Lichmera indistincta 286
Limnocorax flavirostra 121
Limnoctites rectirostris 212
Limnodromus griseus 132
Limnornis curvirostris 212
Limosa lapponica 130
 limosa 131
Lioptilus chapini 262
Lobipes 135
Lochmias nematura 214
Locustella naevia 264
Loddigesia mirabilis 179
Lonchura castaneothorax 307
Lophaetus occipitalis 100
Lophitis 124
Lophoictinia isura 94
Lopholaimus antarcticus 149
Lophonetta specularioides 82
Lophophorus impejanus 112
 lhuysii 113
Lophortyx californica 109
Lophostrix cristata 28, *164*
Lophozosterops javanica 285
Lophura ignita 113
 leucomelana 113
Loriculus philippensis 154
Lorius amabilis 151
Loxia curvirostra 304
Loxops coccinea 298
Lullula arborea 233
Luscinea luscinea 255
 megarhynchus 255
Lybius leucomelas 200
 rolleti 200
Lycocorax pyrrhopterus 317
Lymnocryptes minimus 132
Lyrurus tetrix 108

Machetornis rixosus 223
Macrodipteryx longipennis 172
 vexillarius 172
Macronectes giganteus 57
Macronyx ameliae 238
 croceus 138
Malaconotus cruentus 245
 lagdeni 245
Malacopteron albogulare 260
Malacoptila panamensis 197
MALURINAE 268
Malurus cyaneus 268
 melanocephalus 268

INDEX OF LATIN NAMES

Manacus manacus 227
Manucodia comrii 318
Margaroperdix madagascariensis 111
Margarops fuscatus 252
Margarornis squamiger 212
Mayrornis versicolor 275
Megadyptes antipodes 51
Megalaima chrysopogon 199
  lagrandieri 199
MEGAPODIDAE 106
Megapodius laperouse 106
Megarhynchus pitangua 224
Melaenornis pannelaina 271
Melanerpes formicivorus 205
  rubricapillus 206
Melanochlora sultanea 279
Melanocorypha calandra 232
Melanospiza richardsoni 291
MELEAGRIDIDAE 116
Meleagris gallopavo 116
Melichneutes robustus 201
Melidectes leucostephes 287
Melierax canorus 97
Melilestes megarhynchus 286
Meliphaga chrysops 287
  lewini 287
  montana 287
MELIPHAGIDAE 286
Melithreptus albogularis 287
  validirostris 287
Mellisuga helenae 179
Melophus lathami 289
Melopsittacus undulatus 153
Melopyrrha nigra 291
Menura alberti 231
  novaehollandiae 231
MENURIDAE 231
Merganetta armata 85
Mergus albellus 88
  australis 88
  cucullatus 88
  merganser 88
  serrator 89
MEROPIDAE 189
Meropogon forsteni 189
Merops apiaster 189
  bulocki 189
  nubicus 189
  ornatus 189
MESITORNITHIDAE 117
Mesitornis unicolor 117
  variegata 117
MESOENATIDAE 117
Metopidius indicus 126
Micrastur ruficollis 102
Microcochlearius josephinae 225
Microhierax melanoleucos 102
Micromonacha lanceolata 198
Micropsitta geelvinkiana 152
  meeki 152
Milvago chimango 102

Milvus migrans 94
  milvus 13, 94
MIMIDAE 251
Mimus dorsalis 251
  polyglottos 251
Mino coronatus 312
Mirafra africana 232
  javanica 232
Molothrus ater 302
MOMOTIDAE 188
Momotus momota 188
Monarcha godeffroyi 275
  melanopsis 275
MONARCHINAE 274
Monasa flavirostris 198
Monias benschi 117
Monticola brevipes 256
  saxatilis 256
Montifringilla nivalis 309
Morus 63
Motacilla 236, 237
  alba alba 237
  a. yarelli 237
  cinerea 237
  clara 238
  flava 238
  troglodytes 13
MOTACILLIDAE 95, 236
Muscicapa latirostris 272
  striata 272
MUSCICAPIDAE 222, 253
MUSCICAPINAE 271
Muscisaxicola maculirostris 222
Muscivora tyrannus 223
Musophaga rossae 159
MUSOPHAGIDAE 158
MUSOPHAGIFORMES 157
Myadestes townsendi 255
Myagra atra 274
  inquieta 275
Mycteria ibis 71
  lencocephala 71
Myioborus ornatus 297
Myioparus plumbeus 272
Myiopsitta monachus 156
Myiornis ecaudatus 225
Myiozetetes granadensis 224
Myrmeciza goeldii 216
Myrmecocichla nigra 256
Myrmornis torquata 216
Myrmotherula axillaris 215
  klagesi 215
Myzomela erythrocephala 286
  pulchella 287

Nannopterum harrisi 64
Napothera atrigularis 260
Nectarinia alinae 283
  buetticoferi 283
  famosa 283
  lotenia 283
  pulchella 283

NECTARINIIDAE 283
Neodrepanis coruscans 221
  hypoxantha 221
Neophema bourkii 153
  pulchella 153
Neotis denhami 124
Nesasio solomonensis 167
Nesoctites micromegas 204
Nesomimus trifasciatus 251
Nesopsar nigerrimus 300
Nesotriccus ridgwayi 224
Nestor meridionalis 152
Netta erythrophthalma 86
  rufina 86
Ninox jacquinoti 166
Nipponia nippon 73
Nonnula ruficapilla 198
Nothoprocta kalinowski 49
Notiochelidon cyanoleuca 235
Notornis mantelli 122
Nucifraga columbiana 322
Numenius americanus 130
  arquata 14, 130
  borealis 130
  madagascariensis 130
  phaeopus 130
  tahitiensis 130
Numida meleagris mitrata 18, 115
  m. meleagris 19, 115
NUMIDIDAE 115
Nyctea scandiaca 165
NYCTIBIIDAE 169
Nyctibius grandis 170
  griseus 170
Nycticorax leuconotus 69
  nycticorax 69
Nycticryphes semicollaris 125, 127
Nystalus maculatus 197

Oceanites oceanicus 59
Oceanodroma markhami 60
Ocyphaps lophotes 148
Odontophorus gujanensis 109
  balliviani 110
Odontorchilus cinereus 249
Oena capensis 148
Oenanthe monticola 256
  oenanthe 256
OPISTHOCOMIDAE 116
Opisthocomus hoazin 116, 157
Oreoica gutturalis 275
Oreophasis derbianus 107
Oreornis chrysogenys 287
Oreortix pictus 109
ORIOLIDAE 312
Oriolus cruentus 312
  oriolus 312
Ortalis vetula 107
ORTHONYCHINAE 258
Orthonyx spaldingi 259
Orthorhamphus 136

INDEX OF LATIN NAMES

Orthotomus sutorius 267
Ortygospiza atricollis 306
Ortyxelos meiffrenii 118
OTIDAE 124
Otis tetrax 124
Otus albogularis 28, *164*
   alfredi 164
OXYRUNCIDAE 226
Oxyruncus cristatus 226
Oxyura australis 89
   jamaicensis 89
   leucocephala 89
   vittata 89

Pachycare flavogrisea 276
Pachycephala lorentzi 276
   pectoralis 276
PACHYCEPHALINAE 275
Pachyptyla desolata 58
Pachyramphus marginatus 229
Padda oryzivora 307
Pagodroma nivea 59
Palmeria dolei 298
Pandion haliaetus 101
PANDIONIDAE 101
Panurus biarmicus 263
Paradisaea apoda 319
PARADISAEIDAE 317
Paradoxornis alphonsianus 263
   ruficeps 263
PARADOXORNITHINAE 262
Paramythia montium 282
Pardalotus punctatus 282
   quadrigintus 282
PARIDAE 277
Parotia carolae 319
Parula americana 296
PARULIDAE 295
Parus ater 278
   atricapillus 278
   caeruleus 278
   cristatus 278
   elegans 278
   major 278
   montanus 278
   palustris 279
   rufescens 279
Passer domesticus domesticus 308
   d. italiae 308
   melanurus 309
   montanus 309
   suahelicus 309
PASSERIFORMES 29, *208*
Passerina caerulea 293
   ciris 293
Pavo cristatus 115
Pediocetes 109
PEDIONOMIDAE 118
Pedionomus torquatus 118
Pelagodroma marina 60
PELECANIDAE 62
PELECANIFORMES 61, 62

Pelecanoides garnotii 60
   urinatrix 60
PELECANOIDIDAE 60
Pelecanus erythrorhynchos 62
   occidentalis 62
   onocrotalus 61, 63
Peltohyas australis 137
Penelope purpurascens 107
Perdicula manipurensis 111
Perdix hodgsoniae 111
   perdix 111
Pericrocotus brevirostris 240
   flammeus 240
Perissocephalus tricolor 230
Pernis apivorus 93
   celebensis 93
Petrochelidon pyrrhonota 236
Petroica archboldi 273
   goodenovi 273
Petronia petronia 309
Phacellodomus rufifrons 213
Phaenicophaeus leschenaultii 161
Phaethon lepturus 62
   rubricauda 62
PHAETHONTIDAE 62
Phaethornis anthophilus 176
   gounellei 177
   superciliosus 177
Phainopepla nitens 247
Phainoptila melanoxantha 247
PHALACROCORACIDAE 64
Phalacrocorax africanus 64
   atriceps 64
   bourgainvillii 64
   carbo 64
   colensoi 65
   melanoleucos 65
   punctatus 65
Phalaenoptilus nuttalli 171
PHALAROPODIDAE 134
Phalaropus fulicarius 135
   lolatus 135
   tricolor 135
Phalcoboenus albogularis 101
Phaps elegans 148
Pharomachrus mocino 182
PHASIANIDAE 109
Phasianus colchicus *114*, 162
Philepitta castanea 220
PHILEPITTIDAE 220
Philetairus socius 308
Philohela 132
Philomachus pugnax 134
Phleocryptes melanops 212
Phloeoceastes melanoleucos 205
Phodilus prigoginei 28, *164*
Phoeniconais minor 75
Phoenicoparrus andinus 75
   jamesi 75
PHOENICOPTERIDAE 74
PHOENICOPTERIFORMES 75
Phoenicopterus ruber 75

PHOENICULIDAE 191
Phoeniculus aterrimus 191
   bollei 191
   purpureus 191
Phoenicurus phoenicurus 255
Phrygilus patagonicus 290
Phyllastrephus flavostriatus 242
   terrestris 242
Phylloscopus collybita 265
   sibilatrix 266
Phytotoma raimondii 230
   rutila 231
PHYTOTOMIDAE 230
Pica pica 321
Picathartes gymnocephalus 262
PICIDAE 203
PICIFORMES 195, 196
Picoides dorae 206
   major 206
   medius 207
   minor 207
   stricklandi 207
   tridactylus 207
Piculus chrysochloros 204
Picumnus olivaceus 203
   spilogaster 203
Picus canus 205
   viridis 205
Pinaroloxias inornata 291
Pinarornis plumosus 254, 316
Pinicola enucleator 304
Pipilo erythrophthalmus 291
Pipra erythrocephala 226
   rubrocapilla 227
Pipreola riefferii 229
PIPRIDAE 226
Piprites griseiceps 227
Piranga rubra 293
Pithecophaga jefferyi 99
Pitta angolensis 219
   brachyura 219
   erythrogaster 220
   iris 220
   kochi 220
   phayrei 220
Pittasoma michleri 216
PITTIDAE 219
Pityriasis gymnocephala 246
Platalea ajaja 74
   alba 74
   flavipes 74
   leucorodia 67, 74
   minor 74
   regia 74
Platycercus elegans 153
Platyrinchus coronatus 225
Plectrophanes 290
Plectrophenax nivalis 290
Plectropterus gambensis 88
Plegadis falcinellus 74
PLOCEIDAE 307
PLOCEINAE 308

Plocepasser donaldsoni 308
Ploceus bojeri 309
  cucullatus 310
  philippinus 310
Pluvianus aegyptius 136
Pluvialis apricaria 128
  dominica 128
  squatarola 128
PODARGIDAE 169
Podargus papuensis 169
  strigoides 168, 169
Podica senegalensis 123
PODICEPEDIDAE 54
PODICEPEDIFORMES 54
Podiceps auritus 54
  cristatus 55
  pelzelnii 55
  ruficollis 55
Podilymbus gigas 55
Poephila guttata 306
Pogoniulus bilineatus 199
Polihierax semitorquatus 102
Polioptyla caerulea 264
Polyborus plancus 101
Polyplectron chalcurus 114
Polysticta stelleri 85
Pomatorhinus erythrogenys 260
Pophyrio porphyrio 122
Porphyrolaema porphyrolaema 228
Porphyrula martinica 122
Porzana carolina 121
  porzana 121, *119*
  pusilla 121
Premnoplex brunnescens 213
Prinia atrogularis 266
  erythroptera 266
Prionochilus olivaceus 282
PRIONOPIDAE 243
Prionops alberti 244
  plumata 244
Probosciger aterrimus 151
Procellaria parkinsoni 58
PROCELLARIIDAE 56
PROCELLARIIFORMES 56
Procnias alba 227, *230*
  tricaranculata 230
Prodotiscus regulus 201
Progne dominicensis 235
Promerops cafer 288
Prosthemadera novaeseelandiae 288
Protonotaria citrea 297
Prunella collaris 253
  modularis 253
PRUNELLIDAE 252
Psalidoprocne pristoptera 236
Psaltriparus minimus 277
Psarisomus dalhousiae 209
Psarocolius atrovirens 299
  viridis 300
  wagleri 300
Pseudocalyptomena graueri 208
Pseudochelidon eurystomina 234

sirintarae 234
PSEUDOCHELIDONIDAE 234
PSITTACIDAE 151
PSITTACIFORMES 150
Psittacula cyanocephala 154
  krameri 154
Psittacus erithacus 154
Psittirostra psittacea 298
Psophia crepitans 119
  leucoptera 120
  viridis 120
PSOPHIIDAE 119
Psophodes olivaceus 259
Pteridophora alberti 319
Pternistis swainsoni (or *Francolinus*) 13, *110*
Pterocles burchelli 146
  namaqua 146
  personatus 147
PTEROCLIDAE 146
PTEROCLIDIFORMES 145
Pterocnemia pennata 43
Pterodroma cahow 59
  phaeopygia 59
  solandri 59
Pteroglossus mariae 202
  pluricinctus 202
Pteropodocys maxima 239
Pteroptochos tarnii 218
Ptilinopus luteovirens 149
PTILOGONATIDAE 246
Ptilogonis cinereus 247
Ptilolaemus tickelli 192
PTILONORHYNCHIDAE 316
Ptilonorhynchus violaceus 317
Ptiloris victoriae 318
Ptychoramphus aleuticus 144
Pucrasia macrolopha 113
Puffinus gravis 58
  pacificus 58
  tenuirostris 59
PYCNONOTIDAE 241
Pycnonotus nigricans 241
  xantholaemus 241
Pycnoptilus floccosus 270
Pygoscelis adeliae 50
Pyriglena leuconota 216
Pyrocephalus rubinus 223
Pyrrhocorax graculus 322
  pyrrhocorax 322
Pyrrhula pyrrhula 305
Pyrrhuloxia 292
Pyrrhura hoffmanni 155

Quelia quelia 310
Quiscalus niger 302

Rallicula leucospila 120
RALLIDAE 120
Rallus aquaticus 120
  caerulescens 120
  limicola 120

longirostris 120
  pectoralis 120
RAMPHASTIDAE 201
Ramphastos aurantiirostris 203
  swainsonii 203
Ramsayornis fasciatus 287
Recurvirostra americana 134
  avosetta 134
RECURVIROSTRIDAE 134
Regulus regulus 266
  satrapa 266
REMIZIDAE 277
Remiz musculus 277
  pendulinus 277
Rhabdornis inornatus 281
  mystacalis 281
RHABDORNITHIDAE 281
Rhamphocoris clot-bey 15, *232*
Rhea americana 43
RHEIDAE 43
RHEIFORMES 43
Rheinardia ocellata 115
Rhinocrypta lanceolata 218
RHINOCRYPTIDAE 218
Rhipidura fuliginosa 273
  opistherythra 273
  phoenicura 273
  rufifrons 273
RHIPIDURINAE 273
Rhodostethia 140
Rhynchopsitta pachyrhyncha 155
RHYNOCETIDAE 123
Rhynochetos jubatus 123
Riparia paludicola 235
  riparia 235
Rostramus sociabilis 93
Rostratula benghalensis 127
ROSTRATULIDAE 126
Rupicola peruviana 228
  rupicola 228
RYNCHOPIDAE 142
Rynchops albicollis 142
  flavirostris 142
  nigra 142

SAGITTARIIDAE 92
Sagittarius serpentarius 92
Salpinctes mexicanus 249
Salpornis spilonota 281
Sarcogyps calvus 96
Sarkidiornis melanotus 87
Saurothera merlini 161
Saxicola torquata 256
Sayornis saya 222
Scelorchilus albicollis 218
Scenopoeetes dentirostris 316
Schiffornis turdinus 227
Sclerurus mexicanus 214
SCOLOPACIDAE 129
Scolopax minor 132
  rusticola 132
SCOPIDAE 71

INDEX OF LATIN NAMES 347

Scopus umbretta 71
Scotopelia peli 165
   ussheri 165
Scytalopus megallanicus 219
   panamensis 219
Seiurus aurocapillus 296
Selasphorus platycercus 179
   rufus 179
Selenidera maculirostris 202
Seleucides melanoleuca 318
Semnornis frantzii 199
Sericornis maculatus 270
   nigroviridis 270
Sericulus bakeri 317
Serinus canaria 303
   flaviventris 303
   serinus 303
Serpophaga cinerea 225
Sialia sialis 255
Sitta canadensis 279
   europaea 279
   whiteheadi 279
Sittasomus griseicapillus 210
SITTIDAE 279
Smicrornis brevirostris 269
Smithornis rufolateralis 208
Somateria mollissima 85
Speirops lugubris 285
Spelaeornis troglodytoides 260
Spermophaga ruficapilla 305
Sphecotheres flaviventris 313
   vieilloti 313 '
SPHENISCIDAE 50
SPHENISCIFORMES 50
Spheniscus demersus 51
   mendiculus 51
Sphenocichla humei 260
Sphenorhynchus 72
Sphyrapicus ruber 206
Spilornis holospilus 96
Spizaetus nipalensis 100
   ornatus 101
Spizella arborea 290
Spizixos canifrons 241
Sporophila albogularis 290
   schistacea 291, 313
Stachyris rudolphei 260
Steatornis caripensis 169
STEATORNITHIDAE 169
Steganopus 135
Stephanoaetus coronatus 101
STERCORARIIDAE 138
Stercorarius longicaudus 138
   maccormicki 139
   pomarinus 139
   skua 139
Sterna anaethetus 140
   bergii 141
   caspia 141
   dougallii 141
   forsteri 141
   fuscata 141
   hirundo 141
   nilotica 141
   solida 140
   trudeaui 141
Stictonetta naevosa 85
Stiphrornis erythrothorax 254
Strepera graculina 316
Streptopelia decaocto 147
   senegalensis 147
   turtur 148
STRIGIDAE 28, *164*
STRIGIFORMES 28, *163*
Strigops habroptilus 153
Strix aluco 166
Struthio camelus 41, 42
STRUTHIONIDAE 42
STRUTHIONIFORMES 41, 42
Sturnella magna 301
   neglecta 301
STURNIDAE 28, *310*
Sturnus roseus 311
   vulgaris 311
Sula bassana 63
   leucogaster 63
   sula 63
SULIDAE 63
Surnia ulula 163, *165*
Synallaxis albescens 212
Sylvia atricapilla 265
   communis 265
   melanocephala 265
Sylvietta rufescens 267
SYLVIINAE 263
Syrmaticus elliotti 114
   humei 114
   reevesii 114
Syrrhaptes paradoxus 145, *146*
   tibetanus 146

Tachornis furcata 176
Tachycineta bicolor 235
Tachyeres brachypterus 82
   patachonicus 83
   pteneres 83
Tadorna ferruginea 82
   tadorna 82
   variegata 82
Talegalla cuvieri 106
Tangara cyanoptera 294
   nigroviridis 294
Tanysiptera danae 187
Tauraco corythaix 158
   hartlaubi 158
   leucotis 158
   livingstonii 159
   ruspoli 159
   schuettii 159
Teledromas fuscus 219
Teleonema filicauda 227
Tephrodornis pondicerianus 241
Terpsiphone atrocaudata 274
   corvina 274
   viridis 274
TERSINAE 295
Tersina viridis 295
Tetraogallus himalayensis 110
TETRAONIDAE 107
Tetrao parvirostris 108
Tetraophasis szechenyii 110
Tetrastes 108
Thalassornis leuconotus 89
Thamnophilus nigriceps 215
THINOCORIDAE 137
Thinocorus orbignyianus 138
   rumicivorus 138
THRAUPINAE 293
Thraupis cyanoptera 294
Threskiornis aethiopica 73
   melanocephalus 73
   molucca 73
THRESKIORNITHIDAE 71, 72
Thripadectes rufobrunneus 213
   virgaticeps 213
Thryothorus atrogularis 250
   maculipectus 250
Tichodroma murina 280
Tigrisoma lineatus 70
Timalia pileata 261
TIMALIINAE 259
TINAMIDAE 48
TINAMIFORMES 48
Tinamus guttatus 48
Tityra cyana 229
Tockus alboterminatus 192
   deckeni 192
   griseus 192
TODIDAE 187
Todirostrum nigriceps 225
Todopsis cyanocephala 269
Todus angustirostris 188
   mexicanus 188
   todus 188
Toxorhamphus poliopterus 286
Toxostoma curvirostre 252
   lecontei 252
   rufum 252
Trachyphonus darnaudii 200
   vaillantii 200
Tragopan caboti 112
   melanocephalus 112
   satyra 112
   temminckii 112
Tregallasia leucops 272
Treron australis 148
Trichastoma cinerieceps 259
   tickelli 259
Trichoglossus chlorolepidotus 151
   flavoviridis 151
Tricholaema 200
Trigonoceps occipitalis 96
Tringa glareola 131
   melanoleuca 131
   nebularia 131
   ochropus 131

solitaria 131
TROCHILIDAE 176
Troglodytes aedon 250
  t. troglodytes 13, *250*
  t. zetlandiius 250
TROGLODYTIDAE 249
Trogon collaris 182, *183*
  mexicanus 183
  viridis 183
TROGONIDAE 182
TROGONIFORMES 182
TURDINAE 18, *253*
Turdoides jardinei 261
  nipalensis 261
Turdus albocinctus 257
  merula 257
  migratorius 257
  olivaceus 257
  philomelos 257
  pilaris 258
  poliocephalus 258
  torquatus 258
  viscivorus 258
TURNICIDAE 118
Turnix melanogaster 118
  suscitator 118
  sylvatica 118
Tympanuchus cupido 108
  pallidicinctus 108

phasianellus 109
TYRANNIDAE 222
Tyranniscus bolivianus 226
Tyrannus crassirostris 223
  tyrannus 223
Tyto alba 28, *163*
  tenebricosa 28, *164*
TYTONIDAE 28, *163*

Upupa epops 185, *191*
UPUPIDAE 191
Uraeginthus angolensis 305
Uria aalge 143
  lomvia 143
Uroglaux dimorpha 28, *166*
Urotriorchis macrourus 98

Vanellus chilensis 127
  spinosus 128
  vanellus 128
Vanga curvirostris 246
VANGIDAE 246
Vermivora pinus 296
  virginiae 296
Vestiaria coccinea 298
Vidua macroura 307
  paradisea 308
VIDUINAE 307
Vireo belli 299

olivaceus 299
VIREONIDAE 299
Viridonia virens 298
Vultur californianus 92
  gryphus 91, *92*

Wilsonia canadensis 297
Woodfordia superciliosa 285

Xanthocephalus xanthocephalus 301
Xenicus gilviventris 221
  longipes 221
Xenopirostris polleni 246
Xenops minutus 213
Xiphidiopicus percussus 207
Xiphocolaptes albicottis 210
Xipholena punicea 228
Xiphorhynchus guttatus 210
  spixii 211

Zavattariornis stresemanni 321
Zeledonia coronata 254
Zoothera cinerea 257
ZOSTEROPIDAE 284
Zosterops chloris 284
  pallida 284
  palpebrosa 284
  senegalensis 285
  wallacei 285